Servant-Leadership, Feminism, and Gender Well-Being

Servant-Leadership, Feminism, and Gender Well-Being

How Leaders Transcend Global Inequities through
Hope, Unity, and Love

EDITED BY

Jiying Song, Joe Walsh, Kae Reynolds,
Jennifer Tilghman-Havens, Shann Ray Ferch,
Larry C. Spears

SUNY
PRESS

Cover image courtesy of photographer Qing Yin.

Published by State University of New York Press, Albany

For information, contact State University of New York Press, Albany, NY
www.sunypress.edu

Library of Congress Cataloging-in-Publication Data

Name: Song, Jiying, 1976– editor.
Title: Servant-leadership, feminism, and gender well-being : how leaders
    transcend global inequities through hope, unity, and love / [edited by]
    Jiying Song, Joe Walsh, Kae Reynolds, Jennifer Tilghman-Havens, Shann
    Ray Ferch, Larry C. Spears.
Description: Albany, NY : State University of New York Press, [2022] |
    Includes bibliographical references and index.
Identifiers: LCCN 2022005749 | ISBN 9781438490175 (hardcover : alk. paper) |
    ISBN 9781438490182 (ebook) | ISBN 9781438490168 (pbk. : alk. paper)
Subjects: LCSH: Leadership. | Servant leadership. | Feminism.
Classification: LCC HD57.7 .S4588 2022 | DDC 658.4/092—dc23/eng/20220617
LC record available at https://lccn.loc.gov/2022005749

10 9 8 7 6 5 4 3 2 1

Contents

Section II: The Courageous Wholeness of Servant-Leadership

Section III: The Spiritual Beauty of Servant-Leadership

Section IV: The Art and Science of Servant-Leadership

Illustrations

Figures

Tables

Foreword

Servant-Leadership and Equality

LARRY C. SPEARS

This servant-leadership anthology, *Servant-Leadership, Feminism, and Gender Well-Being: How Leaders Transcend Global Inequities through Hope, Unity, and Love*, is a beautiful collection of writings. It makes a very strong case for servant-leadership as a compelling approach to leadership and service that also provides a powerful and unifying way forward for women and men. The chapters in this compilation offer up a deep wellspring of wisdom, powerful questions, and helpful practices for all who desire to grow as aspiring servant-leaders.

The term *servant-leadership* was first coined in a 1970 essay by Robert K. Greenleaf (1904–1990) titled *The Servant as Leader*. Greenleaf spent most of his organizational life in the field of management research, development, and education at AT&T. Following a forty-year career there, he founded the Center for Applied Ethics in 1964 and enjoyed a second career that lasted another twenty-five years. In 1985, the Center for Applied Ethics was renamed the Robert K. Greenleaf Center, where I served as president and CEO and as senior fellow and president emeritus from 1990 to 2007.

During those years, I edited or coedited five volumes of writings by Robert Greenleaf: *On Becoming a Servant-Leader* (1996), *Seeker and Servant* (1996), *The Power of Servant-Leadership* (1998), *Servant Leadership: 25th Anniversary Edition* (2002), and *The Servant-Leader Within* (2003). Working together with others, I have also coproduced a series of nine servant-leadership anthologies: *Reflections on Leadership* (1995), *Insights on Leadership*

(1998), *Focus on Leadership* (2002), *Practicing Servant-Leadership* (2004), *The Spirit of Servant-Leadership* (2011), *Conversations on Servant-Leadership* (2015), *Servant-Leadership and Forgiveness* (2020), *Global Servant-Leadership* (2021), and this latest volume, *Servant-Leadership, Feminism, and Gender Well-Being* (2022).

Since 1970, more than a half million copies of Robert Greenleaf's books and essays have been sold worldwide. Slowly but surely, his writings on servant-leadership have helped to transform both people and organizations around the world. In many ways, it may be said that the times are only now beginning to catch up with Robert Greenleaf's visionary call to servant-leadership. The idea of servant-leadership, now in its sixth decade as a concept bearing that name, continues to create a quiet revolution around the world.

But what does servant-leadership entail? Who *is* a servant-leader? Greenleaf said that the servant-leader is one who is a servant first and a leader second. In *Servant Leadership: A Journey into the Nature of Legitimate Power and Greatness,* the 25th anniversary edition, Greenleaf (1977/2002) writes,

> The servant-leader is servant first. . . . It begins with the natural feeling that one wants to serve, to serve first. Then conscious choice brings one to aspire to lead. . . . The difference manifests itself in the care taken by the servant—first to make sure that other people's highest priority needs are being served. The best test . . . is this: Do those served grow as persons? Do they, *while being served,* become healthier, wiser, freer, more autonomous, more likely themselves to become servants? *And,* what is the effect on the least privileged in society? Will they benefit or at least not be further deprived? (p. 27; emphasis in original)

The words *servant* and *leader* are usually thought of as being opposites. In deliberately bringing those two words together in a meaningful way, Robert Greenleaf gave birth to the paradoxical term *servant-leader.* His writings on the subject of servant-leadership helped to get this global movement started, and his views have had a profound and growing effect on many organizations and thought leaders. Organizations such as AFLAC, Chick-fil-A, The Container Store, Starbucks, Southwest Airlines, Synovus Financial Corporation, TDIndustries, and many more are recognized today for nurturing servant-led cultures. These institutions and others have been encouraged and supported by a long list of servant-leadership thought leaders such as James Autry, Cheryl Bachelder, Warren Bennis, Ken Blanchard, Peter

Block, John Carver, Stephen Covey, Max DePree, Shann Ferch, Don Frick, John Horsman, James Kouzes, Parker Palmer, M. Scott Peck, Peter Senge, Margaret Wheatley, and Danah Zohar, to name but a handful of today's cutting-edge authors and advocates of servant-leadership.

In 1992, I conducted a study of Robert Greenleaf's writings. From that analysis, I was able to codify a set of 10 characteristics that Greenleaf wrote about in various writings, and which he considered as being central to the development of servant-leaders. These are listening, empathy, healing, awareness, persuasion, conceptualization, foresight, stewardship, commitment to the growth of people, and building community. My analysis showed these to be the ones that Greenleaf mentioned most often in his writings, and which led me to compile them into a list and to begin to write about them. While these 10 characteristics of servant-leadership are by no means exhaustive, they do serve to communicate the power and promise that this concept offers to servant-leaders who are open to its invitation and challenge. Like Robert Greenleaf, I am convinced that it is possible to become an increasingly authentic servant-leader through the conscious development of these and other characteristics.

It is helpful to understand that servant-leadership starts within each one of us, and that it is first and foremost a personal philosophy and commitment that we can choose to practice in any environment. If we understand Greenleaf's best test as the fundamental understanding of servant-leadership, then it becomes clear that the choice to seek to practice servant-leadership is ours to make. Our personal embracing of servant-leadership does not require the approval of our supervisor or our organization's chief executive. We don't need anyone's permission to personally do our best to act as a servant-leader. It is our choice.

Something similar can also be said of understanding and practicing feminism and gender equality through servant-leadership.

For some people, the word *servant* may prompt an initial negative connotation due to the oppression that many people—especially women, people of color, and LGBTQ—have historically endured. However, upon closer analysis many come to appreciate the inherent spiritual nature of what Greenleaf intended by the pairing of *servant* and *leader*. The startling paradox of the term *servant-leadership* serves to prompt new insights.

Here are just a few examples of commentary on servant-leadership by women leaders in their writings on servant-leadership.

Cheryl Bachelder (2018), former CEO of Popeyes Louisiana Kitchen, writes of six servant-leadership principles that guided their actions:

- We are passionate about what we do.

- We listen carefully and learn continuously.

- We are fact-based and planful.

- We coach and develop our people.

- We are personally accountable.

- We value humility.

Juana Bordas has written,

> Many women, minorities and people of color have long tradi-
> tions of servant-leadership in their cultures. Servant-leadership
> has very old roots in many of the indigenous cultures. Cultures
> that were holistic, cooperative, communal, intuitive and spiritual.
> These cultures centered on being guardians of the future and
> respecting the ancestors who walked before. (as cited in Spears,
> 1995, p. 12)

Women leaders are writing and speaking about servant-leadership as
a leadership philosophy that is appropriate for both women and men to
embrace. Patsy Sampson, former president of Stephens College in Columbia, Missouri, is one such person. She wrote, "So-called (service-oriented)
feminine characteristics are exactly those which are consonant with the very
best qualities of servant-leadership" (as cited in Spears, 1995, p. 12).

Danah Zohar (1997), in her book *Rewiring the Corporate Brain*, had
this to say:

> To qualify as servant-leaders in the deepest sense, I think that
> leaders must have four essential qualities.
>
> - They must have a deep sense of the interconnectedness of life
>   and all its enterprises.
>
> - They must have a sense of engagement and responsibility, a
>   sense of "I have to."
>
> - They must be aware that all human endeavor, including business,
>   is a part of the larger and richer fabric of the whole universe.

- And perhaps most important of all, servant leaders must know what they ultimately serve. They must, with a sense of humility and gratitude, have a sense of the Source from which all values emerge. (p. 153)

Margaret Wheatley (2015), author of *Leadership and the New Science* and many other books, has written:

A few phrases come to mind from a wonderful gospel song, "We are the ones we've been waiting for." This is the time for which we have been preparing, and so there is a deep sense of call. Servant-leadership is not just an interesting idea, but something fundamental and vital for the world, and now the world that truly needs it. The whole concept of servant-leadership must move from an interesting idea in the public imagination toward the realization that *this is the only way we can go forward*. I personally experience that sense of right-timeliness to this body of work called servant-leadership. I feel that for more and more of us we need to realize that it will take even more courage to move it forward, but that the necessity of moving it forward is clear. It moves from being a body of work to being a movement—literally a movement—how we are going to move this into the world. I think that will require more acts of courage, more clarity, more saying *this has to change now*. I am hoping that it *will* change now. (p. 119; emphasis in original)

As the authors in this anthology make clear, the decision to seek equality, and to embrace both feminine and masculine qualities as servant-leaders, is to be found within ourselves.

Servant-Leadership, Feminism, and Gender Well-Being reveals many pathways available to people and institutions desiring a better way of working together, coupled with greater acceptance of one another. It also shows how servant-leadership attributes of healing, listening, awareness, community building, and others can be used as an antidote to some of our current inequities. So many caring people are working to break down negative beliefs, and to infuse our relationships through serving and leading.

Servant-Leadership, Feminism, and Gender Well-Being is a wise and hopeful book.

References

Bachelder, C. (2018). Serve the people. In K. Blanchard & R. Broadwell (Eds.), *Servant leadership in action: How you can achieve great relationships and results* (pp. 225–230). Berrett-Koehler Publishers.

Greenleaf, R. K. (2002). *Servant leadership: A journey into the nature of legitimate power and greatness* (L. C. Spears, Ed.; 25th anniversary ed.). Paulist Press. (Original work published 1977)

Spears, L. (1995). Introduction: Servant-leadership and the Greenleaf legacy. In L. C. Spears (Ed.), *Reflections on leadership: How Robert K. Greenleaf's theory of servant-leadership influenced today's top management thinkers* (pp. 1–14). John Wiley & Sons.

Wheatley, M. J. (2015). Interviewed by Larry C. Spears and John Noble. In S. R. Ferch, L. C. Spears, M. McFarland, & M. R. Carey (Eds.), *Conversations on servant-leadership: Insights on human courage in life and work* (pp. 99–120). SUNY.

Zohar, D. (1997). *Rewiring the corporate brain: Using the new science to rethink how we structure and lead organizations*. Berrett-Koehler Publishers.

Preface

Servant-Leadership: A Holistic Life

JIYING SONG AND SHANN RAY FERCH

The sharing of joy, whether physical, emotional, psychic, or intellectual, forms a bridge between the sharers which can be the basis for understanding much of what is not shared between them, and lessens the threat of their difference.

> I am not free while any woman is unfree,
> even when her shackles are very different from my own.

—Audre Lorde (Lorde, 2007, pp. 132–133)

A primary reason for the general malaise and lack of human connection experienced by so many in contemporary society coincides with a loss of joy. With both East and West currently facing widespread personal, relational, and existential losses, the question of what it means to live in and be developed by a real community and to authentically encounter what might be called a sense of home is haunting. Pervasive patriarchy has produced great loneliness, degradation, and desolation in the human community. *Servant-Leadership, Feminism, and Gender Well-Being: How Leaders Transcend Global Inequities through Hope, Unity, and Love* is comprised of authors whose prophetic vision shows leadership in opposition to command-and-control styles and in holistic alignment with the quest to help heal the human community.

In Greenleaf's terms, the true community is a result of servant-leaders working to meet the most ultimate needs of those with whom they come into contact. The result of meeting such needs is that others grow wiser, more free, more healthy, and more autonomous. In Greenleaf's conception, in a good relational environment, a good home community from which to live and move, people are liberated toward the best sense of healthy humanity and therefore become better able to serve, and the least privileged of society are benefited or at least not further deprived. Juana Bordas, a Latina leader known for her vitality and profound advancement of servant-leadership in the contemporary leadership landscape, also calls people to a deeper sense of home. She refers to servant-leadership as having a powerful base in ancient and contemporary collectivist cultures, the will to serve being the foundation for the collective's trust in a person or group's ability to lead. Bordas (2007) recognizes a profound communal broadening and deepening in current national, and by extension, international life: "The rapidly increasing cultural and racial diversity . . . is challenging leadership to better reflect the values and worldviews inherent to our multicultural society" (p. ix). She notes a more holistic and diverse sense of leadership in families and communities will only be affirmed "when the voices, values, and contributions of all . . . are integrated into mainstream leadership" (p. ix).

In a world where leaders and organizations face global pandemics and power conflicts, patriarchy and gender dualism still prevail, be it in the East or in the West. Gender stereotyping and the glass ceiling continue to affect humanity's conceptualizations of leadership (Barreto et al., 2009; Eagly & Sczesny, 2009; Olcott & Hardy, 2006; Parsons, 2019; Reynolds, 2013, 2014, 2020). The ill effects of patriarchy are deeply rooted and ubiquitous, and often overlooked by both men and women (Johnson, 1997). In the ancient Chinese philosophy of the cosmos, males are heaven while females are earth, males are *qian* while females are *kun*, and males are *yang* while females are *yin* (Bao, 1987). This was dichotomous but equal; there was neither high nor low between *yin* and *yang* (Bao, 1987). It was not until the Han Dynasty (around 100 BC) that *yin* and females were degraded to be inferior and subjected to *yang* and males (Bao, 1987). This ideology led to women's foot-binding, concubinage, arranged marriage, and deprival of education in ancient China (Bao, 1987). Women were subdued based on the ascendancy of patriarchy, the focus on the contradictory aspects of *yin* and *yang*, and the elevation of *yang* (Bao, 1987; Xie, 1916/2011). It set the norms for Confucianism and controlled Chinese people for two millennia. Having stressed the equally and mutually complementary character of *yin-yang*, some scholars paved the way for the women's egalitarian movement in nineteenth-century China (Bao, 1987; Xie, 1916/2011).

In the West, embedded in male-focused interpretations of the Bible as well as the more atheistic influx of industrialism, hypercapitalism, reductive science, and empire, patriarchy has been a powerfully controlling and degrading set of conceptual tools used to maintain, enforce, contest, and adjudicate social order (Miller, 2017). Notably, a well-discerned vision of spiritual life, be it in Buddhism, Islam, Judaism, Confucianism, or Christianity, has the seeds of equality and dignity for all people, but in most traditional forms of religious interpretation an undue focus on the maleness of God, women's subjugation, and hierarchy with regard to people, church, temple, or mosque is still prevalent (Ruether, 1989). Women have been excluded from leadership roles in many religious bodies based on certain interpretations of honored scriptures (Cowles, 1993; Howe, 1982). People might think that this issue has been less intense in recent history because egalitarians have made progress, but many men as well as women throughout the world, religious or otherwise, still take this stance. The Council on Biblical Manhood and Womanhood (1988) clearly states in its Danvers Statement: "Some governing and teaching roles within the church are restricted to men" (Affirmations 6.2). Despite many scholars' vigorous efforts of interpreting the Bible in a more discerning historical context (Bailey, 2000; Belleville, 2003; Kroeger, 1979; Wright, 2004), gender discrimination prevails in religious leadership in China and the United States (Song, 2018, 2019). Atheistic, agnostic, and nonreligious leadership worldwide embodies a similar calcification of gender discrimination, as systemic sexism, homophobia, racism, and classism still pervasively dominate the systems of the modern world economically and structurally.

Patriarchy relates to excluding women from (certain) leadership roles (Barreto et al., 2009; Cowles, 1993; Eagly & Sczesny, 2009; Ferch, 2020; Howe, 1982; Jakobsh, 2004; Olcott & Hardy, 2006; Parsons, 2019; Reynolds, 2013, 2014, 2020; Tilghman-Havens, 2018), sexual harassment and violence against women (Bao, 1987; Bloomquist, 1989; Griffith, 2004; Miller, 2017; Ruether, 1989), and femicide and child abuse (Kennedy, 2000; Parkinson et al., 2012; Redmond, 1989; Tailor et al., 2014; Tran, 2020). Given the long traditions of patriarchy, many organizations today are still male dominated, with the assumption that these organizations are gender-neutral and their structures asexual (Jakobsh, 2004). With these assumptions and systems of entrenched power, both men and women are conditioned to maintain the status quo (Jakobsh, 2004). That which can be named as feminine is often subdued, degraded, dominated, or made invisible by the masculine in China as well as in the West.

When I (Jiying) worked in China, I was promoted to leadership positions later than my male colleagues because I am a woman and assumedly would need to spend more time to take care of my family, which would hinder my performance at work. Later, when I became the operation director and was recruiting graduates for my company, I tended to choose female students only if they had higher degrees (master's vs. bachelor's) or much more experience than their male peers. I did not do it out of intentionally discriminating against women, instead, I thought it was to serve the interest of a gender-neutral corporation. I was conditioned by the male-dominant perspective to maintain the status quo, and I lacked the discernment necessary at the time to resist and seek to transform oppressive systems into liberatory systems (hooks, 1985; West, 2014).

Audre Lorde, poet, warrior, lesbian, leader, and freedom fighter, changed the world with her intrepid spirit. Her critique of patriarchy stands as a beacon of light in the dark of dominance and oppression: "The master's tools will never dismantle the master's house. They may allow us to temporarily beat him at his own game, but they will never bring about genuine change" (Lorde, 2007, p. 110). What the mind of the rational perceives, the heart of the mystery transcends. Who has not wandered in the dark of night and wondered at the night sky? Night, being the only time during the sun's daily orbit when we can witness that which is beyond our atmosphere. We are found then, even when we may feel lost. Humility accompanies mystery. From of old, when a divine antagonist was wrestled for a blessing, those who wrestled with the divine understood that God dwells in deep darkness. Theologians sometimes then referred to God as the Awful One, the one who repels and attracts, beyond our spare and limited knowing, into greater humanity, sometimes granting us the will to die for others, even those we do not know, in order to bestow on humanity a more elegant, graceful, generous, and loving existence.

We believe servant-leadership, in its ethic of love, care, and service to the least privileged, is a potential antidote to patriarchal binds because servant-leadership "espouses a nonhierarchical, participative approach to defining organizational objectives and ethics that recognizes and values the subjectivity and situatedness of organizational members" (Reynolds, 2014, p. 57). It can be "a driving force for generating discourse on gender-integrative approaches to organizational leadership" (p. 51). Since Greenleaf coined the term *servant-leader*, the debate over its paradox has been ongoing. Eicher-Catt (2005) claimed the apposition of servant with leader was associated with subjugation and domination, respectively, and instantiates a paradoxical discourse game that perpetuates male-centric patriarchal norms rather than neutralizing gender bias. Reynolds (2014) proposed that Eicher-Catt's (2005) critique adds to a quality deconstructive discourse; however, Reynolds (2014) argued that the paradoxical linguistic term *servant-leader* in its authentically embodied contextual foundations is not a disguise for male-centric norms, as Eicher-Catt (2005) claimed, but a complementary and harmonious sense of wholeness across the gender spectrum.

Reynolds analyzed Spears' (2002) 10 characteristics to examine servant-leadership constructs in terms of gender. Reynolds (2014) argued that six of the ten characteristics distinguish servant-leadership from other forms of leadership, whereas the other four are more in line with traditional notions of leadership. Foresight, conceptualization, awareness, and persuasion can be characterized as leadership behaviors that are often associated with the more traditionally masculine aspect of leadership, whereas stewardship, listening, empathizing, healing, commitment to people's growth, and building community are predominantly needs-focused and other-oriented, and thus comprise more feminine-attributed aspects of leadership (Reynolds, 2014). These two sets of characteristics, when pursued through seeking to "make things whole" as Greenleaf espoused, are complementary, not oppositional as Eicher-Catt (2005) claimed. How can we discern and develop the feminine and masculine within every leader?

According to Greenleaf (1977/2002), servant-leaders are "*healers* in the sense of *making whole* by helping others to a larger and nobler vision and purpose than they would be likely to attain for themselves" (p. 240; emphasis in original). Healing is underappreciated in leadership (Barbuto & Wheeler, 2006). It is "the most rare and perhaps the most needed characteristic of leaders today" (Ferch, 2012, p. xi). A hallmark of a servant-leader is that "they heal others, and they do so through mature relationship to self, others, and God" (p. 72). A central essence of servant-leadership is the commitment to making oneself, others, organizations, and relationships whole. Of course healing and making society whole takes great moral effort in community with others, as feminist leaders such as bell hooks, Judith Butler, Angela Davis, and Juana Bordas attest. Such healing can be said to be a byproduct of the self-awareness, listening, empathy, and community building envisioned in servant-leadership. This sense of wholeness resonates with Tutu's (1998) understanding of community: "A person is a person through other persons" (p. 19).

This sense of wholeness also resonates with the way of *yin-yang* in ancient Chinese literature:

> As for yin and yang, they are the Way of heaven and earth, the fundamental principles [governing] the myriad beings, father and mother to all changes and transformations, the basis and beginning of generating life and killing, the palace of spirit brilliance. (Unschuld et al., 2011, p. 95)

Lao Tzu (about fourth or sixth century BC) said, "All the myriad things carry the Yin on their backs and hold the Yang in their embrace, deriving their vital harmony from the proper blending of the two vital Breaths" (Lao Tzu, 2005, p. 49). *Yin* and *yang* cannot exist without each other. They are a complementary and harmonious oneness. This oneness, wholeness, across gender, culture, and context, is the heart of servant-leadership, the curative element capable in small and large ways of healing patriarchy, imperialism, and dominant culture's inherent conscious and unconscious dominance.

How can we build the safety, love, wisdom, and sustenance of healthy life together? What will this beloved community, to borrow the elegance of Coretta Scott King and Martin Luther King, Jr., look like? Acknowledging the beauty, grace, elegance, and power of the gender spectrum, its integration, freedom, and wholeness, is a joyful expression. *Servant-Leadership, Feminism, and Gender Well-Being* seeks to affirm the depths of leadership found in a gender-integrative approach, thereby helping leaders honor wholeness at home, at work, in person-to-person relationships, organizationally, nationally, and internationally, across the gender spectrum. The world seeks wholeness, even as self-embedded lifestyles and desperation strike at the core of our ability to create community and give to others a sense of home in which love and power remain in balance, and openness, humility, strength, and vulnerability are one.

In looking closer at this dynamic as a man, I (Shann) find servant-leadership challenges my will to power with a coinciding and more profound will to love. Vulnerability can be painful, but it is required for healthy community. I grew up in Montana, in a home filled with music, basketball, hunting, and fishing. Having served as a panelist on the US National Endowment for the Humanities Research Division, as well as for the US National Endowment for the Arts as a literature fellow, I've come to admire both the great sense of inquiry found in social science as well as the depth of art and human potential found in works of true literary merit. The loss of home is a recurrent theme in the contemporary literature of America. Sometimes downplayed or ignored, most often revealed as fractured or fragmented or wrecked, the sense of loss is pervasive and painful and raises questions about human nature, my own experience of manhood in the context of home, and the nature of servant-leadership. In this section of the preface I want to consider polyvalent meanings of manhood, and what servant-leadership might have to say about masculinity in contemporary times.

My father turned seventy recently.

"I guess the Lord saw fit to bless me," he said, and it wasn't only about the seventy years, it was about the wilderness. In a given season, a Montana hunter might bring home a deer, perhaps an elk. Many people in Montana feed their families on the steak, hamburger, sausage, and jerky that arrives after an animal is rendered and processed. My family lived mainly on deer as I grew up. In his seventieth year my father brought home two turkeys, an elk, two deer, two antelope, and a mountain goat. The mountain goat he found in the Crazy Mountains, north of the Beartooth Range, a hunt he made alone in the high country, cresting ridges and plateaus, rock walls and escarpments, at higher than 10,000 feet. He went farther than expected in order to approach from above and shoot the animal behind the shoulder on a steep slant from 300 feet.

The animal collapsed and slid a great distance down a narrow chute. It took time and great caution to reach the goat where it came to rest across a razor uplift of rock. There my father straddled a rock spine and stood over an expanse of sky as he proceeded to bone out the animal. He knew he would need to work fast. In a treacherous pathless country, being caught coming down the mountain after dark is not pleasant. In his precarious position, field dressing a mountain goat, a job that normally takes my father forty-five minutes, took more than two hours. With a hunting knife, a sharpening tool, and a small bone saw he worked to quarter the animal, remove the meat, and take the cape and horns. Finally, with the sun on a hard lean toward last light, the heavy pack was ready and he began the descent. The Crazy Mountains are a dramatic and isolated "island" range east of the Great Divide, north of Big Timber, Montana. They lie in Sweet Grass County between the Musselshell and Yellowstone Rivers. Just after dusk my father emerged on the flat below the mountains, made his way to his truck, and returned home.

For years, my father and I could not express our weaknesses to one another. Nor could we easily express our tenderness. In those years, conflict was hot and full of wrath and mostly irresolvable, but in later life, love came to us and taught us the nature of forgiveness. Roxane Gay (2014), the dynamic and truth-telling feminist and nationally renowned writer, said strength is made perfect in weakness. Purposefully echoing the New

Testament book of Corinthians, she gives masculinity a new lens from which to view power. Power not as force but as vulnerability, a strength that emerges through weakness. The physical landscape of Montana, as well as the interior landscape of people, gives a small glimpse into the reality of how we give and how we ask forgiveness. The land can sometimes be an echo of how we change, and especially how we love. In America there is sometimes a pervasive lack of vision regarding the masculine and the feminine. Across the gender spectrum, many who identify most with masculine traits do not have words for their relationship to women or to men. Here, when combined with a wordless or muted interior, the Montana landscape evokes an even more isolate and rugged exterior, often resonant of the stylistic characteristics of a man's own physicality. A man's generational family line, his temperament, his response to abuse or violence or sustained trauma, all this is embedded in a Western landscape as bleak as it is beautiful, as fatal as it is enervated with life. The result, for those who cannot find words to express feelings, is often a potent bend toward that which is harsh, desolate, violent, and deadly. As a result, some men live physically loud and largely defunct familial lives. Or in a countershadow, many men shun emotional engagement and carry an ultimate sense of apathy toward that which is lovely and true in the lives of others. Such men live empty and void lives that are also often experienced as meaningless. Such men become leaders blind to gender integration, and blind to the possibilities of servant-leadership. Often they unconsciously or consciously forward an antiethic of command and control. In violence or apathy, the unhealthy masculine cuts off the feminine and succeeds in harming relationships with women and other men. Even if it can be said that all of us benefit from a healthy and in fact exquisite balance of the feminine and the masculine, many men find it very difficult to reach toward the feminine within their own masculinity, and many women find it equally difficult to reach toward the masculine within their own womanhood. As a clinical psychologist working with couples for more nearly 30 years, I've found balancing courage with tenderness, and love with legitimate power, is necessary for both the feminine and the masculine to relate on an in-depth level throughout the complexity and fluidity of contemporary gender formulations. Servant-leadership, when engaged with sincerity, humility, and the will to change, provides just such a balance.

Broken relationships, fractured families, the border of despair, the fall from grace. On the more masculine side of the continuum I've found those who reject grace or fall short of grace tend to live in violence or ennui toward self and others. Truly, there is a hard fall for people who reject grace. At the same time, in my experience a deep desire to return and atone exists in the lifeblood of the masculine in America. I've come to understand that almost all men yearn for grace and, in fact, love from the women and men in their lives. I believe most men yearn for an authentic sense of home, yet without grace and love a life of pain and unwieldy consequence tracks them, often in predatory fashion.

The mystery of life and the hope for love is irrevocable and is felt even in men whose interiority can often appear more mountain-like than human. Cold, distant, massive in darkness or density, far removed from the intimacies of daily life, such men suffer. Still, in the heart of hearts, I've learned men crave something higher. If you have encountered wilderness, you know the great respect, awe, and fear wilderness commands, and at the same time you know the intimacy wilderness imparts without measure. In a similar way, I believe the men of the West, even those who appear to be the hardest or most emotionally apathetic and void, desire a pathway toward grace, and if they somehow are given to set out on this path, they tend to traverse the landscape bravely and with endurance. I believe leadership espousing and embodying a healthy sense of gender integration can be realized through seeking to understand the tremendous depths of servant-leadership. Certainly, some leaders never open their eyes or soul enough to begin the journey back from a fractured sense of self and others into a loving community, yet those leaders who dare are beloved in their families and communities.

As a man, I believe men need atonement.

In order to find such atonement, our will is required. Our will to be mentored by women and men who are exquisite servant-leaders, who balance authentic love with power for others, and who generate in us and others greater health, wisdom, freedom, and autonomy, as well as a greater will to serve.

In atonement, people are restored to a sense of home.

In my own home, because of my wife and the heart we share with our three daughters, there is a spirited love for poetry, story, music, and dance. When I met Jennifer, I began to experience life more fully. She feels deeply and is an elegant and complex leader, thinker, writer, and reader who meets the world with tenacity and belief in immanent possibility. A fully expressed person is a wonder to encounter—the woman or man capable of understanding, embracing, and transcending their own weaknesses or their own shadow, while also attending to the light. Jennifer is such a person. I think of the capacity to live in balance as an everyday miracle: balance involves not only embodying darkness, as we are wont to do, but also transcending our individual and collective darkness by living toward light, as is our shared hope. From this encounter with an articulated sense of the healing qualities of the feminine and the masculine, I believe the essence of home becomes more present to us.

Home is a place of peace, reunion, and reconciliation, where love, discernment, gravity, gentleness, wisdom, power, and beauty reside. Home, rather than dislocation or displacement, draws us to the affirmative reality of what it means to be human. That home could be the original sacredness of the Native American traditions in Montana such as those of the Northern Cheyenne or the Blackfeet or the Sioux, or the many other powerful sovereign nations of Montana, or it could be a sense of home that heralds from a far homeland such as my own heritage in Czechoslovakia or Jiying's heritage in China. Home can be found anywhere in the world, in the heart of the community we hope in and for which we openly seek a healing that will reverse the descent of the present and take us into the vitality of a more responsible future. Home is acknowledged or embraced, challenged, divided, attacked, or subdued as a result of the level of ego we may have in our lives at a given time, or depending on the level of atrocity we may have suffered in our families, nationally or culturally.

When my father came home from the mountains he was received with open arms. We thought with gratitude of how he went at seventy into the heart of a rough and often relentless landscape. In the house, the evening settled in and he cooked a meal for us. My mother prayed, and we received her grace. My wife read to us from sacred texts, enjoining us to bless others with the blessings we'd been given. We celebrated how good it is to be alive and wild as we gazed with open eyes on the beauty of the wilderness in this world.

There is a pernicious displacement of people today.

And there is also the hope of returning home.

Emotional and spiritual wilderness is sometimes equally as treacherous as physical wilderness. In the mix of Native American and Euro-American culture in Montana and in the American West, imaginative and essential life comes of care and discipline, brokenness and surrender, and the honoring of one another's cultures while also directly facing the atrocities of the present and the past. Servant-leaders take us toward the atonement we need to become more whole. Honoring place and people and history with a commitment to truth telling aimed at restoring the sense of one-to-one relationship, between people, and between cultures heals the nations, and heals the world. Of ultimate value is an understanding of love and power, the atrocities and massacres and grave harms, the pervasive human rights abuses as well as the reconciliations that have transpired in Montana history, in American history as a whole, and throughout the world. Integration of both feminine and masculine ways of knowing, seeing, and being is a lodestar. In the unhealthy home, as in the lived experience and embodiment of personal, organizational, or global dysfunction, the nature of the masculine as it appears in society presently is often something that either steps forth in greed or remains apathetically dormant and is therefore unconsciously violently projected or silently subduing, rather than something that is contemplative, given in dignity and received with dignity. Listening is diminished or in fact destroyed. I believe the healing of the masculine involves receiving the influence of the feminine, of home, and of the will to be honorable, integral, intimate, and authentically life-giving in the center of culture and country.

As editors of this collection of works so elegant and fierce, in *Servant-Leadership, Feminism, and Gender Well-Being* we sing a song of joy. In this song the melody is a kind of prophecy, envisioning a home, an international community of life, where love and strength go hand in hand, and safety and peace are the result. Consider bell hooks, the profound and powerful black feminist American thought leader:

> Visionary feminism is a wise and loving politics. It is rooted in the love of male and female being, refusing to privilege one over the other. The soul of feminist politics is the commitment to ending patriarchal domination of women and men, girls and boys. Love cannot exist in any relationship that is based on domination and coercion. Males cannot love themselves in patriarchal culture if their very self-definition relies on submission to patriarchal rules. When men embrace feminist thinking and practice, which emphasizes the value of mutual growth and self-actualization in all relationships, their emotional well-being will be enhanced. A genuine feminist politics always brings us from bondage to freedom, from lovelessness to loving. To love well is the task in all meaningful relationships, not just romantic bonds. (hooks, 2000, pp. 123–124)

Here we are restored to the gifts of an integrated sense of the feminine and the masculine toward mutual influence, personally and collectively. The book speaks of healing, wholeness, and the return to oneness rather than fragmentation in family, culture, and nations. In this language, humanity generates not only exceptional holistic leadership but also grace, forgiveness, reparations, restoration, and mercy. Each chapter in this anthology first appeared in the *International Journal of Servant-Leadership*. We are grateful to Gonzaga University and SUNY Press for support over the years in publishing the *International Journal of Servant-Leadership*.

How can we integrate the lost aspects of ourselves, often socialized by gender calcification, so as to recover wholeness? How can we discern and develop the fluid wholeness of the feminine and the masculine within leaders? *Servant-Leadership, Feminism, and Gender Well-Being* offers a new path, interwoven with countless paths that have come before and those yet to come. We've collected evidence of servant-leaders crossing gender boundaries and integrating gendered traits and behaviors. Feminist ways of knowing, honoring both feminine and masculine giftedness, deepen the holistic foundation of servant-leadership. By integrating female perspectives with male perspectives, a paradigm shift in leadership theory through avenues aligned with holistic servant-leadership can move organizations from hierarchy-driven, rules-based, and authoritative models to value-driven, follower-oriented, and participative models. In this book we hope you find others to walk with you into the wilderness that is circumscribed by people committed to listening, deep serving, and holistic leading. We hope you find peace, the strength to endure and overcome, the joy found with others in freedom and liberatory practices, and the grace that comes of enduring friendship.

May each poem, essay, and research discovery be a light to you on your way.

References

Bailey, K. E. (2000). Women in the New Testament: A Middle Eastern cultural view. *Theology Matters, 6*(1), 1–11.

Bao, J. (1987). Yin yang xue shuo yu fu nv di wei [The idea of *yin-yang* and women's status in China]. *Han Xue Yan Jiu, 5*(2), 501–512. http://ccsdb.ncl.edu.tw/ccs/image/01_005_002_01_07.pdf

Barbuto, J., & Wheeler, D. (2006). Scale development and construct clarification of servant leadership. *Group & Organization Management, 31*(3), 300–326.

Barreto, M., Ryan, M. K., & Schmitt, M. T. (Eds.). (2009). *The glass ceiling in the 21st century: Understanding barriers to gender equality*. American Psychological Association.

Belleville, L. L. (2003). Exegetical fallacies in interpreting 1 Timothy 2:11–15. *Priscilia Papers, 17*(3), 3–9.

Bloomquist, K. L. (1989). Sexual violence: Patriarchy's offense and defense. In J. C. Brown & C. R. Bohn (Eds.), *Christianity patriarchy and abuse: A feminist critique* (pp. 62–69). The Pilgrim Press.

Bordas, J. (2007). *Salsa, soul, and spirit: Leadership for a multicultural age.* Berrett-Koehler.

The Council on Biblical Manhood and Womanhood. (1988). Danvers statement. https://cbmw.org/about/danvers-statement

Cowles, C. S. (1993). *A woman's place? Leadership in the church.* Beacon Hill.

Eagly, A. H., & Sczesny, S. (2009). Stereotypes about women, men, and leaders: Have times changed? In M. Barretto, M. K. Ryan, & M. T. Schmitt (Eds.), *The glass ceiling in the 21st century: Understanding barriers to gender equality* (pp. 21–47). American Psychological Association.

Eicher-Catt, D. (2005). The myth of servant-leadership: A feminist perspective. *Women and Language, 28*(1), 17–25.

Ferch, S. R. (2012). *Forgiveness and power in the age of atrocity: Servant leadership as a way of life.* Lexington Books.

Ferch, S. R. (2020). Eros and logos: Servant-leadership, feminism, and the critical unities of gender well-being. *The International Journal of Servant-Leadership, 14*(1), 157–186.

Gay, R. (2014). *Bad feminist: Essays.* Harper Perennial.

Greenleaf, R. K. (2002). *Servant leadership: A journey into the nature of legitimate power and greatness* (L. C. Spears, Ed.; 25th anniversary ed.). Paulist Press. (Original work published 1977)

Griffith, R. M. (2004). *Born again bodies: Flesh and spirit in American Christianity.* University of California Press.

hooks, b. (1985). *Feminist theory: From margin to center.* South End.

hooks, b. (2000). *Feminism is for everybody: Passionate politics.* Routledge.

Howe, E. M. (1982). *Women and church leadership.* Zondervan.

Jakobsh, D. R. (2004). Barriers to women's leadership. In G. R. Goethals, G. J. Sorenson, & J. M. Burns (Eds.), *Encyclopedia of leadership* (pp. 77–81). SAGE.

Johnson, A. G. (1997). *The gender knot: Unraveling our patriarchal legacy.* Temple University Press.

Kennedy, M. (2000). Christianity and child sexual abuse—the survivors' voice leading to change. *Child Abuse Review, 9*(2), 124–141.

Kroeger, C. C. (1979). Ancient heresies and a strange Greek verb. *The Reformed Journal,* 12–15.

Lao Tzu. (2005). *Tao teh ching.* J. C. H. Wu (Ed. & Trans.). Shambhala.

Lorde, A. (2007). *Sister outsider: Essays and speeches.* Crossing.

Miller, P. (2017). *Patriarchy.* Routledge. https://doi.org/10.4324/9781315532370

Olcott, D., & Hardy, D. W. (Eds.). (2006). *Dancing on the glass ceiling: Women, leadership, and technology.* Atwood Publishing.

Parkinson, P. N., Oates, R. K., & Jayakody, A. A. (2012). Child sexual abuse in the Anglican church of Australia. *Journal of Child Sexual Abuse, 21*(5), 553–570. https://doi.org/10.1080/10538712.2012.689424

Parsons, N. E. (2019). *Women are creating the glass ceiling and have the power to end it.* WSA Publishing.

Redmond, S. A. (1989). Christian "virtues" and recovery from child sexual abuse. In J. C. Brown & C. R. Bohn (Eds.), *Christianity patriarchy and abuse: A feminist critique* (pp. 70–88). The Pilgrim Press.

Reynolds, K. (2013). *Gender differences in messages of commencement addresses delivered by Fortune 1000 business leaders: A content analysis informed by servant-leadership and the feminist ethic of care* [Doctoral dissertation]. http://foley.gonzaga.edu/

Reynolds, K. (2014). Servant-leadership: A feminist perspective. *The International Journal of Servant-Leadership, 10*(1), 35–63.

Reynolds, K. (2020). Do women stand back to move forward? Gender differences in top US business leaders' messages of servant-leadership. *The International Journal of Servant-Leadership, 14*(1), 487–523.

Ruether, R. R. (1989). The Western religious tradition and violence against women in the home. In J. C. Brown & C. R. Bohn (Eds.), *Christianity patriarchy and abuse: A feminist critique* (pp. 31–41). The Pilgrim Press.

Song, J. (2018). *Face management and servant-leadership: A hermeneutic phenomenological study of Chinese and American Christian church leaders* [Doctoral dissertation, Gonzaga University].

Song, J. (2019). Understanding face and shame: A servant-leadership and face management model. *Journal of Pastoral Care and Counseling, 73*(1), 19–29. https://doi.org/10.1177/1542305018825052

Spears, L. C. (2002). Introduction: Tracing the past, present, and future of servant-leadership. In L. C. Spears & M. Lawrence (Eds.), *Focus on leadership: Servant-leadership for the twenty-first century* (pp. 1–16). Wiley.

Tailor, K., Piotrowski, C., Woodgate, R. L., & Letourneau, N. (2014). Child sexual abuse and adult religious life: Challenges of theory and method. *Journal of Child Sexual Abuse, 23*(8), 865–884. https://doi.org/10.1080/10538712.201 4.960633

Tilghman-Havens, J. (2018). The will to (share) power: Privilege, positionality, and the servant-leader. *The International Journal of Servant-Leadership, 12*(1), 87–128.

Tran, D. Q. (2020). Toward a servant-led response rooted in forgiveness and restorative justice in the Catholic clergy sexual abuse scandal and cover-up. In J. Song, D. Q. Tran, S. R. Ferch, & L. C. Spears (Eds.), *Servant-leadership and forgiveness: How leaders help heal the heart of the world* (pp. 187–210). SUNY.

Tutu, D. (1998, Feb). Desmond Tutu (Z. Jaffrey, Interviewer). *The Progressive, 62,* 18–21.

Unschuld, P. U., Tessenow, H., & Zheng, J. (Eds. & Trans.). (2011). *Huang Di nei jing su wen: An annotated translation of Huang Di's inner classic—basic questions* (Vol. 1). University of California Press.

West, C. (2014). *Black prophetic fire: In dialogue with and edited by Christa Buschendorf.* Beacon Hill.

Wright, N. T. (2004). Women's service in the church: The biblical basis. http://ntwrightpage.com/2016/07/12/womens-service-in-the-church-the-biblical-basis/

Xie, W. (2011). *Zhong guo fu nv wen xue shi* [History of Chinese women's literature]. China Renmin University Press. (Original work published 1916)

Introduction

Servant-Leadership and Breaking Free of Gendered Categorizations

JOE WALSH, KAE REYNOLDS, AND
JENNIFER TILGHMAN-HAVENS

Section I by Joe Walsh

I remember the morning vividly. As I gaze outside at the fall colors, painting the University of Minnesota maroon and gold, I try to contain my nervous excitement for the impending philosophy course on knowledge and society. The epistemological discussions promised to happen were a constant source of generative energy for my college-aged self recently coming to terms with my attraction to other men and constantly questioning how identity is constructed by the self and by others. The first question raised this class period caught me off guard. In a room filled with inquisitive and inspiring minds, a student seeking to test the limits of social construction asks about how trans persons sexually identify. The presumption of their prompt comes from a binary gender perspective in which sexuality is also limited to either same- or opposite-gendered attraction and performance. The idea perplexed the room. Given a transitive gender identity, there came several invites for further information into this hypothetical situation. While I felt too threatened to engage with the conversation as a discreet gay man, I couldn't help but wonder what the dialogue would look like if instead of asking about the different identities assumed by society and our classroom,

1

the question was posited directly to this hypothetical person about their definition of their sexuality.

Too paralyzed to truly study for the rest of the lesson that day, the details in my memory are blank after this conversation. The prospect of a listening society that dares first to ask for a self-expression of identity rather than imposing a construction a priori onto our relationship with each other continued to ring in my mind. Such a subversion of the social construction of gender and sexuality, as I would later read and become engrossed in, lies at the heart of a leader that chooses to listen first and place emphasis upon the needs, well-being, and wholeness of the community over themselves. Considering the topic of Greenleaf's (1977/2002) liberating servant-leadership philosophy as it relates to the feminist movement within leadership studies, I see just how a closely related queer studies seeks insight into similar questions.

To better explore the impact that a true servant-leadership philosophy offers is to deepen our understanding of different ways of knowing—to move beyond the traditionally masculine definitions of leadership and engage meaningfully with feminist ways of knowing, which embrace both the feminine and masculine qualities of relating to one another, not as discrete states of being but as fluid polarities of wholeness. Hegemonic masculinity, which reigns over societal perceptions of authority and the conflation of leadership, asserts a leader-centric ontological claim (Heasley, 2005). The servant-leader philosophy seeks an understanding of leadership that is emergent within the interconnected nature of the community rather than from the authoritarian power and traits of the singular leader (Northouse, 2015).

Drawing inspiration from Herman Hesse's character Leo in *Journey to the East*, Robert K. Greenleaf recognized a needed paradigm shift in the ways society interacted with one another (Greenleaf, 1977/2002). Calling for *seekers* who are able to better identity the highest priority needs of the individual and society, Greenleaf recognized a moral ontological dilemma posing a crisis of leadership—the ways people relate to one another is too wrought with coercion and a blasé attitude toward the potentiality of one's neighbor. A *leader-first* mentality acts outside of their own consciousness, and the servant as leader who is motivated by the highest needs and noble pursuits actively engages within the positionality of their leadership practice in order to decenter themselves. The servant-leader does not attend to the needs of their followers as a means to an end, nor in an attempt to garner a false trust and increase a perception of connectivity or debt toward a group.

A servant-leader carries a philosophy that posits the highest needs, desires, and dreams of all, especially the least privileged, as the epitomized end.

A leader-centric philosophy acts as an imposition of a singular vision onto a community, much like the societal insistence on sexual definitions. A queer epistemology intentionally inquires about the needs, desires, and identity of the followers first. Queer epistemology is akin to the servant-leader philosophy in that both respect an individual's ownership of their identity first.

Greenleaf (1998) writes that a leader has the responsibility to concern oneself with those who are less privileged in society, and to address and remove inequalities. Yet, as the animating writing of Matthew Williams and Jennifer Tilghman-Havens as they appear in this text shows, servant-leadership theory is strictly limiting when identity work is not integrated, and a diversity of voices is missing. The cannon of servant-leadership continues to grow, and the writings contained within this anthology contribute to the ever-widening perspective of how the author's positionality directly relates to the theoretical and practical aspects of leadership.

As Greenleaf (1977/2002) coins the term *servant-leader* in his 1970 essay "The Servant as Leader," the feminist movement also gains momentum seeking liberation for all against the toxicity of a patriarchal system in which only wealthy white men are recognized as a legitimate and complete persons (hooks, 1984/2015). Greenleaf's (1977/2002) conception of legitimate power coming from relationship, and an authentic leader being one who chooses to serve first, creates a driving force for generative social interactions of leadership. The often-quoted best test of leadership, investigating whether those served are improved in their quality of life, are able to choose and live freely, and are themselves able and inspired to serve others, coincides directly with the feminist movement. To treat the person as whole means to embrace both the masculine and feminine and requires an epistemology that extends beyond reductive categorization. The whole person is an entity larger than labels, even those ubiquitous labels such as gender, and requires the servant as leader to see beyond the constraints of predefined social constructions.

A new way of seeing the world brings with it a promise of transformation. The servant as leader, embracing a listening-first disposition, is able to harvest a transformation of the ways in which we limit ourselves and our relations. Dr. Shann Ray Ferch, in his chapter "Eros and Logos," writes about the unification of the gendered ways of knowing that are too often considered rivals: for all genders to construct within themselves and their communities a synthesis of the feminine and masculine. Remarking on Greenleaf's poetic essays on the prophetic nature of the servant-leader, Ferch highlights how thinking outside of a strictly empirical construct creates opportunity for equitable, liberatory, and loving kindness paradigms, as opposed to reinforcing toxic masculinity and other colonizing practices.

Greenleaf's (1977/2002) assertion that the phenomenon of leadership has the responsibility to concern oneself with those who are less privileged in society, and to address and remove inequalities, walks in tandem with feminist and queer theory. In the nexus of servant-leadership, feminist, and queer philosophies is the idea that one's societally imposed identity ought not to limit a person's ability to emerge and speak with legitimate power and engage with leadership (Frick, 2004). The choice to define and exclusively construct society through the use of identity categories is inherently limiting to the human potential and reduces the generative possibilities of our social interactions. "If we can free ourselves from assuming the inevitability of some form of gender, then combinations of femininity and masculinity—and of same-gender or other gender desire—do not represent the only human possibilities" (Jackson, 2005, p. 33).

To be queer is to defy what is considered as traditional social constructions. "The nontraditional male presents an unknown. The difference demands justification and explanation. 'Non' requires an invention of self" (Heasley, 2005, p. 115). Queer epistemology directly challenges the linear logic of the postenlightenment social world, forcing a reconsideration of the social contract based on a loving axiomatic tradition. The inherent contradiction of the queer into normalized society threatens a perceived paradox, what Derrida considers aporia (Rasche, 2011).

The construction of servant-leadership, by intentionally joining the typically subservient *servant* with the connotatively assertive and ruling *leadership*, acts in kind with *queer* as a living paradoxical construction. For Greenleaf (1977/2002), to serve is fundamentally to listen—not limited to listening as a passive approach to following directions but rather listening to the natural transformations, yearnings, and potentialities of all those around us. The leader, in contrast, is characterized by the ability to decide and to declare to others the direction for moving forward. The connection between listening for the direction and shouting the direction for the future is found in the ways Greenleaf shapes the servant-leader as being in touch with the emerging future. Considering the foresight to be the "lead" of leadership, the hyphenation of *servant-leadership* acts to ease the aporetic understanding of what it means to be a natural servant and legitimate leader (Wallace, 2007).

As I reflect back on the lessons I gained from my experience in the epistemology discussion, and recognize the ways in which seeming contradictions around cultural understandings of gender and sexuality embolden an oppressive definition toward even hypothetical persons, I see just how powerful embracing a queer identity and worldview can be. As a leadership philosophy, queer epistemology elevates the liberatory forces that seek to break free of colonization, toxic masculinity, and archaic understandings of leadership as a phenomenon found in a specific type of hierarchy rather than as an emergent phenomenon within social relationships. Servant-leadership walks in step with queer philosophy, with the stunningly courageous feminist thinkers, and is primed for cutting-edge research to create new ways of seeing the world and each other.

Section II by Kae Reynolds

In my early years as a career academic, I attended a conference for servant-leadership, and I recall distinctly a rather awkward moment. One of the keynote speakers had opened the floor for questions, and a woman from the audience stood up and said two things. First, she commented on how curious it was that people find servant-leadership so revolutionary: women had been engaging in this form of leadership for generations. There was scattered laughter and applause in the room. Secondly, she commented on how the distinguished panel of keynote speakers was exclusively male and white. This time, there was a viscous moment of silence. For me, a person who tends to avoid conflict, this was excruciatingly awkward: but what a moment to relish. I admire this woman for having the courage to create a publicly awkward moment.

Conflict is awkward. We are experiencing these moments of awkwardness and discomfort increasingly, as the silenced masses leverage the tools of modern society both to expose the injustices entrenched and enacted through inequality, and to reveal the darkness and pain in the hearts of those who feel oppressed by enlightenment. The awkwardness of conflict is penetrating many areas of disagreement, as crisis after crisis sets in: whether a "Me Too" hashtag, a BLM protest, or decrying *covidiocy*, the public arena is flooded with awkward encounters of conflicting views and values. We are living in an age of crisis; yet crisis can bring key revelations as to the entwinement of human relationships and opportunities for transformation that have failed (Branicki, 2020).

Echoing the words of Shann Ray Ferch from his chapter in this anthology: we are harmed. Indeed, we are harmed; we are all harmed. We are hurt; we are indignant; we are suffering. We are all harmed because we are all inherently vulnerable. We face challenges, among these, the struggle for equality—not just for women, but with an understanding of a critical feminist philosophy that strives toward dignity for all marginalized groups. To better deal with these conflicts, we need better means to push through the awkwardness and get us to the other side without hurting each other: a consistent and intentional pursuit of integration. We need a language for taming conflict, holding environments for suspending vulnerability, and protocols for shaping resilience to ease the journey on rocky paths along which egos, hearts, minds, and souls are scattered.

People who wield political and economic power often appear to forget the vulnerable nature of humanity. They are under the illusion of immortality, existing in bubbles of false invincibility. Prime ministers, presidents, Hollywood moguls, and everyday toxic individuals permit themselves to harm others with hateful words and spiteful acts, dismissing their behavior as "jokes," "banter," "satire," or "alternative truths." But words hurt. Mere facial expressions hurt. The mere presence of an oppressor hurts. All forms of communication have intention, motivation, meaning, and impact. Those who wield and enact power must recognize the impact of their language, and the moral imperative to dismantle inequality and division. If the masked knife-throwing magician no longer cares to avoid impaling the lovely assistant, don't we need to ask ourselves: are our psyches evolving such that we no longer desire to escape harm and instead voraciously lust after schadenfreude? Even if we tire of "political correctness," we need people to stop being political-correctness snowflakes and start being more "woke" to the cult of carelessness enacted through the collusion of social violence and systems of androcentricity.

The post-truth society is both blessed and plagued by the paradox of transparency, which reveals both individual worthiness and collective cruelty. Standing by as we watch a person be degraded, assaulted, even murdered is symbolic of the collusion of which we are all guilty through our ignorance, indifference, and inaction. Our globalized and technologically interconnected society has created a hyperpublic town square of ubiquitous soapboxes. It has simultaneously empowered the masses to become their worst selves behind masks of technology-enhanced anonymity. The solipsists create anarchy and chaos by labeling everything except their own truth as "fake" and are so bold as to refuse to mask their toxicity. By daring to get awkward, those who shackle themselves in the stockades of social media, defying collusion to take a stand, subject themselves to invisible hands that freely and proudly sling rotting insults and putrefied death threats.

Marshall (2002) stated, "Integrity is doing the right thing when you don't have to—when no one else is looking or will ever know" (p. 142). Curiously, despite technology enabling us all to be looking all the time, it seems that collective integrity is fading, as the firing squads are shrouded in anonymity, firing at will for all who will look on. More than ever, in a postcare global arena, as we all throw ourselves to the proverbial lions, society needs a beacon. We need a code. A code for human potential, a code for embracing the social imperative of human existence and human survival. That beacon is the inalienable right to human dignity. May we vigorously pursue integration with intent and commitment by mounting the beacon of human dignity on a three-pillar foundation: appreciative inquiry, an ethic of care, and servant-leadership. Appreciative inquiry can provide the language for conflict mediation; servant-leadership, the culture, norm and protocol for resilience; and an ethic of care, the framework for managing vulnerability. This structure to uphold the beacon of human dignity should keep us right so that we can resist using conflict to destroy each other.

Crisis creates consequences for well-being and opportunities for learning. Instead of deploying weapons of mass division and mass humiliation, we choose to deploy the tools of appreciative inquiry and commit to what is life-affirming, not life-destroying:

> The task of AI is the penetrating search for what gives life, what fuels developmental potential, and what has deep meaning—even in the midst of the tragic. In so many times of disruption, there is always the radically increased potential to summon our better humanity. (Cooperrider & Fry, 2020, p. 269)

Gilligan (2011) challenged society to resist losing our humanity and losing the grounds that make us human: the capacity for empathy, for relationality—the capacity to care. We must practice caring responsiveness. The difference between a caring approach to crisis management and the traditional, rational approach lies first in the criteria for success: qualitative value (e.g., quality) of care and relationships versus a cost-benefit, cost-loss calculation of human and financial costs; second in the aim or purpose of the crisis response: social transformation (e.g., learning and progress toward improving quality of life and social justice) versus a return to normalcy; and third, in the means or praxis of the response (e.g., ongoing attention to relationships versus performance goals) (Branicki, 2020). With a care ethics approach, communities can promote the stability, efficacy, connectedness, and affirmative learning necessary to emerge stronger (Dückers et al., 2017).

In times of crisis, servant-leadership not only has potential for meeting the emotional and psychological needs of its recipients but can also enhance resilience:

> Leaders with a high level of resilience are able to respond in positive ways to crises their organizations may encounter and, by exhibiting that resilience and those positive responses, are able to increase the level of resilience of those around them. (Eliot, 2020, p. 12)

The inherent core of all ethical action must be to do no harm; and the inherent core of leadership must be to empower each other, enhance relationality, and build resilience. The leaders we choose must commit to deploying appreciative inquiry, servant-leadership, and an ethic of care to harness the generativity of conflict to strengthen our collective values, including the pursuit of equality.

With this anthology, we aspire to get awkward and raise awareness of the crisis of care exemplified in leadership inequality. We aspire to challenge assumptions of neoliberal capitalism and provide insight into the alternative pathways that appreciative inquiry, care ethics, and servant-leadership can provide both in times of crisis and in times of perceived normalcy. It is our hope with *Servant-Leadership, Feminism, and Gender Well-Being* to inspire and equip our readers with language to approach conflict with courage, to stand and create the awkwardness we need to evolve.

Section III by Jennifer Tilghman-Havens

As I consider the major issues facing our nation and the world, the social ills that plague us are increasingly the result of divisive binaries that inhibit our ability to engage with one another as a human community. The binaries of black/white, male/female, liberal/conservative, and so forth drive wedges between us, exactly at a moment in history when coming together to face the dangers before us (i.e., climate change, COVID-19, racism) presents our only chance at ensuring human and ecological flourishing. The term *leadership*, at its root, arises from the Old English word *laedon*—to take someone upward or forward, and *schaeppen*—to create something of deep value. Leadership at its best is bringing others together to move forward on a journey to create something deeply meaningful. This is what our world craves deeply—leaders to guide us toward creating a new, more equitable, more just and sustainable society. Too often our culture equates leadership with power, but the power associated with leading others on a meaningful journey cannot be decoupled from the wisdom to guide the path with care so that all may be included. Love must be part of the leading. A leader takes others with them because they care deeply for those being led, and they care for the valued project being envisioned together. Servant-leadership is an approach to leadership that aligns with these ideals. At the heart of servant-leadership is a profound invitation for leaders to embrace their fullest humanity and to honor that humanity in those around them, for the good of the whole.

Within this understanding of servant-leadership, examination of social identity is central. Each of us is called to reflect upon the inner dynamism of our interior life to notice both an embedded oppressor and embedded oppressed within us—aspects of our identity or family history that have been historically or culturally privileged and identities that have been marginalized (Ferch, 2012). The inner work of integrating these complex aspects of our identity is crucial to effective leadership that is integrative and liberatory for all. Robert Greenleaf's own countercultural vision is that leaders who have historically been advantaged will hand over their power so that those without out it can lead. This is a key aspect of servant-leadership. He asks, "What is the effect on the least privileged in society? Will they benefit or at least not be further deprived?" (Greenleaf, 1977/2002, p. 27). Where historically rooted dynamics of privilege and power are at play (for instance, in a mixed male-female boardroom, or in a diverse classroom led by a white teacher), traditionally advantaged leaders are invited into ongoing critical self-reflection to examine their ability to either disrupt or reinforce dominant norms. In whatever situation they find themselves in, leaders are invited to take part in critical self-examination: what are the privileges that, without my own awareness, can manifest themselves in toxic ways in this situation? Servant-leadership invites dominant-identity leaders to step back, to listen, to bring their full empathy, and to invite otherwise silenced voices for the benefit of the least privileged. This process in turn allows for the full humanity of each individual to arise and be added to the chorus of voices toward a richer, integrated harmony for all.

There is a very real cost to women and people of color when leaders neglect to see and validate the fullness of their contributions. For many women and people of color, lack of visibility within movements or organizations requires them to hustle and achieve more than male counterparts in order to be acknowledged as leaders (Lazarus & Steigerwalt, 2018). Attempting to make oneself visible and "seen" can lead to overcompensating, giving long hours, and sacrificing time at home and with family. In my own professional life, I work at an institution whose leadership history has until somewhat recently traditionally heralded white, male, clerical leaders. To compensate for not embodying the expected quality of a leader at my institution, I was intent to fulfill all my roles perfectly. Bowles and McGinn (2005) call this "reactive role management" (p. 202), a coping strategy used by many women and people of color who decide to meet every demand required by the various roles they embody in order to "meet the mark" that was not initially built for them in a white, male-dominated society. Sometimes reactive role management requires females and leaders of color to become "superpeople" to feel as though they are doing enough (Bowles & McGinn, 2005).

Servant-leadership is meant to be liberating for those being led. Servant-leadership that is deeply shaped by personal and social identity echoes themes of what I call "liberatory leadership," drawing upon the wisdom and theory of bell hooks (1984/2015) and Paolo Freire (1972). Within a liberatory approach to leadership, dominant-identity leaders (men, straight folks, and white-identifying leaders) engage in a process of liberating themselves from narrowly conceived visions of privilege. In turn, they are able to create conditions within organizations where others are liberated from unjust systems and welcomed fully as they are. Nondominant-identity leaders are invited into full participation at all levels of organizations and begin to be freed from internalized limiting self-conceptions, finding their authentic voice. Within this vision, integration becomes possible as women find liberation toward fully embracing their experience and gifts, and men find liberation in a new, more integrated masculinity. White leaders begin to examine the historical and current privileges of their white identity, and look to the wisdom and expertise of historically marginalized communities as guides in the journey toward the deeper meaning, justice, and truth to heal and unify our broken world.

References

Bowles, H. R., & McGinn, K. L. (2005). Claiming authority: Negotiating challenges for women leaders. In D. M. Messick & R. M. Kramer (Eds.), *The psychology of leadership: New perspectives and research* (pp. 191–208). Lawrence Erlbaum Associates.

Branicki, L. J. (2020). COVID-19, ethics of care and feminist crisis management. *Gender, Work & Organization, 27*(5), 872–883. https://doi.org/10.1111/gwao.12491

Cooperrider, D. L., & Fry, R. (2020). Appreciative inquiry in a pandemic: An improbable pairing. *The Journal of Applied Behavioral Science, 56*(3), 266–271. https://doi.org/10.1177/0021886320936265

Dückers, M. L. A., Yzermans, C. J., Jong, W., & Boin, A. (2017). Psychosocial crisis management: The unexplored intersection of crisis leadership and psychosocial support. *Risks, Hazards & Crisis in Public Policy, 8*(2), 94–112. https://doi.org/10.1002/rhc3.12113

Eliot, J. L. (2020). Resilient leadership: The impact of a servant leader on the resilience of their followers. *Advances in Developing Human Resources.* Advance online publication. https://doi.org/10.1177/1523422320945237

Ferch, S. R. (2012). *Forgiveness and power in the age of atrocity: Servant leadership as a way of life.* Lexington Books.

Freire, P. (1972). *Pedagogy of the oppressed* (M. Ramos, Trans.). Sheed and Ward.

Frick, D. (2004). *Robert K. Greenleaf: A life of servant leadership.* Berrett-Koehler.

Gilligan, C. (2011). *Joining the resistance.* Polity Press.

Greenleaf, R. K. (1998). *The power of servant leadership: Essays* (L. C. Spears, Ed.). Berrett-Koehler.

Greenleaf, R. K. (2002). *Servant leadership: A journey into the nature of legitimate power and greatness* (L. C. Spears, Ed.; 25th anniversary ed.). Paulist Press. (Original work published 1977)

Heasley, R. (2005). Crossing the borders of gendered sexuality: Queer masculinities of straight men. In C. Ingraham (Ed.), *Thinking straight: The power, the promise, and the paradox of heterosexuality* (pp. 109–130). Routledge.

hooks, b. (2015). *Feminist theory: From margin to center.* Routledge. (Original work published 1984)

Jackson, S. (2005). Sexuality, heterosexuality, and gender hierarchy: Getting our priorities straight. In C. Ingraham (Ed.), *Thinking straight: The power, the promise, and the paradox of heterosexuality* (pp. 15–38). Routledge.

Lazarus, J., & Steigerwalt, A. (2018). *Gendered vulnerability: How women work harder to stay in office.* University of Michigan Press.

Marshall, C. W. (2002). *Shattering the glass slipper: Destroying fairy-tale thinking before it destroys you.* Prominent Publishing.

Northouse, P. G. (2015). *Leadership: Theory and practice* (7th ed.). Sage.

Rasche, A. (2011). Organizing Derrida organizing: Deconstruction and organization theory. In H. Tsoukas & R. Chia (Eds.), *Philosophy and organization theory* (pp. 251–280). Emerald Group Publishing.

Wallace, D. (2007). The power of a hyphen: The primacy of servanthood in servant-leadership. In S. R. Ferch & L. C. Spears (Eds.), *The spirit of servant-leadership* (pp. 166–169). Paulist Press.

SECTION I

THE FEMINIST ESSENCE OF SERVANT-LEADERSHIP

Chapter 1

The Poetry of Servant-Leadership
I Walked This Earth

PATRICIA VALDÉS

I bend toiling the land. I go on strike to feed my children . . . to serve my family.
I stand to claim land, land that belongs to the poor . . . to serve my community.
I speak against the government. I am jailed and tortured . . . to serve my country.
I walk to protest the killing of my people . . . to serve humanity.
Some say I am *loca* . . . crazy
. . . I should stay home.
Some say I should not go out to the plaza.
. . . I will go into exile.
Some say they will kill my spirit . . . my body.
Some said I was only a woman, *solo una mujer* . . .
Others . . . perhaps the ones that join the struggle . . .
They know that service, passion, and love were my guides.
They said I walked this earth . . . woman leader . . . a servant-leader.

Chapter 2

The Poetry of Servant-Leadership

You Like to Fly at Night . . .

NADINE CHAPMAN

You like to fly at night
the calmest time and cool
no threat of thermals   downdrafts

For you the elements connect
at angles far above the earth
Despite motion sickness
fear of heights
I must scope the North Sky
night dance with you
across a floorless stage

A midnight sun blazes
over the Alaska Range
At cruising altitude
we burst onto the Yukon Basin
Double vision
In your face joy fractures fear
and carries me away

Chapter 3

Servant-Leadership

A Feminist Perspective

KAE REYNOLDS

At the heart of this chapter is the notion that servant-leadership has potential as a feminism-informed, care-oriented, and gender-integrative approach to organizational leadership. Although there is a significant body of literature on feminist and gender-based interpretations of leadership, the same is not true for servant-leadership. The main contributors to date include Crippen's (2004) narrative inquiry of three women servant-leaders, Eicher-Catt's (2005) feminist critique of servant-leadership, Oner's (2009) and Barbuto and Gifford's (2010) empirical studies of gender differences in servant-leadership, and Ngunjiri's (2010) phenomenological study of African women servant-leaders.

This chapter expands the conceptual development of servant-leadership through a feminist framework. The intent is to explore whether the servant-leadership philosophy has potential as a gender-integrative mode of leadership. Gaps in previous research are addressed through a broader scope of feminist analysis and inquiry to servant-leadership. The analyses unfolds as a literature review building on discussions of gender and feminist perspectives of leadership and servant-leadership in the context of leadership theory, gender, and feminist critique.

Feminist Perspectives on Leadership

Traditional perspectives of leadership assume inherent systems of influence and structure for human organization (Chin, 2007). Northouse (2007) offered an example of a typical definition of leadership from a popular textbook: "Leadership is a process whereby an individual influences a group of individuals to achieve a common goal" (p. 3). Smircich and Morgan (1982) offered a definition of the leadership process from a feminist perspective: "Leadership is realized in the process whereby one or more individuals succeed in attempting to frame and define the reality of others" (p. 258). Based on the notion that a person (or group) mobilizes systems of power (framing and defining reality) over other(s) toward the achievement of a goal (framed and defined by whom?) through human organization, leadership especially merits interpretation from a feminist perspective.

In my experience of studying leadership, my fellow colleagues have often expressed common misconceptions about what feminism comprises. There seems to be confusion about what a feminist perspective entails. Some have assumed that if a woman authors a paper, she has implicitly represented a feminist (i.e., a woman's) perspective. Others have assumed that if the participants in a study are exclusively women, or if the study includes gender as a variable, these studies have necessarily adopted a feminist perspective. If this were true, there would be a plethora of feminist research in the field of leadership. Obviously, this is not the case. Whether or not a piece of leadership research adopts a feminist perspective is not necessarily determined by the gender or sex of the scholar or the gender or sex of research participants, nor is the inclusion of gender or sex as a variable a determining factor of a feminist perspective. Only if the researcher employs feminism as the interpretive framework would a study or theoretical piece constitute a feminist perspective (Hesse-Biber, 2007).

To demonstrate these assumptions as misconceptions, I conducted an experimental search of scholarly peer-reviewed journals using the resources from the Foley Center Library at Gonzaga University in the databases Academic Search Premier, Business Source Premier, PsychInfo, SocIndex, ERIC, and Communication and Mass Media Complete. I initially entered the keyword *leadership* in the subject field and the term *gender* in the title field of the search interface, which yielded 608 results. Entering the term *feminist* in the text field (indicating a full-text search—i.e., do the authors even consider feminism?) to refine the search reduced the number of hits to 65 articles. Entering the term *feminist* in the abstract field (indicating a strong focus in the paper on feminism) narrowed the results to just 19 hits (this search was executed on March 23, 2011). Therefore, of 608 articles claiming the subject *leadership* with *gender* as a motivating keyword for the title, only 19 made *feminism* a sufficiently central concern to merit its discussion in the abstract. This, in my view, demonstrates that although including biological sex or gender as a variable may generate knowledge that includes women, it does not necessitate a feminist perspective.

Differences between women and men can be measured quantitatively or interpreted qualitatively; however, whether the research adopts a feminist perspective depends on the questions asked (Hesse-Biber, 2007), the conceptual framework (Brooks & Hesse-Biber, 2007), and the interpretation of results in relation to a feminist agenda (Miner-Rubino & Jayaratne, 2007). The degree to which gendered power systems become a central theme in a piece of scholarship can be considered an indication of convergence with feminist interpretation (Hesse-Biber & Leavy, 2007). Acknowledging where gender differences are perceived and can or cannot be verified is a first step toward questioning why they exist, in what context they exist, what systems create them, and how strategies toward integration can be devised.

There are several ways researchers and theorists have approached examining leadership in the context of feminism. One is to use perceived gender differences in leadership as a foundation for feminist interpretation, such as understanding the glass ceiling (Eagly & Sczesny, 2009). Another way is to question and challenge the systems of gender operating in leadership, for example, through phenomenological study of the meaning of leadership (Parker, 2005). Yet another way is to deconstruct gendered language and gendered systems that construct perceptions of leadership (Calás & Smircich, 1991). The following is a brief review of these three common approaches to the study of gender in leadership.

Gender Differences in Leadership

Extensive research has been conducted concerning gender differences in leadership styles (Eagly & Carli, 2004). Eagly and Johnson (1990) and Eagly et al. (2003) conducted meta-analyses of empirical studies on gender differences in leadership styles. Both of these meta-analyses produced findings that reinforced the traditional assignment of gender-bound attributes (Eagly & Carli, 2004). Results showed that women and men tended to differ in their application of democratic and participative style (more typical of women) versus an authoritative and directive style (more typical of men) (Eagly & Johnson, 1990). In addition, women exceeded men on measures of transformational behavior, individual consideration, and contingent reward (Eagly et al., 2003). Through interpretation of research findings, Eagly and her colleagues have contributed significantly to understanding the sources of difference. Part of this work included turning the focus to the glass-ceiling phenomenon (Eagly & Sczesny, 2009), gender congruity, stereotyping, and discrimination, as well as the creation of a new metaphor for women's challenges in aspiring to leadership: the labyrinth (Eagly & Carli, 2004). Much mainstream research on gender in leadership, however, remains limited to examining gender differences between women and men as leaders and lacks critical interpretation (Ford, 2005).

Women's Leadership

Since roughly the last decade of the twentieth century, research on how women lead has become more frequent. Making women the primary subjects of study has been a process through which scholars contributed to the inclusion of women in leadership research. Qualitative studies on women leaders have also often supported stereotypical gender notions. One well-known author who brought the subject of women leaders into mainstream discussion is Helgesen (1995). In her book, Helgesen described women's methods of leadership as striking more of a balance than men's. The balance was largely driven by self-care, relationships, and social concern (Helgesen, 1995). Madden (2007) claimed that collaboration is "the most prominent theme" in feminist leadership (p. 192). This claim was supported by Fine (2007, 2009), who described collaboration as giving voice, listening, empowering, and team building. Fine (2007) also concluded that the women in her study "discursively constructed a vision of leadership through *a moral discourse of leadership*" (p. 182). The four principles of leadership the women in Fine's (2007) study described were making a positive contribution, collaboration, open communication, and honesty in relationships. Discussion of citizenship, community, information sharing, ethics, and attending to relational aspects of leading supported emergent themes. In her study of African American women leaders, Parker (2005) produced findings that reinforced several of Fine's (2007) themes. Parker's (2005) study also added a dimension of interactive leadership described as communicating knowledge (information sharing), being accessible, and role modeling. Parker revised Fine's (2007) version of making a positive contribution as "leadership through boundary spanning" (Parker, 2005, p. 84) that challenges fixed ideas of organizational boundaries and extends responsibility to community needs.

The insight gained from exclusively studying women's practice of leadership on the one hand created a space for opening up the androcentric matrix of leadership. On the other hand, the danger of perpetuating essentialist assumptions of the gender paradigm remains. In response to this warning, Fine (2007) stated, "Discussion of the research on women's leadership . . . is not intended to essentialize women. . . . The values expressed in the research on women and leadership suggest new ways of theorizing about leadership" (pp. 181–182). By focusing exclusively on women's perspectives of leadership, the field was able to gain new insights and new possibilities for constructing leadership that had been previously ignored by a male-biased perspective.

Gendered Power Relations in Leadership

Some poststructural feminist and critical scholars (Billing & Alvesson, 2000; Brady & Hammett, 1999; Calás & Smircich, 1991; Johanson, 2008; Kark, 2004; Smircich & Morgan, 1982) who have addressed leadership in a broader organizational context focus primarily on the language of leadership. Discourse analysis and deconstruction are their main tools for interpretation. Such deconstruction feminist analyses of leadership have revealed how leadership discourse is contained within an androcentric matrix. Echoing Eisler (1994), Johanson (2008) pointed out that leadership discourse is not only attributed with masculinity by default, but that in attempts to appear gender-neutral, they also fail to acknowledge the feminine gendering of new parameters for effective leadership behavior. Findings from Johanson's (2008) experimental study showed that although contemporary leadership theories may describe and espouse "arguably feminine" behaviors (p. 784), implicit theories of leadership remain strongly stereotypically male. Johanson's results supported Eagly and Carli's (2004) conclusions about gender congruence in leadership. Because the role of leader is still so strongly associated with maleness, women encounter discrimination when displaying leadership behaviors that are not congruent with acceptable degrees of masculinity in women (Eagly & Carli, 2004).

Viewing leadership through a gendered lens also reveals how the notion of leadership is romanticized. Meindl et al. (1985) asserted that by romanticizing leaders and the effects of leadership, followers are better able to cope with organizational ambiguity. Such romantic fantasies and adherence to the mystery of leadership add a satisfying sense of myth to leadership, which permits followers to ascribe responsibility for events and outcomes to the leaders (Meindl et al. 1985). In their analysis of leadership as seduction, Calás and Smircich (1991) pointed out how leadership embodies desire. Corrupt leadership—as opposed to ethical leadership—seduces and misleads followers (Calás & Smircich, 1991). They qualified this analogy further in the sexualized context: whereas a leader is by default a man, a seductress is by default a woman. Such sexualized observations reveal male bias and a heterosexual framework in the leadership matrix. In this way, deconstruction feminist perspectives allow for a critical reflection of how gendered hierarchies of power are implicit in supposedly neutral leadership discourse. This idea will be discussed in connection with servant-leadership later in this chapter.

Summary

This brief review of gender and feminist perspectives of leadership points out several ideas that are important for developing the discussion of servant-leadership and feminism. First, underlying assumptions about leadership and gender generally tend to reflect historical gender stereotyping. Second, failing to acknowledge supposedly feminine aspects of leadership as feminine perpetuates the androcentric gendering of leadership. Third, the continued labeling of traditionally feminine behaviors as feminine is unacceptable for deconstruction feminism. To formulate a gender-integrative perspective of leadership, it is necessary to envision leadership behaviors and attitudes as exclusive to neither women nor men. Indeed, describing gender differences within an androcentric matrix of leadership may only perpetuate essentialist assumptions of gender differences based on biological determinism. Nevertheless, it is equally important to reveal how gender socialization has affected women's perspectives and practices of leadership to open up possibilities for changing the gender hierarchy of leadership. Discovering gender differences in leadership, studying leadership in a gender vacuum, and deconstructing the gendered nature of leadership tend to reinforce instinctive beliefs that evolve through cultural gender socialization. Ultimately, all this work has established is that gender as a social construct permeates leadership phenomena within an androcentric matrix and continues to be reinforced by gendered discourse. As such, the question remains, how do we move beyond gendered leadership toward gender-integrative leadership?

Servant-Leadership

Servant-leadership literature credits Robert K. Greenleaf with coining the term *servant-leadership* in the essay *The Servant as Leader* from 1970 (Beazley, 2003). This vision emerged out of Greenleaf's experiences in the business world (Spears, 2003). Greenleaf (1977/2002) credited his inspiration of the leader as servant to the fictional character Andres Leo in Hesse's (1956/2003) *Journey to the East*. Leo, initially characterized as a servant, was later revealed as a leader who served others. This image prompted Greenleaf to document his ideas in essays that were later published.

Servant-leadership has as its focus the mutually determinate development of individuals and strengthening of community (Spears, 2003, p. 19). Greenleaf (1977/2002) clearly identified the developmental needs of followers and community needs as the driving forces of servant-leadership. The centrality of this needs-focused attitude includes the validity of individual needs (van Dierendonck & Heeren, 2006). In a servant-led organization, people take priority over issues (Stone et al., 2003). The attitude of the servant-leader is that of an equal who accepts the imperfection of others and oneself and is able to see the potential for growth and healing (Greenleaf, 2003). The servant-leader's first impulse is to listen, and first desire is to serve (Greenleaf, 1977/2002), such that beneficial transformation occurs in the followers (Greenleaf, 2003). In his essay on servant-leadership, forgiveness, and social justice, Ferch (2004) noted that the human capacities to discern one's own faults, to seek and grant forgiveness, and to heal relationships are central ideas of servant-leadership. Servant-leadership in this way asserts that genuinely building up people's spirits and abilities also builds community; the formation and achievement of organizational objectives follow.

The servant-leader exercises integrity and care, applies foresight and cognitive capacity to shape activity, and provides opportunity in the best interest of followers (Greenleaf, 2003, p. 65). Greenleaf also stressed the importance of an attitude of social justice (Ferch, 2004) and moral integrity in the servant-leader. The basic assumption of servant-leadership questions the structure-bound and prevailing image of leaders as dominating and being served by followers. The notion of the leader serving others, regardless of status or structural power, challenges culturally persistent norms of leadership as a manifestation of hierarchies (Page & Wong, 2000). Greenleaf (2003) thus turned the predominant vision of organizational hierarchy—with leaders at the top of the pyramid—upside down (Page & Wong, 2000). Servant-leadership advocates flattened structures, collaborative leadership, individual initiative, and commitment (Greenleaf 2002). The servant-leader acts as primus inter pares, "first among equals" (p. 74), and is thus shielded from the isolation and immense burden of sole responsibility. By promoting shared leadership and follower-centered leadership, Greenleaf proposed to demythologize (p. 70) and deromanticize (p. 41) the heroic lone-wolf leader. Each individual employee is summoned to exercise mutually reinforcing servant-leadership: organizational members for institutions and for each other, and institutions for social responsibility within communities and social justice globally (Greenleaf, 2003, p. 37).

Theoretical work in servant-leadership has also led to empirical work. Some of the most comprehensive reviews of servant-leadership models and instruments were conducted by van Dierendonck (2010), van Dierendonck and Heeren (2006), and van Dierendonck and Nuijten (2011). For the purposes of this literature review, I have summarized the arguments of van Dierendonck and Nuijten (2011) underlying their operationalization of distinguishing constructs of servant-leadership. In their development of a new servant-leadership model, van Dierendonck and Nuijten described eight constructs, which, they asserted, solved some of the deficiencies of previous models and differentiate servant-leadership from other leadership models. These constructs are empowerment, accountability, standing back, humility, authenticity, courage, forgiveness (interpersonal acceptance), and stewardship (p. 251–252). Within these constructs, I identified some underlying values and attitudes as follows. A relational focus is evident in the constructs of empowerment, forgiveness, and accountability. Power sharing and participative aspects of leadership are represented in the constructs of standing back and stewardship, as well as empowerment and accountability. The capacity for adequately distributing one's own personal resources and downplaying self-promotion can be interpreted from the constructs of empowerment, accountability, standing back, and forgiveness. An attitude to ethics and social justice is implied in the constructs of humility, authenticity, courage, and forgiveness.

In summary, I assert that the overarching elements of servant-leadership can be expressed as (a) valuing people, relationships, and community above issues; (b) sharing power and decision making in human organization; (c) finding balance between well-being and performance; and (d) placing ethics and social justice above delusions of personal and in-group grandeur. The purpose of the subsequent sections is to develop a deeper understanding of servant-leadership, its assets and its flaws, and to highlight aspects of servant-leadership. The following discussion looks at servant-leadership first through two frameworks of leadership theory: transformational leadership and ethical leadership. In the following, I presented servant-leadership through the lens of gender, analogous to the preceding section on feminist perspectives of leadership. This review included critiques of servant-leadership and foremost a discussion of critical feminist deconstruction of servant-leadership.

Servant-Leadership in the Context of Leadership

Transformational Leadership

Leadership theory has sometimes characterized servant-leadership as a sub-category of transformational leadership (Reinke, 2004; Stone et al., 2003). In Burns's (1978) original conceptualization, he described transformational leadership as having the capacity to raise followers' motivation to transcend individual needs and advance collective purposes. Burns's description framed transformational leadership as capable of increasing the moral attitude of followers (Graham, 1995). When Bass (1999) operationalized transformational leadership into four dimensions—individualized consideration, intellectual stimulation, inspirational motivation, and idealized influence—it led to transformational leadership shifting focus to a model driven by elevating organizational goals and performance standards above the "selfish" needs of followers (p. 13). Bass saw the transformational leader as the dominant force for determining collective organizational objectives and subsequently aligning followers' needs with them (p. 13). Transformational leadership also emphasizes organizational results according to Reinke (2004). Although servant-leadership might express certain constructs of transformational leadership, the focus is different.

Servant-leadership clearly identifies the developmental and community needs of followers as the driving force and includes the validity of individual needs (Greenleaf, 1977/2002; van Dierendonck & Heeren, 2006). In an environment of servant-leadership, people take priority over issues (Stone et al., 2003). The servant-leader, in contrast to the transformational leader, aligns organizational objectives with human needs (Mayer et al., 2008;

Stone et al., 2003). As organizational goals fulfill the needs of those served, beneficial transformation occurs in the organizational members (Greenleaf, 2003), and consequently the community and society. This alignment can be attributed to the servant-leader's first impulse to listen and first desire to serve (Greenleaf, 1977/2002). In this way, servant-leadership addresses issues of subjectivity and the situatedness of organizational members differently from transformational leadership. Although transformational leadership, as described by Bass (1999), also expresses other-centered constructs such as intellectual stimulation and individual consideration, transformational leadership differs from servant-leadership in its focus on organizational objectives and preference to value performance above human need. The debate about human needs versus organizational goals in leadership places the ethical component of leadership in the foreground.

Ethical Leadership

Prosser (2010) delivered a compelling argument that servant-leadership is better understood as a philosophy of leadership than as an academic theory or leadership model. Indeed, Greenleaf's (2003) vision of servant-leadership was not originally developed through academic scholarship. The philosophy perspective of servant-leadership supported the categorization of servant-leadership under the subheadings of normative and ethical leadership by Johnson (2008) and Northouse (2007), respectively. Indeed, theoretical discussion of servant-leadership has often referenced ethical frameworks such as *agapáo* (Ayers 2008; Patterson & Stone, 2004), virtue ethics (Lanctot & Irving, 2007), and the five major religious worldviews (Kriger & Seng, 2005). Graham (1995) presented an early analysis of servant-leadership in an ethical framework in the context of Kohlberg's (1994) stages of moral development. Graham (1995) summarized, "Servant leaders serve their followers best when they model and also encourage others not only to engage in independent moral reasoning, but also to follow it up with constructive participation in organizational governance" (p. 51). In Graham's assessment, transformational and servant-leaders encourage followers to engage in postconventional moral reasoning. The suggestion is that leaders promote followers' moral development by operating from a standpoint of superior morality. This assertion is more congruent with Burns's (1978) description of the transformational leader's moral imperative to operate at higher levels of moral reasoning and elevate others to higher levels of moral behavior.

In contrast to the implications of Graham's (1995) assessment, Patterson (2004) asserted that servant-leaders possess an attitude of humility. Greenleaf (2003) stressed the importance of an attitude of social justice and moral integrity in the servant-leader in relation to those served. Greenleaf encouraged all organizational members to serve others' needs such that those served are at least no worse off than before. He also emphasized the need for servant-leaders to engage in self-reflection and regeneration to ensure that self-care is not neglected. In the context of self-care and concern for others' needs, the attitude of self-in-relation (Fletcher, 2004) present in servant-leadership promotes a relational ethic of leadership that is much stronger than in transformational leadership. Neither the hierarchical structure of a Kohlbergian pure justice approach to moral reasoning (Graham, 1995) nor the hierarchical structure of a Bass-Burnsian concept of determining organizational objectives adequately characterize a servant-leadership approach to those served or the one serving. The subjectivity of those-served takes on a powerful position in the servant-leadership process. By virtue of the servant-leader attitudes of stewardship, listening, and building community (Spears, 2002) the situatedness of those served is assigned higher ethical value than in transformational leadership.

A Gender Perspective of Servant-Leadership

By linking two terms that traditionally denote subordination (servant) and domination (leader), Greenleaf (2003) disrupted a long-established understanding of power structures. From a feminist perspective, such disruption is part of the process toward achieving gender equity. However, paradoxes create ambiguities that demand interpretation. As such, servant-leadership provides an interesting playing field for exploring gender-integrative approaches to leadership. The following provides a discussion of the paradox of servant and leader from a gender perspective.

The assumption that leadership is embedded in hierarchies often goes unquestioned (Iannello, 1992), as do many systems within predominantly masculinized contexts, such as organizations (Madden, 2007). That top-down hierarchies in organizations often remain unquestioned is a claim echoed in feminist perspectives of the gender hierarchy. In her deconstruction of servant-leadership rhetoric, Eicher-Catt (2005) pointed out that the feminine and the masculine, based on traditional gender hierarchies, are associated with subjugation and domination, respectively. In her interpretation, the aspect of servant would be equivalent to the feminine, and the aspect of leader equivalent to the masculine. This observation by Eicher-Catt serves as a fundamental framework for examining servant-leadership constructs in terms of gender.

Among the vast literature on servant-leadership, both academic and popular, one of the most often cited and relatable interpretations of servant-leadership constructs came from Spears (2002). From his readings of Greenleaf, Spears defined a set of 10 characteristics that he believed to be the core of servant-leader behavior and activity: listening, empathizing, healing, practicing stewardship (serving the needs of others), exercising commitment to the growth of people, building community, foresight, conceptualization, awareness, and persuasion (Spears, 2002). In my view, six of the characteristics distinguish servant-leadership from other forms of leadership, and the other four are more strongly associated with traditional notions of leadership (Reynolds, 2011). These distinguishing characteristics, or behaviors, are practicing stewardship, listening, empathizing, healing, exercising commitment to the growth of people, and building community. The other group comprises foresight, conceptualization, awareness, and persuasion. Leadership theory provides some theoretical and empirical support for my claim, which I outlined briefly in a previous publication and reiterate here in greater depth.

Based on several predominant findings of leadership scholars, the behaviors—foresight, conceptualization, awareness, and persuasion—of servant-leadership can be described as *leader* behaviors (Reynolds, 2011). For example, through a comprehensive analysis of research and theoretical work on servant-leadership, van Dierendonck (2010) related aspects of these four characteristics to the key characteristic *providing direction*. "Providing direction" is one of the main entries in *Merriam-Webster*'s definition of *leading* and virtually synonymous with the concept of leadership ("Leading," n.d.). Later, van Dierendonck and Nuijten (2011) related this key characteristic to their constructs of servant-leadership Courage and Accountability. Van Dierendonck (2010) clarified this connection as follows:

> A servant-leader's take on providing direction is to make work dynamic and "tailor made" (based on follower abilities, needs, and input). In this sense, providing direction is about providing the right degree of accountability. . . . It can also imply creating new ways or new approaches to old problems. (p. 8)

Historically, leadership theory offered a variety of models that define leadership in terms of traits and behaviors. Leadership trait theory defined *forward-looking* as one of the most dominant leadership traits (Northouse, 2007). This trait—forward-looking—corresponds, in my interpretation, to Spears's (2002) servant-leader characteristic *foresight*. Concepts from theories of visionary leadership also provided support. For example, Kouzes and Posner (2002) and Sashkin and Sashkin (2003) both described transformational leadership in models sometimes referred to as visionary leadership. Their concept of vision, in my view, can be equivocated with *foresight* (Reynolds, 2011).

The servant-leader characteristic of *conceptualization* can also be associated with concepts from transformational leadership theory (Reynolds, 2011). Conceptualization can be thought of as a certain kind of cognitive ability, a trait that has been described in leadership theory by both Sashkin and Sashkin (2003) and Kouzes and Posner (2002). Other traits and behaviors from leadership theory, such as competence and knowledge of the business (Kouzes & Posner, 2002), can be attributed to cognitive ability. Competence, the ability to conceptualize options and solutions cognitively, is often associated with intelligence and critical thought (Reynolds, 2011). In his operationalization of transformational leadership, Bass (1999) included the construct of intellectual stimulation as an aspect of leadership. In this way, conceptualization, cognitive capacity, knowledge, and intelligence are applied to stimulate other organizational members intellectually (Reynolds, 2011).

The servant-leadership characteristic *awareness* is also an aspect of transformational leadership. Awareness can be understood as both self-awareness and awareness of the (business) environment. Krishnan and Arora (2008) noted that transformational leadership had a high correlation with the constructs self-awareness and public self-consciousness, an awareness of the self and part of a social environment. Kouzes and Posner (2002) asserted that leadership also includes the ability to assess environmental influences. This claim was supported by a study of transformational leadership and situation awareness conducted by Eid et al. (2004) in a military setting. Eid et al. described situation awareness as a construct that includes, for example, perception, memory, and schemas (p. 204). They found that transformational leadership actually predicted situation awareness.

Persuasion is the fourth characteristic of servant-leadership described by Spears (2002) that can be associated with transformational leadership. Several other behaviors that have been associated with leadership can be understood as elements of persuasive behavior (Reynolds, 2011). Specifically, the constructs alignment, inspiration, assertiveness, and influence, which are also strongly associated with change leadership (Gill, 2003), indicate persuasion in leadership. The leadership construct of assertiveness surfaced out of trait theory (Northouse, 2007). In his operationalization of transformational leadership, Bass (1999) described dimensions that included inspirational motivation and idealized influence. Kouzes and Posner (2002) included in their model the behavior of inspiring others, which also aligned with Bass's (1999) construct of inspirational motivation. Change leadership scholars, such as Gill (2003) and Kotter (1996), wrote extensively about the importance of alignment, for example, aligning followers' goals with organizational goals. Other studies also supported the importance of inter-personal influence in transformational leadership. For example, Eid et al. (2004) found that transformational leadership also predicted interpersonal influence. Foresight, conceptualization, awareness, and persuasion are aspects of servant-leadership that I asserted can be characterized as leader aspects (Reynolds, 2011).

Thus, building on Eicher-Catt's (2005) observation of gendered notions associated with the terms *servant* and *leader*, I argue that these characteristics can also be associated with socialized gendered notions of behavior. The previous discussion of gender in leadership demonstrated the strong asso-ciation of leadership with the masculine. Numerous gender assessments of leadership supported the claim that leadership is still predominantly associated with male socialization (Coleman, 2003) and masculinity, despite cultural differences in the construction of masculinity and leadership (Fine, 2007). It follows that the leader characteristics of servant-leadership would comprise the more traditionally masculine aspect of leadership. Further support of my conceptualization of gender in servant-leadership was provided by Barbuto and Gifford (2010). They noted in their study of sex differences in servant-leadership dimensions that these four servant-leader characteristics—foresight, conceptualization, awareness, and persuasion—are predominantly associated with agency and masculine behavior.

The following presents a discussion of servant characteristics as the feminine aspect of servant-leadership. In the context of servant-leadership, Oner (2009) examined aspects of leadership typically associated with servant-leadership in Turkish business employees. She described these characteris-tics—empathy for others, authentic listening, nurturance, and caring—as feminine. Barbuto and Gifford (2010) pointed out that needs-focused and other-centered characteristics are more strongly associated with feminine behavior. These traditionally feminine socialized behaviors, I argue, are embedded in what Northouse (2007) delineated as the relationship-oriented aspects of leadership (in contrast to the task-oriented aspects). Integrative behaviors—such as dialogue and nonviolent conflict resolution—also traditionally belong to the realm of feminine socialization (Eisler, 1994). In leadership theory terms, they could be understood as what Howell (1988) called *socialized leadership* aspects. The six servant-leader characteristics described by Spears (2002) that can be associated with the feminine aspect of gender are also predominantly needs-focused and other-oriented: listening, empathizing, healing, practicing stewardship (serving the needs of others), exercising commitment to the growth of people, and building community (Reynolds, 2011). In van Dierendonck and Nuijten's (2011) model, the five constructs of empowerment, humility, standing back, stewardship, and forgiveness also represented socialized aspects of behavior as opposed to personalized aspects.

Although these observations might support Eicher-Catt's (2005) assertions that, from a gendered perspective, serving is predominantly associated with femininity and leading with masculinity, they need not be associated with the negative aspects associated with gendered notions. For example, Eagly et al. (2003) noted that some of the more negative masculine aspects of leadership (in particular transactional leadership) and organizations include hierarchical power structures, coercive power, and focus on competition. Other negative aspects of leadership have been described in charismatic leadership theory. For example, Conger and Kanugo (1998) warned of the dangers associated with the self-centered and manipulative nature of charismatic leadership. Other scholars have differentiated between ethical and unethical transformational leaders (Bass & Steidlmeier, 1999; Howell, 1988; Howell & Avolio, 1992), who consistently differ in terms of socialized versus personalized interests and motivations, respectively. The leader aspects of the servant-leader outlined above—awareness, conceptualization, persuasion, and foresight—may be congruent with a general concept of leadership, but these aspects do not necessarily imply coercive domination or manipulation associated with negative leadership aspects. Indeed, I argue that, when combined with the servant facets of leadership, the leader facets suggest ethical, socialized leadership.

Following this same line of thinking, the more traditionally feminine aspects of servant-leadership also need not be confined to negative connotations. Keshet et al. (2006) noted that the descriptive nature of gendered notions stereotypically views women and behaviors associated with the feminine as weak and submissive. Similar negative connotations of the concept *servant* were outlined by Eicher-Catt (2005). Van Dierendonck (2010) noted that although servant-leadership has some overlap with models of self-sacrificing leadership, he also asserted that self-determination is an essential condition of servant-leader behavior. He argued that a self-determined leader does not seek power for its own sake and as a result has a stronger capacity to distribute personal resources in a healthy manner. In this way, self-sacrifice is not sacrifice or self-denial at all. Servant-leaders, through the capacity to fulfill their own basic psychological needs and by virtue of the lack of self-centeredness and desire to dominate (van Dierendonck, 2010), are willing and able to forgo the typically ostentatious rewards of power and position. In addition, the servant-leader aspects of accountability, stewardship, and empowerment (van Dierendonck, 2010; van Dierendonck & Nuijten, 2011) contradict the claim that serving in servant-leadership could be associated with placating or self-degrading connotations of coerced subservience.

Based on previous arguments about behaviors traditionally associated with female socialization, it would follow that listening, empathizing, and empowering others might be considered signs of weakness in a leader. Whether or not these arguably traditionally feminine aspects of servant-leadership are considered passive or active, signs of weakness or of strength, appears to be unimportant considering the power of gender role congruity. Eagly and Karau (2002) reported that the consequences of perceived incongruity with gender roles in the leadership context cause women to be evaluated less favorably as leaders and as potential leaders in general. Few would argue that the feminine characteristics of servant-leadership are undesirable behaviors in either women or men. Indeed, Johanson (2008) reported that male leaders could successfully integrate feminine behaviors into their leadership. Apparently, men can integrate positive feminine behaviors without violating gender role congruity. Nevertheless, evidence of constraints imposed on women as leaders, as posited by gender role congruity theory (Eagly & Karau, 2002) and critical skepticism over the potential and effectiveness of servant-leadership in the business environment (Johnson, 2008; Showkeir, 2002) tend to support the assertion that feminine behavior is negatively perceived in leadership.

In the previous discussion, I outlined arguments supporting my claim that the characteristics distinguishing servant-leadership from other leadership perspectives are traditionally feminine-attributed aspects of servant-leadership. It follows that servant-leadership adds more feminine-gendered behaviors to the leadership matrix. Although from the feminist deconstruction standpoint represented by Eicher-Catt (2005) this condition of servant-leadership might not be congruent with feminist objectives, I argue that the servant-leadership perspective can nevertheless serve as a driving force for generating discourse on gender-integrative approaches to organizational leadership. The aspects of servant and leader need not necessarily be loaded with the hierarchical connotations of subjugation and domination. They can also be understood as an integration of common, desirable human behavior and activity.

Women and Feminism in Servant-Leadership Literature

Numerous women have contributed to the body of literature and research on servant-leadership (see the anthologies Spears, 1995, 1998b; and Spears & Lawrence, 2002, 2004 for examples of female servant-leader essayists; and Crippen, 2004; Dannhauser & Boshoff, 2006; Graham, 1995; Ngunjiri, 2010; Parolini et al., 2009; Patterson, 2004; Stone et al., 2003; and Reinke, 2004 for examples of female scholars in the field of servant-leadership). Nevertheless, management literature that explicitly discusses women or examines feminist issues through the study of servant-leadership is rare. The contributions in the following examples of Crippen (2004) and Ngunjiri (2010) are worth mentioning in this context.

Crippen (2004) presented a historical narrative inquiry and content analysis of pioneer women in Manitoba, Canada. In her analysis, Crippen pointed out especially how the opportunities for women's leadership were severely constrained in the pioneer era. Such constraints were symptomatic of socially imposed gender hierarchies of the era. Nevertheless, by adopting attitudes and behaviors that are central to servant-leadership, Crippen asserted that these pioneer women were able to exercise great influence on their communities. Ngunjiri (2010) presented a compelling account of black female servant-leaders in her qualitative study of African women leaders. Ngunjiri asserted that by operating within the heterosexual matrix of their socialized subjectivity, African women leaders are able to deconstruct the constraints of oppressive systems. The women in Ngunjiri's study reconstructed their leadership as tempered radicals and critical servant-leaders and used their servant-leader approach to foster social change and pursue social justice.

These contributions represent some groundbreaking qualitative work to include women explicitly in the study of servant-leadership, to discuss women servant-leaders in the context of oppressive conditions, and to construct perspectives of the potential outcomes of servant-leadership in terms of social change and social justice. Both of these studies exemplify the strength that a servant-leader perspective afforded women in their situated position. The Manitoba pioneer women and the African women leaders also provide examples that meet Parker's (2005) appeal to incorporate resistance to injustice as a dimension of leadership.

Crippen (2004) and Ngunjiri (2010) used feminist frameworks in their studies and as such pioneered feminist analysis in servant-leadership. In their qualitative work, they represented servant-leadership through the experiences of women as a positive force. Their critical feminist voices spoke more to a social criticism of systems that expect women to lead like men or not lead at all. Eicher-Catt (2005), in contrast, voiced a critical feminist deconstruction of servant-leadership that equated servant-leadership with systems of male dominance as opposed to dismantling androcentric concepts of leadership. The following is an in-depth review and discussion of Eicher-Catt's critique.

Critique of Servant-Leadership

Servant-leadership has been criticized on a variety of levels. Some critiques have addressed structural elements of servant-leadership as a leadership theory. For example, Eicher-Catt (2005) claimed servant-leadership lacks a coherent conceptual framework. Van Dierendonck (2010) and van Dierendonck and Heeren (2006) echoed this critique, noting that servant-leadership research and conceptualization have lacked an integrated theoretical development. In the past, servant-leadership has been criticized for the lack of empirical support (Northouse, 2007) to ground servant-leadership in evidence-based research. Indeed, servant-leadership was not originally developed through research-based scholarship. In response to such critique and popular interest, numerous scholars (Barbuto & Wheeler, 2006; Laub, 1999; Liden et al., 2008; Page & Wong, 2000; Patterson, 2004; van Dierendonck, 2010) in recent years have made efforts to advance the conceptualization and operationalization of servant-leadership into theoretical models, research models, and instruments. Greenleaf's leadership perspective has been broadly integrated into empirical leadership research (van Dierendonck, 2010) and scholarly dialogue on ethics in leadership (Patterson, 2008). Nevertheless, as Johnson (2008) pointed out, servant-leadership continues to be met with cynicism in terms of practical application.

Despite the increasing interest in servant-leadership research models, instruments, and empirical studies, only a handful of peer-reviewed articles have made gender a central category of analysis (Barbuto & Gifford, 2010; Oner, 2009), studied women in servant-leadership (Crippen, 2004; Ngunjiri, 2010), or adopted a feminist perspective (Eicher-Catt, 2005). For my discussion of critical analysis concerning servant-leadership, I would like to focus on feminist criticism of servant-leadership. Eicher-Catt's (2005) deconstruction of servant-leadership addressed substantive and normative flaws from a feminist perspective. In the next section, I review the deconstruction feminist perspective that servant-leadership is perpetuating structures of gender domination. Then I offer the suggestion that, from a different feminist perspective, servant-leadership can be conceptualized as a gender-integrative approach. By offering a different perspective, this study provides a foundation for addressing the normative and contextual factors of leadership that continue to hinder women's rise to equitable representation in the executive ranks of business and moving both women and men beyond existing categories to integrative thinking.

Feminist Deconstruction of Servant-Leadership

The purpose of deconstruction is primarily to reveal otherwise obscure meaning in language and behavior as driven by implicit, unobtrusive power dynamics (Billing & Alvesson, 2000; Kark, 2007). In this spirit, Eicher-Catt (2005) presented a critical feminist deconstruction of servant-leadership. She grounded her main arguments in discursive analysis of the term *servant-leadership* and the rhetorical appeal to pathos in servant-leadership discourse. The following is a summative review of Eicher-Catt's analysis.

The paradox of the servant-leader for the gendered interpretation of Eicher-Catt (2005) lies in the historical assignment of the feminine to *servant* and the masculine to *leader*. Eicher-Catt asserted further that servant-leadership discourse is both deceptively ambiguous and deceptively gender-neutral. Based on instruments of discourse analysis, she claimed that the linking of servant and leader, instead of neutralizing gendered connotations, actually accentuates essentialist notions of gender. In rhetorical terms, she stated that the term *servant-leadership* can be described as a trope or a figurative term, and in this case a mutually constraining term. The ambiguity and perceived innocence of the term, she continued, leads to language games in which organizational members experience a kind of linguistic anarchy. This assumingly strategically created confusion, Eicher-Catt posited, allows those in power to manipulate the other organizational members. Because discursively the term *leader* is unambiguous in the organizational context, the term *servant* becomes the marked term, or the term that is defined through a dominant or default term. A typical example of this semiotic relationship is found in the terms *man* and *woman*, in which *man* is the generalized default term and *woman* is the marked other that is defined in terms of not-man. Therefore, Eicher-Catt stated, the term *servant-leader* reinforces the one-way relationship characterized by the hierarchical arrangement of domination-submission because the term manifests an either/or logic. She claimed leaders must give privilege to one interpretation or the other, since if they were not to privilege one, the rules of the leadership game would change. In her conclusion, Eicher-Catt asserted that the cultural essentialization of masculine and feminine would not allow servant-leadership discourse to be gender-neutral or genderless. The illusion of gender neutrality would actually increase the effect of gender oppression.

Oner (2009) contradicted Eicher-Catt's (2005) assertion, claiming that the gender-integrative character of servant-leadership offered women opportunities for liberation in terms of leadership. Oner (2009) addressed the ideas of gender neutrality versus gendering in servant-leadership through an empirical study in Turkey. She claimed that principles typically associated with servant-leadership, such as ethics, service, trust, sense of community, and shared leadership, contributed to the gender neutrality of the leadership perspective because they contradict typically masculine aspects of leadership. Oner explained that Turkish society is considered a feminine and hierarchical society in Hofstedian terms. In her assessment, the notion of a nurturing *masculine* (paternalism) tended to be negatively interpreted in leadership literature. The results of Oner's (2009) survey of middle management employees in a Turkish business context showed evidence that servant-leadership is, indeed, gendered. Her main assertion stated that servant-leadership is gendered in the sense that servant-leadership is perceived as a blend of feminine and masculine qualities of leadership. In conclusion, Oner postulated that the feminized version of leadership, such as servant-leadership, brings certain aspects of benevolence to the foreground of the leadership phenomenon, which, if practiced actively, could open up the matrix of leadership for women.

The strength in Eicher-Catt's (2005) critique lies primarily in arguments concerning gendered connotations of leadership and of serving. As noted earlier, the concept of *servant* is typically associated with subjugation, whereas the concept of *leader* is associated with domination (Eicher-Catt, 2005). Her deconstruction of servant-leadership echoed the arguments and discussion previously presented concerning leadership as a predominantly male-gendered construct. In addition, Eicher-Catt (2005) made salient aspects of servant-leadership that are predominantly female-gendered. These arguments were brought forth previously in feminist and critical analyses of gender differences in leadership. The problem with gendered notions of leadership (and servant-leadership) resides in the largely unquestioned hierarchical value order of female versus male. Despite the new consciousness of feminine behaviors as tolerable if not desirable in leadership (Johanson, 2008), behavior typically and traditionally associated with female performativity (Butler, 2004) continues to be devalued. Upvaluing the experiences and characteristics of the oppressed by celebrating and advocating their integration into the dominant belief systems and social structures within which the oppression was devised carries with it the danger of perpetuating existing and unquestioned assumptions and systems (Eicher-Catt, 2005).

Spears (1998a) noted that the paradoxical combining of servant and leader has been criticized often for its connotations. Spears, however, interpreted serving and leading as a complementary, harmonious dualism rather than a hierarchical, dichotomous tension. Greenleaf (2003) acknowledged the mutual constraining nature of servant and leader in his statement "One cannot serve as one leads" (p. 45). He also spoke to the choice that the servant-leader must make. However, his framing of the choice excluded the possibility that those who lead first cannot serve. Complacency, he argued, prevented those who have the disposition to serve and the capacity to lead, yet still choose not to lead. For Greenleaf, the choice between serving and leading is not a question of when, as implied by Eicher-Catt (2005), but a question of whether and why. The person who is by impulse a servant first and chooses not to take on the leadership role, or who chooses to follow leader-first types, is complacent. A true servant-leader must serve first and make a conscious decision to take on the role and responsibility of leading through serving. If we accept Eicher-Catt's (2005) assertions to be as true as Greenleaf's, then the problem of women being underrepresented in business leadership would be a matter of complacency and the cultural inability to reconcile gendered notions of leadership.

A further strength of Eicher-Catt's (2005) critique is the danger she sees in the normative nature of servant-leadership discourse. She noted that the spiritual and religious ideology of servant-leadership discourse used the rhetorical tool of pathos (emotional appeal). By constructing a sort of evangelical vision of organizational leadership, Eicher-Catt warned of the discursive practices associated with religious doctrine that particularly marginalize women and other groups. She cited feminist theologians who also argued that Judeo-Christian doctrine sustains the condition of male domination:

> While on the surface the language [of servant-leadership] appears
> to promote an innocent ethic of resistance to standardized, per-

haps oppressive, leadership practices, it operates by a logic of rhetorical substitution that maintains, or at least can maintain, those oppressive practices. One standardized, prescriptive ethic of leadership is replaced by another. (Eicher-Catt, 2005, p. 23)

Instead of offering a new vision of leadership with horizontal ideology, Eicher-Catt (2005) asserted that servant-leadership discourse merely reproduced a prescriptive, androcentric concept of leadership infused with religious dogma.

Van Dierendonck (2010) outlined numerous similarities servant-leadership shares with theories of ethical leadership. Hamilton and Bean (2005) also noted that servant-leadership is viewed as a normative leadership ethic. Because of Greenleaf's background (Greenleaf was a white, US American male, a devoutly Christian Quaker, and a corporate business executive) it is easy to interpret servant-leadership as a vehicle of Western, Christian, capitalistic, hegemonic discourses. Without explicitly managing the meaning of Greenleaf's religious references to Christian stories, confusion may arise. Hamilton and Bean (2005), for example, described the dilemma of transporting servant-leadership for leadership development at a British subsidiary of Synovus Financial Corporation and the necessity to manage meaning in context. Synovus' British colleagues were confused about the religious undertones in servant-leader literature, as a recent law in Great Britain had restricted the expression of religion in the workplace (Hamilton & Bean, 2005). In a public, business-related context, associating leadership discourse with Christian doctrine devalues its potential (Reynolds, 2011). From a perspective of critical theory, it is not unusual to assume that servant-leadership perpetuates patriarchal religious norms. In a pluralistic society such as the United States and in an increasingly globalized community, normative leadership perspectives may well be advised to maintain a secular stance. Proponents of servant-leadership therefore must be equipped to manage normative meaning across cultural contexts.

The deconstruction of servant-leadership makes clear that servant-leadership, as a leadership perspective, philosophy, or ethic, is vulnerable to abuse, as is any ethical guideline, leadership model, or power relationship. In this way, feminist theory offers a lens to question and revise cultural assumptions while revealing the unethical nature of the gendering of power (Kark, 2004, 2007). Romanticizing Greenleaf and servant-leadership is as dangerous as romanticizing any leader or leadership model. Deconstruction feminist interpretations of leadership and servant-leadership warn of mixed messages and gender blindness in the language of servant-leadership discourse.

Conclusion

While one can hardly claim that servant-leadership was born of feminist theorizing, some of its foundational concepts are compatible with feminist theory. Despite the fact that his writing lacked mastery of feminist discourse and purposeful intention of addressing gender or feminist issues, Greenleaf's vision of servant-leadership included values that are compatible with feminism. Transformational leadership, as described in the preceding sections, suggests a hierarchy of organizational priorities over human needs and a hierarchy of moral reasoning to be imposed on organizational members. Feminist perspectives of leadership point out hierarchies of gender, power, and hegemonic discourses that perpetuate gender performativity in the context of leadership in organizations. The questions remain: Who decides what the organizational needs are? What counts as ethical? Who decides what behaviors are acceptable for women or men and what effective leadership is? Servant-leadership espouses a nonhierarchical, participative approach to defining organizational objectives and ethics that recognizes and values the subjectivity and situatedness of organizational members. Feminist critique and a gender perspective can also inform servant-leadership through the appeal to integrate the female experience with male experience, subordinated experience with dominant experience. A paradigm shift in leadership theory driven by a paradigm shift of gender values could move organizations from models of hierarchy-driven, rules-based models of dominance and authoritativeness to more holistic, value-driven, follower-oriented and participative models. Further scholarly interpretation from various spiritual worldviews, philosophical paradigms, and interpretive perspectives—such as feminism—can continue to extend Greenleaf's vision as a vehicle for advancing social change and social justice agendas in contemporary and future organizational life. Feminist theories, no matter which strain of feminism they may espouse, have the potential to further enrich theoretical development, research agendas, and political agendas in leadership and servant-leadership.

References

Ayers, M. R. (2008, August). *Agapáo in servant-leadership* [Paper presentation]. The Servant Leadership Roundtable. Regent University, Virginia Beach, VA.

Barbuto, J. E., & Gifford, G. T. (2010). Examining sex differences of the servant leadership dimensions: An analysis of the agentic and communal properties of the Servant Leadership Questionnaire. *Journal of Leadership Education, 9*(2), 4–21.

Barbuto, J. E., & Wheeler, G. T. (2006). Scale development and construct clarification of servant leadership. *Group and Organization Management, 31*(3), 300–326.

Bass, B. M. (1999). Two decades of research and development in transformational leadership. *European Journal of Work and Organizational Psychology, 8*(1), 9–32.

Bass, B. M., & Steidlmeier, P. (1999). Ethics, character, and authentic transformational leadership behavior. *The Leadership Quarterly, 10*(2), 181–217.

Beazley, H. (2003). Forward. In H. Beazley, J. Beggs, & L. C. Spears (Eds.), *The servant-leader within: A transformative path* (pp. 1–12). Paulist Press.

Billing, Y. D., & Alvesson, M. (2000). Questioning the notion of feminine leadership: A critical perspective on the gender labeling of leadership. *Gender, Work and Organization, 7*(3), 144–157.

Brady, J. F., & Hammett, R. F. (1999). Reconceptualizing leadership from a feminist postmodern perspective. *The Review of Education/Pedagogy/Cultural Studies, 21*(1), 41–61.

Brooks, A., & Hesse-Biber, S. N. (2007). An invitation to feminist research. In S. N. Hesse-Biber & P. L. Leavy (Eds.), *Feminist research practice: A primer* (pp. 1–24). Sage.

Burns, J. M. (1978). *Leadership.* Harper and Row.

Butler, J. (2004). *Undoing gender.* Routledge.

Calás, M. B., & Smircich, L. (1991). Voicing seduction to silence leadership. *Organization Studies, 12*(4), 567–602.

Calás, M. B., & Smircich, L. (2009). Feminist perspectives on gender in organizational research: What is and is yet to be. In D. Buchanan & A. Bryman (Eds.), *The Sage handbook of organizational research methods* (pp. 246–269). Sage.

Chin, J. L. (2007). Overview: Women and leadership: Transforming visions and diverse voices. In J. L. Chin, B. Lott, J. K. Rice, & J. Sanchez-Hucles (Eds.), *Women and leadership: Transforming visions and diverse voices* (pp. 1–18). Blackwell.

Coleman, M. (2003). Gender and the orthodoxies of leadership. *School Leadership and Management, 23*(3), 325–339.

Conger, J. A., & Kanungo, R. N. (1998). *Charismatic leadership in organizations.* Sage.

Crippen, C. L. (2004). *Three women pioneers in Manitoba: Evidence of servant-leadership* [Unpublished doctoral dissertation]. University of North Dakota.

Dannhauser, Z., & Boshoff, A. B. (2006). The relationships between servant leadership, trust, team commitment, and demographic variables [Paper presentation]. The Servant Leadership Roundtable. Regent University, Virginia Beach, VA.

Eagly, A. H., & Carli, L. L. (2004). Women and men as leaders. In J. Antonakis, A. T. Cianciolo, & R. J. Sternberg (Eds.), *The nature of leadership* (pp. 297–301). Sage.

Eagly, A. H., Johannesen-Schmidt, M. C., & van Engen, M. L. (2003). Transformational, transactional, and laissez-faire leadership styles: A meta-analysis comparing men and women. *Psychological Bulletin, 129*(4), 569–591.

Eagly, A. H., & Johnson, B. T. (1990). Gender and leadership style: A meta-analysis. *Psychological Bulletin, 108*(2), 233–256.

Eagly. A. H., & Karau, S. J. (2002). Role congruity theory of prejudice toward female leaders. *Psychological Review, 109*(3), 573–598.

Eagly, A. H., & Sczesny, S. (2009). Stereotypes about women, men, and leaders: Have times changed? In M. Barretto, M. K. Ryan, & M. T. Schmitt (Eds.), *The glass ceiling in the 21st century: Understanding barriers to gender equality* (pp. 21–47). American Psychology Association.

Eicher-Catt, D. (2005). The myth of servant leadership: A feminist perspective. *Women and Language, 27*(1), 17–25.

Eid, J., Johnsen, B. H., Brun, W., Laberg, J. C., Nyhus, J. K., & Larsson, G. (2004). Situation awareness and transformational leadership in senior military leaders: An exploratory study. *Military Psychology, 16*(3), 203–209.

Eisler, R. (1994). From domination to partnership: The hidden subtext for sustainable change. *Journal of Organizational Change Management, 7*(4), 32–46.

Ferch, S. R. (2004). Servant-leadership, forgiveness, and social justice. In L. C. Spears & M. Lawrence (Eds.), *Practicing servant leadership: Succeeding through trust, bravery, and forgiveness* (pp. 225–239). Jossey-Bass.

Fine, M. G. (2007). Women, collaboration, and social change: An ethics-based model of leadership. In J. L. Chin, B. Lott, J. K. Rice, & J. Sanchez-Hucles (Eds.), *Women and leadership: Transforming visions and diverse voices* (pp. 177–91). Blackwell.

Fine, M. G. (2009). Women leaders' discursive constructions of leadership. *Women's Studies in Communication, 32*(2), 180–202.

Fletcher, J. K. (2004). The paradox of post-heroic leadership: An essay on gender, power, and transformational change. *The Leadership Quarterly, 15*(5), 647–661. https://doi.org/10.1016/j.leaqua.2004.07.004

Ford, J. (2005). Examining leadership through critical feminist readings. *Journal of Health Organization and Management, 19*(3), 236–251.

Gill, R. (2003). Change management—or change leadership? *Journal of Change Management, 3*(4), 307–318.

Graham, J. W. (1991). Servant-leadership in organizations: Inspirational and moral. *The Leadership Quarterly, 2*(2), 105–119.

Graham, J. W. (1995). Leadership, moral development, and citizenship behavior. *Business Ethics Quarterly, 5*(1), 43–54.

Greenleaf, R. K. (2002). *Servant leadership: A journey into the nature of legitimate power and greatness* (L. C. Spears, Ed.; 25th anniversary ed.). Paulist Press. (Original work published 1977)

Greenleaf, R. K. (2003). *The servant-leader within: A transformative path* (H. Beazley, J. Beggs, & L. C. Spears, Eds.). Paulist Press.

Hamilton, F., & Bean, C. J. (2005). The importance of context, beliefs, and values in leadership development. *Business Ethics: A European Review, 14*(4), 336–347.

Helgesen, S. (1995). *The female advantage: Women's ways of leadership*. Doubleday Currency.

Hesse, H. (2003). *The journey to the East*. Picador. (Original work published 1956)

Hesse-Biber, S. N. (2007) Feminist research: Exploring the interconnections of epistemology, methodology, and method. In S. N. Hesse-Biber (Ed.), *Handbook of feminist research: Theory and praxis*. Sage.

Hesse-Biber, S. N. (2010). *Mixed methods research: Merging theory with practice*. The Guilford Press.

Hesse-Biber, S. N., & Leavy, P. L. (2007). *Feminist research practice: A primer*. Sage.

Howell, J. M. (1988). Two faces of charisma: Socialized and personalized leadership in organizations. In J. A. Conger, & R. N. Kanungo (Eds.), *Charismatic leadership* (pp. 213–236). Jossey-Bass.

Howell, J. M., & Avolio, B. J. (1992). The ethics of charismatic leadership: Submission or liberation? *Academy of Management Executive, 6*(2), 43–54.

Iannello, K. P. (1992). *Decisions without hierarchies: Feminist interventions in organizational theory and practice*. Routledge.

Johanson, J. C. (2008). Perceptions of femininity in leadership: Modern trend or classic component? *Sex Roles, 58*(11–12), 784–789.

Johnson, C. E. (2008). *Meeting the ethical challenges of leadership: Casting light or shadow*. Sage.

Kark, R. (2004). The transformational leader: Who is (s)he? A feminist perspective. *Journal of Organizational Change Management, 17*(2), 160–176.

Kark, R. (2007). Re-thinking organizational theory from a feminist perspective. In L. E. Lucas (Ed.), *Unpacking globalization: Markets, gender, and work* (pp. 191–204). Lexington Books.

Keshet, S., Kark, R., Pomerantz-Zorin, L., Koslowsky, M., & Schwarzwald, J. (2006). Gender, status and the use of power strategies. *European Journal of Social Psychology, 36*(1), 105–117. https://doi.org/10.1002/ejsp.287

Kohlberg, L. (1994). Kohlberg's original study of moral development. In B. Puka (Ed.), *Moral development: A compendium* (Vol. 3). Garland.

Kotter, J. P. (1996). *Leading change*. Harvard Business Review Press.

Kouzes, J. M., & Posner, B. Z. (2002). *The leadership challenge: How to get extraordinary things done in organizations*. Jossey-Bass.

Kriger, M., & Seng, Y. (2005). Leadership with inner meaning: A contingency theory of leadership based on the worldviews of five religions. *The Leadership Quarterly, 16*(6), 771–806.

Krishnan, V. R., & Arora, P. (2008). Determinants of transformational leadership and organizational citizenship behavior. *Asia-Pacific Business Review, 4*(1), 34–43. http://rkvenkat.org/pooja_abr.pdf.

Lanctot, J. D., & Irving, J. A. (2007, July). Character and leadership: Situating servant leadership in a proposed virtues framework [Paper presentation]. The Servant Leadership Research Roundtable. Regent University, Virginia Beach, VA.

Laub, J. (1999). *Assessing the servant organization: Development of the servant organizational leadership assessment (SOLA) instrument* [Unpublished doctoral dissertation]. Florida Atlantic University.

Liden, R. C., Wayne, S. J., Zhao, H., & Henderson, D. (2008). Servant leadership: Development of a multidimensional measure and multi-level assessment. *The Leadership Quarterly, 19*(2), 161–177.

Madden, M. E. (2007). Strategic planning: Gender, collaborative leadership, and organizational change. In J. L. Chin, B. Lott, J. K. Rice, & J. Sanchez-Hucles (Eds.), *Women and leadership: Transforming visions and diverse voices* (pp. 192–208). Blackwell.

Mayer, D. M., Bardes, M., & Piccolo, R. F. (2008). Do servant-leaders help satisfy follower needs? An organizational justice perspective. *European Journal of Work an Organizational Psychology, 17*(2), 180–197.

Meindl, J. R., Ehrlich, S. B., & Dukerich, J. M. (1985). The romance of leadership. *Administrative Science Quarterly, 30*(1), 78–102.

Merriam-Webster. (n.d.). Leading. In *Merriam-Webster.com dictionary*. Retrieved April 5, 2013 from https://www.merriam-webster.com/dictionary/leading

Miner-Rubino, K., & Jayaratne, T. E. (2007). Feminist survey research. In S. N. Hesse-Biber, & P. L. Leavy, *Feminist research practice: A primer* (pp. 293–325). Sage.

Ngunjiri, F. W. (2010). *Women's spiritual leadership in Africa: Tempered radicals and critical servant leaders*. SUNY Press.

Northouse, P. G. (2007). *Leadership: Theory and practice* (4th ed.). Sage.

Oner, H. (2009, April). *Is servant leadership gender bound in the political arena?* [Paper presentation]. Annual meeting of the Midwest Political Science Association 67th Annual National Conference, Chicago, IL. http://www.allacademic.com/meta/p364186_index.html

Page, D., & Wong, P. T. P. (2000). A conceptual framework for measuring servant leadership. In S. Adjibolosoo (Ed.), *The human factor in shaping the course of history and development* (pp. 69–109). University Press of America.

Parker, P. S. (2005). *Race, gender, and leadership: Re-envisioning organizational leadership from the perspectives of African American women executives*. Lawrence Erlbaum.

Parolini, J., Patterson, K., & Winston, B. (2009). Distinguishing between transformational and servant leadership. *Leadership & Organization Development Journal, 30*(3), 274–291.

Patterson, K. A. (2004, August). Servant leadership: A theoretical model [Paper presentation]. The Servant Leadership Research Roundtable. Regent University, Virginia Beach, VA.

Patterson, K. A., & Stone, A. G. (2004, August). Servant-leadership: Examining the virtues of love and humility [Paper presentation]. The Servant Leadership Roundtable. Regent University, Virginia Beach, VA.

Prosser, S. (2010). *Servant leadership: More philosophy, less theory* [Essay]. The Greenleaf Center for Servant Leadership.

Reinke, S. J. (2004). Service before self: Towards a theory of servant-leadership. *Global Virtue Ethics Review, 5*(3), 30–57.

Reynolds, K. (2011). Servant-leadership as gender-integrative leadership: Paving a path to gender-integrative organizations through leadership education. *Journal of Leadership Education, 10*(2), 155–171.

Sashkin, M., & Sashkin, M. G. (2003). *Leadership that matters: The critical factors for making a difference in people's lives and organizations' success.* Berrett-Koehler.

Showkeir, J. D. (2002). The business case for servant-leadership. In L. C. Spears & M. Lawrence (Eds.), *Focus on leadership: Servant-leadership for the twenty-first century* (pp. 153–165). John Wiley and Sons.

Smircich, L., & Morgan, G. (1982). Leadership: The management of meaning. *The Journal of Applied Behavioral Science, 18*(3), 257–273.

Spears, L. C. (Ed.) (1995). *Reflections on leadership: How Robert K. Greenleaf's theory of servant-leadership influenced today's top management thinkers.* John Wiley and Sons.

Spears, L. C. (1998a). Introduction: Tracing the growing impact of servant-leadership. In L. C. Spears (Ed.), *Insights on leadership: Service, stewardship, spirit, and servant-leadership* (pp. 1–14). John Wiley and Sons.

Spears, L. C. (Ed.) (1998b). *Insights on leadership: Service, stewardship, spirit, and servant-leadership.* John Wiley and Sons.

Spears, L. C. (2002). Introduction: Tracing the past, present, and future of servant-leadership. In L. C. Spears & M. Lawrence (Eds.), *Focus on leadership: Servant-leadership for the twenty-first century* (pp. 1–16). John Wiley and Sons.

Spears, L. C. (2003). Introduction. In H. Beazley, J. Beggs, & L. C. Spears (Eds.), *The servant-leader within: A transformative path* (pp. 13–28). Paulist Press.

Spears, L. C., & Lawrence, M. (Eds.) (2002). *Focus on leadership: Servant-leadership for the twenty-first century.* John Wiley & Sons.

Spears, L. C., & Lawrence, M. (Eds.) (2004). *Practicing servant leadership: Succeeding through trust, bravery, and forgiveness.* Jossey-Bass.

Stone, A. G., Russell, R. F., & Patterson, K. (2003, August). Transformational versus servant leadership—A difference in leader focus [Paper presentation]. The Servant Leadership Roundtable. Regent University, Virginia Beach, VA.

van Dierendonck, D. (2010). Servant-leadership: A review and synthesis. *Journal of Management, 37*(4), 1228–1261. https://doi.org/10.1177/0149206310380462

van Dierendonck, D., & Heeren, I. (2006). Toward a research model of servant-leadership. *International Journal of Servant-Leadership, 2*(1), 147–164.

van Dierendonck, D., & Nuijten, I. (2011). The servant-leadership survey (SLS): Development and validation of a multidimensional measure. *Journal of Business and Psychology, 26*(3), 249–267. https://doi.org/10.1007/s10869-010-9194-1

Chapter 4

Servant First or Survival First?

How Servant-Leaders Lead during COVID-19

JIYING SONG

The year 2020 has been most challenging for many people all over the world. The COVID-19 pandemic has left almost no one's life untouched. George Floyd's death and other race-related incidents also unsettled the world to its core. An ancient lamentation resonates with us today: "How lonely sits the city that once was full of people" (Lamentations 1:1a, NRSV).

The statistics help tell the story of this year. The World Health Organization (WHO, 2020) and Johns Hopkins University and Medicine (2020) has confirmed more than 33 million COVID-19 cases worldwide and more than one million deaths in 216 countries. The United States has more than seven million confirmed cases and more than 200,000 deaths as of September 30, 2020 (Johns Hopkins University and Medicine, 2020; WHO, 2020). The unemployment rate in the United States was 3.7% in August 2019 and skyrocketed to 14.7% in April 2020. By August 2020, the rate was down to 8.4%, but the future is uncertain (US Bureau of Labor Statistics, 2020).

Among all the struggles and grief, leadership is more important than ever. How do servant-leaders react to this cruel reality? What does holistic leadership look like during a crisis? Should organizations serve first or fight for survival first? Should they prioritize people or profit? Are economic responsibilities really the foundation of a corporate's social responsibility? How are we going to serve the sick, the broken, the vulnerable, and the forgotten? How are we going to lead with courage, faith, and grace? Do people with different genders lead differently?

Servant-leadership, in its ethic of love, care, and service to the least privileged, is a potential antidote to patriarchal binds because it can serve as "a driving force for generating discourse on gender-integrative approaches to organizational leadership" (Reynolds, 2014, p. 51). During a crisis, leaders need foresight and awareness (traditionally a masculine aspect of leadership) as well as listening, empathy, and caring for people (more feminine-attributed aspects of leadership) (Reynolds, 2014). How can we discern and develop the feminine and masculine within every leader? Servant-leadership, "as a feminism-informed, care-oriented, and gender-integrative approach to organizational leadership" (p. 35), can offer a holistic and responsible way of leading during crises. Honoring both feminine and masculine giftedness can deepen the holistic foundation of servant-leadership. Unfortunately, gender studies of servant-leadership are limited (Barbuto & Gifford, 2010; Crippen, 2004; Eicher-Catt, 2005; Lehrke & Sowden, 2017; Ngunjiri, 2010; Oner, 2009; Reynolds, 2013, 2014; Song, 2018).

This study examines the lived experience of three female and three male servant-leaders during the COVID-19 pandemic through a hermeneutic phenomenological study to explore the essence of corporate social responsibility (CSR) and crisis leadership through the lens of servant-leadership. Prior to this study, to my knowledge, no hermeneutic phenomenological research of CSR and crisis leadership has been conducted during the COVID-19 pandemic. This study documents how servant-leaders led during this unprecedented time; it collects leadership challenges and experiences, helps leaders reflect upon their own leadership, explores successful leadership traits, and offers insights for business leaders across gender.

In this chapter, literature is reviewed in the areas of crisis leadership, corporate social responsibility, and servant-leadership. Following is a discussion of this study's methodology, methods, participants, findings, suggestions, limitations, and recommendations for further research. This chapter ends with conclusions.

Literature Review

Crisis Leadership

People tend to consider crisis as negative, as something to be avoided at all costs. The *Oxford English Dictionary* (2020) defines *crisis* as "a vitally important or decisive stage in the progress of anything; a turning-point; also, a state of affairs in which a decisive change for better or worse is imminent." This definition resonates with its Chinese translation "危机"— danger and opportunity.

A crisis can also be defined as "an event that affects or has the potential to affect the whole organization" (Mitroff, 2004, p. 6). This COVID-19 pandemic definitely put all kinds of organizations under crisis scrutiny. The challenges of this crisis are its power as an unprecedented turning point and its large scale of uncertainty. Whether an organization is being able to act creatively to avoid/mitigate the danger or exploit/enhance the opportunity will set the stage for their success or failure in the long run, if not immediately. Some businesses clearly benefited from the crisis. The usage of eClinicalWorks Telehealth increased 1400% within three weeks at the beginning of the COVID-19 pandemic and exceeded 1.5 million daily minutes in April 2020 (eClinicalWorks, 2020). In June 2020, at its annual developer conference, Apple announced that it is going to bring handwashing detection to the Apple Watch, among other new features (Eadicicco, 2020). *Be creative.*

Crisis leadership differs from crisis management in that the latter focuses on a mechanistic or tactical aspect of a leader's role in crisis, whereas the former is more systematic and proactive (Gigliotti & Fortunato, 2017). In terms of crisis management, Kerrissey and Edmondson (2020) listed what good leadership looks like during this pandemic: acting with urgency, communicating with transparency, taking responsibility and focusing on solving problems, and engaging in constant updating. These actions serve as a tactical aspect of leadership, and thus are good crisis management strategies rather than crisis leadership. However, when the authors propose "tapping into suffering to build meaning" (para. 22), they highlighted a more systematic and proactive approach to lead during crises: "We believe that leadership is strengthened by continually referring to the big picture as an anchor for meaning, resisting the temptation to compartmentalize or to consider human life in statistics alone" (para. 24). Scott Cowan (2014), president of Tulane University during Hurricane Katrina, offered 10 principles for crisis leadership: Do the right thing, seek common ground, marshal facts, understand reality, aim high, stand up for your beliefs, make contact, innovate, embrace emotion, and be true to core values. Among these 10 principles, "seek common ground" and "be true to core values" serve to direct people to the bigger picture. *Build meaning.*

Leaders tend to protect their own or their organizations' reputation during a crisis. Gigliotti and Fortunato (2017) argued, "Crisis leadership involves more than simply saying the right things to the right audiences to uphold the reputation of an institution in the face of crisis" (p. 311). Rather, crisis leadership calls for "a more expansive understanding of the types of risks that a unit, department, or institution faces—and a continual emphasis on personal and institutional learning at all phases of the crisis process" (p. 311). In short, crisis leadership calls for a learning attitude rather than solely preserving a reputation. Given the amount of uncertainty during a crisis, leaders must be open to learn, be transparent, and be able to say, "I don't know." This approach takes humility, a contrast to traditional leadership in which people expect leaders to have all the answers in their pockets. Humility and honesty build trust in the leader-follower relationship. Leaders, as well as organization, have to be open and learn together. *Be open.*

Crisis preparation remains a top priority for leaders (Gigliotti & Fortunato, 2017). "If things far away don't concern you, you'll soon mourn things close at hand" (Confucius, 2014, p. 121). Jacobs and Chase (2021) claim that operations and supply chain strategic planning requires risk management. The International Risk Governance Council (2019) was established in 2003 to provide policy makers, regulators, and key decision makers with evidence-based recommendations about risk governance. However, most of risk management and crisis preparation did not consider a global pandemic. Gigliotti and Fortunato (2017) compiled a list of crisis taxonomies (p. 305), including human errors and natural disasters, but their list did not include a global pandemic. COVID-19 is not the first pandemic in recent human history. Past pandemics include the 1918 pandemic (H1N1 virus), the 1957–1958 pandemic (H2N2 virus), the 1968 pandemic (H3N2 virus), and the 2009 pandemic (H1N1pdm09 virus) (CDC, 2018). When organizations were hit by the COVID-19 pandemic, it was not that they did not prepare—they did not prepare to this extent. Facing a toilet paper shortage in May 2020, P&G's chief product supply officer, Julio Nemeth, said, "We are prepared for thousands of different events, from cybersecurity attacks to earthquakes to fire. . . . But we were not prepared for all of those happening at the same time, which is what the pandemic brought to us" (as cited in Wieczner, 2020). *Be prepared.*

Resilience is a term used often during a crisis. The European Commission (2016) has defined resilience as "the ability of an individual, a community or a country to cope, adapt and quickly recover from stress and shocks caused by a disaster, violence or conflict" (p. 1). This pandemic is challenging our community resilience, which focuses on the "reflective dimension of communities to deal with external shocks in their social structure and bounce back, strengthening their internal cohesion, their resources and sustainability to future shocks" (Estêvão et al., 2017, p. 11). However, community resilience is not about returning to previous conditions or bouncing back after a disaster but about taking collective actions to reduce the negative impact and strengthen the community for the future (Cuervo et al., 2017). After record-breaking production, P&G's team was considering business process reengineering to redesign their supply chain for a more volatile environment (Wieczner, 2020), which calls for being adaptable or agile. Agile or hybrid (a mix of agile and traditional) approaches to project management had more than 20% higher success rates than traditional ones in terms of stakeholder satisfaction (Reich, 2019). According to the Project Management Institute and Agile Alliance (2017), the leadership theory underpinning agile approaches is servant-leadership:

> Agile approaches emphasize servant leadership as a way to empower teams. Servant leadership is the practice of leading through service to the team, by focusing on understanding and addressing the needs and development of team members in order to enable the highest possible team performance. . . . Servant leadership is not unique to agile. But once having practiced it, servant leaders can usually see how well servant leadership integrates into the agile mindset and value. (pp. 33–34)

Agile approaches offer a framework for delivering maximum value (meeting the expectations of high quality and speed from stakeholders) in a complex, uncertain environment. *Be agile.*

In summary, these five principles of crisis leadership emerge: be creative, build meaning, be open, be prepared, and be agile.

Corporate Social Responsibility

Long before the term *corporate social responsibility* was coined, leaders and businesses had been searching for ways to make a positive contribution to society (Blowfield & Murray, 2008). With the rise of the concept of CSR, some people argued that profit maximization should remain the dominant purpose of business (Levitt, 1958) and that social issues are not the concerns of businesspeople (Friedman, 1962). In 1991, Freeman and Liedtka called for abandoning the concept of CSR because it had become "a barrier to meaningful conversations about corporations and the good life" (p. 92). In spite of these oppositional voices, CSR still prevails. The focus of CSR has shifted from the role of business leaders to the behavior of companies, to environmental concerns, and to corporate citizenship (Blowfield & Murray, 2008). Thus, Blowfield and Murray (2008) assert that "no single definition is sufficient to capture the range of issues, policies, processes, and initiatives" of CSR (p. 16). The European Commission (2011) redefined CSR as "the responsibility of enterprises for their impacts on society and outlines what an enterprise should do to meet that responsibility" (para. 3). The European Commission states its strategy on CSR:

> [To] help enterprises achieve their full potential in terms of creating wealth, jobs and innovative solutions to the many challenges facing Europe's society. It sets out how enterprises can benefit from CSR as well as contributing to society as a whole by taking greater steps to meet their social responsibility. (para. 1)

A four-part definition of CSR was developed by Carroll in 1979 and has been widely used since then. Carroll (1991) suggests that four kinds of social responsibilities constitute total CSR: economic (be profitable), legal (obey the law), ethical (be ethical), and philanthropic (be a good corporate citizen). In 1991, Carroll shaped the four-part definition into the form of a CSR pyramid. He described it as follows:

> It portrays the four components of CSR, beginning with the basic building block notion that economic performance undergirds all else. At the same time, business is expected to obey the law because the law is society's codification of acceptable and unacceptable behavior. Next is business's responsibility to be ethical. At its most fundamental level, this is the obligation to do what is right, just, and fair, and to avoid or minimize harm to stakeholders (employees, consumers, the environment, and others). Finally, business is expected to be a good corporate citizen. This is captured in the philanthropic responsibility, wherein business is expected to contribute financial and human resources to the community and to improve the quality of life. (para. 19)

In 2016, Carroll took another look at the four-part definitional framework upon which the pyramid was created. He admitted that some issues had been raised about the applicability of his CSR pyramid in different global, situational, and organizational contexts (Carroll, 2016). Feminist scholar Spence (2016) examined Carroll's CSR pyramid through the ethic of care and feminist perspectives; she indicates that Carroll's categories represented a masculinist perspective.

Carroll's (1991) hierarchical design of CSR set economic responsibilities or being profitable as the foundation of CSR, supporting the idea of Levitt (1958): profit maximization should be the dominant purpose of business. Carroll's (2016) CSR pyramid suggests that business should fulfill its social responsibilities in a sequential fashion, starting with being profitable, then obeying the law, then being ethical, and then being a good corporate citizen (even though he emphasized that the pyramid was supposed to be seen as an integrated, unified whole rather than different parts). This sequential fashion could be misleading or used as an excuse in terms of meeting a corporate's social responsibilities. Where is the end of being profitable and the beginning of social responsibility? This question does not mean that a socially responsible business cannot or should not make profits. A social business model is to benefit economically disadvantaged or marginalized people/communities while being financially sustainable not through dona- tions or charity but through its own economical sustainability (Osberg & Martin, 2015; Thompson & Doherty, 2006; Yunus et al., 2010). Yunus et al. (2010) placed a profit-maximizing business and a social business at two ends of the spectrum of profit maximization and social impact.

Starbucks is an example of a company that integrated CSR with sustainability. Starbucks (2005) defines a responsible company as "one that listens to its stakeholders and responds with honesty to their concerns" (p. 1). Apparently, Freeman's (1984) stakeholder theory influenced Starbucks in terms of being socially responsible as thinking about stakeholders as customers, employees, suppliers, communities, and shareholders. In its 2019 "Global Social Impact Report," Starbucks (2020) emphasized its CSR focus as "being people positive, planet positive, and profit positive" (p. 4). Starbucks' CSR focus has moved from stakeholders to 3Ps (people, planet, profit). Elkington (2018) coined the term *triple bottom line* referring to people, planet, and profit in 1994. It is "a sustainability framework that examines a company's social, environment, and economic impact" (para. 4). However, Elkington recalled this term in 2018 and claimed that it needed some fine-tuning. He believed that the triple bottom line had been wrongly used because many corporations had been measuring its sustainability goals only in terms of profit. In order to keep the well-known 3Ps and its true meaning of sustainability, Kraaijenbrink (2019) suggested using "prosperity" to replace "profit." Kraaijenbrink hoped to broaden the scope of economic impacts within the 3Ps while drawing attention away from profit as the only legitimate goal.

Grameen Danone Food Limited (GDFL) is another example of a business centered on CSR and sustainability. GDFL is a joint venture by Group Danone, the largest food company in France, and Grameen Bank, established by the Bangladeshi economist Muhamad Yunus. GDFL "aims to fight poverty and malnutrition in Bangladesh and to create positive social impact throughout its value cycle" (Danone, 2020, para. 1). After the initial investment is returned to the investors, any profit gained through the operations will be reinvested in the company itself (Yunus et al., 2010). GDFL affects 300,000 children in Bangladesh and has created sustainable revenues for 500 farmers, 200 local women, and 117 van pullers who distribute the products (Danone, 2020). GDFL has made people, planet, and prosperity (of local communities) the inner core of its business, and CSR (economic, legal, ethical, and philanthropic responsibilities) its outer core. Using the layers of the earth as a metaphor (figure 4.1), I propose that 3Ps and CSR should be the core of business (figure 4.2).

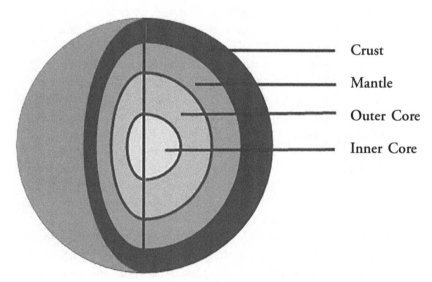

Figure 4.1. Layers of the Earth.

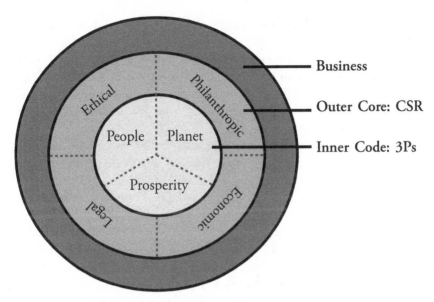

Figure 4.2. 3Ps and CSR as the Core of Business.

The dimensions of CSR are aligned with the goals of for-profit organizations as well as many nonprofit ones (Ferris, 1998; Waters & Ott, 2014). Kincaid (2017) pointed out that the lack of affirmations and the ineffective attempt to convey a meaningful message of CSR has hindered a genuine movement of building socially responsible organizations. However, this global pandemic has provided a great opportunity for businesses to move toward a more authentic CSR (He & Harris, 2020). This study examined the practice of CSR in one for-profit and five nonprofit organizations during the COVID-19 pandemic.

Servant-Leadership

Servant-leadership is not a new concept, even though 2020 is the 50th anniversary of Robert K. Greenleaf (2003) coining the term *servant-leader*. In ancient China, the best leader was regarded as one who served and nurtured others without contending with them and helped people accomplish things without taking credit: "The highest form of goodness is like water.

Water knows how to benefit all things without striving with them" (Lao Tzu, 2005, p. 17). According to Judeo-Christian tradition, Jesus, as the son of God, emptied himself and took the form of a servant (Philippians 2:6–7). Preaching the kingdom of his father, Jesus led the way as a teacher, a sage, and a servant (Morse, 2008): "Whoever wishes to become great among you must be your servant, and whoever wishes to be first among you must be slave of all" (Mark 10:43–44).

Greenleaf was a Quaker thinker and servant-leader. Retired from his career as director of management research at AT&T, he founded the Center for Applied Ethics in 1964 and devoted his life to leadership studies. In 1970, he published "The Servant as Leader," a landmark essay that used the term *servant-leader* (for the original 1970 edition, see Greenleaf, 2003). Drawing from his experiential leadership practice and deep Quaker spirituality, he coined and defined the term *servant-leadership*: "The servant-leader *is* servant first. . . . It begins with the natural feeling that one wants to serve, to serve *first*. Then conscious choice brings one to aspire to lead. That person is sharply different from one who is *leader* first" (Greenleaf, 1977/2002, p. 27; emphasis in original). Greenleaf explained how we can identify servant-leaders:

> Do those served grow as persons? Do they, *while being served*, become healthier, wiser, freer, more autonomous, more likely themselves to become servants? *And*, what is the effect on the least privileged in society; will they benefit, or, at least, not be further deprived? (p. 27; emphasis in original)

In Greenleaf's writings, Spears (2002) has identified 10 characteristics of a servant-leader: listening, empathy, healing, awareness, persuasion, conceptualization, foresight, stewardship, commitment to the growth of people, and building community.

Based on Spears's (2002) 10 characteristics of a servant-leader and my research study, I constructed a servant-leadership model (figure 4.3). Empathy, listening, awareness, and forgiveness contribute to healing; healing, listening, and reflexivity (with conceptualization) lead to the growth of entheos; and the growth of entheos results in better awareness (Song, 2020). *Entheos* comes from the Greek word ἐνθεος, which literally means "in God." By *entheos*, Greenleaf (2003) meant "the power actuating one who is inspired" (p. 118). These characteristics of servant-leadership interweave with one another to bring out better awareness in servant-leaders, so they tackle

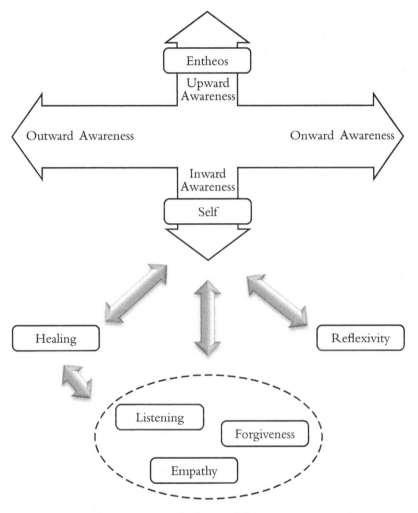

Figure 4.3. Servant-Leadership Model (source: Song, 2020).

whatever issues are in front of them. Inward awareness (i.e., self-awareness) can help leaders understand their own strengths, weaknesses, emotions, and concerns, as well as the impacts of their actions. Upward awareness (i.e., spirit awareness) can shape a leader's entheos and nurture his or her oneness and wholeness. Outward awareness (i.e., other awareness, relation awareness, and situation awareness) can move a leader toward stewardship, including persuading people through word and deed, committing to the growth of people, and building community. A person with relation awareness and situation awareness is able to identity situational, historical, religious, cultural, and social elements in a complex situation. All of these forms of awareness take place with onward awareness (i.e., time awareness), and the awareness of the future leads to foresight (Song, 2020).

In the 1970s, Greenleaf (1977/2002) observed that "the sense of business responsibility is inadequate for the influence that business wields" (p. 66). This statement is even more true today. For years Greenleaf made the strongest pleas he could for major institutions to "become affirmative (as opposed to passive or reactive) servants of society" (p. 170). In 1974, the first unequivocal response came to him from a large multinational business (Greenleaf, 1977/2002). In his proposal to the directors of this company, Greenleaf said, "If directors want a more socially responsible company . . . they should start the process by becoming more responsible directors" (p. 175). As a socially responsible company founded in 2006, GDFL is the result of the efforts of two responsible leaders—Franck Riboud and Muhammad Yunus (Danone, 2020).

Greenleaf (1977/2002) recognized that the core reason so few businesses serve well is found "not in business institutions; rather, it is in the attitudes, concepts, and expectations regarding business held by the rest of society" (p. 149). People inside and outside business do not love business institutions (Greenleaf, 1977/2002). Greenleaf claimed, "Businesses, despite their crassness, occasional corruption, and unloveliness, *must be loved* if they are to serve us better" (p. 149; emphasis in original). How can you love an institution? You cannot. You love the people, and the people are the institution (Greenleaf, 1977/2002). A centerpiece of Greenleaf's work and writing is the principle of love (Tilghman-Havens, 2018). Van Dierendonck and Patterson (2015) argued that compassionate love is an antecedent to servant-leadership and the cornerstone of the servant-leader and follower relationship. If a mechanistic cog-and-wheel perspective of institution is replaced by an organic servant-led perspective, traditional, hierarchy-driven, and command-and-control leadership models will yield to participative, value-driven, and people-oriented models. When you are asked, "What are you in business for?," you can use Greenleaf's (1977/2002) words to answer: "I am in the business of growing people" (p. 159).

But how can servant-leaders be loving and responsible during a crisis, such as this COVID-19 pandemic? I was hoping to find out through this hermeneutic phenomenological study.

Methodology, Methods, and Participants

The purpose of this hermeneutic phenomenological study is to explore the essence of corporate social responsibility and crisis leadership through the lens of servant-leadership during the COVID-19 pandemic with a sample of business leaders in the United States. I adopted a qualitative approach because it is able to bring unanticipated perspectives into the study, instead of being tightly prescribed; in addition, it can provide a holistic picture of the phenomenon, rather than looking for causal relationships among variables (Creswell, 2013).

This study employs semistructured interviews to gain an in-depth understanding of the lived experience of business leaders during the COVID-19 pandemic. I obtained institutional review board approval and participants' informed consent before collecting the data. A background question sheet was used before the interview to collect participants' demographic information. A one-hour interview session via Zoom was conducted with each participant to understand their lived experience. The interviews were recorded and transcribed. I conducted a first cycle of open coding and a second cycle of pattern coding during data analysis using ATLAS.ti.

The qualifications of this study's participants include having diverse experiences of the topic under study (Laverty, 2003), the ability to articulate their experiences (Colaizzi, 1978; van Kaam, 1966; van Manen, 2016), and the willingness to participate (Laverty, 2003; van Kaam, 1966). I found my participants through the connections of the editors of the *International Journal of Servant-Leadership*. The organizations of these participants either explicitly or implicitly integrate servant-leadership into their missions and visions. The sample size in hermeneutic phenomenological research can vary from one to hundreds (Creswell, 2013; Dukes, 1984; Polkinghorne, 1989). This study's sample is comprised of three male and three female American business leaders who were willing and able to articulate their business management experiences during the COVID-19 pandemic (table 4.1). Pseudonyms were used in all data for the sake of confidentiality.

Findings and Discussion

Four major themes emerged from the interviews with the six participants: (a) care and concern for other people were overwhelming across all partic-

Table 4.1. Participants' Background Information

	Luis	John	Luke*	Mary	Bella	Sara
Gender	Male	Male	Male	Female	Female	Female
Age	48	53	40	52	51	65
Ethic Identity	Hispanic	Caucasian	Caucasian	Caucasian	Caucasian	Caucasian/ Hispanic
Education	Master's degree	Master's degree	PhD	PhD	Master's degree	PhD
Religion	Christian	Christian	Christian	Christian	Christian	Christian
Size of the Organization	800 employees	320 employees	400 employees/ 5 partners	1,800 employees	9 full-time and 400–500 employees seasonal	2,300 employees
Business Type	Nonprofit	Nonprofit higher education	Nonprofit higher education/ for-profit	Nonprofit higher education	For-profit	Nonprofit higher education
Position and Years	CEO, 3 years	President, 13 years	Professor, 11 years/managing partner, 9 years	Vice provost, 16 years	COO, 4 years	Chancellor, 10 years

*Luke works for two organizations at the same time.

ipants; (b) the five principles of crisis leadership were well supported; (c) the model of 3Ps and CSR as the core of business was partially supported; and (d) not all elements of Song's (2020) servant-leadership model were reflected during the interviews.

Theme One: Care and Concern for Other People

All participants were asked about their engagement with stakeholders during the COVID-19 pandemic. Both female and male participants showed great care and concern for other people at the personal and institutional level, emotionally as well as financially. Sara emphasized "the dignity of every human being." "No one really cares how much you know until they know how much you care," John quoted. John cancelled two crucial fundraising events out of safety concerns:

> We actually are not going to do either one of those events this fall because we think it's going to be too risky for the population of individuals who come for that, those who are in the most vulnerable population. . . . So those are just a few ways that we're trying to be sensitive to alumni, parents, friends, supporters, and fans in every one of those situations.

Before the pandemic, Luis had to divest six million dollars' worth of programs at his institution, a move that involved substantial layoffs. After the divestment, they were able to serve 2,000 more people (clients). But caring for employees laid off was one of his institution's major concerns during the reconstruction process, as Luis explains:

> When we divested of programs, we worked very diligently with other organizations and encouraged them to hire the individuals that used to be with us. It's just incredible the way the team really paid so much attention and focus on that so that those individuals could have a job. So that was a big part of our focus and our effort; it was not to just get out of those programs because it was going to be good for us. There was an overwhelming concern for the people we serve and how they were going to be served through another organization.

During the COVID-19 pandemic, Luis had to furlough 60 more individuals. This move was painful:

We believe in serving our staff, and some of our staff are no longer with us. So that's hard for us because we feel that they are part of our family. We love them. We care very much for them and we're sad that they can't be with us today. . . . [It is] painful for those individuals; painful for us that we need to separate with [them]. . . . I started making those calls. . . . I just wanted to thank them for the tremendous work that they have done in some cases for years: improving the health and well-being of the people we serve and making significant contributions to this organization. . . . They were very appreciative. They learned so much from the organization, they were treated so well, they [had] nothing but good to say about [us]. So I thought it was important for me to just thank them, but then I heard a lot of just really positive feedback as a result of making those calls.

Mary's institution supported its employees during the pandemic:

We have in fact been able to pay those employees who are unable to work from home because their job isn't conducive to that. So even though they have been home since mid-March, they are getting their full paycheck because of our care and sense of responsibility for them as [our] employees.

Both Sara and Luke's institutions serve students from diverse socioeconomic backgrounds. During this pandemic, they knew that some students did not have a laptop or the Internet at home, so they provided these students with computers or hot spots for Internet. Sara's institution also provided food through food banks to help students and families in need. Luke pointed out, "The question as leaders we should always be asking is, 'What does this person need from me?'"

Luke summarized five changes to make things better for students: keep it simple, create engagement (for online learning), be flexible, reach out and follow up, and get feedback. Luke encouraged conversations in his class to serve students:

I've had a couple classes that it didn't cover a bunch of content, but we certainly talked about what people are doing and it's not always me saying "Let me help." There will be another student say, "Hey Jeff, I can help with that, and send me a message and we can help you." So it's just kind of opened the door of conversations that I think are healthy and necessary for some people.

Sometimes care was shown through voluntary financial sacrifice. Sara's employees were willing to take a pay cut for everyone so that no one would be laid off. Similarly, Bella sacrificed her own paycheck to help her employees:

> We just laid out everyone's plan and then I'm taking the brunt of the hit. I . . . significantly lowered my paycheck to help the team to make sure that everybody gets across the line. . . . I've been blessed. We'll just do what we can. . . . Money is dirt and used to grow beautiful things. . . . That doesn't mean much if you don't grow something beautiful with it.

These accounts confirm that love can serve as an antidote to leading out of fear and scarcity (hooks, 2000; Patterson, 2010).

Theme Two: Five Principles of Crisis Leadership

Based on the literature review, I suggested five principles of crisis leadership: be creative, build meaning, be open, be prepared, and be agile. All five principles were supported through the interviews. Both female and male participants showed equal attention to building meaning, being prepared, and being agile; female participants tended to be more open and talked less about innovation than male participants (see figure 4.4).

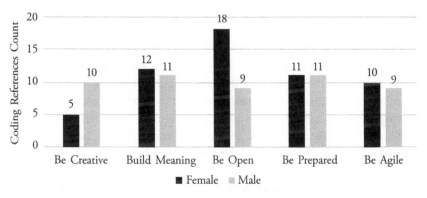

Figure 4.4. Five Principles of Crisis Leadership Coding References Count.

BE CREATIVE

This global pandemic pushed innovation to the top of these leaders' agendas. Luke said, "If we want to survive . . . we have to rethink the entire business model." Bella told her team, "We're going to have to think outside the box as far as how we do business." Mary told me that her faculty members were "redesigning their courses, redelivering the course through various media that they felt would be more responsive to students." Affected by state budget cuts, Sara asked, "How to generate new revenue so that . . . we don't have to depend on the state as much? . . . A lot of innovation, saying, 'let's do something new and different.'" Luis's institution has already benefited from innovation,

> On the revenue side, we implemented a Telehealth. So in February of this year we had zero Telehealth with zero revenue. Today [June 2020] it comprises about 70 to 80% of our community-based services and about $400,000 to $500,000 of revenue per month. . . . The implementation of Telehealth provided us [with] the vehicle to serve thousands in the community that would not have been served if it weren't for that platform.

BUILD MEANING

All of my participants are Christians. Faith is an essential part of their meaning building and sense making. They considered their jobs as God's calling and connected this calling with their institution's mission, vision, and values. They held on to this calling especially during this crisis. Sara told me that faith affected everything she did in every way because "a part of my faith . . . is this kind of a preferential love of the poor and so one of the things is to help the people who need it most." Luke pointed out that "the people who are really well grounded . . . are able to weather the storm [i.e., COVID-19] because they are grounded to some values that are meaningful and real . . . anchored to a set of . . . core values." Mary went through the reconstruction of a program with mission in mind, "to really understand that our mission was to make the world a better place to educate leaders that the world so desperately needs." She believes in chaos theory:

> We as humans need to have something happen for us to be willing to rethink who we are, what we do, how we do it, and

how we can do it better. So most of the time when things get difficult, I, like most humans, will on occasion say, "This is just so hard and I don't have it in me anymore to continue to do this work." But in those moments, I just say, "You know, things happen for a reason. There will be some good that will come from this. And we will become a better place. We will become a better institution."

When Bella became the new leader of her organization, the leadership paradigm shifted from a hierarchical to a participative model. She created a new culture and established the discipline of "delight in difficulty":

> We wrote on the board "delight in difficulty," so that was kind of our slogan. . . . First step, number one, as soon as I hear [bad news], I'm going to take a big breath and I'm going to say, "Thank you, God." And then we're going to call the team together and we're going to pray together. We're going to say, "We're going to delight in this and we're going to trust God to have good come out of this." And that's been a huge discipline. . . . Who would have known about the pandemic? Having that discipline in place allowed for us to hit this tsunami without capsizing. . . . [You] can't do that if you don't believe that there's something beyond you.

BE OPEN

All participants admitted that they did not have all the answers during the COVID-19 pandemic and that they were open to learn and ask for help. Having a learning attitude assumes humility and leads to innovation and collaboration. The section "Be Creative" already demonstrated some learning attitudes from these leaders and their institutions. All participants highly valued teamwork and collaboration during crises. Bella said, "The hardest piece was there was no playbook for this. It was so outside the rule box. . . . We were troubleshooting all the time, which is really exhausting. I think our team just handled it really, really well." John admitted that at the beginning of COVID-19, "We didn't really know what we didn't know. We're just trying to learn more about the pandemic." He tried to surround himself with the brightest people who were fully committed to the mission of his institution:

> I don't have all the answers. . . . Other people are going to help me make good decisions. We're not going to get it right every day. We're not going to make the decision right now. We're not going to get every decision correct, but we're going to try to do so from the standpoint of living out our mission and loving others with a Christ-like love, even in the hard decisions.

When Luis first became the CEO of his current organization, he was facing a two-million-dollar loss from the previous year. He was open to learning:

> I started at the organization asking five questions: What are the biggest challenges the organization is facing? Why are we facing those challenges? What are some of our biggest opportunities for growth? What do we need to do to leverage those opportunities? And if you were me, what would you focus your attention on? It is the answers and insights to those questions that led to the development of a strategic plan that led to the transformation that we're going through right now.

Sara learned from every role and in every situation prior to the pandemic, and kept learning during COVID:

> There is a real openness to learning and doing what we need to do. . . . Lots of lessons about how to communicate, how to stay united and focused, how to respond to legitimate fear or concern about health and safety, and then the very legitimate questions about the quality of learning and the experience for students. . . . Every institution is going to have to do this, to look at the business model. How do we make it sustainable? What are new things you have to do? What are things we should stop doing? . . . Sometimes hardships bring opportunities that we don't see. . . . Once we face it, we learn things.

BE PREPARED

All participants were prepared in certain ways for crisis: strategic planning, attention to early alerts, timely decisions, and contingency plans. Long-term strategic planning sets the organization on the right track for success and survival. Before the pandemic, John's institution finished prioritizing

its academic programs in order to strengthen the institution; Mary reconstructed some programs into a new school to "make it even stronger and
more accessible and more nationally and internationally reaching." Two years
ago, Luis divested six million dollars' worth of programs, resulting in serving
2,000 more people and shifting the organization from deficit to profit. He
said, "We had to make those changes in order to position us for success."
When the pandemic hit, Luis said,

> We have done some divestments during this time too. That is
> going to position us to do more good for more people because it's
> smart, it's strategic, and we have to make those decisions for the
> greater good of the organization and our community. . . . Instead
> of us losing 3.6 million dollars by the end of the year, we're
> going to be millions positive.

When early alerts of a crisis arose, these leaders were prepared and took
action quickly. When 911 occurred, Sara took immediate action to keep
her Middle Eastern students safe and then to facilitate conversations among
students to avoid misunderstanding. Rather than ignore the potential conflict,
she called attention to it and got people to communicate, thus building
respect and understanding. At the beginning of COVID-19, John sent
students home immediately with all of their belongings. Mary required all
study abroad students to return home at an early stage in spite of complaints
and uncertainties. Bella said,

> We kind of got some indication around March like something
> is not right. . . . I could have been thinking like "This doesn't
> seem right. This seems more significant." So I met with the
> team. . . . I said, "Okay, let's take this to the most dire extreme. If
> we can't . . . what are the things that we really want of ourselves
> to look back on to be known for?" . . . We kind of went to the
> full extreme talking about . . . how we want to navigate this.

Luke shared that one of his friends used up his own rainy day account so
that he didn't have to fire anyone during the COVID-19 pandemic. Luke
commented,

> One of Greenleaf's principles was foresight. And foresight doesn't
> necessarily mean you know what's going to happen, but it means

you're looking ahead far enough to know something could happen, right? And so I think the people who had foresight have listened well, whose general demeanor is about building others up. I think it's a kind of just-been-tested leadership that they've done pretty well with. I think some of the others have had a lot harder time.

BE AGILE

Speaking of the COVID-19 pandemic, all participants talked about resilience, flexibility, and adaptability. "As a professor," Luke said, "I [have to] be flexible."

> I need to be completely available to my students. . . . I give them my cell phone number. . . . I've got to meet them where they are and they are on their phones like all the time. And so I tell them, "You can text me. You can call me. You can email me. You do what works for you and I'm okay with it."

John was impressed by the resiliency of his employees:

> You learn a lot about people when you go through hard times or challenges together. And what I learned about our faculty and staff is just how resilient they are and even our students as well. How resilient they are and how much people love this college.

Mary saw the potential for changes in her institution:

> I didn't think we would ever [make certain changes in the organization]. Now given what has happened, I wouldn't say that anymore. I think there will be some room for flexibility. . . . We are up to something that is challenging and difficult now, but something that will ultimately leave us with some realities to help us be better able to do our work and to be more resilient.

Sara called for entrepreneurship:

> I'm very, very grateful for how much and how quickly all of our team, our faculty and staff and administration[,] just jumped in to make things happen for the students. . . . [Students] are

adapting and they're happy to be on campus, and so it's very fascinating to me that their adaptation has been fast. . . . I don't think we're going to go back to how it was, and so I think that is a long-lasting impact of the pandemic. I think that we will all need to be more entrepreneurial.

Bella considers this pandemic as a mini Ice Age: everything will be very different when we come out of it. She said, "I think greater flexibility is the name of the game. Like we're just going to have to be really flexible, flexible with ideas, flexible with implementation. Try it out, experiment, be as flexible as we can." Luis said,

> What I have seen now is our ability to adapt very quickly. . . . Hundreds of people are working from home. And then also we adapted our staffing model based on productivity. This has forced us to kind of rightsize the organization, something that could have maybe taken a three-year process. We were able to accelerate and do that more quickly. . . . I think this pandemic showed the strength of this leadership team and the organization and how we're able to overcome this unprecedented challenge, something we've never seen ever in our lifetime. . . . Not only overcome it, but also in a substantial way, make this organiza-tion better . . . because we were able to adapt, innovate, and collaborate.

Theme Three: The Model of 3Ps and CSR as the Core of Business

I suggested that socially responsible organizations should make people, planet, and prosperity the inner core of its business, and CSR (economic, legal, ethical, and philanthropic responsibilities) its outer core. This model was partially supported through the interviews. Both female and male participants paid equal attention to people, prosperity, and economic and philanthropic responsibilities; only one woman talked about planet value; two women and one man touched on legal responsibilities, and one woman and two men on ethical responsibilities (see figure 4.5).

Through this research study, people or social value reflected through Theme One was definitely part of the inner core for these institutions. Planet or environmental concern was only mentioned once by Sara: "Whatever we do in one part of the world impacts the other part of the world." This problem came from one of the limitations of this study—all participants

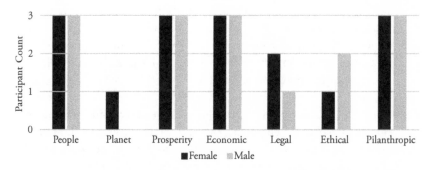

Figure 4.5. The Model of 3Ps and CSR as the Core of Business Participant Coding Count.

were in a service business. I will discuss more about research limitations later.

Prosperity, according to Kraaijenbrink (2019), is realized through economic impacts such as employment, innovation, and taxes. Caring for people, not only physically and emotionally but also financially, contributes to these people's prosperity. Bella cut her own pay in order to help her employees. At Sara's institution, everyone was willing to take a pay cut so that no one would be laid off. For the prosperity of the community they served and their institution, Luis had to divest some programs before the pandemic. Luis did not simply lay people off; he tried to connect with them and help them get hired by other companies. Being creative through implementing Telehealth enabled Luis's institution to serve more community members and brought in hundreds of thousands dollars of revenue per month during the pandemic. John's, Luke's, and Luis's institutions received greater support from their donors during the pandemic, and they were very grateful for that. All participants shared the value of a good team and partnership. Sara told me the story of how local businesses would rather sacrifice their sales to help teachers protect students from gang violence. "It takes a village," she said. Prosperity is more than just economic value; it is people and community being prosperous with the support from one another. It is the "flourishing of all" (Tilghman-Havens, 2018, p. 120). It is bell hooks's (1984) vision of "reorganizing society so that the self-development of people can take precedence over imperialism, economic expansion, and material desires" (p. 26). It is Tutu's (1998) *ubuntu*, "a person is a person through other persons" (p. 19).

All participants were under the pressure of economic responsibilities. They talked about their financial difficulties due to the pandemic, gaining or losing financial support, and serving their students or clients through funding or refunding. Strategic planning and foresight had strengthened some institutions before the pandemic hit. Through learning and innovation, these leaders strove to stabilize their institutions and increase revenue. Three participants touched on legal responsibilities during the interviews, while three mentioned being ethical and doing what is right. Luke said, "Choose the harder right instead of the easier wrong." Luis explained why he had to furlough some people due to the pandemic:

> If you look at the organization as a whole and our responsibility to our mission, the viability of the organization, and the people we serve, we feel that we did the right thing and we can justify the thing even though it's painful.

All participants assumed philanthropic responsibilities through their institution's mission and values to give back to society and to improve the quality of life. This result is partially due to two limitations of this study: five out of six participants are from nonprofit businesses, and all participants were identified as servant-leaders.

Theme Four: Servant-Leadership Model

Not all elements of the servant-leadership model in figure 4.3 were present in every interview. All female and male participants exhibited listening, empathy, and awareness; only one woman talked about forgiveness, and two women showed reflexivity; nobody touched on healing (see figure 4.6). The themes of serving and loving others were strong across all participants.

Forgiveness was mentioned by only one female participant, but it was a life-changing experience and the foundation upon which to build the culture of her institution. All participants demonstrated listening, since they were open to learning and asking for help. Although communication is an important skill for servant-leaders, "intense and sustained listening" is even more important because "true listening builds strength in other people" (Greenleaf, 1977/2002, p. 235, 31). As discussed in Theme One, they all showed great empathy toward other people during a crisis. "People grow taller when those who lead them empathize" (p. 35). Only two women touched on reflexivity by inviting the team to reflect on what they

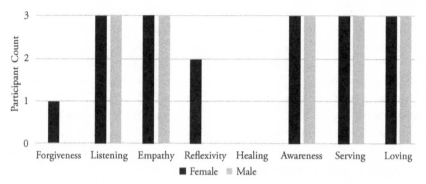

Figure 4.6. Servant-Leadership Model Participant Coding Count.

did and what they could have done better. Nobody talked about healing during the interviews.

All participants demonstrated the four dimensions of awareness. Upward awareness (i.e., spirit awareness) was exhibited through their faith and meaning making during a crisis. *Entheos* was in the center of their upward awareness. This study confirms that spirituality can be a crucial component to leadership effectiveness (Howard, 2002; Ngunjiri, 2010). Inward awareness (i.e., self-awareness) was shown through participants' awareness of their own emotions (such as fear, stress, sadness, disappointment, embarrassment, sorrow, discomfort, and gratefulness) and limitations (by saying "I don't have all the answers"). Palmer (1998) emphasized the importance of a leader's self-awareness: a leader "must take special responsibility for what's going on inside his or her own self, inside his or her consciousness, lest the act of leadership create more harm than good" (p. 200).

All participants exhibited outward awareness: other awareness through care and concern for other people, relation awareness through teamwork and partnership, and situation awareness through paying attention to early alerts and being prepared. Onward awareness (i.e., time awareness), especially foresight, was reflected through being prepared and being creative. "Foresight is the 'lead' that the leader has" (Greenleaf, 1977/2002, p. 40). A lack of foresight in the past may result in an unethical action in the present (Greenleaf, 1977/2002).

The code group *serving others* had the most coding counts—34 times with all participants. This prevalence verified that the participants were servant-leaders; however, this result was due to the limitation of this study—all participants were from service businesses. They served others through owning personal responsibility, being patient with one another, understanding others' needs, thinking of others first, being flexible and adaptable, providing better service, making hard decisions, building networks to help others, cutting their own pay, and demonstrating care and love. As John said, "Don't think less of yourself, but . . . think of yourself less."

No matter female or male, the participants all appreciated others' love to their institutions and showed great love to the poor, to the people they served, and to their institutions. Mary said, "I think it is all because of our love for the work that we do and the institution that we serve." For Sara, it is "a preferential love of the poor and so one of the things is to help the people who need it most." John told me, "We found out how much people really love this place [through the pandemic]." Luke's love for his students was evident during the pandemic: "I've got to be available. I've got to be flexible. And ultimately I've got to think about 'What is it that my students most need from me?'" When Bella was facing leadership transition and people leaving, she said, "That was a huge transition for me to help the team not only to transition people out" but also "to help them feel deeply loved and part of our community and not forgotten." Luis encountered similar challenges. He said, "We love them. We care very much for them and we're sad that they can't be with us today." Luis also shared how much his employees loved the people they served and how they tried to connect with these people. He said, "The service, the love, and the care that we have for a client continues [during the pandemic]." The love of people and institution also generated discourse on gender-integrative approaches to leadership (Reynolds, 2014). When Bella became the leader of her institution, she considered,

> How do I change team culture from a dominated personality style to more of a shared vision? . . . It was more like . . . the pyramid: ideas were generated from him [former leader] and then they were executed by others. And I really needed everyone to become more vocal, more engaged, more influential in the decision making rather than just saying yes.

Suggestions, Limitations, and Recommendations for Further Research

Based on these findings and development of theory, some suggestions may be helpful to leaders. First, the five principles of crisis leadership—be creative, build meaning, be open, be prepared, and be agile—can help leaders navigate dire times, but the foundations of these principles should be built ahead of time. In other words, these principles will be valuable only if leaders establish them with foresight. Foresight enables servant-leaders to understand the lessons from the past, see and rise above events in the present, and foresee the consequences of a decision in the indefinite future (Greenleaf, 1977/2002; Spears, 2010).

Second, the model of 3Ps and CSR as the core of business can offer valuable insights to business leaders even though the application of planet value and legal and ethical responsibilities were not extensive in this study. This model, using the layers of the earth analogy, overcame the hierarchical and sequential limitations of Carroll's (1991) CSR pyramid. This model also integrated Elkington's (2018) 3Ps into CSR. Positioning people, prosperity, and planet as the inner core and economic, legal, ethical, and philanthropic responsibilities as the outer core of business provides business leaders with a sustainable model for socially responsible success.

Last but not least, listening, empathy, awareness, and foresight are crucial characteristics for a servant-leader, especially during crises. Luke said, "I think servant leadership is . . . a way of life that helps you stay grounded." This research also supports the idea that awareness has four dimensions: inwardness, upwardness, outwardness, and onwardness (Song, 2020).

Some limitations emerged from my study, and further research is needed. First, all of my participants were from service business, and five of them worked for nonprofit organizations. This sample could have predicted the overwhelming evidence of concerns for other people and serving others. The results may not be identical for leaders from all business types. Second, planet value was not evident in this study due to the limitation of my sample and my interview design. All participants worked in service business; therefore, environmental concerns were not part of my interview protocol. Third, legal and ethical responsibilities were not extensive in this study because they were not built into my interview protocol. The purpose of this research was to explore the lived experience of servant-leaders during the COVID-19 pandemic, not to test the model of 3Ps and CSR as the core of business. Generalization is not the purpose of hermeneutic phenomenological studies, but transferability is important for the theories of crisis leadership, CSR, and servant-leadership. Because of these three limitations, further research in for-profit merchandising and manufacturing business fields is needed to enrich the understanding of crisis leadership,

CSR, and servant-leadership and to test the model of 3Ps and CSR as the core of business.

Conclusions

Servant first or survival first? How do servant-leaders lead during the COVID-19 pandemic? The purpose of this hermeneutic phenomenological study was to examine the lived experience of both female and male servant-leaders during the COVID-19 pandemic and to explore the essence of corporate social responsibility and crisis leadership through the lens of servant-leadership. Three male and three female business leaders from one for-profit and five nonprofit organizations participated in the interviews. Through data analysis, four major themes emerged: care and concern for other people were overwhelming across all participants, the five principles of crisis leadership were well supported, the model of 3Ps and CSR as the core of business was partially supported, and not all elements of Song's (2020) servant-leadership model were reflected during the interviews.

This research does not answer all the questions asked during a global pandemic, but does provide leaders with insights on how to lead in crisis and how to build a socially responsible organization. First, the five principles of crisis leadership—be creative, build meaning, be open, be prepared, and be agile—used with foresight, can be valuable tools to help leaders navigate crisis. This study confirms that both female and male leaders lead well during a crisis through building meaning, being prepared, and being agile; female leaders tend to be more humble and open, while male leaders tend to focus more on innovation. Second, by integrating Elkington's (2018) 3Ps into CSR, I suggested a new model to replace Carroll's (1991) CSR pyramid: people, prosperity, and planet as the inner core and economic, legal, ethical, and philanthropic responsibilities as the outer core of business. This new model was partially supported due to some limitations of this study. Further research is needed to test this model, but this study shows that both female and male leaders value people, prosperity, and CSR responsibilities.

Finally, during a crisis, servant-leaders demonstrated the desire to serve, a love of others, and the characteristics of listening, empathy, awareness, and foresight across different genders. This study proves that servant-leaders honor both feminine and masculine giftedness and lead through a gender-integrative approach. The significance of this study is to enrich the understanding of crisis leadership, CSR, and servant-leadership across gender and to provide the model of 3Ps and CSR as the core of business. This study offers insights and tools for business leaders to lead during crises.

References

Barbuto, J. E., & Gifford, G. T. (2010). Examining sex differences of the servant leadership dimensions: An analysis of the agentic and communal properties of the Servant Leadership Questionnaire. *Journal of Leadership Education, 9*(2), 4–21.

Blowfield, M., & Murray, A. (2008). *Corporate responsibility: A critical introduction.* Oxford University Press.

Carroll, A. B. (1979). A three-dimensional conceptual model of corporate performance. *The Academy of Management Review, 4*(4), 497–505. https://doi.org/10.2307/257850

Carroll, A. B. (1991). The pyramid of corporate social responsibility: Toward the moral management of organizational stakeholders. *Business Horizons, 34*(4).

Carroll, A. B. (2016). Carroll's pyramid of CSR: Taking another look. *International Journal of Corporate Social Responsibility, 1*(3), 1–8. https://doi.org/10.1186/s40991-016-0004-6

Centers for Disease Control and Prevention (CDC). (2018). Past pandemics. https://www.cdc.gov/flu/pandemic-resources/basics/past-pandemics.html

Colaizzi, P. F. (1978). Psychological research as the phenomenologist views it. In R. S. Valle & M. King (Eds.), *Existential-phenomenological alternatives for psychology* (pp. 48–71). Oxford University Press.

Confucius. (2014). *Analects* (D. Hinton, Trans.). Counterpoint.

Cowan, S. (2014). The inevitable city: The resurgence of New Orleans and the future of urban America. Palgrave Macmillan.

Creswell, J. W. (2013). *Qualitative inquiry and research design: Choosing among five approaches* (3rd ed.). Sage.

Crippen, C. L. (2004). *Three women pioneers in Manitoba: Evidence of servant-leadership* [Doctoral dissertation]. University of North Dakota.

Cuervo, I., Leopold, L., & Baron, S. (2017). Promoting community preparedness and resilience: A Latino immigrant Community-Driven project following hurricane sandy. *American Journal of Public Health, 107*(S2), S164. doi:10.2105/AJPH.2017.304053

Danone. (2020). Danone communities: Grameen Danone, fighting against malnutrition in Bangladesh. https://www.danone.com/integrated-annual-report-2019/sustainable-projects/danone-communities-grameen.html

Dukes, S. (1984). Phenomenological methodology in the human sciences. *Journal of Religion and Health, 23*(3), 197–203. https://doi.org/10.1007/BF00990785

Eadicicco, L. (2020, June 22). Apple just unveiled major upgrades to the iPhone, its own chips for Macs, and much more. Here's everything Apple announced at its biggest event of the year. *Business Insider.* https://www.businessinsider.com/apple-wwdc-2020-keynote-live-blog-ios-14-watchos-announcements-2020-6

eClinicalWorks. (2020, April 10). eClinicalWorks' healow Telehealth usage exceeds 1.5 million aily minutes mid COVID-19 pandemic. https://www.eclinicalworks.com/healow-telehealth-usage-exceeds/

Eicher-Catt, D. (2005). The myth of servant leadership: A feminist perspective. *Women and Language, 27*(1), 17–25.

Elkington, J. (2018, June 25). 25 years ago I coined the phrase "triple bottom line." Here's why it's time to rethink it. *Harvard Business Review.* https://hbr.org/2018/06/25-years-ago-i-coined-the-phrase-triple-bottom-line-heres-why-im-giving-up-on-it

Estêvão, P., Calado, A., & Capucha, L. (2017). Resilience: Moving from a "heroic" notion to a sociological concept. *Sociologia, Problemas E Práticas, 85,* 9–25. https://doi.org/10.7458/SPP20178510115

The European Commission. (2011, October 25). Corporate social responsibility: A new definition, a new agenda for action. https://ec.europa.eu/commission/presscorner/detail/en/MEMO_11_730

The European Commission. (2016). Resilience—European civil protection and humanitarian aid operations. https://ec.europa.eu/echo/what/humanitarian-aid/resilience_en

Ferris, J. M. (1998). The role of the nonprofit sector in a self-governing society: A view from the United States. *International Journal of Voluntary and Nonprofit Organizations, 9*(2), 137–151. https://doi.org/10.1023/A:1022048504194

Freeman, R. E. (1984). *Strategic management: A stakeholder approach.* Pitman Publishing.

Freeman, R. E., & Liedtka, J. (1991). Corporate social responsibility: A critical approach. *Business Horizons, 34*(4), 92–98.

Friedman, M. (1962). *Capitalism and freedom.* University of Chicago Press.

Gigliotti, R. A., & Fortunato, J. A. (2017). Crisis leadership: Upholding institutional values. In B. D. Ruben, R. D. Lisi, & R. A. Gigliotti (Eds.), *A guide for leaders in higher education: Core concepts, competencies, and tools* (pp. 299–323). Stylus.

Greenleaf, R. K. (2002). *Servant leadership: A journey into the nature of legitimate power and greatness* (L. C. Spears, Ed.; 25th anniversary ed.). Paulist Press. (Original work published 1977)

Greenleaf, R. K. (2003). *The servant-leader within: A transformative path* (H. Beazley, J. Beggs, & L. C. Spears, Eds.). Paulist Press.

He, H., & Harris, L. (2020). The impact of Covid-19 pandemic on corporate social responsibility and marketing philosophy. *Journal of Business Research, 116,* 176–182. https://doi.org/10.1016/j.jbusres.2020.05.030

hooks, b. (1984). *Feminist theory: From margin to center.* South End Press.

hooks, b. (2000). *All about love: New visions*. William Morrow.

Howard, S. (2002). A spiritual perspective on learning in the workplace. *Journal of Managerial Psychology, 17*(3), 230–242. https://doi.org/10.1108/02683940 210423132

International Risk Governance Council. (2019). About IRGC. https://irgc.org/about/

Jacobs, F. R., & Chase, R. B. (2021). *Operations and supply chain management* (16th ed.). McGraw-Hill.

Johns Hopkins University and Medicine. (2020, September 30). Coronavirus Resource Center. https://coronavirus.jhu.edu

Kerrissey, M. J., & Edmondson, A. C. (2020, April 13). What good leadership looks like during this pandemic. *Harvard Business Review.* https://hbr.org/2020/04/what-good-leadership-looks-like-during-this-pandemic

Kincaid, M. (2017). Sticky like butter: The language surrounding corporate social responsibility is uninspiring and therefore not embraced. *The International Journal of Servant-Leadership, 11*(1), 257–276.

Kraaijenbrink, J. (2019, December 10). What the 3Ps of the triple bottom line really mean. *Forbes.* https://www.forbes.com/sites/jeroenkraaijenbrink/2019/12/10/what-the-3ps-of-the-triple-bottom-line-really-mean/#43b926dd5143

Lao Tzu. (2005). *Tao teh ching* (J. C. H. Wu, Ed.). Shambhala.

Laverty, S. M. (2003). Hermeneutic phenomenology and phenomenology: A comparison of historical and methodological considerations. *International Journal of Qualitative Methods, 2*(3), 21–35. https://doi.org/10.1177/160940690300 200303

Lehrke, A. S., & Sowden, K. (2017). Servant leadership and gender. In C. J. Davis (Ed.), *Servant leadership and followership: Examining the impact on workplace behavior* (pp. 25–50). Palgrave Macmillan.

Levitt, T. (1958). The dangers of social responsibility. *Harvard Business Review, 36,* 41–50.

Mitroff, I. I. (2004). *Crisis leadership: Planning for the unthinkable*. Wiley.

Morse, M. (2008). *Making room for leadership: Power, space, and influence*. IVP Books.

Ngunjiri, F. W. (2010). *Women's spiritual leadership in Africa: Tempered radicals and critical servant leaders*. SUNY Press.

Oner, H. (2009, April). *Is servant leadership gender bound in the political arena?* [Paper presentation]. Annual meeting of the Midwest Political Science Association 67th Annual National Conference, Chicago, IL.

Osberg, S. R., & Martin, R. L. (2015). Two keys to sustainable social enterprise. *Harvard Business Review, 93*(5), 86–94.

Oxford English Dictionary. (2020). Crisis. In *Oxford English Dictionary*. https://www-oed-com.georgefox.idm.oclc.org/

Palmer, P. J. (1998). Leading from within. In L. C. Spears (Ed.), *Insights on leadership: Service, stewardship, spirit, and servant-leadership* (pp. 197–208). John Wiley & Sons.

Patterson, K. (2010). Servant leadership and love. In D. van Dierendonck & K. Patterson (Eds.), *Servant leadership: Developments in theory and research* (pp. 67–76). Palgrave Macmillan.

Polkinghorne, D. E. (1989). Phenomenological research methods. In R. S. Valle & S. Halling (Eds.), *Existential-phenomenological perspectives in psychology: Exploring the breadth of human experience: With a special section on transpersonal psychology* (pp. 41–60). Plenum.

Project Management Institute and Agile Alliance. (2017). *Agile practice guide.* Project Management Institute.

Reich, B. H. (2019). Beyond the triangle: Delivering value in an agile world. https://www.projectmanagement.com/webinars/508290/Beyond-the-Triangle—Delivering-Value-in-an-Agile-World.

Reynolds, K. (2013). *Gender differences in messages of commencement addresses delivered by Fortune 1000 business leaders: A content analysis informed by servant-leadership and the feminist ethic of care* [Doctoral dissertation]. http://foley.gonzaga.edu/

Reynolds, K. (2014). Servant-leadership: A feminist perspective. *The International Journal of Servant-Leadership, 10*(1), 35–63.

Song, J. (2018). *Face management and servant-leadership: A hermeneutic phenomenological study of Chinese and American Christian church leaders* [Doctoral dissertation]. http://foley.gonzaga.edu/

Song, J. (2020). Awareness, healing, and forgiveness: Servant-leaders help heal the heart of the world. In J. Song, D. Q. Tran, S. R. Ferch, & L. C. Spears (Eds.), *Servant-leadership and forgiveness: How leaders help heal the heart of the world* (pp. 9–36). SUNY.

Spears, L. C. (2002). Introduction: Tracing the past, present, and future of servant-leadership. In L. C. Spears & M. Lawrence (Eds.), *Focus on leadership: Servant-leadership for the twenty-first century* (pp. 1–16). Wiley.

Spears, L. C. (2010). Character and servant leadership: Ten characteristics of effective, caring leaders. *The Journal of Virtues & Leadership, 1*(1), 25–30.

Spence, L. (2016). Small business social responsibility: Expanding core CSR theory. *Business and Society, 55*(1), 23–55.

Starbucks. (2005). *Starbucks 2004 corporate social responsibility report.* https://www.starbucks.com/responsibility/global-report

Starbucks. (2020). *Starbucks 2019 global social impact report.* https://stories.starbucks.com/uploads/2020/06/2019-Starbucks-Global-Social-Impact-Report.pdf

Thompson, J., & Doherty B. (2006). The diverse world of social enterprise: A collection of social enterprise stories. *International Journal of Social Economics, 33*(5/6), 361–375.

Tilghman-Havens, J. (2018). The will to (share) power: Privilege, positionality, and the servant-leader. *The International Journal of Servant-Leadership, 12*(1), 87–128.

Tutu, D. (1998, February). Desmond Tutu (Z. Jaffrey, Interviewer). *The Progressive, 62*, 18–21.

US Bureau of Labor Statistics. (2020, September 4). The employment situation—August 2020. https://www.bls.gov/news.release/empsit.toc.htm

van Dierendonck, D., & Patterson, K. (2015). Compassionate love as a cornerstone of servant leadership: An integration of previous theorizing and research. *Journal of Business Ethics, 128*(1), 119–131. https://doi.org/10.1007/s10551-014-2085-z

van Kaam, A. (1966). *Existential foundations of psychology.* Duquesne University Press.

van Manen, M. (2016). *Phenomenology of practice.* Routledge.

Waters, R. D., & Ott, H. K. (2014). Corporate social responsibility and the nonprofit sector: Assessing the thoughts and practices across three nonprofit subsectors. *Public Relations Journal, 8*(3), 1–18. http://www.prsa.org/Intelligence/PRJournal/Vol8/No3/

Wieczner, J. (2020, May 18). The case of the missing toilet paper: How the coronavirus exposed U.S. supply chain flaws. *Fortune.* https://fortune.com/2020/05/18/toilet-paper-sales-surge-shortage-coronavirus-pandemic-supply-chain-cpg-panic-buying/

World Health Organization. (2020, September 30). Coronavirus disease: COVID-19 Pandemic. https://www.who.int/emergencies/diseases/novel-coronavirus-2019

Yunus, M., Moingeon, B., & Lehmann-Ortega, L. (2010, April–June). Building social business models: Lessons from the Grameen experience. *Long Range Planning, 43*(2–3), 308–325. https://doi.org/10.1016/j.lrp.2009.12.005

Chapter 5

The Women's Project—A Power Balance Issue in the Core of a Spanish Feminist Organization

A Case Study Inquiry through the Lens of Servant-Leadership and Feminism

CARLA PENHA-VASCONCELOS

The Women's Project (TWP) is a Spanish based nonprofit organization that hired an external consultant to analyze its organizational conflict between the main leaders and its members. TWP requested consultancy services to present a background case study about the organization through the lens of different philosophical approaches that can pose a series of reflective questions that may be used to initiate an internal dialogue toward practicing conflict resolution and a healing process of self-care.

The consultant presents the final report with a background case study called *The Women's Project—A Power Balance Issue at the Core of a Feminist Organization* with two philosophical analyses. The first analysis uses a servant-leadership lens, which is a new philosophical perspective to TWP. This analysis focuses on the ideas of using power, practicing trust, and applying the 10 characteristics of servant-leadership. The second analysis uses a feminist organizational lens following the organization's feminist self-identification. This analysis focuses on a feminist leadership process of distributing power based on the idea of the organization's collective way of leading. The consultant concludes with a brief reflection on the intersection between servant-leadership and feminist analyses regarding the organization's background and conflict. This paper suggests that servant-leadership and feminist lenses are compatible approaches toward creating a practical inquiry that may help this women's organization in facing its internal conflict scenario while encouraging sustainable growth.

Case Study Background

The Women's Project is a nonprofit organization created in 2015 by a group of Latin American women who shared an interest in participatory spaces to strengthen the visibility of Latin American women's political, social, and cultural capabilities in Barcelona, Spain. The organization was created in a Spanish national context where even though many Latin American immigrant women are dual citizens, there is still little visibility or recognition of their contributions in their host countries (European Anti-Poverty Network, 2015, p. 83). Foreign women in Europe are almost an "anonymous subject," many times not acknowledged or recognized by governments and society. They are offered mainly entry-level jobs or minimal wages (in niche markets) and subsidized programs geared toward welfare.

In this context, TWP works to highlight and emphasize the roles of these women, who in their daily lives develop political, social, and cultural contributions not only to their social environment but also to European society as a whole. Since its first meetings in 2015, the organization has been gradually consolidating in the process of a multidisciplinary combining of several cultures, knowledges, and perspectives and in a collective creation promoting global citizenship. The organization also adopts an intercultural approach when promoting interaction among women from different cultural backgrounds and cultures, and an intersectional approach recognizing differences among women, especially considering their race, sexuality, class, and nationality. TWP works from the city of Barcelona as a meeting place for women. The group was established as a nonprofit organization with a rotating election system for the president, the main coordinator, and multiple group leaders (including employees and volunteers). The members are all women from diverse nationalities and backgrounds. TWP works with and for migrant women from Latin America in Europe.

According to a feminist leadership process, the organization was created based on the idea of the collective way of leading in the community. This means that each woman who is part of the group displays leadership skills and practices according to specific moments and projects, always with the dynamic of dialoguing and sharing the "leader" role in synchrony with the organization's values. Following this collective feminist philosophy, the election of a president, a coordinator, and group leaders is a formal procedure, but the hierarchical legal structure (requested per law) is not supposed to be taken as fixed or to create dynamics of superiority and subordination inside the organization.

The main objectives of the organization include creating training areas and promoting initiatives that amplify the voices of women as political actors; providing financial credits to women's projects in Spain; building bridges and networks among women from different contexts; developing advocacy work from an intersectional, multidisciplinary, creative, and advocacy perspective; and creating a learning process in collaboration with organizations and institutions while fostering bonds of sisterhood in harmony with peace, equality, and justice.

The feminist values of the organization are collaboration and sisterhood; horizontality in dynamics of power; communication and group care; a shared commitment to opposing mechanisms and structures of oppression and domination; recognition and respect for diverse capabilities and skills; collective and individual empowerment; professionalism; multidisciplinary and interdisciplinary work; respect; visibility in transnational reality; and a collective financial decision-making processes.

In 2017, two years after TWP's creation, the organization was already well established and recognized by Spanish society. The group was managing various projects for the community and the Catalan government. This resulted in unexpected expense increases. The management of the budget and expense that were usually discussed during meetings in a democratic decision-making process (by vote) started to follow a different system. The president of the organization canceled most of the budget assemblies, using the justification that the members were extremely busy with their new projects, and no members were openly questioning or complaining about the new unilateral decision-making system.

A year passed, and in 2018, the main coordinator started to openly question the new system and the president's decisions regarding the budgets. She revealed that the organization's annual report was not specifying projects' expenses and that the final numbers were ambiguous. During a general assembly, the president explained that she was doing her best according to the organization's values and that the credits issued to women's projects were not always paid back as the organization expected. Following this explanation, the main coordinator started to demand meetings to openly discuss the annual report and the budget numbers that were supposedly not correctly justified. She argued that the TWP feminist leadership process was not being respected, that the president was not following the values of horizontality in dynamics of power, as she was making important decisions without the members' consultation and voting. Moreover, the coordinator declared that the lack of clarity around budget and financial decisions was not acceptable in a feminist collective organization.

A month later, a series of assemblies took place to audit the organization collectively. On one side, the president was continuously posing her justifications around a lack of support when she was working with budgets and making financial decisions. She affirmed that nobody in the organization had the time or desire to work with her when she asked for help, and for this reason she had to make many decisions by herself. On the other side, the coordinator continued to demand clear and detailed explanations about budgets and the president's financial decisions. After noticing an open conflict between the president and the main coordinator, many members started to develop a narrative of confrontation, seeming to affirm that the president was creating excuses that could not justify the lack of financial clarity the organization was facing. Finally, after two months of assemblies, the organization had a divided climate, with half of the members supporting the coordinator and the other half supporting the president. The lack of trust, accountability, and horizontality in power were the main issues discussed inside the assemblies and meetings and outside the organization.

Servant-Leadership Analysis

The servant-leadership philosophy emerged in the 1970s when Robert K. Greenleaf initiated a discussion about the need for "a better approach to leadership, one that puts serving others—including employers, customers, and community—as the number one priority" (Spears, 2011, p. 10). Greenleaf (1977/2002) highlighted the focus on the developmental needs of followers and the community first. In this sense, Spears (2011) affirmed that "servant leadership emphasizes increased service to others, a holistic approach to work, promoting a sense of community, and the sharing of power in decision making" (p. 10).

Organizations that apply a servant-leadership approach view people as the priority over organizational issues (Reynolds, 2014). Greenleaf

(1977/2002) referred to a servant-led organization as one that serves and focus on the growth of its people first. According to Greenleaf, the first impulse of servant-leadership practice is listening and serving. The ultimate goal is to transform the ones being served, a transformation in the lives of the less privileged in society. Ferch's (2004) interpretation of Greenleaf's sense of putting the person and the community first "places servant-leadership firmly in the contemporary landscape of the family, the workplace, and the global pursuit of social justice" (p. 235). In this framework of pursuing social justice, we consider the application of a servant-leadership philosophy in a feminist organization such as TWP because, as Reynolds (2014) explained, "servant-leadership has potential as a feminism-informed, care-oriented, and gender-integrative approach to organizational leadership" (p. 36).

Women's orientation toward the care and support of others first illustrates a servant-leadership practice, but it is essential to recognize that women are expected by society to place the needs of others before their own (Gilligan, 1982). Servant-leadership has not yet developed a critical feminist discourse that deconstructs women's expectations and traditional feminine essentialization in society. However, its genuine commitment to the use and sharing of power for good and the advocacy for a dynamic of full partici-pation at all levels of organizations (Tilghman-Havens, 2018) is compatible with feminist principles of transforming social relations of power in societal structures (Batliwala, 2013). Furthermore, servant-leadership foundational principles espouse "a non-hierarchical, participative approach . . . that rec-ognizes and values the subjectivity and situatedness of organizational mem-bers" (Reynolds, 2014, p. 57) and model a "self-examination and action on behalf of those who are unheard or underrepresented by traditional power structures," (Tilghman-Havens, 2018, p. 88), which shows compatibility with feminist ideals that advocate for the need of hearing and amplifying the voices, understandings, and experiences of those who are the most subjugated and invisible in society (McClish & Bacon, 2002).

Even though TWP formally has a president as the main leader of the organization, in its essence, the group questions a hierarchical leadership structure and refuses to have a leader that dominates and exercises cohesive power. Its leadership is based on distributing power according to the idea of the organization's collective way of leading, with its members displaying individual leadership skills and practices according to specific moments and projects. Regarding this, Showkeir (2002) affirmed that "central to servant-leadership is power and its use" (p. 153). According to Reynolds (2014), servant-leadership implies "the notion of the leader serving others, regardless of status or structural power, [and] challenges culturally persistent norms of leadership as a manifestation of hierarchies" (p. 41). In this sense, TWP advocates for a horizontal structure and collaborative leadership that include individual initiatives. These are practices that promote a shared and people-centered leadership which coincides with servant-leadership ideals that focus on the development of its members while strengthening the entire community (Spears, 2003).

Regarding the issue of power, the consultant starts a series of reflective questions: How could TWP use power as an instrument "to create opportunity and alternatives so that individuals may choose and build autonomy?" (Greenleaf, 1977/2002, p. 41). What is the organization doing to avoid the practice of "coercive power used to dominate and manipulate people?" (p. 41). What are the mechanisms the organization can develop to be more alert in detecting covert and subtly manipulative coercive power in its practices? These questions are framed toward incentivizing reflections regarding the practices of coercive power that create organizational conflicts.

In contrast to coercive power, servant-leadership focuses on "persuasive power [that] creates opportunities and alternatives so individuals can choose and build autonomy" (Showkeir, 2002, p. 153). Servant-led organizations rely on persuasion practices, in which the servant-leader seeks to convince others through building a consensus (Spears, 2010). Servant-leadership practices the distribution of organizational power while believing in the need to keep individuals' rights and responsibilities connected to the accountability of the entire community. In this sense, it is necessary to invite and engage individuals in conversations about the decision-making processes. Thinking about distributing power, the consultant asks TWP: How is the organization changing the underlying assumptions and beliefs it holds about an individual's contributions toward achieving collective goals? How is the organization expecting personal accountability toward the purposes of the group? How does the organization support freedom and accountability in the sense of people being free to choose how to serve the group?

Regarding the trust issues, Greenleaf (1977/2002) affirmed that "everyone in the institution has a share in building trust. The administrators have the major responsibility for institutional performance that merits trust" (p. 115). Trust and respect are higher ethical factors that give strength to all institutions (Greenleaf, 1977/2002). Therefore, the consultant asks TWP: What are the personal values, convictions, and ethical positions that drive trust for the organization? What are TWP's beliefs about motivating trust while leading its people?

While thinking about how TWP will create a dialogue to answer all of the previous questions, the consultant suggests a reflection based on servant-leadership's 10 characteristics (Spears, 2004). The consultant believes that the development of these characteristics by TWP leadership can create a servant-leadership approach to positive change, appropriate use of power, and improvement of trust and accountability within the organization. The characteristics are listening, empathy, healing, awareness, persuasion, conceptualization, foresight, stewardship, commitment to people's growth, and building community.

Listening

According to Greenleaf (1991), "true listening builds strength in other people" (p. 8). Servant-leaders, in their deep commitment to serving first, emphasize the need to practice intentional listening toward identifying people's will (Burkhardt & Spears, 2004). According to Spears (2004), "Listening also encompasses getting in touch with one's own inner voice and seeking to understand what one's body, spirit, and mind are communicating" (p. 13). Hence, the leadership of TWP should reflect on how communication with its members is developed. The questions put to TWP are: Is TWP leadership listening attentively to the ones they serve? How can TWP create dynamics of listening and reflection?

Empathy

Greenleaf (1977/2002) explained empathy as "the imaginative projection of one's own consciousness into another being" (p. 33). It is through practicing authentic listening that the characteristic of empathy will emerge. Spears (2004) stated that "servant-leaders strive to understand and empathize with others" (p. 13). A servant-leadership organization should emphasize developing leadership that is empathetic to the voices and needs of its people. Therefore, the consultant asks: How is TWP listening to the beliefs and expectations of its members? What are TWP's beliefs about morale and motivation in the group? What can TWP do to develop empathy among its people?

Healing

Spears (2004) stated that "heal[ing] is a powerful force for transformation and integration" (p. 13). The emphasis on the need for healing individually and collectively is considered a strength of the servant-leadership philosophy. Burkhardt and Spears (2004) explained that "servant-leaders recognize that they have an opportunity to help make whole those with whom they come in contact" (p. 72). In the conflictive context of TWP, applying a healing process while listening and being emphatic can help TWP find reconciliation and wholeness again. Thus, it is important to ask: How can TWP claim a healing role while serving its members and mission?

Awareness

Spears (2004) stated that "general awareness, and especially self-awareness, strengthens the servant-leader" (p. 14). Achieving awareness helps to understand power, ethics, and values in a more holistic way and in different situations (Burkhardt & Spears, 2004). Regarding TWP's background and conflict, it is important to look toward seeing things as an interconnected system of relations, values, power, and ethics. Therefore, the consultant asks the following questions: How does TWP create and practice awareness as its organizational basis? How can TWP develop an awareness of its essential interdependent values while considering its connection and disconnections to its problems?

Persuasion

Servant-leadership relies on persuasion while convincing and building consensus in the decision-making process. Burkhardt and Spears (2004) explained that "Greenleaf uses this term to distinguish between leadership that relies on positional authority and coercion, in contrast to leadership that works through a process of influence, example, and moral power" (p. 78). In this sense, the consultant asks: What can TWP do to create an attitude of persuasion? How can TWP practice persuasion as its organizational basis?

Conceptualization

Spears (2004) explained that "the ability to look at a problem or an organization from a conceptualizing perspective means that one must think beyond day-to-day realities" (p. 14). Servant-leadership emphasizes practicing a balance between broader-based conceptual thinking and a day-to-day operational approach (Burkhardt & Spears, 2004). In this sense, the consultant asks: How is TWP balancing its conceptual feminist framework with its day-to-day operations?

Foresight

Spears (2004) explained that "foresight is a characteristic that enables the servant-leader to understand the lessons from the past, the realities of the present, and the likely consequence of a decision for the future" (p. 15). This characteristic is directly connected to conceptualization ideas, and highlights the capacity to relate the actions of the present time to the future. Regarding this, the consultant asks: How is TWP balancing its core purpose with the construction of meanings and practices beyond its daily routines to move toward a sustainable future?

Stewardship

Burkhardt and Spears (2004) stated that people "play a significant role in holding trust for the greater good of society" (p. 73). Spears (2004) also affirmed that "Servant leadership, like stewardship, assumes first and foremost a commitment to serve the needs of others. It also emphasizes the use of openness and persuasion rather than control" (p. 15). Hence, the consultant asks: What are TWP leadership members doing to create a dynamic of trust within the organization? Is TWP assuming first and foremost a commitment to serve the needs of its people using openness and dynamics of trust?

Commitment to the Growth of People

Burkhardt and Spears (2004) affirmed that a "servant leader is deeply committed to the personal, professional, and spiritual growth of everyone within an organization" (p. 73). This commitment to people's growth means focusing on improving their lives through the provision of opportunities, the recognition of capabilities, and the maximization of potentialities (Burkhardt & Spears, 2004). In this sense, the consultant asks: How is TWP taking an interest in its members' personal and professional growth? How is TWP truly encouraging members to be involved in the decision-making process throughout all leadership levels?

Building Community

Burkhardt and Spears (2004) stated that "no organization could be oriented to serve if it lacked its own sense of internal cohesion and purpose" (p. 87). Therefore, servant-leadership emphasizes a strong sense of community, and the need to seek community from within the organization. Hence, the consultant finally asks: Do members of TWP feel a strong sense of community? How can TWP leadership develop a sustainable community connection that can remain strong, even when facing conflictive situations?

Feminist Philosophical Analysis

While reviewing different feminist approaches, the consultant identified that feminist poststructuralist and postmodernist perspectives consider "organizing as the discursive mobilization of power/knowledge resources" (Gherardi, 2003, p. 215). These feminist approaches emphasize critiques of ideas of knowledge construction and the role of discourse in sustaining hegemonic power in societal structures (Gherardi, 2003).

Frost and Elichaoff (2014) affirmed that poststructuralism perceives "knowledge as socially produced, unstable, and contextualized, [and that] an emphasis is placed on language and discourse" (p. 44). Poststructuralism challenges universalistic ideas, the idea of "a truth," social male constructions, and the power of patriarchy in language, discourses, and social practices (Frost & Elichaoff, 2014). Poststructural feminism explores how multiple intersectionalities of gender, race, class, and sexuality, among others, coconstruct one another (Collins, 1998). It is a conceptual framework that helps uncover the subjectivities and hidden dominant practices in organizations (Holvino, 2010).

Frost and Elichaoff (2014) explained that "postmodernist thinking proposes that instead of the existence of one essential truth, there are multiple subjective, relative truths of personal construction" (p. 43). Postmodern feminism questions the concepts of rationality and knowledge and the existence of universal values (Alvarez, 2001). Thus, it questions the universal category of women (Gherardi, 2003). Postmodern feminism highlights the plurality of women's experience resulting from different intersectionalities that led them to various social understandings which create different ways of producing knowledge. This approach claims that there is no unique woman's voice and focuses on deconstructing power within discourses while claiming attention to voices that would otherwise continue marginalized.

Applying poststructuralist and postmodernist feminist lenses, the consultant proposes that TWP should first inquire about the discursive mobilization of power and knowledge within the organization. In this sense, it is significant to explore the organization's knowledge regarding its feminist values of sisterhood and shared commitment to oppose mechanisms and structures of oppression. The organization should ask its members: How is the organization adopting these values? How is the knowledge of its feminist values and practices being constructed and mobilized inside the organization? These questions consider the assumption that sisterhood is based on the idea of women joining in action and banding together to support one another while committing to fight domination and oppression and respecting the diversity among them.

Moreover, the assumption about how power is distributed in an organization plays a significant role in organizational complexity. The power balance in a feminist group should guarantee its equity, fluidity, and flexibility. Thus, TWP should ask itself: How is the organization discussing and practicing the ideals of mobilization and the distribution of power? How do the members and leaders assess whether their values create arenas of power within the organization?

In approaching collaborative organizational practices within The Women's Project, it is important to inquire if and how members' multiple social identities intersect with power relations, and how this may affect internal collaborative practices. In this sense, the consultant asks: Do women members from different backgrounds, experiences, and previous collaborative practices help to shape how the organization decides to organize and share dynamics of power? How does the organization respect and create a positive legitimation of diversity and difference among its members? And how does the organization uncover privileges and discrimination and oppressions among its members? This intersectional approach questions an essentialist and universal collective experience of "woman," focusing instead on the importance of recognizing and uncovering women's complex realities, which are shaped not by a single axis of social inequality but by many axes that coconstruct one another through relational processes organized by power relations (Acker, 1999; Yuval-Davis, 2006). Thus, a postmodern feminist approach with intersectionality is applied to "understand[ing] all dimensions of power relations" (Collins & Bilge, 2016, p. 3) intersecting with women's social identities and affecting women's collaborations within the organization. It is about determining how members of this organization understand their individual and collective identities, challenge the status quo, and whether and how they aim to transform power relations among themselves and across systems of power. This means looking at transformative possibilities arising within their collaborative phenomena (Collins & Bilge, 2016). A feminist intersectional praxis provides a framework to make visible the inequalities and differences in power relations within the group and among its members (Collins, 1995). It helps uncover the privileges and oppressions that shape individual and group experiences (Goikoetxea, 2017). It also provides a tool to highlight the similarities that diverse people and groups share, which also helps establish alliances and coalitions (Goikoetxea, 2017).

Finally, while looking toward analyzing how organizational conflict starts with the confrontation between the president and coordinator and ends by dividing the organization into two sides creating conflict among all members, TWP should ask its members: To whom do both the leaders and its members speak, and to whom are they accountable? Which voices of the organization (with its leaders and members) are acknowledged or silenced? These questions are based on the assumption that all members, while sharing the value of horizontality in the dynamics of power, should practice accountability and communication all times. However, as the case presents, both the president and the coordinator's particular discourses were constructed using the specific knowledge and power of their positions, positions that were legitimized by their access to mechanisms such as the budget and financial reports, while other members who supposedly should have had the same access to these mechanisms were somehow passive agents. Based on these facts, the consultant believes the organization must answer the question: Which steps should TWP follow to ensure that communication and accountability are assured during all stages, especially during decision-making phases? Finally, the consultant asks: How does TWP plan to manage access to mechanisms that can eventually create or legitimize discourses and practices that promote the construction of coercive and conflictive structures?

Conclusion

Regarding The Women's Project case study conflict scenario, the application of a servant-leadership perspective first highlights how TWP's values and practices are in synchrony with this philosophy. Second, it inquires about organizational practices that would avoid coercive power and develop persuasive power to achieve collective goals first. Third, it inquires about the values, convictions, and ethical positions that drive trust in the organization. Finally, it asks questions of TWP based on the application of the 10 characteristics of the servant-leadership philosophy.

Using a feminist perspective, the case study inquires about the discursive mobilization of power and knowledge inside the organization while considering sisterhood values and shared commitment and how members' multiple social identities may intersect with power relations. In addition, it asks about accountability and the matter of which voices are acknowledged or silenced during all processes, especially during the decision-making phases. Finally, it emphasizes the need to explore the issues of accessing mechanisms that can create coercive or conflictive discourses and structures.

In conclusion, to initiate an internal dialogue toward practicing internal conflict resolution and a healing process of self-care among TWP members and its leadership, the organization can apply an inquiry praxis intersecting both servant-leadership and feminist lenses. The servant-leadership approach to power practices, organizational values, ethical positions, and the 10 characteristics of servant-leadership can complement an in-depth internal critical thinking analysis using the feminist lens. This intersection may help TWP explore the roots of particular discourses of knowledge and power that create conflict among its members.

References

Acker, J. (1999). Rewriting class, race, and gender: Problems in feminist rethinking. In M. M. Ferree, J. Lorber, & B. B. Hess (Eds.), *Revisioning gender* (pp. 1–36). Sage.

Alvarez, S. (2001). Feminismo radical. In E. Beltran, V. Maquiera, S. Alvarez, & C. Sanchez (Eds.), *Feminismos: Debates teoricos contemporaneous* (pp. 104–114). Ciencias Sociales Alianza Editorial.

Batliwala, S. (2013). Clearing the conceptual cloud: Feminist leadership for social transformation. In S. Batliwala (Ed.), *Engaging with empowerment: An intellectual and experimental journey* (pp. 171–227). Women Unlimited.

Burkhardt, J. C., & Spears, L. C. (2004). Servant leadership and philanthropic institutions. In L. C. Spears & M. Lawrence (Eds.), *Practicing servant leadership: Succeeding through trust, bravery, and forgiveness* (pp. 71–89). Jossey-Bass.

Collins, P. H. (1995). Symposium: On west and Fernmaker's "doing difference." *Gender & Society, 9*(4), 491–494.

Collins, P. H. (1998). It's all in the family: Intersection of gender, race, and nation. *Hypatia, 13*(3), 62–82.

Collins, P. H., & Bilge, S. (2016). *Intersectionality.* Polity.

European Anti-Poverty Network. (2015). Más visibilidad de las mujeres en la Estrategia EU-2020—Informe Final. https://www.eapn.es/ARCHIVO/documentos/documentos/1462537660_eapn_invisibilidad_mujeres_2016_.pdf

Ferch, S. R. (2004). Servant-leadership, forgiveness, and social justice. In L. C. Spears & M. Lawrence (Eds.), *Practicing servant leadership: Succeeding through trust, bravery, and forgiveness* (pp. 225–239). Jossey-Bass.

Frost, N., & Elichaoff, F. (2014). Feminist postmodernism, postructuralism, and critical theory. In S. J. N. Hesse-Biber (Ed.), *Feminist research practice: A primer*. Sage.

Gherardi, S. (2003). Feminist theory and organization theory: A dialogue on new bases. In H. Tsoukas & C. Knudsen (Eds.), *The Oxford handbook of organization theory: Meta-theoretical perspectives* (pp. 210–236). Oxford University Press.

Gilligan, C. (1982). *In a different voice: Psychological theory and women's development.* Harvard University Press.

Goikoetxea, I. G. (2017). ¿Un neologismo a la moda? Repensar la interseccionalidad como herramienta para la articulación política feminista. *Revista Investigaciones Feministas, 8*(1), 73–93.

Greenleaf, R. K (1991). *The servant as leader.* The Greenleaf Center for Servant Leadership.

Greenleaf, R. K. (2002). *Servant leadership: A journey into the nature of legitimate power and greatness* (L. C. Spears, Ed.; 25th anniversary ed.). Paulist Press. (Original work published 1977)

Holvino, E. (2010). Intersections: The simultaneity of race, gender and class in organizations studies. *Gender, Work & Organization, 17*(3), 248–277.

McClish, G., & Bacon, J. (2002). Telling the story her own way: The role of feminist standpoint theory in rhetorical studies. *Rhetoric Society Quarterly, 32*(2), 27–55.

Reynolds, K. (2014). Servant-leadership: A feminist perspective. *The International Journal of Servant Leadership, 10*(1), 35–63.

Showkeir, J. D. (2002). The Business case for servant-leadership. In L. C. Spears & M. Lawrence (Eds.), *Focus on leadership: Servant-leadership for the 21st century* (pp. 153–166). John Wiley & Sons.

Spears, L. C. (2003). Introduction. In H. Beazley, J. Beggs, & L. C. Spears (Eds.), *The servant-leader within: A transformative path* (pp. 13–28). Paulist Press.

Spears, L. C. (2004). The understanding and practice of servant-leadership. In L. C. Spears & M. Lawrence (Eds.), *Practicing servant leadership: Succeeding through trust, bravery, and forgiveness* (pp. 9–24). Jossey-Bass.

Spears, L. C. (2010). Character and servant leadership: Ten characteristics of effective, caring leaders. *The Journal of Virtues & Leadership, 1*(1), 25–30. https://www.regent.edu/acad/global/publications/jvl/vol1_iss1/Spears_Final.pdf

Spears, L. C. (2011). Introduction: The spirit of servant-leadership. In S. R. Ferch & L. C. Spears (Eds.), *The spirit of servant-leadership* (pp. 7–20). Paulist Press.

Tilghman-Havens, J. (2018). The will to (share) power: Privilege, positionality, and the servant-leader. *The International Journal of Servant-Leadership, 12*(1), 87–128.

Yuval-Davis, N. (2006). Intersectionality and feminist politics. *European Journal of Women's Studies, 13*, 193–210.

Chapter 6

Eros and Logos

Servant-Leadership, Feminism, Poetry, and the Critical Unities of Gender Well-Being

SHANN RAY FERCH

The feminist warrior poet Audre Lorde died in Saint Croix in 1992. She lived as a freedom fighter seeking to serve the deepest needs of people in order to create a more just world. Her critique of dominant patriarchy resounds: "The master's tools will never dismantle the master's house. They may allow us to temporarily beat him at his own game, but they will never enable us to bring about genuine change" (Lorde, 2007, p. 110). In the truest sense of the word, Lorde led people and nations into greater love and freedom. With her life and poetry she showed how the legitimate power associated with serving the highest-priority needs of others can help heal the heart of the peoples of the world, especially the least respected or those Cornel West (2014) identifies as the wretched of the earth, a moniker imbued with clarion transparency by Frantz Fanon: the least of these being those we are unified with, indebted to, and with whom we share humility, *humus*, the earth that bears the imprint of our feet and the hope of a more humane existence. Ill patriarchal tendencies wound the world, leaving in their wake power abuses of all forms, severe lack of emotional intelligence, hyperrational lack of love, a history of genocide, and the aftereffects of the generational narcissistic injury so prevalent in America today. Lorde, a self-described "black, lesbian, mother, warrior, womanist, poet" who lived and created through directly challenging intersectional injustice, wrote in *The Black Unicorn*,

> and when we speak we are afraid
> our words will not be heard
> nor welcomed
> but when we are silent
> we are still afraid
> So it is better to speak
> remembering
> we were never meant to survive (Lorde, 1995, p. 32)

Her boldness helps us overcome our fears, and draws me to a question asked of me by the inimitable Nike Imoru, a North Londoner raised in Nigeria, an exceptional casting director, and the first woman and person of color to gain a tenured position in the Theatre Department at Hull in the United Kingdom (when she was only twenty-eight). Like Audre, Nike's presence is water from a deep well.

The question: what is your understanding of the masculine in America?

Lest we, like the structurally racist system in which we are embedded, become too binary or too set on defining gender, it's good to be reminded that the amount of feminine or masculine in each person chromosomally is a mystery, a uniquely conceived blend in every individual. We house within us the nonbinary dualism or rather multivalent multiplicity of a feminine/masculine artistic and biological notion, a circularity of which no one can claim full knowledge. Art sings and science confirms humanity's inability to control, contain, or fully name ultimate truth. With that humility in mind, in light of unrelenting systemic patriarchal power imbalances, an extreme mediocrity exists in much of the masculine in America today, characterized by emptiness, impoverished relational capacity, an overblown or underdeveloped sense of self, and a life with others that is often devoid of meaning. Such men are filled with things like excess media, sexual objectification, emotional shallowness, and the man's agenda at the expense of others, the age-old establishment of overt and covert patriarchal footing. No words for feelings. Violence. Privilege for privilege's sake, which results in decadence, and in the end decay, and finally death. The Western world is currently experiencing this decadence, decay, and death. Carl Jung (1959) gave a lucid and fear-invoking expression of the masculine and the feminine. In Jung's conception the masculine is symbolized as the logos, which he referred to as the power to make meaning, to be meaningful, and to be experienced as meaningful by loved ones and by the collective soul around us. Not the superrational man, incapable of emotion or regret, but the person who lives well, loves well, and is well loved. A question then rises, how many men do you know who are experienced as meaningful in their relationships with women and men, with their children, with others?

A modern practitioner of a form of leadership called servant-leadership, Robert K. Greenleaf, embodied lesser-known aspects of holistic living such as prophesy, foresight, healing, and the will to better society, often through personal and collective sacrifice. Not servant as slave or as subservient, but servant to the highest-priority needs of others, a concept referred to by black thought leader Lea E. Williams (2009) as reserved for those we consider *servants of the people*. Through this subtle embodiment in both life and poetry, let alone the ambiguous term *leadership*, a subtle authentic force is exerted: the dynamic, steadying, and fiercely graceful impulse toward atonement, reparations, and forgiveness at the core of humanity. Greenleaf died in 1990, just two years before Audre Lorde. The true test of our humanity and whether we truly serve, love, and lead, according to Greenleaf (1977/2002), is that others around us become more wise, more free, more autonomous, more healthy, and better able to serve others; and the least privileged of society are benefited, or at least not further deprived. I often think Greenleaf is describing not just leaders across the disciplines but especially the quietly profound people, transgressive poets, and spiritual prophets through whom we've encountered a more generous sense of life.

Greenleaf's test, difficult to administer, and worthy of humanity's most hard-won humility, utterly lays low the white supremacist patriarchal regime bell hooks (2000) so eloquently detailed in *Feminist Theory: From Margin to Center*. In hooks's understanding, aligned with Greenleaf's best test of human nature, we are authentically whole if we are simultaneously broken. In a form of existential vitality and surrender, awareness, foresight, and healing accompany us. This way of living or leading, as a person, as a poet, removes power from our hands and acknowledges that legitimate moral and relational gravity resides in the hands of the beloved other. I can't bend my family members' or friends' arms behind their backs and force them to tell others I've become less toxic or more loving, more whole. I've either done the life work required and their voice resounds freely or I need to seek more healing. In equal measure this is true not just of individuals but of nation states and all privileged or toxically dominant cultures. Groups small or large who listen and respond to beloved others' subtle and direct demands for atonement through reparations enter the restorative essence to which life inherently calls the human community.

Greenleaf (1977/2002) believed in Camus's call to "create dangerously," and did so by generating the beautiful freedom of consensus through listening and responding to the highest priority needs of others. In his telling essay on Robert Frost's (1947) poem "Directive," Greenleaf showed not only his strengths in linear thinking but also his uncommon gifts with regard to nonlinear, mystery-based, and more circular aspects of wisdom more readily associated with poets and painters than with business practitioners or social scientists, and in so doing, he opened the door for leaders to take greater responsibility for their own humanity and for humanity as a whole. Often the linear or rational is projected to be primarily associated with the masculine, while circular or mystery-based ways of knowing are projected to be primarily associated with the feminine. To be a leader responsible for the healing so vitally important to the wholeness of individuals and society, the mystery of gender well-being along the he-she-they continuum, and the reality of repair, forgiveness, and making things right or whole again comes forth from the shadows, illumining often obscured and ancient truths.

Greenleaf's (1977/2002) essay "The Inward Journey" from his *Servant Leadership: A Journey into the Nature of Legitimate Power and Greatness* contains an elegant, artistic, and in many respects circular, or mystery-based, look at the nature of the servant-leader. In the essay, Greenleaf relates how his reading Frost's "Directive" deepened his understanding of the courageous and wise presence of the servant as leader, be that leader woman, man, or elsewise positioned on the gender continuum.

Notably, the burgeoning of more linear or "rational/positivist" ways of knowing as found in quantitative research in servant-leadership conducted by Liden (Hu & Liden, 2011; Liden et al., 2015; Liden et al., 2016; Liden et al., 2014; Liden et al., 2008; Panaccio et al., 2015), van Dierendonck (Sousa & van Dierendonck, 2016, 2017a, 2017b; van Dierendonck et al., 2017; van Dierendonck & Nuijten, 2011; van Dierendonck et al., 2014), and many others has revealed weighty implications for servant-leadership across many dimensions of human experience. This body of research significantly fortifies and brings to the fore the new quantitative frontier of servant-leadership understandings, leading the field in unforeseen directions while contributing invaluable new knowledge.

That said, more circular or "mystery-based qualitative/interpretivist" studies in servant-leadership perform a different function—again, a function aligned less with linear or superrational knowledge than with poetic or symbolic knowledge. Quantitative research, in its emphasis on numerical reliability, validity, and generalizability at the expense of more intimate individual and collective expressions of human capacity, cannot, by definition, draw on the empirical grounding in lived experience found in qualitative research (Crotty, 1998; Denzin & Lincoln, 2011; van Manen, 1990, 2016). Privileging the linear/rational over the circular/mystery generates profoundly masculinist holes in our collective knowledge, and often continues a toxic diminishment of that which is not rational or linear. In effect, favoring quantitative knowing over qualitative knowing reifies toxic masculinity, colonizing practices, and the inherent inequities and human rights abuses so rampant in dominant cultures that lack the awareness to be not only equitable and liberatory but loving, as true relational and emotional intelligence demands. Quantitative research typically disallows, or rather occludes, the researcher from acknowledging and challenging personal biases, a research practice that is a common requirement for qualitative studies. This refusal to acknowledge and detail personal bias can often prevent leaders from hard-earned self-knowledge, and thus dominant culture blindness or "head in the sand" occlusion can be a shadow force or unconscious frailty in much quantitative research and oppressive patriarchal leadership. This results in calcification, brittleness, and eventual fracture of the knowledge base. Certainly, research using qualitative, quantitative, and mixed methodologies is necessary for more complete and robust understanding of servant-leadership. The gift of in-depth, well-designed, and deeply informed qualitative studies in servant-leadership offers the opportunity to expose our blind spots as people and leaders, and to bring us to a more intimate understanding of ourselves, others, and the world.

To understand the world more intimately, a move toward greater wholeness and healing, and deeper understanding, is required. Both poets and researchers, women and men and beloved others, can lead us there.

Though the extent of Greenleaf's personal connection with Pulitzer Prize winner in poetry Robert Frost is unknown, they did know each other, and spent time in each other's presence. The possibility that they directly influenced one another's thought is apparent, and becomes a compelling thread in the history of leadership studies. Consider this moment, relayed by Greenleaf (1977/2002):

> In a group conversation with him [Frost] one evening, he digressed on the subject of loyalty. At one point I interjected with: "Robert,

that is not the way you have defined loyalty before." He turned to me with a broad friendly grin and asked softly, "How did I define it?" I replied, "In your talk on Emerson a few years ago, you said, 'Loyalty is that for the lack of which your gang will shoot you without benefit of trial by jury.'" To this man who had struggled without recognition until he was forty, and then had to move to England to get it, nothing could have pleased him more in his old age than to have an obscure passage like this quoted to him in a shared give-and-take with non-literary people. (p. 326)

In Greenleaf's (1977/2002) "engagement" with Frost's poem, he affirmed the necessity of a prophetic, circular orientation in going further into the depths of human awareness: "Our problem is circular: we must understand in order to be able to understand. It has something to do with awareness and symbols" (p. 329). Throughout history, such symbolic knowledge, though not solely feminine, can often be ascribed more naturally to the feminine. Symbolic understanding is formless, cannot be linearized, and cannot be understood by simple 1-2-3 progressions. Rather, it is absorbed; it is an element of life and leadership in which the servant-leader chooses to become willingly submerged:

Awareness, letting something significant and disturbing develop between oneself and a symbol, comes more by being waited upon rather than by being asked. One of the most baffling of life's experiences is to stand beside one who is aware, one who is looking at a symbol and is deeply moved by it, and, confronting the same symbol, to be unmoved. Oh, that we could just be open in the presence of symbols that cry out to speak to us, let our guards down, and take the risks of being moved!

The power of a symbol is measured by its capacity to sustain a flow of significant new meaning. The substance of the symbol may be a painting, a poem or story, allegory, myth, scripture, a piece of music, a person, a crack in the sidewalk, or a blade of grass. Whatever or whoever, it produces a confrontation in which much that makes the symbol meaningful comes from the beholder.

The potentiality is both in the symbol and in the beholder. (Greenleaf, 1977/2002, p. 329)

From the broad foundations of qualitative research, thought leaders in human nature such as Heidegger (1962), Arendt (2006), Husserl (1970), Weil (2018), Gadamer (1975/2004, 1976), and Ricoeur (1981) have spoken of the impossibility of knowing humanity without knowing oneself. Qualitative research helps us find a more accessible avenue toward increased self-awareness: through symbol, depth, and meaning. The need to name, articulate, and bracket one's own biases in the attempt to show the lived human experience more clearly is inherent to qualitative research, even as it generally remains obscured in quantitative research. By extension, the person with a leader-first mentality, often mired in self-aggrandizement without foreknowledge, ambition at the expense of love and service, and an inappropriate power drive obscuring or negating authentic intimacy, generally lacks healthy self-awareness. The leader-first leader has limited or no capacity to name his or her own faults, let alone invite others to influence, challenge, or help correct them. In this light, Greenleaf's (1977/2002) prophetic truths—warning individuals, communities, and nations against the leader-first mentality—take on pivotal and, in fact, essential meaning.

Reynolds's (2013) qualitative study through a feminist lens used content analysis methodology to better understand speeches delivered by fifty of the top female and male American business leaders whose companies made *Fortune* best-of lists. She took a profound and precise deep dive into whether gender differences among prominent American business leaders support the conceptualization that servant-leadership is a gender-integrative mode of leadership and found servant-leadership gender integration intuitively and qualitatively true. In her study, no overall gender distinctions were expressed in the main servant-leadership characteristics, but important gender differences were observed: for example, women spoke more about humility and standing back in leadership, whereas men highlighted accountability; and female speakers considered the motivation to lead as an ethical drive and a choice, whereas male speakers articulated it as an obligation (Reynolds, 2013).

Eicher-Catt's (2005) quick dismissal of the gender-integrative essence of servant-leadership was exposed by Reynolds's more in-depth read of the necessary counterintuitive alignment of the terms *servant* and *leader*, purposely chosen by Greenleaf (1977/2002). Not only was Greenleaf's work explicitly not associated with being subservient, enslaved, or in a one-down position to dominant culture, toxic masculinity, or facile conceptions of gender, his approach was directly aimed at deconstructing such command-and-control leadership and replacing it with the prophetic notion that people will eventually refuse to be led by anyone but the kind of leader (he, she, or they) who is a healer, who is known as one who helps shape people and society, women and men and all people along the gender continuum, toward greater health, wisdom, autonomy, freedom, and service of the least privileged of the human community. The servant-first ethos of legitimate leaders is shown in the will to put others' highest-priority needs first—their vitality, wholeness, autonomy, freedom, wisdom, and health—placing others' well-being above one's own or the organization's economic, power, or ambition-oriented goals (Greenleaf, 1977/2002). By understanding the ways of life required to lead others in this way, as "primus inter pares"—a form of circular leadership in which each person is seen as equal—servant-leaders become crucial unifiers of others throughout the gender continuum. Of course, such understanding is hard won, requires long-term self-development, and demands substantial moral and personal effort in communion with others who help lead the way to deeper more communal expressions of humanity. Notably, Eicher-Catt (2005) is determined to examine *servant* and *leader* for their undertones, deconstructing the toxicity such terms can often embody. But notably, and of significant detriment to her own critical analysis, she appears to perform her deconstruction without recognizing the previous more humane, discerning, and multilayered deconstruction Greenleaf already arrived at through his own critical analysis of toxic American leadership propensities.

In Reynolds's (2013) study, gender differences found in her qualitative analysis could reify gender congruency expectations if read without critical gender understanding. To counteract such reification, her study presented evidence of female leaders combining care orientation and relationality (typically feminine aspects of leadership) with courage and contrarian thinking (typically masculine aspects) and evidence of male leaders combining accountability and risk taking (typically masculine aspects) with forgiveness and being attuned to others' needs (typically feminine aspects). Reynolds concluded that servant-leadership combines both feminine and masculine aspects of leadership.

Furthermore, Eicher-Catt (2005) proposed that the serving aspect of servant-leadership is associated with submissive femininity, and the leading aspect with oppressive masculinity. Reynolds (like Greenleaf, whose work predates Eicher-Catt) challenged Eicher-Catt's framework, revealing her conclusions with regard to servant-leadership to be largely based on her perception of the words *servant* and *leader* and not on Greenleaf's own interpretations of these words. Greenleaf's interpretations return the words to their original and imperative communal meanings (serving and leading others through healthy self-sacrifice by sacrificing ego, power, and ambition for the good of the community, especially the community's children, elders, and most marginalized peoples), affirming the value of the words *servant* and *leader* across gender, culture, time, and context. Reynolds analyzed Spears's (2002) 10 characteristics to examine servant-leadership constructs in terms of gender. She argued that 6 of the 10 characteristics distinguish servant-leadership from other forms of leadership, whereas the other 4 characteristics are more in line with traditional notions of leadership (Reynolds, 2014). These 6 distinguishing characteristics are stewardship, listening, empathizing, healing, commitment to the growth of people, and building community; the other 4 are foresight, conceptualization, awareness, and persuasion. Reynolds asserted that foresight, conceptualization, awareness, and persuasion can be characterized as leader behaviors, and are often associated with the more traditionally masculine aspect of leadership. The 6 distinguishing characteristics of servant-leadership, in contrast, are predominantly needs-focused and other-oriented, and thus, for Reynolds, comprise the feminine-attributed aspects of leadership.

Eicher-Catt (2005) claimed, from her particular feminist perspective, that the apposition of *servant* with *leader*, associated with subjugation and domination, respectively, instantiates a paradoxical discourse game that perpetuates male-centric patriarchal norms rather than neutralizing gender bias. Reynolds (2014) agreed that Eicher-Catt's (2005) critique reveals otherwise obscure discursive and behavioral meanings and hidden cultural assumptions that sometimes lie at the core of the words *servant* and *leader*. However, Reynolds (2014) exposed how Eicher-Catt lacked the will to go deeply into Greenleaf's original texts in order to find the more central discursive and deconstructive reality that is ascribed to Greenleaf's sense of "making things whole" across gender, culture, and context. Reynolds (2014) argued that the combination of servant facets and leader facets of servant-leadership does not automatically confirm the negatives Eicher-Catt associated with gendered notions but, on the contrary, provides a model of ethical and gender equity-enhancing leadership: "Servant-leadership espouses a nonhierarchical, participative approach to defining organizational objectives and ethics that recognizes and values the subjectivity and situatedness of organizational members" (p. 57). Servant-leadership can serve as "a driving force for generating discourse on gender-integrative approaches to organizational leadership" (p. 51).

Reynolds (2014) proposed that the paradoxical linguistic term *servant-leader* is not a disguise for male-centric norms, as Eicher-Catt (2005) claimed, but a complementary and harmonious dualism. My colleague and associate editor of the *International Journal of Servant-Leadership*, Dr. Jiying Song, wrote,

This dualism resonates with the concepts of *yin* and *yang*, which represent female and male, respectively, in ancient Chinese literature.

> As for yin and yang, they are the Way of heaven and earth, the fundamental principles [governing] the myriad beings, father and mother to all changes and transformations, the basis and beginning of generating life and killing, the palace of spirit brilliance. (Unschuld, Tessenow, & Zheng, 2011, p. 95)

Lao Tzu (2005) said, "All the myriad things carry the Yin on their backs and hold the Yang in their embrace, deriving their vital harmony from the proper blending of the two vital Breaths" (p. 49). *Yin* and *yang* cannot exist without each other. They are a contradictory yet complementary unit. Women were degraded in ancient China based on the ascendancy of patriarchy, the focus on the contradictory aspect of *yin* and *yang*, and the elevation of *yang* (Bao, 1987). The same kind of degradation still exists in the leadership field today. Having stressed the equally and mutually complementary character of *yin-yang*, some scholars paved the way for the women's egalitarian movement in nineteenth-century China (Bao, 1987). Likewise, this is what Reynolds (2013, 2014) and many other servant-leadership scholars are doing—elevating complementary aspects of gender without neglecting the contradictory aspects. Carrying yin and holding yang in intimate embrace, leaders learn to forgive more readily and more deeply, and help others gain the vital harmony so often missing in today's families, organizations, and nations.

Through a discussion of the complementary character of *yin-yang* and servant-leader elements, without ignoring the contradictory aspects, leaders may establish harmony and gender-integrative models wherever they serve. Although the results of Reynolds's (2013) study indicated that gender stereotyping continues to affect conceptualizations of leadership, her study also provided evidence of servant-leaders crossing gender boundaries and integrating gendered traits and behaviors. As Reynolds (2014) noted, by integrating the female perspective with a male perspective, a paradigm shift in leadership theory (through avenues inherent to servant-leadership) has the capacity to move organizations from hierarchy-driven, rules-based, and authoritative models to value-driven, follower-oriented, and participative models with gender balance. (Song & Ferch, 2020, pp. xxii–xxiii)

This brings me, in these postmodern days, to the good involved in multiple views, and to the Jesuit and Quaker notions, identifiably feminist, of the need for persuasion rather than coercion, listening rather than overtalking, and the timeless truth that among many good possibilities the mature person seeks the ultimate good for others. We affirm Jung's (1959) typology as well as the current complexities that exist in human relations by noticing that each of us have both feminine and masculine within us, and to the extent that we hide or subdue either of these, we harm ourselves and others.

Jung conceived of the feminine as the eros, but not the blown-out glammed and glitzed porn culture of American media and Westernized masculine agendas. Neither is it the critical, enraged, contempt-focused feminine at odds with the masculine. Rather, he conceptualized the eros as the womblike existence that gives peace, the life-giving sacrificial essence willing to undergo great suffering in order to preserve more authentic life, the wild mystery at odds with all who might try to come against the child, the family, the collective, or the future. For me, Mochis comes to mind, the Cheyenne woman warrior whose ferocity is legendary. After the Sand Creek Massacre in the late 1800s in which US cavalry slaughtered the Cheyenne, Mochis took up the axe and fought as a warrior and killed many for eleven years until she was captured and shipped by train to Florida, where she was incarcerated by the US Army as a prisoner of war. My mother comes to mind, with her bravery and her heart of forgiveness, and my wife, with her vivacity and wisdom. Not to mention my Czech grandmother. In our family, we call her the Great One. Each of these, in their own way, reflects bell hooks's (2001) liberatory ethic founded in critical race theory and Judith Butler's (2006) restorative wisdom founded in critical feminism aimed at overthrowing prejudicial supremacist patriarchal regimes. What rises from this overthrow, through revolutionary love and leadership, is a communal existence closer to dialogue than monologue, closer to care than apathy or alienation, and closer to peace than war.

It is increasingly more clear now how often the masculine seeks to subdue and overtake the feminine. The masculine is infatuated with a pseudo-eros, an eros he himself has pumped up to proportions that amount to oblivion. That brand of masculine cannot face its own feminine, for to do so would shatter him, and he would then have to integrate the feminine, honor the feminine, and truly love the feminine in order to be healed and made whole. In like fashion the feminine has often usurped the masculine, setting itself against the masculine through bitter alienation or outright hatred, a form of condemnation that amounts to giving the masculine pariah status, often naming the masculine as meaningless or absurd not only in the core of relationships but also at national and international levels. That form of feminine cannot face its own masculine, for to do so would be too shattering and would then require the feminine to integrate the masculine, to take him in with care and enduring affection as well as legitimate healing-oriented power, to truly love in order to be healed and made whole. In my experience working with women and men as a systems psychologist, we carry mutual desolation in our hands. Women and men are made of bone and blood, heart and spirit. I believe understanding and love are required if we are to embrace and heal the feminine and the masculine inside ourselves and in our relationships with others.

Modern-day prophets such as bell hooks, Audre Lorde, Angela Davis, and Judith Butler see far into the mystery, depicting men who are often disintegrated, void, violent, and at odds with the feminine, and, in effect, at odds with themselves. Some of these men, including many men I know, desire to move and change and become capable of giving and receiving love. In symbiotic conflict with the harsh masculine, Lorde, hooks, Davis, and Butler also note that many women live silenced or enraged, embittered, and integrally ill at ease with the masculine. Some of these women also desire an unfolding that results in unity over fragmentation. But to become humble often requires being humbled. I know such women and men, whose shadows extend and do harm, and who are sometimes blessed to come into what bell hooks (2001) calls "redemptive love," and who have wept at the beauty that exists when they let themselves be broken and let themselves emerge from that long darkness into something new.

I hope to be with them when the dawn comes.

In my own life the humility to surrender or submit to the redemptive love hooks refers too has often been elusive, and pride too present. I am reminded of how silent and songlike, how contemplative and prayerful, the writing life is. "You must grasp life in its depths," Van Gogh said. In response, the poet crafts poems, the novelist novels, and the short story writer stories that show love and respect for the grand, ominous landscapes of humanity and the world. The result is rigorous honesty with regard to the shadow and light in women and men, in families of all forms, profoundly diverse in the interior life and the life of the collective. There has long been a philosophy that says the landscape, and people, grind you up and spit you out, so watch out or your head might get taken off. The mountains kill you. The animals kill you. Your family kills you. Life kills you.

Yet in reading hooks and Lorde, this feels too absolute, too darkly nihilistic to me.

I'm reminded that the artist who serves humanity serves life.

The artist who serves life, serves love.

In the wake of authentic love comes a deeply felt sense of dignity. Internationally, I find this dignity often attends a holistic conception of the Divine. Cornel West (2014) spoke of W. E. B. Du Bois's (*The Souls of Black Folk*) spirituality, saying Du Bois was "more of a prophet than most Christians or religious Jews or religious Buddhists and so on, because . . . he was able to sustain himself spiritually without the apparatus of tradition" (p. 59). West noted with hardy respect how Du Bois didn't succumb to the reductionistic (and in fact, masculinist) bias of scientific positivism and the kind of narrow Darwinism plagued by "the more sophomoric atheists like . . . Christopher Hitchens, Richard Dawkins, and others who reduce the rich Darwin to narrow scientism. Darwin is the brook of fire through which we all must pass" (p. 99). West's uniquely revolutionary Christianity, underlined by his visions of healthy antiimperialist Marxism, given in everyday life through loving acts of service and the willingness to die for the wretched of the earth, calls on Western powers, especially America, to overthrow the militarism, materialism, racism, and poverty imperialism produces, nightshades that have always bred greater patriarchy, sexism, classism, homophobia, and xenophobia. Poisons. In West's sisterhood with bell hooks, I find a genuine sense of heartfelt welcome, identification with the love, justice, and truth embodied by their conception of Christ in the real world, and transmitted by the soul of Christ in historical and present-day Christianity. This Christianity fights for the freedom of others through truth, justice, and love, including the will to die for friends and strangers, and, in the words of Nâzim Hikmet (1994), Marxist and transcendent Islamic poet, the willingness to die even for those you know nothing of. This Christ, of which Cornel West, James Cone (*The Cross and the Lynching Tree*), and bell hooks speak, is not bound by undue optimism or facile understandings of grace but sees clearly into the murky oblivion at the core of humanity, the Beckett-drawn existential emptiness of our collective evil, and stands courageously against it even to the point of death. Being a believer in Christ, like West (2014), I find it "true that my atheistic brothers and sisters do not accept conceptions of God linked to love and justice as I do. But atheistic movement can be one of the carriers of prophetic tradition" (pp. 125–126). A community mosaic colored by love, truth, justice, beauty, and goodness, the transcendentals of which the Jesuits (or "little Christs") speak across time, space, and belief (or antibelief, being another kind of conviction), religious or otherwise, is a community of loving devotion. Of course, like all systems, be it the multiverse of faith traditions worldwide, the uncounted systems in our individual and collective family lives, or the systems of work, government, and public life through which we encounter the world, when rigid, inflexible, and calcified, or when boundaryless, enmeshed, or entangled, trouble and suffering are the result.

Yes, we are harmed. Yes, we die. We all know these truths. Yet death can be met with love, and trauma with dignity: this we often overlook. Just as life can be embraced with healthy abandon, and togetherness with wisdom. I've been embedded in the mountains and rivers and skies of Montana, showing me there exists not merely the reality of my vain or vapor-like existence but also the reality of an enduring sense of generosity, perhaps eternal, and with it, an abiding intimacy, despite and even within the presence of evil, decadence, decay, and death. In bell hooks and Audre Lorde I've found prose and poetry that does not ignore or forego or turn a blind eye to the presence of human evil but rather reaches for light in the presence of evil.

To find light in the presence of evil involves foresight.

In great literature, foresight is ever present.

In poor literature, just as in unhealthy individuals and families, I find foresight lacking or nonexistent. In healthy art, as in healthy people, the wilderness of the human heart beckons us toward love. I think of foresight differently as a psychologist than I would if I was trained in another field. When a psychologist lacks foresight the costs are high. People may descend into suicide, or ramp toward homicide. Outside of troubling mental health deficits, even in "normal" people a lack of foresight is a symbol of relational disorder. Though painful to face, when we lack foresight, life holds us responsible. For dominant culture, consequence is a difficult concept, specifically in present-day America, where it is so easy to be irresponsible across the spectrum: in the family or at work, and on a larger scale in the way America engages with the marginalized and with other countries. Being that America, like all nations, contains manifold complexities, when we lack foresight collectively the results are ruinous. There is a need to hone our capacity for foresight, so when I think about it from a psychological perspective, I think, how can we train ourselves toward greater foresight?

And when I think of art, I ask how can we hone foresight in our artistic leanings?

Examples from the Gottman Institute's research on relationships (J. M. Gottman, 1995, 1999; J. M. Gottman & DeClaire, 2002; J. S. Gottman, 2004) provide greater clarity. Their work shows a level of foresight never before realized in social science. In three to five minutes a Gottman-trained therapist can predict at a 95% rate how likely a couple is to fracture or descend further into negative sentiment override, a level of negative feeling and experience in which the relationship is plagued by impending dissolution rather than essential unification (J. M. Gottman, 1995, 1999; J. S. Gottman, 2004). The institute's founder, John Gottman, and his wife, Julie, also discovered that 80% of men who divorce all share one character quality, and that 80% of women who divorce share a different but mutually reinforcing character quality (J. M. Gottman, 1995, 1999; J. S. Gottman, 2004).

So what is it?

According to the Gottmans' research, 80% of men who divorce refuse to receive the influence of the feminine, and 80% of women who divorce have contempt for the masculine (J. M. Gottman, 1995, 1999; J. S. Gottman, 2004).

Such an imploding dynamic in human relations then becomes pure foresight when it is turned toward health: women who relate well affirm and love the masculine; and men who relate well receive the influence of the feminine and love the feminine. The whole person who relates well listens to and loves both the feminine and the masculine. In light of this, some suffering, generationally bound, is unavoidable, while other suffering, when met with foresight, becomes predictable and can be turned away from.

Again, a calcified system, too set on defining women and men, forecloses on mystery and keeps us from the crucial discernment that the amount of feminine or masculine in each person chromosomally is beyond our limited understanding and comprises an individual and communal field of unknowing, gracefully eluding the entrapment of the rational. Notably, the Gottmans' research (J. M. Gottman, 1995, 1999; J. S. Gottman, 2004) is tied to a systemic way of looking at the world, and has proven to be of significance across age, gender, and sexual orientation; if I am this type of person, I'm generally going to attract that type of person. If I don't receive the influence of others, I attract contempt and evoke relational dissolution. If I am full of contempt, I attract people who are defensive, who put up a wall in their interactions with me, and who often refuse to receive my influence. Again, I evoke dissolution. The same principles are reflected in organizational life, national policy, and global interactions. If I'm cynical, I tend to attract opposition. If I'm depressed or angry at the world, anxious, or difficult to relate to, I tend to attract an equal but opposing desultory force. Similarly, the person who is humble or graced with common sense and self-responsibility tends to attract healthiness in others. In other words, we attract to ourselves the same level of maturity we have attained. In psychological understanding, this is the disturbing fundamental foresight that you join with or marry an equal level of dysfunction as yourself across time, space, race, religion, socioeconomic status, gender, and sexual orientation.

In like fashion, art that embodies despair, showing contempt for light, gives despair to the world. Such art lacks foresight not because it speaks of death but because it silences, effaces, or erases life. In this sense, great literature counters the homicidal and suicidal tendencies of humanity, with deeper humanity. Be it through comedy or tragedy, through descent or transcendence, or both, great art endures because it is fully human without reducing life's inherent mystery.

Many of the more curative psychological truths fall under the wing of foresight. We all understand some of these, such as: the only person in the world you can change is yourself. But there are also unwritten truths not as readily discovered that prove helpful not just in life but in discerning the processes involved in creativity. For example, a primary finding of systems psychology states that when you change yourself, others around you have to change. An interesting axiom, and a potent one. So, for example, if in my relationships with others I get more defensive or more fortified or more rigid or more severe in the coming months, it's generally predictable how people will respond to me: they will probably say something like, "What's going on?," "I don't like this very much," or "I wish he wasn't so difficult to be with." The outlay is also generally predictable. I'm going to make people irritated and, eventually, different types of responses beyond irritation will come my way, like anger, frustration, and attacks on my character. Certain results follow when I become less mature, less fully human.

I believe much of current literary art, by cascading into or becoming overfocused on less responsible expressions, contains less moral gravitas, and therefore less humanity. In other words, as a person and as an artist, I can't give what I don't have. If I don't have much love in my heart, I don't have much love to give, and my art will lack the depths associated with love. In contemporary literature, where ancient tragedy is the overlord of ancient comedy, readers experience a poverty of love. Yet in great art, love rises through tragedy, attends to the voicelessness and desperation of which tragedy speaks, and still sings.

However, if a person changes in order to become more whole, the result is not generally what we think. It doesn't mean life suddenly tips over into healthy relationships. Why? Because all change must be tested. Our very biology tests change and requires homeostasis, challenging whether we are really going to change or not. Changing to a more full way of life or more fully developed moral character will receive resistance from others, because integrity requires endurance. Integrity is the difference between what is called first-order and second-order change. In first-order change, the system changes for a bit and then pops back to the same shape it was in before, maintaining its original homeostasis; in second-order change, the system changes for the long-term, others affirm the changes, and the changes eventually become aligned toward relational health as the system accomplishes a new more holistic homeostasis.

Greenleaf (1977/2002) had a wonderful grasp of foresight and the robust futures associated with foresight. He believed that not only are people responsible to have foresight but that they are individually responsible to create collective responsibility for foresight so that families, communities, and nations can experience greater health, wisdom, freedom, and autonomy, and the least privileged of society are benefitted or at least not further deprived. In a larger sense the question is daunting: will we gather the foresight we need to meaningfully address the current state of the globe, the volatile ways we relate to each other, our apathy and our lack of individual and collective well-being?

In art, as in life, our lives depend on the answer.

How did the Gottmans come to understand foresight? How did they become capable of predicting such significant relational fulcrums? First, they discovered that we either bind each other in mutual dysfunction or free each other into greater health. Then they began to break the mutual dysfunction or function down into its component parts, to the level of behaviors, words, voice tone, facial expression, patterns of action, patterns of inaction, resistances, energies, attitudes, motivations . . . the myriad ways people relate to each other. They analyzed the thoughts that drive our words, the motives that shape our facial expressions signifying the interior engine behind our thoughts (J. M. Gottman, 1995, 1999; J. M. Gottman & DeClaire, 2002; J. S. Gottman, 2004). The Gottmans helped open the door to consciousness, to the ways we love or lack love, both subtle and direct.

For the artist, such knowledge is akin to grace.

A fortified, defended, protected, critical, fearful, angry, troubled self inevitably attracts a similarly troubled person. And a self of contentment, peace, discipline, responsibility, community, forgiveness, change, and love attracts like qualities in others. When we gain momentum toward greater wholeness, eventually critical mass is reached and the system surrenders to authentic change: the community, then, has drawn itself into a deeper expression of life. Foresight, a distilled form of personal and collective awareness, leads us to the imaginative capacity to surrender to a deeper sense of our shared humanity.

So how did the Gottmans make such foolproof predictions about the ascent or decline of love? They realized that foresight has much to do with a person's facial expressions—they started to see certain critical elements in people's faces, like what drove them to become flooded, reactive, and conflictual rather than clear-minded, emotionally discerning, or at peace. People's faces showed their reactive emotions, and specific facial expressions became predictors, also revealed in the tone and general wording of the spoken voice and the thoughts driving that voice. How did the Gottmans train to achieve such foresight? John Gottman went to France and studied for two years under the world's foremost facial expression expert (J. M. Gottman, 1999).

His journey to France awakens me as an artist and makes me think, who would we study under regarding artistic foresight? Whose narratives can we find to mentor us in the symmetry of love and power? Shadow and light? Good and evil? I ask myself, how might I surrender to the study of life through the tragedy and uplift great artists carry in their hands? Can I listen fervently enough?

The gap between conceiving of and bringing something to fullness is wide when we consider the light-speed pace of everyday society. Contemplative stability is needed. Quiet wisdom. Sable brilliance is powerful, and somehow aligned with or embedded in the illumination that comes up through darkness, like the light of a candle, or a forest fire at night. Avoiding or denying the reality of either darkness or light makes art opaque and weakly envisioned.

In opening our eyes, in facing others with dignity, we see shadow and light.

Deeply conceived, fiercely imagined literary art embraces the tension between shadow and light, ingesting it and not running from it. Not fleeing, blocking, ignoring, or denying the tension but seeking to create weighty resolutions that build to a culminating and unifying force.

We know from personal and communal experience, and from scientific study, that it takes a long time to change personal character. According to family systems research, it takes a generational family system about fifteen years to move from a living death to fully expressed life together. As a systems psychologist, that's why transitional figures in the generations are so important. Instead of alcoholism, alcoholism, alcoholism, when we find one person who pursues the emotional well-being required not just for sobriety but for depth of life, that person has the capacity to change the generational structure into the future. In organizations and nations, instead of overambition, overdominance, or overuse of power down through the generations, we need a transitional generation: critical density and critical mass, a tipping point into a new and better way of being, where authentic love and authentic power go hand in hand. The Truth and Reconciliation Commission in South Africa, People Power 1 and 2 in the Philippines, the Velvet Revolution in Czechoslovakia, the reconciliation ceremonies of the Nez Perce at the site of the Big Hole Massacre, and the Cheyenne and Arapaho at the site of the Sand Creek Massacre, as well as the American civil rights movement are examples of a transitional generation reaching critical mass and changing the world.

Similarly, a transitional generation, capable of great foresight, is needed in American literary art. Narrative too weighted toward nihilism lacks love and therefore lacks power, and narrative too weighted toward sentiment lacks power and therefore lacks love. The literary artists who balance love and power today call us back from dissolution and loneliness and lead us to new wellsprings of human connection. From them we receive value and intimacy, and in their presence we are renewed.

In the art of the poem, the short story, and the novel, the gap in American discernment regarding intimacy shows itself in the violence of men toward women, toward other men, and toward themselves. This is the shadow of which bell hooks and Paulo Freire (1990) speak, the age-old patriarchal house of dominance and victimhood in which we all reside regardless of gender, race, or creed. The loss of our mothers and fathers has left us wounded and hungry to enact either violence or apathy against ourselves and others. Men in America forfeit their sense of the feminine, and so their masculinity is either overexpressed or underexpressed in response to this society-wide epidemic. A blotting out of the feminine results in the fear of intimacy, and the inability to address the spiritual side of life. The art that hails from a deformed sense of masculinity further divides women and men. Overexpressed masculinity symbolizes the death of the feminine and prevents men and women from coming together on mutually inviting, mutually loving, and mutually powerful terms. When a man loses or cuts off his sense of the feminine, it is as if he has experienced the early death of his mother, a death from which all men find it very difficult to recover.

Similarly, a woman who has a truncated sense of the masculine lives as if she has experienced the premature death of her father, a loss that resounds throughout the lifespan. So the grief we bear is the grief of severe loss. Such death is not only untimely but psychically excruciating. Women in America forfeit their sense of the masculine, and so their feminine ethos is either overexpressed or underexpressed. Hatred for the masculine also results in the fear of intimacy and the erasure of access to a more sacred or divine unity. Understanding that personal and biological gender expression, sexual expression, and sexual orientation are natural, complex, and beautiful, the void between the feminine and the masculine (multitudinously defined, as the feminine/masculine dynamic should be) in American art signals the death of the beloved across all gender and sexual dimensions, and it is precisely this alienation between the feminine and the masculine that carries pervasive hopelessness in its wake.

Great art, in contrast, transforms us.

A unified feminine/masculine dynamic leads people and nations into greater foresight. This embrace, the feminine for the masculine and the masculine for the feminine, is rarely seen in contemporary American literary art, and speaks to a disintegration at the core of nations. Movements in modernism and early postmodernism, and the styles of fortification men and women crowd themselves with, have prevented people and nations from knowing how to love both womanhood and manhood. Contemporary literature overflows with characters characterized by moral malaise, sexual ego, sexual cutoff, or sexual degradation; emotional ego and cutoff, or degradation; grim thinking, crass consciousness, and dismal representations of relationship in which discernment (or foresight) and relational intimacy are denied or deemed a fraud. In this sense, art must attend to or pass through the existential emptiness that inheres in the present age. How a writer chooses to navigate this passage reveals the writer's vision of humanity.

The notion of an abiding intimacy, championed by bell hooks (2001), Viktor Frankl (1997), and many others, suggests something I find to be much more believable than the cynicism, nihilism, and facile atheism that characterizes much of contemporary Western literature. How much faith does it take to believe life conspires against you and annihilation is existence? I think it takes a great deal more faith to convince myself harm and ill will are the only reality than it does to open my eyes to the inviolability of life, the virtue of others, and authentic love. The experience of love, like the experience of a smile, achieves almost immediate affirmation of the existence of a transcendent essence in the world.

In the shadow of the Holocaust, Frankl (1997) had the gall to say this: "The salvation of [humanity] is through love and in love. I understood how a [person] who has nothing left in this world still may know bliss, be it only for a brief moment, in the contemplation of [the] beloved" (p. 85). Frankl also echoed the basic intimacy of our biology when he said:

> Consider the eye. The eye, too, is self-transcendent in a way. The moment it perceives something of itself, its function—to perceive the surrounding world visually—has deteriorated. If it is afflicted with a cataract, it may "perceive" its own cataract as a cloud; and if it is suffering from glaucoma, it might "see" its own glaucoma as a rainbow halo around lights. Normally, however, the eye doesn't see anything of itself.
>
> To be human is to strive for something outside of oneself. I use the term "self-transcendence" to describe this quality behind the will to meaning, the grasping for something or someone outside oneself. Like the eye, we are made to turn outward toward another human being to whom we can love and give ourselves.
>
> Only in such a way do people demonstrate themselves to be truly human.
>
> Only when in service of another does a person truly know his or her humanity. (p. 85)

Like Viktor Frankl, Audre Lorde lived in accord with revolutionaries of freedom and those who abandon themselves to love everywhere. She addressed injustices of racism, sexism, classism, heterosexism, and homophobia. Her voice resounds today, the song of a poet who leads us to greater wisdom, health, autonomy, connection, freedom, and communion. Her art unites us in the warm home of her essential understanding and sends us back into the world prepared not only to see more clearly but to love more deeply, not only to challenge but to bring healing. "Pain is important," she said, "how we evade it, how we succumb to it, how we deal with it, how we transcend it" (as cited in Hall, 2004, p. 16). "Revolution is not a one-time event" (Lorde, 2007, p. 140).

References

Arendt, H. (2006). *Eichmann in Jerusalem: A report on the banality of evil.* Penguin Classics.

Bao, J. (1987). Yin yang xue shuo yu fu nv di wei [The idea of *yin-yang* and women's status in China]. *Han Xue Yan Jiu, 5*(2), 501–512. http://ccsdb.ncl. edu.tw/ccs/image/01_005_002_01_07.pdf

Butler, J. (2006). *Gender trouble: Feminism and subversion of identity.* Routledge Classics.

Cone, J. H. (2013). *The cross and the lynching tree.* Orbis.

Crotty, M. (1998). *The foundations of social research: Meaning and perspective in the research process.* Sage.

Denzin, N. K., & Lincoln, Y. S. (2011). Introduction: The discipline and practice of qualitative research. In N. K. Denzin & Y. S. Lincoln (Eds.), *The Sage handbook of qualitative research* (4th ed., pp. 1–20). Sage.

Eicher-Catt, D. (2005). The myth of servant-leadership: A feminist perspective. *Women and Language, 28*(1), 17–25.

Frankl, V. (1997). *Man's search for ultimate meaning.* Basic Books.

Freire, P. (1990). *Pedagogy of the oppressed.* Continuum.

Frost, R. (1947). *Steeple bush.* Henry Holt and Company.

Gadamer, H. (1976). *Philosophical hermeneutics* (D. E. Linge, Ed. & Trans.). University of California Press.

Gadamer, H. (2004). *Truth and method* (J. Weinsheimer & D. G. Marshall Trans.). (2nd, rev. ed.). Continuum. (Original work published 1975)

Gottman, J. M. (1995). *Why marriages succeed or fail: And how you can make yours last.* Simon and Schuster.

Gottman, J. M. (1999). *The marriage clinic: A scientifically based marital therapy.* W. W. Norton & Company.

Gottman, J. M., & DeClaire, J. (2002). *The relationship cure: A five-step guide to strengthening your marriage, family, and friendships.* Random House.

Gottman, J. S. (Ed.). (2004). *The marriage clinic casebook.* W. W. Norton & Company.

Greenleaf, R. K. (2002). *Servant leadership: A journey into the nature of legitimate power and greatness* (L. C. Spears, Ed.; 25th anniversary ed.). Paulist Press. (Original work published 1977)

Hall, J. W. (Ed.) (2004). *Conversations with Audre Lorde.* University Press of Mississippi.

Heidegger, M. (1962). *Being and time* (J. Macquarrie & E. Robinson, Trans.). Blackwell.

Hikmet, N. (1994). *Poems of Nâzim Hikmet* (R. Blasing & M. Konuk, Trans.). Persea Books.

hooks, b. (2000). *Feminist theory: From margin to center* (2nd ed.). South End Press.

hooks, b. (2001). *All about love: New visions.* Harper Paperbacks.

Hu, J., & Liden, R. C. (2011). Antecedents of team potency and team effectiveness: An examination of goal and process clarity and servant leadership. *Journal of Applied Psychology, 96*(4), 851–862. https:/doi.org/10.1037/a0022465

Husserl, E. (1970). *The crisis of European sciences and transcendental phenomenology: An introduction to phenomenological philosophy* (D. Carr, Trans.). Northwestern University Press.

Jung, C. G. (1959). *Aion: Researches into the phenomenology of the self.* Princeton University Press.

Lao Tzu. (2005). *Tao teh ching* (J. C. H. Wu, Ed. & Trans.). Shambhala.

Liden, R. C., Fu, P., Liu, J., & Song, L. (2016). The influence of CEO values and leadership on middle manager exchange behaviors: A longitudinal multilevel examination. *Nankai Business Review International, 7*(1), 2–20. https:/doi.org/10.1108/NBRI-12-2015-0031

Liden, R. C., Wayne, S. J., Liao, C., & Meuser, J. D. (2014). Servant leadership and serving culture: Influence on individual and unit performance. *Academy of Management Journal, 57*(5), 1434–1452. https:/doi.org/10.5465/amj.2013.0034

Liden, R. C., Wayne, S. J., Meuser, J. D., Hu, J., Wu, J., & Liao, C. (2015). Servant leadership: Validation of a short form of the SL-28. *The Leadership Quarterly, 26*(2), 254–269. https://doi.org/10.1016/j.leaqua.2014.12.002

Liden, R. C., Wayne, S. J., Zhao, H., & Henderson, D. (2008). Servant leadership: Development of a multidimensional measure and multi-level assessment. *The Leadership Quarterly, 19*(2), 161–177. https://doi.org/10.1016/j.leaqua.2008.01.006

Lorde, A. (1995). *The black unicorn: Poems.* W. W. Norton and Company.

Lorde, A. (2007). *Sister outsider: Essays and speeches.* Crossing.

Panaccio, A., Henderson, D. J., Liden, R. C., Wayne, S. J., & Cao, X. (2015). Toward an understanding of when and why servant leadership accounts for employee extra-role behaviors. *Journal of Business and Psychology, 30*(4), 657–675. https://doi.org/10.1007/s10869-014-9388-z

Reynolds, K. (2013). *Gender differences in messages of commencement addresses delivered by Fortune 1000 business leaders: A content analysis informed by servant-leadership and the feminist ethic of care* [Doctoral dissertation]. http://foley.gonzaga.edu/

Reynolds, K. (2014). Servant-leadership: A feminist perspective. *The International Journal of Servant-Leadership, 10*(1), 35–63.

Ricoeur, P. (1981). *Hermeneutics and the human sciences: Essays on language, action, and interpretation* (J. B. Thompson, Ed. & Trans.). Cambridge University Press.

Song, J., & Ferch, S. R. (2020). Preface: The forgiveness ethos of servant-leadership. In J. Song, D. Q. Tran, S. R. Ferch, & L. C. Spears (Eds.), *Servant-leadership and forgiveness: How leaders help heal the heart of the world* (pp. xiii–xxxv). SUNY.

Sousa, M., & van Dierendonck, D. (2016). Introducing a short measure of shared servant leadership impacting team performance through team behavioral integration. *Frontiers in Psychology, 6,* 1–12. https:/doi.org/10.3389/fpsyg.2015.02002

Sousa, M., & van Dierendonck, D. (2017a). Servant leaders as underestimators: Theoretical and practical implications. *Leadership & Organization Development Journal, 38*(2), 270–283. https:/doi.org/10.1108/LODJ-10-2015-0236

Sousa, M., & van Dierendonck, D. (2017b). Servant leadership and the effect of the interaction between humility, action, and hierarchical power on follower engagement. *Journal of Business Ethics, 141*(1), 13–25. https:/doi.org/10.1007/s10551-015-2725-y

Spears, L. C. (2002). Introduction: Tracing the past, present, and future of servant-leadership. In L. C. Spears & M. Lawrence (Eds.), *Focus on leadership: Servant-leadership for the twenty-first century* (pp. 1–16). Wiley.

van Dierendonck, D., & Nuijten, I. (2011). The servant leadership survey: Development and validation of a multidimensional measure. *Journal of Business and Psychology, 26*(3), 249–267. https:/doi.org/10.1007/s10869-010-9194-1

van Dierendonck, D., Sousa, M., Gunnarsdóttir, S., Bobbio, A., Hakanen, J., Pircher Verdorfer, A., . . . & Rodriguez-Carvajal, R. (2017). The cross-cultural invariance of the servant leadership survey: A comparative study across eight countries. *Administrative Sciences, 7*(2), 1–11. https:/doi.org/10.3390/admsci7020008

van Dierendonck, D., Stam, D., Boersma, P., de Windt, N., & Alkema, J. (2014). Same difference? Exploring the differential mechanisms linking servant leadership and transformational leadership to follower outcomes. *The Leadership Quarterly, 25*(3), 544–562. https:/doi.org/10.1016/j.leaqua.2013.11.014

van Manen, M. (1990). *Researching lived experience: Human science for an action sensitive pedagogy.* SUNY.

van Manen, M. (2016). *Phenomenology of practice.* Routledge.

Weil, S. (2018). *Love in the void: Where God finds us.* Plough Publishing House.

West, C. (2014). *Black prophetic fire: In dialogue with and edited by Christa Buschendorf.* Beacon Hill.

Williams, L. E. (2009). *Servants of the people: The 1960s legacy of African American leadership* (2nd ed.). Palgrave Macmillan.

Chapter 7

The Will to (Share) Power

Privilege, Possibility, and the Servant-Leader

JENNIFER TILGHMAN-HAVENS

As an administrator at a university, I find myself reflecting on the cycles of years that mark the time our students walk the sidewalks of our campus. As one considers the last four years for our traditional graduating seniors, the formational national landscape that emerges is a critical one. As first-year students, they watched protests erupt in Ferguson, Missouri, over the shooting of high school graduate Michael Brown (Bosman & Fitzsimmons, 2014) and immigration debates across Europe due to the Syrian refugee crisis (Robins-Early, 2015). As sophomores, they learned of the intended oil pipeline across the indigenous land of the North Dakota Standing Rock Tribe, a hate-inspired shooting in a Charleston black church, and the rising candidacy of the first female presidential contender (Chozich, 2015; Horowitz et al., 2015; Thorbecke, 2016). While juniors, they participated in an election that voted into the Oval Office a white billionaire TV star who bragged about assaulting women, questioned the birthplace of the former president, called Latinos "rapists," and instituted a ban on travel from Muslim nations (Fahrenthold, 2016; Lopez, 2018). And as seniors, our students witnessed a white supremacy rally in Charlottesville, Virginia, the rollback of DACA legislation, the demonizing of kneeling NFL football players who protest police brutality toward African Americans, and an unprecedented movement among women to call out male aggression in a united chorus of "#MeToo" (Hoffman & Belson, 2017; Romo et al., 2017; Shugerman, 2017; Stohlberg & Rosenthal, 2017). Our students' education has been intensely shaped by a nation conflicted about race, gender, power, and privilege and desperate for leadership to guide it toward equality, health, and wholeness (Massingale, 2017).

If effective leadership aims to heal the divides that plague our local, national, and global community, then leaders of dominant gender, race, and class (including myself) must examine unearned privilege in order to actively lead organizations toward greater justice. Because the range of complicity by leaders in our historical and current societal injustices is vast, leadership models must take seriously the leader's positionality, inviting examination of one's participation in both the shadow and light sides of our collective history and one's embodiment of both the "imbedded oppressor" and the "imbedded oppressed" (Ferch, 2017). At the heart of the servant-leadership model are values that invite the servant-leader to lean into self-examination and action on behalf of those who are unheard or unrepresented by traditional power structures. If deployed holistically and adopted with an eye toward positionality, servant-leadership has the potential to make a major contribution to healing the injustices that divide our nation and world. Throughout this chapter, I will be referencing both critical race theory and feminist theory as points of intersection with theories of leadership. The term *privilege*, composed of the Latin roots for the concepts *private* and *law*, describes the conferral of advantages, status, resources, and access to one social group and the denial or ration of these same advantages to those lower in the hierarchy (Adams et al., 1997).

An examination of white privilege recognizes racial privilege that is unearned, while male privilege focuses on unearned privilege related to gender. Other privileges that invite examination include ability, sexual orientation, age, and religion, among others. For the purposes of this chapter, I adopt the following terms used by Adams et al. (1997): *advantaged, privileged*, and *dominant* describe groups with access to social power, while *disadvantaged, marginalized*, and *subordinated* describe groups who are blocked or thwarted from access to social power. No terms will serve to fully elucidate the complexities of our individual and social identities, but these terms focus on the structured roles and impacts of an oppressive system, highlighting the inequalities that are systemic rather than attributes of individual people (Adams & Bell, 2016).

The Problem of Unexamined Privilege

How did this problem of unexamined privilege within leadership arise? A survey of the widely adopted leadership models over many decades reveals that the study of leadership has historically been undertaken by white males (Rost, 1991; Vetter, 2010). A Google search of "authors of leadership theory" brings up 22 images of leadership theorists, all of whom are white and 17 of whom are male. Due to the fact that leadership is often confused with management, and that white males are prevalent within the demographic of managers and positional leaders in our nation and world (Jones, 2017), it is no surprise that the vast majority of leadership theory has emerged through this dominant lens. However, a leadership theory that ignores the leader's identity and positionality (as well as that of the followers) faces challenges in its viability in practice. Anthropologists Wren and Faier (2006) argue that "bypassing the impact of the multiple, overlapping, and competing levels of leader and follower identities (age, gender, race, nation, community, etc.) ignores the fundamental elements of the human tradition" (p. 8). Many scholars have emphasized the importance of integrating critical race theory into leadership models, especially in the area of education (DeMatthews, 2016; Giles, 2010; Kezar, 2002; Kezar & Lester, 2010). However, leadership theory as applied to corporate or organizational contexts has largely ignored the identity of the leader. Northouse's (2013) textbook *Leadership: Theory and Practice* includes a chapter titled "Culture and Leadership" but lacks a leadership theory that includes a critical race perspective. Similarly, this oft-used scholarly compilation of leadership theories confines the topic of "women and leadership" to one chapter and fails to make any reference to feminist leadership as a viable model. Dugan's (2017) recently published text *Leadership Theory: Cultivating Critical Perspectives* brings a critical lens to traditional leadership theories, and attempts to remedy the lack of leadership scholarship regarding race and gender by fore-fronting critical inquiry and identity awareness for the leader as she/he advances social, political, or scientific goals. As lenses of race and gender have only more recently influenced the development of leadership theory, it is unsurprising that the positionality and identity of the leader have been largely absent within dominant theories.

The myth of the archetypal leader as the "Great Man" continues to persist in the commonly held perception of the leader. However, one does not have to look beyond the covers of recent newspapers to realize that many men assumed to be "great" leaders by our society have fallen short of the lofty ideal ascribed to them, having manipulated and even assaulted the women they lead (Almukhtar et al., 2018). The roots of this power-and-control leadership style run deep. Philosophers such as Nietzsche (1966) paved the way for a leadership centered in power and control of others. Nietzsche unabashedly claimed that the will to power frames the human condition. In *Beyond Good and Evil*, he described all that lives as striving to "grow, to gain ground, attract to itself and acquire ascendency—not owing to any morality or immorality, but because it lives, and because life is precisely Will to Power. Exploitation . . . is a consequence of the intrinsic Will to Power" (section 259). Through a feminist and critical race lens, what Nietzsche posits reinforces white male oppression. To argue that the human condition necessarily centers on a will to power emboldens the dominant in oppressing the marginalized. Nietzsche (2012) wrote in *The Birth of Tragedy* that there is "nothing more terrible than a barbaric slave class who have learned to regard their existence as an injustice, and now prepare to avenge, not only themselves, but all generations" (p. 65). Although troubling, I believe Nietzsche was trying to name honestly the traps that humans, and especially nonmarginalized classes of people, can fall into: a sense of their own self-righteousness and an utter disregard for marginalized communities.

The legacy of Nietzsche's philosophy influences our current context. Just as Nietzsche (1966) believed sympathy "to be in very bad taste" (section 293), one sees this distaste for sympathy in presentations by popular conservative campus speakers such as Ben Shapiro, who convince willing audiences that white privilege is a farce, and that one simply needs to take control of his own life in order to succeed. He proclaimed in a 2017 presentation:

> [White privilege] is an absolute outright lie. . . . There's another reason some people fail and some people succeed, because some people make better decisions than other people and some values are better than other values. . . . White privilege isn't a reality. It is a cowardly way to blame someone else for your failures to live up to decent responsible standards. (Shapiro, 2017)

Cawthon (2002) warns that leaders like Shapiro find support in Nietzsche's philosophy to justify the idea that the weak are somehow a burden to the strong, whose superiority emerges from the strength of their will. Shapiro, and others like him, argue that history and policy have no relevance, rendering sympathy and historical contextual analysis unnecessary.

His cultural shaming toward personal responsibility reinscribes a colonial mindset that releases from responsibility individuals advantaged by their race, class, and gender. He reinforces a false binary between "all white people are to blame" and "the oppressed are entirely to blame" for the realities of racial disparities in our nation, erecting false barriers to mutual understanding. An effective leader collapses paradoxes such as these, understanding both one's complicity and one's possibility for creating solutions and healing through their leadership.

An Answer to Nietzsche

The increasing disparity between rich and poor, the violence perpetrated against African Americans, the erasure of the Native Peoples from the collective conscious, the rise of white supremacy, and the emerging allegations of rampant sexual assault and exploitation expose the failure of the "will to power" as the driving force for survival. Ferch (2012) stated that "the command-and-control leadership of nation states has resulted in the shunted and often malignant personality of dominant cultures" (p. 19). New leadership approaches are warranted for historically privileged leaders. hooks (1984, 2000) and Frankl (2000, 2014) each provide powerful answers to Nietzsche. If Nietzsche's (1968) hypothesis is that the human condition reflects a will to power, hooks and Frankl suggest the alternative: that the human condition is collectively yearning for a loving, meaningful will to *share* power. hooks (2000) invites leaders to reflect on both love and truth, reminding us that "the heart of justice is truth-telling" (p. 33). Shapiro's arguments conceal the fullness of the truth regarding the historical and social contexts that have shaped communities of color and discount the effect of white privilege and racism. A fuller truth is required to move us toward healing.

Massingale (2010), in his book *Racial Justice and the Catholic Church*, highlights crucial features of racism in the context of the post–civil rights era. He argues that an understanding of racism that is limited to individual acts of hatred or discrimination is far too narrow. He posits that racism has become a normative, unquestioned part of our culture, "a set of shared beliefs and assumptions that undergirds the economic, social, and political disparities experienced by different racial groups" (p. 24). He outlines the ways that this culture (if unquestioned) makes assumptions about where the burdens and benefits of society belong. His work aligns with other modern cultural theorists who help us navigate unconscious, or tacit, transference of cultural expectations. Barnlund (2013) refers to a collective cultural frame of reference that goes unseen or touched but that affects all ways of life. He warns that "as long as people remain blind to the sources of their meaning, they are imprisoned within them" and encourages an awakening of individual and communal critical awareness (p. 299). Chamberlain (1976) describes racism as "an unconscious, unreflective meaning system resting upon symbols of color and sex which are deeply embedded in the fears and anxieties of white Americans" (p. 353). Racism festers within prisons of unawareness. Feminist Judith Butler (2015) also points to the normativity that blinds individuals to deeper truths, positing that "to be a subject at all requires first finding one's way with certain norms that govern recognition—norms we never choose and that found their way to us and enveloped us with their structuring and animating cultural power" (p. 40). Racism or gender discrimination may not be something that leaders consciously choose, but it may be reproduced unconsciously by them in the absence of intentionality or when invoked by insecurity or fear.

hooks's (2000) remedy for managing these embedded fears is to return to love. She suggests that to "return to love, to know perfect love, we surrender the will to power" (p. 221). Although the will to power may provide the illusion of having triumphed over fear, love can truly drive out fear (hooks, 2000). I would argue that in order to love others fully, we even need to love the *fear* in the other and to accompany one another into the shadow places where fear resides. Once we have acknowledged our fears and vulnerabilities together—enough to love the fear in the other—then we can move beyond unjust divisions and structures.

Holocaust survivor, physician, and author Victor Frankl (2000, 2014), who suffered immeasurably as a result of an intentional system of domination, unchecked privilege, control, and brutality, also offers a counterpoint to Nietzsche. Frankl (2000) believed that the will to power serves as a substitute for "a frustrated will to meaning" (p. 89). For Frankl (2014), humankind is united by a common will to a common meaning fulfilled by self-transcendence, which he names the "essence of existence" (p. 33). This self-transcendence can bring about a necessary and, Frankl notes, healthy tension as one examines his/her conscience to notice a responsibility to one another. One of Frankl's (2000) most poignant insights for our day is that as a culture, we have embraced monotheism (the belief in one god), but not monanthropism, the willingness to embrace the reality of one humanity. He echoes Massingale's lament for a culture that breeds racism: "If we only broadened our horizon we would notice that we enjoy our freedom, but we are not yet fully aware of our responsibility" (Frankl, 2014, p. 73). This is especially true for people traditionally privileged by the structures of our culture, in particular those of us who are white. Frankl (2000) believes that education—and I would argue leadership—"must see its assignment as refining the individual's conscience" in an era where values are no longer commonly held (p. 119). Frankl points to the importance of mining one's unconscious spiritual depths as an antidote to the will to power, as these depths are where important existential choices are made. One could argue that the choice for members of advantaged groups to examine privilege is such an existential choice.

Many contemporary leaders inspire our culture to refine its conscience around race and privilege. Feminist scholar Peggy McIntosh's (2003) work "White Privilege: Unpacking the Invisible Knapsack" is reflection on and enumeration of the many ways that white people in the United States reap societal benefit simply because of the color of their skin. She lists numerous daily effects of unearned white privilege and invites the reader to note which benefits are afforded them due to their skin color. This kind of examination by a leader is crucial if she sees herself as a healing agent in our divided culture. Ijeoma Oluo (2017), editor-at-large of the *Establishment*, a media platform run and funded by women, speaks and writes to white audiences about whiteness and the importance of examining white privilege: "Every time you go through something, and it's easy for you, look around and say, 'Who is it not easy for? And what can I do to dismantle that system?'" (para. 5). In the area of literary criticism, American novelist Toni Morrison (1992), in her work *Playing in the Dark: Whiteness and the Literary Imagination*, invites white writers and readers of fiction to notice biases in classical and current works of literature that portray people of color as embodiments of the fears of white authors instead of characters whose own rich and complex personhood was honored. English scholar Eula Biss (2015) invites whites to think about whiteness not only as an identity but also as a moral problem. Biss (2015) disagrees with Nietzsche's vilification of guilt as a killjoy, arguing instead for the proper role of guilt in forming the conscience as one considers the harm of unquestioned whiteness. Public thinker and writer Ta-Nehisi Coates (2017) has also written extensively on white privilege and white supremacy, arguing that "the point of white supremacy . . . is to ensure that that which all others achieve with maximal effort, white people (particularly white men) achieve with minimal qualification" (para. 5). He describes the ways the privileges and care and concern afforded lower-class whites in the recent election cycle belied the fact that

African American communities with similar long-standing concerns have consistently been ignored. Coates (2014) and many others recall historical decisions that have led us to our current state—for instance, the government-sanctioned practice of "redlining" in communities of color, which kept minoritized communities from being able to secure stable FHA-backed mortgages, leaving communities of color in cycles of debt for generations, while white communities watched equity accrue in their suburban homes. It is not coincidence that these once redlined Chicago neighborhoods now suffer from greater poverty and violent crime than other boroughs in my still-segregated hometown Chicago (Semuels, 2018).

Within the realm of religion and Christianity, Fletcher (2017) examines the perpetuation of white privilege in our Christian stories and symbols, in her efforts to draw attention to the sin of white supremacy. Bishop Edward Braxton (2017) calls for truth telling about the "flaw at the foundation" of US history in the enslavement of free African people as well as the recent police shootings of unarmed African Americans. Braxton calls on people of faith to learn the truth of our collective and current history—especially the genocide of Native Peoples and the mass incarceration of African American males. He emboldens white communities to refuse to remain silent about continued racial injustice. These leaders of thought and word and action can serve to inspire leaders of dominant identities to examine their privilege and to claim their proper positionality as they lead us toward a hopeful future.

The Challenges and Possibilities of Servant-Leadership

Positionality theory emerged in the 1980s alongside the important feminist scholarship of Sandra Harding (1991). It posited that multiple identities (such as race, gender, and class) shape and reinforce individual perspectives (Collins, 1986; Haraway, 1991). Since one's identities are complex, fluid, and contextually bound, they vary in their relationship to how power is structured within a culture or society. As Kezar and Lester (2010) argue, leadership beliefs and actions are shaped by one's identity, context, and access to power; therefore, one's subjectivity—or, I would argue, one's objectification—is formed through the effects of one's positioning. Ferch (2012) reminds us that unawareness of our personal and communal cultural identity perpetuates unconscious and conscious loathing of those whom we deem "different" from ourselves—a loathing, if coupled with power, leads to domination and oppression. A leadership theory appropriate to the current national context needs to take seriously the positionality of the leader, not to reinforce the oppressor/oppressed binary but to reconcile it, taking into account the self-responsibility of the leader for examining his or her role in furthering social and racial justice. Paolo Freire's (1972) crucial work *Pedagogy of the Oppressed* shaped the education of marginalized communities and played a crucial role in the emergence of liberation theology worldwide. Our current times beg for a "Pedagogy (or Leadership) of the Oppressor," which would require those aligned with historical oppression to "unlearn" approaches that dominate others and instead to move out of complicity into true community.

What leadership approach, then, can guide the actions of the leader who engages in this critical reflection of privilege and power? McIntosh (2003) invites a similar natural and vital question in her article about white privilege as she considers, "Having described it, what will I do to lessen or end it?" (p. 1). It is insufficient for a leader to engage simply in the *examination* of privilege, when ultimately it is the use of their power to transform systems toward racial equality that will make the greatest difference for our society. Mainstream leadership models provide minimal guidance here. In James MacGregor Burns's (1978) transformational leadership theory, the leader serves as a strong role model, creates a true connection with followers, and raises the level of morality in both leader and follower in order to contribute to the common good. Authentic leadership relies on self-awareness, internalized perspective, balanced processing, and relational transparency as its four primary characteristics (Walumbwa et al., 2008). Various ethical theories within the discipline of leadership encourage altruism, utilitarianism, and respect for people (Northouse, 2013). However, no single conception of leadership relies on positionality, critical race, and feminist theory as its backbone.

Robert Greenleaf's (1970) model of the "servant-leader" presents an opportunity for leaders to examine privilege and to employ a set of behaviors that can overturn systems of oppression and dominance. I offer here that the effectiveness in the utilization of the servant-leadership model within diverse environments depends on two factors: (1) the positionality of the leader, and (2) the context of the organization. As this chapter attempts to highlight both the opportunities and challenges of utilizing a servant-leadership model, the Jesuit lens found in *The Spiritual Exercises of Saint Ignatius* serves as a helpful tool. Saint Ignatius of Loyola (1963) proposed that an authentic discernment about how to act (and, I propose, how to lead) should invite the discerner or leader to name honestly one's consolations—the places of hope, gratitude, and possibility within an option for consideration—and to name honestly one's desolations—the places of unease, limitation, and unfreedom—within the topic being discerned. As I reflect on Greenleaf's servant-leadership model regarding its potential to address the problem of unexamined privilege, I experience both consolation and desolation, as described here.

Consolations. First, the very foundational values that undergird the servant-leadership model lead one to a self-examination on unearned privilege. The values of listening, empathy, healing, awareness, the commitment to the growth of people, and building community are especially pertinent in this regard (Spears, 2002). Second, Robert Greenleaf believed that able leaders could emerge from every segment and strata of society, regardless of their position, education, income, ethnicity, or religion (Frick, 2004). A devout Quaker, Greenleaf's inspiration for his servant-leadership model was the historical Jesus, who befriended those rejected by society, and who called out domination and control tactics on the part of religious leaders. The "best test" of servant-leadership, according to Greenleaf (1970), is whether those served grow as persons to become healthier, wiser, and more free (p. 6).

Third, Greenleaf (1977) calls leaders to a "legitimate power" that respects the dignity of others, especially those without privilege. Greenleaf writes that a leader has the responsibility to concern oneself with those who are less privileged in society, and to address and remove inequalities. He suggests that the central question in leadership is whether "other people's highest priority needs are being served" (p. 27). Frick recalled Greenleaf's speech to Ohio Fellows in April 1967, in which Greenleaf asserts, "We all do have the obligation, because we are educated and intelligent, to care for the less fortunate. It is not simply a matter of charity; everybody should be charitable. Obligation is a consequence of privilege" (as cited in Frick, 2004, p. 233). Greenleaf's commitments reflect the commitments of leaders throughout history who are afforded advantages and have used their power for the good of others, leading by example in the effort to upend systems and policies that obstruct opportunities for those of disadvantaged status. In their book *White Men Challenging Racism*, Thompson, Schaefer, and Brod (2003) uphold this kind of leadership as they enumerate examples of historically advantaged groups who not only unmask the role they have played in maintaining the status quo but who articulate the moral and societal cost of an unequal society and invite justice-oriented action. Greenleaf's servant-leadership model would support this engagement.

Fourth and finally, the servant-leader relies on self-responsibility. Greenleaf believed in leadership that is honest, loving, and responsible (Frick, 2004). Greenleaf (1998) writes, "Responsible people build. . . . They are moved by the heart; compassion stands ahead of justice. The prime test of whether an act is responsible is to ask, 'How will it affect people? Are lives moved toward nobility?' " (p. 96). Ferch (2012) describes it this way:

> The natural tendency of humanity is to externalize blame for a given communal conflict—but the life of love sustains the truths that heal us and we begin to internalize self-responsibility for system health rather than externalize blame; in this context, the family as well as in work, and even in the course of nations, resilience and moral power, infused by love, breathe life into the system. (p. 48)

Leadership that takes responsibility for the health of the whole serves as a healing corrective as our communities, nation, and world begin to move toward reconciliation for personal and communal pain caused by inequality.

Desolations. The limitations, or desolations, that I notice within this model relate to the positionality of the leader and the context within which the model is employed. First, depending on the gender, race, and social identity of the leader, servant-leadership may or may not be experienced as Greenleaf intended. Several of the characteristics related to servanthood have traditionally been associated with women's roles (listening, empathy, care), which represent a freedom for traditional white males from the hegemonic masculinity that pervades many approaches to leadership, but may reproduce assumptions about women and leaders of color. For men, servant-leadership can provide an antidote to the toxic masculinity so often associated with power and control. People of marginalized identities, however, may not experience these same benefits. Fine and Buzzanell (2000) found that servant-leadership fails to take into consideration the ways in which gender relations may make it a very different process for women and men. Feminist theorist Deborah Eicher-Catt (2005) argues that the servant-leadership model can reinscribe androcentric, patriarchal norms by assuming that the perspective and characteristics of a servant is a *new* standpoint for the (assumed male) leader, as opposed to a set of characteristics already present within leaders of color and women. Although servant-leadership promotes listening and service as primary characteristics of the servant-leader, Bowles and McGinn (2005) found that women are less likely than men to engage in self-promotion or making visible their hard-earned accomplishments, to the detriment of their career advancement. Babcock and Laschever (2003) found that women are also less likely to negotiate for new opportunities, raises, and promotions. Adoption of a servant-leadership approach that prioritizes meeting the needs of others over oneself could continue perpetuate the invisibility of women. Further, the white male servant-leader who leads by serving renounces gender expectations in a way that is remarkable and exemplary, while women who enact the same behaviors are unexceptional (Fine & Buzzanell, 2000). Men may feel freed from restrictive conceptions of masculinity or of leadership to embrace more "feminine" aspects of their personality, but women face a double bind as they both attempt to transgress traditionally "feminine" characteristics, as these are seen as contrary to effective leadership, while trying to embody them as servant-leaders.

Reynolds (2014) submits to the arguments of Eicher-Catt (2005) and others that servant-leadership may not be congruent with feminist objectives because of the danger of perpetuating existing assumptions about gender and power. However, Reynolds (2014) promotes servant-leadership for its potential as a gender-integrative approach that embraces traditionally conceived feminine traits as part of the leadership theory matrix. She argues that because traits traditionally associated with leadership are often also correlated with masculinity, and traits associated with service/servanthood are traditionally associated with the feminine (and, I would argue, marginalized racial and gender identities), the 10 characteristics of the servant-leader delineate along dominant/nondominant lines—foresight, conceptualization, awareness, and persuasion being the "leader/masculine" traits, while listening, empathizing, healing, practicing stewardship, exercising commitment to the growth of people, and building community align with feminine or nondominant identities. Reynolds asserts that these characteristics need not be correlated with oppression and subjugation but rather are commonly desirable traits that most human beings look for in a leader, and sees possibilities for a holistic approach.

This is where organizational and communal context matter. If women and people of color are encouraged to employ the servant-leadership model as singular actors within situations of unequal power dynamics, they may become the servant-leaders Greenleaf envisioned but not be perceived by superiors as exercising leadership. Because the qualities associated with servant-leadership (and servanthood itself) have historically been ascribed to women and people of color, their natural ways of leading may not signal to superiors their readiness for advancement. Bordas (2012) notes in her book *Salsa, Soul and Spirit: Leadership for a Multicultural Age* that Greenleaf might be discouraged today to find many dominant-culture leaders refusing to hand over power to marginalized groups (p. 124). However, he would be uplifted by the presence of many servant-leaders of color working within the context of communities of color, committed to leading with legitimate power for the common good. Bordas describes these leaders as "community servants" and "stewards" (p. 125). Here is where context matters. Because African American, Native, and Latino cultures have historically been rooted in the values consistent with Greenleaf's model (community, public welfare, and addressing unjust social systems), the contexts of these communities celebrate the qualities of the servant-leader (Bordas, 2012).

I argue that a person of color or woman attempting to embody servant-leadership within a dominant-culture organization may not find that her leadership is promoted in the same way. My own professional witness to this is echoed by Marlene Fine, who wrote about her own experience, "I tried to lead by serving—and I failed. Failed—not to serve. I think I served well. But I failed to convince those above me that I was exercising leadership. I remained invisible to those above me" (Fine & Buzzanell, 2000, p. 128). I have observed this dynamic among individuals of nondominant identities in my own organization, and further scholarship is warranted in this area, to ensure that women and people of color who are solo practitioners of servant-leadership are not risking career stagnation.

Toward a Liberatory Model of Leadership

The Dictionary.com "word of the year" for 2017 is "complicit." In their explanation for this choice, Dictionary.com states, "*Complicit* means 'choosing to be involved in an illegal or questionable act, especially with others; having partnership or involvement in wrongdoing.' Or, put simply, it means being, at some level, responsible for something . . . even if indirectly." I would argue that the phrase "even if indirectly" is terribly relevant to an examination of leadership in our times. Few leaders are free from complicity in a global system that continually reinscribes the domination of a powerful few over the "minoritized" many. At the end of her work *Feminist Theory: From Margin to Center*, bell hooks (1984) encourages a "liberatory ideology" that breaks with the current systems of domination, replaces them with love and dialogue, and sees the interconnectedness of all movements toward liberation. bell hooks argues,

> The world we have most intimately known, the world in which we feel "safe" (even if such feelings are based on illusions) must be radically changed. Perhaps it is the knowledge that everyone must change, not just those we label enemies and oppressors, that has so far served to check our revolutionary impulses. (p. 166)

I propose that a model of "liberatory leadership" is needed in our times to uncover personal and communal complicity in structures, practices, and policies that assume a white male norm and ignore potent yet unquestioned assumptions regarding race and gender. Expounding upon Greenleaf's servant-leadership framework and drawing upon bell hooks's insights, a liberatory leadership paradigm would liberate people of color and women from unjust systems and welcome them into full participation at all levels of organization, while also freeing white people from narrowly conceived illusions about whiteness and privilege and inviting men to reconsider narrowly defined hegemonic masculinities. By recognizing and taking seriously the positionality of the leader as well as historical communal contexts, a liberatory leadership paradigm would honor the uniqueness of the capacities of nondominant groups and encourage (as Greenleaf did) a genuine sharing of power with those who have historically been disempowered.

This proposed liberatory leadership framework includes three primary components: theoretical underpinnings that serve as the foundation for the framework, a set of principles for effective leaders (throughout all levels of an organization), and a set of organizational policy and practice considerations. Initial considerations for a model are presented here, although robust input, particularly from traditionally marginalized populations, would be essential to a more thorough examination of a liberatory leadership model, and methods for assessment will need to be explored in future scholarship.

Theoretical Underpinnings

It is important to begin by naming the theoretical underpinnings for a liberatory leadership framework. Critical leadership studies, poststructural feminism, critical race theory, and transdisciplinary theory serve as the scaffolding for the liberatory model. Critical leadership studies is a broad and diverse array of critiques that question the power dynamics and identity constructions through which leadership is received and reproduced and questioned and transformed in the development of leadership theory (Collinson, 2011). Liberatory leadership contributes to this growing body of research as it attempts to confront dominant thinking about leader-follower dynamics and assumed hegemonic perspectives. Poststructural feminist analysis explores the intersectionalities of race, gender, class, and sexualities and the ways these identities "mutually construct one another" (Collins, 1998, p. 63). Poststructural feminism serves an important role because it reveals the subjectivities in organizations; critiques dominant organizational practices; reveals the hidden raced, classed, and gendered dynamics therein; and requires from the practitioner a critical awareness of one's social location as the starting point for their contribution to leadership (Holvino, 2010). Organizational practices emerge from poststructural feminism, as outlined below. Critical race theory explores the relationship between race, power, and structural inequities where racism becomes imbedded, and questions the cultural assumptions at the foundations of the liberal order (Delgado et al., 2017). It arose after the civil rights era, as scholars, lawyers, and activists recognized the stalling of progress toward black liberation and the need for new theories and strategies to uncover and resist racism. Drawing on European philosophers such as Michel Foucault and Jacques Derrida, critical race theory also emerged from the lived experience of individuals such as Sojourner Truth, Cesar Chavez, Martin Luther King, Jr., and others (Delgado et al., 2017). It attempts to rectify what J. King (1991) calls dysconscious racism, "a form of racism that tacitly accepts dominant White norms and privileges," and suggests that a society reorganized without racial privilege is possible only with a fundamental shift in the way racially advantaged groups think about their status, their self-identities, and their conceptions of people of color (p. 135).

Finally, the liberatory paradigm draws upon transdisciplinary theory. The integration of seeming dichotomies and collapsing of paradoxes is crucial in order for a liberatory model to be successfully employed. The unhelpful binaries of "leader vs. follower," "born vs. made," "masculine vs. feminine," "oppressed vs. oppressor," and "individual rights vs. collective good" lock leaders into contrived either/or decisions. Max-Neef (2005) argues that although contemporary human beings know very much, we understand very little, lacking a more comprehensive, deeper way of encountering the world in all its complexity, in order to see the reality of the "unity of all things" (p. 15). Transdisciplinarity invites leadership that is horizontal and inclusive, that takes seriously the impact of decisions for "generations yet to come . . . the planet as a whole . . . an economy as if people matter" (p. 8). This holistic, transdisciplinary thinking is core to liberatory approaches. Although Robert Greenleaf lacked the consciousness of critical race and feminist discourse, Greenleaf's approach also advocated the reconciliation of seeming dichotomies. His vision of a "good society" included individualism amid community, elitism along with populism, both chaos and order. The characteristics of servant-leadership also attempt to reconcile binaries. As Reynolds (2014) posits, they promote traditionally ascribed "feminine" characteristics as a counterbalance to some of the traditional white-male-authored theories of leadership, liberating both men and women from binary categories. A liberatory approach affirms the servant-leadership ideal of the reintegration of the lost feminine and the full embrace by both men and women of societally inscribed "masculine" and "feminine" leadership characteristics, as they engage the fullest spectrum of human emotion, intellect, and activity, regardless of gender. This integration and freedom from gender-inscribed norms makes a more liberatory leadership possible.

Leadership Principles

Inspired by the works of Robert Greenleaf, Paolo Freire, and bell hooks, and distilling core themes from their vast and important works, the liberatory leadership framework offers a set of three guiding principles that inspire the practices of leadership: awareness, a commitment to share power, and love. After extensive study of Greenleaf's original works, Spears (2002) extracted a set of characteristics of the servant-leader, which include listening, empathy, healing, awareness, persuasion, conceptualization, foresight, stewardship, commitment to the growth of people, and building community. While each of these servant-leader characteristics could be employed by a leader committed to liberatory practices, awareness becomes a central principle for effective liberatory work. Self-awareness creates conscious space for reflection on one's identity, history, emotional responses, assumptions, and unconscious biases in order for continuous growth and transformation. This level of self-awareness becomes important in resisting what Hofstede (2011) calls "the collective programming of the mind which distinguishes the members of one group or category from another" and that assumes normativity of the dominant group (p. 3). Greenleaf (1977) recognized that entering into this awareness can produce disturbance as leaders move "below the level of conscious intellect" to mine both the conscious and unconscious mind, to notice the errors inherited by our culture, the "undigested residue of our experience," and the losses sustained but unexamined (p. 340). Discomfort, guilt, or pain arises in distinctive ways for people of dominant positionalities as they become aware of their privilege. Greenleaf

(1977) writes, "Awareness is not a giver of solace—it is just the opposite. It is a disturber and an awakener. Able leaders are usually sharply awake and reasonably disturbed. They are not seekers after solace" (p. 41). Greenleaf recommends that leaders remove what blinds them from reality, even to the point of choosing to lose "what must be lost" (p. 340). This is a particularly poignant directive for societally advantaged groups who want to engage in antiracist or feminist practices that require personal sacrifice. White antiracist author Robin DiAngelo (2018) suggests that as white people awaken to the realities of white privilege and racial inequality, they must build "capacity to sustain the discomfort of not knowing, the discomfort of being racially unmoored, the discomfort of racial humility" (p. 14). For leaders with nondominant identities, the pain of recognizing internalized oppression can also arise, spurring them to examine their internalized bias, recover their personal power, and seek out communities from which they may have become alienated, in order to resist unknowingly passing on to others what they've tacitly acquired (David, 2014). From a place of deep self-awareness, leaders from nondominant groups will discern how to harness and claim their agency. Hofstede (2011) suggests that no matter what our social location might be, critical awareness can rewire the "software of the mind" that assigns meaning to our cultural and gender identities, with the possibility of liberation for all (p. 13). In this way, leaders come to reconcile and make peace with both the imbedded oppressed and oppressor within themselves (Ferch, 2017).

As the liberatory leader engages in deep and continuous practices of self-awareness, he or she recognizes one's own capacity and responsibility to share power with others, especially those who have historically been denied it. Paolo Freire (1972), whose liberatory lens transformed pedagogical practice for underserved communities, promotes dialogue between oppressed and oppressor to bring people together toward greater mutual freedom. This dialogue is an avenue for sharing power, as both oppressed and oppressor gain greater critical consciousness as they work to change society for the better. For Greenleaf (1977), too, power was meant to be shared, as "legitimate" power is exercised only through service to others. He advocated that servant-leaders step back to allow the talents and "genius" of others to come to light. Servant-leadership espouses a "nonhierarchical, participative approach to defining organizational objectives and ethics that recognizes and values the subjectivity and situatedness of organizational members" (Reynolds, 2014, p. 57). Critical leadership studies interrogate the place of power as well, and critiques the persistence within mainstream leadership theory of the distinction between leader and follower (Gronn, 2011). Hofstede (2011) argues that *power distance*, the widespread cultural acceptance of unequal distribution of power, has significant influence within institutions and organizations. Bryson and Crosby (1992) conceive of a shared-power world, where systems of organizational partnerships, coalitions, and collaborations work together toward mutual and long-term gain for the common good. A liberatory model proposes to equalize power relations by acknowledging unequal distributions of power and minimizing power distance by all members of a given organization. The concept of subsidiarity is important in this regard—that those people closest to a given decision have the greatest voice in its discernment. Shared power is also a key principle within many Native American communities. As Okanogan leader Jeanette Armstrong (2002) describes it, "From our point of view, the minority voice is the most important voice to consider in terms of the things that are going wrong, the things that we're not looking after, the things we're not being responsible toward (9:04)." As decisions are made, the Okanogan call forth the voices of the young, the elders, the artists, and the land, recognizing the wisdom these marginalized perspectives offer and sharing power to ensure the sustainability and survival of the Okanogan people (Armstrong, 2002). Liberatory leadership, too, blurs the lines between leader and follower, trusting that leaders exist throughout an organization, and seeking out unheard voices in order that power is shared.

A centerpiece of the work and writing of Greenleaf, Freire, and hooks is the principle of love (hooks, 2000; Miller et al., 2011; Patterson, 2010). Liberatory leadership relies on love as its foundation, as liberatory leaders place people at the center of an organization's focus, choosing to lead and act out of love. Van Dierendonck and Patterson (2015) argue that compassionate love is an antecedent to servant-leadership and that this loving compassion entails considering each individual (or follower) in his or her fullness. Cultural leadership theorists Miller et al. (2011) propose that love was a primary operational tenet of Freire's work as well. hooks (2000) gives depth and fullness to the concept of love, defining it as a combination of "care, commitment, knowledge, responsibility, respect and trust," which must be experienced together in order for the receiver to experience love (p. 7). Love in leadership also serves as an important antidote to operating out of fear and scarcity (hooks, 2000; Patterson, 2010). Even mainstream leadership scholarship is surfacing the primacy of love as central to the practice of effective leadership. Lawrence and Pirson (2015) point out that renewed Darwinian theory is recovering the primacy of the "drive to bond" and the "drive to comprehend" as two primary motives that direct decision making in leadership and serve as important counterweights to the drive to acquire and to defend, traditionally associated with the survival of the fittest. Their research reveals that if a leader is unable to form true caring relationships or to seek to comprehend the experience of another, individuals and organizations suffer. Love that seeks to understand and to connect with others is central to effective liberatory leadership. Alongside awareness that allows us to honestly name our personal and communal realities and shared power that entrusts individuals and communities with agency, love that sacrifices for the growth of another and nurtures the fullest development of each human being defines the liberatory leader.

Organizational Practice Considerations

What would organizational practices within a liberatory leadership framework look like? Holvino (2010) recommends three specific organizational practices that lend themselves to examination of privilege and organizational transformation toward racial and gender justice. First, she suggests giving voice to "hidden stories at the intersections of race, gender, class, sexuality, ethnicity and nation" (p. 263). This truth telling through personal narrative allows for the embodiment of collective histories within individuals, creating space for acknowledgement of painful truths and inspiring motivation to resist reproducing them. Chronicling stories from nondominant perspectives serves as an important counternarrative to assumed norms and can be a vehicle for education about the particularities of the ways discrimination and exclusion are experienced by individuals. It can also serve as fodder for examination of institutional practices that may unknowingly contribute to oppressive experiences. Second, Holvino recommends an analysis of the ways practical, everyday practices within organizations are experienced differently and create advantages or disadvantages based on one's positionality. Honest assessment by diverse constituents about the practical impact of structures and decisions, specifically on women and people of color, enables institutional policy to shift. Finally, Holvino suggests an honest naming of organizational and individual location with regards to background, history, and social context. This includes the exploration of the ways that neocolonial practices, historical social inequities, and patriarchal discriminatory mindsets or contexts can inhibit liberatory practices.

Additional organizational practices that actualize awareness, shared power, and love include proactive hiring and promotion processes that favor diverse candidates; antibias training for all stakeholders of the organization (to enable movement beyond fear and into greater love); policies that support work/life balance, family responsibilities, health, and community engagement; facilitated practices for personal and collective reflection to attend to conscience; creating community partnerships across previously uncrossed barriers; a commitment to seeking ongoing reconciliation and reparations with individuals and communities affected by the organization; and a communal engagement in creative imagination about how to envision a future rooted in justice for all humans as well as the earth.

As the roots of Robert Greenleaf's theory of servant-leadership are grounded in a spirituality inspired by the Judeo-Christian context, consideration of spiritual practice within the liberatory framework is also worth exploration here. Howard (2002) argues that the expansion of interest in spirituality and leadership is one of the greatest areas of interest within practice and research. An Amazon book search for topics related to spirituality and effective leadership in 2018 revealed over 8,000 results. Howard connects spirituality and workplace growth, noting that the transformation of people and organizations requires generativity, courage, and strength, which can be bolstered by spiritual practice. Ngunjiri (2010), in her study of servant-leaders and tempered radicals among African women, found spirituality to be a crucial component to their effectiveness as leaders. The women she interviewed drew upon spiritual practice in three primary ways: as a source of inspiration and direction, as a source of leadership practice, and as a source of courage and strength amid adversity. Ngunjiri found that spirituality served as a "divine inspiration to lead for social justice, a source of fulfillment in the face of performing thankless work, and the impetus for action" (p. 203). The spirituality of these women empowered them to develop a profound critique of the status quo and then to reconstruct and move toward more hopeful and potent possibilities for their communities. Although espousal of religious belief is unnecessary for practitioners of liberatory leadership, spirituality can provide inspiration and courage to leaders as they live out liberatory principles and lead organizations toward practices that are liberating for all.

Conclusion

Civil, corporate, ecclesial, and educational systems cry out for a liberatory leadership that acknowledges positionality and privilege, operates out of both truth and love, shares power, and turns our societies toward the healing and justice they so desperately need for the flourishing of all. This model raises up both hooks's (1984) vision of "reorganizing society so that the self-development of people can take precedence over imperialism, economic expansion, and material desires" (p. 26) and Greenleaf's commitment to use power for good, making sure that means determine ends without justification of unjust practices or the exploitation of human beings (Frick, 2004). The health, freedom, wisdom, and autonomy that Greenleaf (1970) envisioned would be at the center of human organizations. This leadership approach would move our society toward something it has never been—the beloved community, as Martin Luther King (1957) called it, or, in Ignatian terms, "the Magis," that sacred "more" to which we must strive as we envision a just and humane world for future generations.

References

Adams, M., & Bell, L. A. (2016). *Teaching for diversity and social justice* (3rd ed.). Routledge.

Adams, M., Bell, L. A., & Griffin, P. (1997). *Teaching for diversity and social justice: A sourcebook* (2nd ed.). Routledge.

Almukhtar, S., Gold, M., & Buchanan, L. (2018, February 8). After Weinstein: 71 men accused of sexual misconduct and their fall from power. *The New York Times*. https://www.nytimes.com/interactive/2017/11/10/us/men-accused-sexual-misconduct-weinstein.html?_r=0

Armstrong, J. (2002). Human relationship as land ethic. https://www.youtube.com/watch?v=qwNoX3MNisE

Babcock, L. & Laschever, S. (2003). *Women don't ask: Negotiation and the gender divide*. Princeton University Press.

Barnlund, D. (2013). Communication in a global village. In M. Bennett (Ed.), *Basic concepts of intercultural communication* (2nd ed., pp. 281–302). Nicholas Brealey.

Biss, E. (2015, December 2). White debt: Reckoning with what is owed—and what can never be repaid—for racial privilege. *The New York Times*. https://www.nytimes.com/2015/12/06/magazine/white-debt.html?_r=0

Bordas, J. (2012). *Salsa, soul, and spirit: Leadership for a multicultural age: New approaches to leadership from Latino, Black, and American Indian communities* (2nd ed.). Berrett-Koehler Publishers.

Bosman, J., & Fitzsimmons, E. (2014, August 10). Grief and protests follow shooting of a teenager. *The New York Times*. https://www.nytimes.com/2014/08/11/us/police-say-mike-brown-was-killed-after-struggle-for-gun.html

Bowles, H. R., & McGinn, K. L. (2005). Claiming authority: Negotiating challenges for women leaders. In D. M. Messick & R. M. Kramer (Eds.), *The psychology of leadership: New perspectives and research* (pp. 191–208). Lawrence Erlbaum Associates.

Braxton, E. (2017, October 17*). The horizon of possibility, the Catholic Church, and the racial divide in the United States: Old wounds reopened.* Address presented at Catholic Heritage Lecture Series. Seattle University, Seattle.

Bryson, J. & Crosby, B. (1992). *Leadership for the common good: Tackling public problems in a shared-power world.* Jossey-Bass.

Burns, J. M. G. (1978). *Leadership.* Harper & Row.

Butler, J. (2015). *Notes toward a performative theory of assembly.* Harvard University Press.

Cawthon, D. (2002). *Philosophical foundations of leadership.* Transaction Publishers.

Chamberlain, G. L. (1976). A model to combat racism. *Theology Today, 32*(4), 353–364. https://doi.org/10.1177/004057367603200403

Chozich, A. (2015, April 12). Hillary Clinton announces 2016 Presidential bid. *The New York Times.* https://www.nytimes.com/2015/04/13/us/politics/hillary-clinton-2016-presidential-campaign.html

Coates, T. (2014, June). The case for reparations. *The Atlantic.* https://www.theatlantic.com/magazine/archive/2014/06/the-case-for-reparations/361631/

Coates, T. (2017, October). The first white president. *The Atlantic.* https://www.theatlantic.com/magazine/archive/2017/10/the-first-white-president-ta-nehisi-coates/537909/

Collins, P. (1986). Learning from the outsider within: The sociological significance of black feminist thought. *Social Problems, 33*(6), 14–32.

Collins, P. H. (1998). It's all in the family: intersection of gender, race, and nation. *Hypatia, 13*(3), 62–82. https://onlinelibrary.wiley.com/doi/epdf/10.1111/j.1527-2001.1998.tb01370.x

Collinson, D. (2011). Critical leadership studies. In A. Bryman (Ed.), *The SAGE handbook of leadership* (pp. 181–194). Sage.

David, E. J. R. (Ed.). (2014). *Internalized oppression: The psychology of marginalized groups.* Springer Publishing Co.

Delgado, R., Stefancic, J., & Harris, A. (2017). *Critical race theory: An introduction* (3rd ed.). University Press.

DeMatthews, D. (2016). Effective leadership is not enough: Critical approaches to closing the racial discipline gap. *The Clearing House: A Journal of Educational Strategies, Issues and Ideas, 89*(1), 7–13.

DiAngelo, R. (2018). *White fragility: Why it's so hard to talk to white people about racism.* Beacon Press.

Dugan, J. P. (2017). *Leadership theory: Cultivating critical perspectives.* John Wiley & Sons.

Eicher-Catt, D. (2005). The myth of servant-leadership: A feminist perspective. *Women & Language, 28*(1), 17–25.

Fahrenthold, D. (2016, October 8) Trump recorded having extremely lewd conversation about women in 2005. *Washington Post.* https://www.washingtonpost. com/politics/trump-recorded-having-extremely-lewd-conversation-about-women-in-2005/2016/10/07/3b9ce776-8cb4-11e6-bf8a-3d26847eeed4_story.html? utm_term=.a785f849bb67

Ferch, S. R. (2012). *Forgiveness and power in the age of atrocity: Servant leadership as a way of life.* Lexington Books.

Ferch, S. R. (2017, December 1). Class notes from leadership theory presentation. Gonzaga University.

Fine, M., & Buzzanell, P. (2000). Walking the high wire: Leadership theorizing, daily acts, and tensions. In P. M. Buzzanell (Ed.), *Rethinking organizational & managerial communication from feminist perspectives* (pp. 128–156). Sage Publications.

Fletcher, J. H. (2017). *The Sin of white supremacy: Christianity, racism, and religious diversity in America.* Orbis Books.

Frankl, V. (2000). *Man's search for ultimate meaning.* Basic Books.

Frankl, V. (2014). *The will to meaning: Foundations and applications of logotherapy.* Plume.

Freire, P. (1972). *Pedagogy of the oppressed* (M. Ramos, Trans.). Sheed and Ward.

Frick, D. (2004). *Robert K. Greenleaf: A life of servant leadership.* https://ebookcentral.proquest.com

Giles, M. (2010). Howard Thurman, black spirituality, and critical race theory in higher education. *The Journal of Negro Education, 79*(3), 354–365. http:// www.jstor.org/stable/20798354

Greenleaf, R. K. (1970). *The servant as leader.* https://www.essr.net/~jafundo/mestrado_ material_itgjkhnld/IV/Lideran%C3%A7as/The%20Servant%20as%20Leader. pdf

Greenleaf, R. K. (1977). *Servant leadership: A journey into the nature of legitimate power and greatness.* Paulist Press.

Greenleaf, R. K. (1998). *The power of servant leadership: Essays* (L. C. Spears, Ed.). Berrett-Koehler.

Gronn, P. (2011). Hybrid configurations of leadership. In A. Bryman (Ed.), *The SAGE handbook of leadership* (pp. 437–454). Sage.

Haraway, D. (1991). *Simians, cyborgs, and women.* Routledge.

Harding, S. G. (1991). *Whose science? Whose knowledge?: Thinking from women's lives.* Cornell University Press.

Hoffman, B., & Belson, K. (2017, October 1.) NFL anthem protests: Players kneel, stand and hear boos. *The New York Times.* https://www.nytimes. com/2017/10/01/sports/nfl-trump-anthem.html

Hofstede, G. (2011). Dimensionalizing cultures: The Hofstede model in context. *Online Readings in Psychology and Culture, 2*(1), 1–26. https://doi.org/10.9707/ 2307-0919.1014

Holvino, E. (2010). Intersections: The simultaneity of race, gender and class in organization studies. *Gender, Work & Organization, 17*(3), 248–277.

hooks, b. (1984). *Feminist theory: From margin to center.* South End Press.

hooks, b. (2000). *All about love: New visions.* William Morrow.

Horowitz, J. Corasaniti, N., & Southall, A. (2015, June 17.) Nine killed in shooting at black church in Charleston. *The New York Times.* https://www.nytimes.com/2015/06/18/us/church-attacked-in-charleston-south-carolina.html

Howard, S. (2002). A spiritual perspective on learning in the workplace. *Journal of Managerial-Psychology, 17*(3), 230–242.

Ignatius. (1963). *The spiritual exercises of Saint Ignatius* (T. Corbishley, Ed.). P. J. Kennedy.

Jones, S. (2017, June 17). White men account for 72% of corporate leadership at 16 of the Fortune 500 companies. *Forbes.* http://fortune.com/2017/06/09/white-men-senior-executives-fortune-500-companies-diversity-data/

Kezar, A. (2002). Reconstructing static images of leadership: An application of positionality theory. *Journal of Leadership Studies, 8*(3), 94–109. https://doi.org/10.1177/107179190200800308

Kezar, A., & Lester, J. (2010). Breaking the barriers of essentialism in leadership research: Positionality as a promising approach. *Feminist Formations, 22*(1), 163–185.

King, J. (1991). Dysconscious racism: Ideology, identity, and the miseducation of teachers. *The Journal of Negro Education, 60*(2), 133–146.

King, M. L., Jr. (1957, April 7). The birth of a new nation [Sermon delivered at Dexter Avenue Baptist Church.]. http://kingencyclopedia.stanford.edu/primarydocuments/Vol4/7-Apr-1957_BirthOfANewNation.pdf

Lawrence, P. R., & Pirson, M. (2015). Economistic and humanistic narratives of leadership in the age of globality: Toward a renewed Darwinian theory of leadership. *Journal of Business Ethics, 128*(2), 383–394.

Lopez, G. (2018, January 14). Donald Trump's long history of racism, from the 1970s to 2018. *Vox.* https://www.vox.com/2016/7/25/12270880/donald-trump-racism-history

Massingale, B. (2010). *Racial justice and the Catholic church.* Orbis Books.

Massingale, B. (2017, November 2). Keynote address on the commitment to justice and reconciliation in the mission of Jesuit Catholic higher education. Association of Jesuit Colleges and Universities Mission and Identity Officer meeting, Fordham University, NY.

Max-Neef, M. (2005). Foundations of transdisciplinarity. *Ecological Economics, 53*(1), 5–16.

McIntosh, P. (2003). White privilege: Unpacking the invisible knapsack. In S. Plous (Ed.), *Understanding prejudice and discrimination* (pp. 191–196). McGraw-Hill.

Miller, P. M., Brown, T., & Hopson, R. (2011). Centering love, hope, and trust in the community: Transformative urban leadership informed by Paulo Freire. *Urban Education, 46*(5), 1078–1099. https://doi.org/10.1177/0042085910395951

Morrison, T. (1992). *Playing in the dark: Whiteness and the literary imagination*. Harvard University Press.

Ngunjiri, F. W. (2010). *Women's spiritual leadership in Africa: Tempered radicals and critical servant leaders*. State University of New York Press.

Nietzsche, F. W. (1966). *Beyond good and evil; prelude to a philosophy of the future* (W. Kaufmann, Ed.). Vintage Books. https://play.google.com/books/reader?id=yas8AAAAYAAJ&pg=GBS.PA226.w.1.1.0

Nietzsche, F. W. (1968). *The will to power* (W. Kaufmann & R. J. Hollingdale, Eds.). Vintage Books.

Nietzsche, F. W. (2012). *Birth of tragedy*. http://public.eblib.com/choice/publicfullrecord.aspx?p=1889782

Northouse, P. G. (2013) *Leadership: Theory and practice* (6th ed.). Sage Publications.

Oluo, I. (2017, October 1). I am drowning in whiteness. *National Public Radio*. http://kuow.org/post/ijeoma-oluo-i-am-drowning-whiteness

Patterson, K. (2010). Servant leadership and love. In D. Van Dierendonck & K. Patterson (Eds.), *Servant leadership* (pp. 67–76). Palgrave Macmillan.

Reynolds, K. (2014). Servant-leadership: A feminist perspective. *International Journal of Servant-Leadership, 10*(1), 35–63.

Robins-Early, N. (2015, October 28). How the refugee crisis is fueling the rise of Europe's right. *Huffington Post*. https://www.huffingtonpost.com/entry/europe-right-wing-refugees_us_562e9e64e4b06317990f1922

Romo, V., Stewart, M., & Naylor, B. (2017, September 5). Trump ends DACA, calls on congress to act. *National Public Radio*. https://www.npr.org/2017/09/05/546423550/trump-signals-end-to-daca-calls-on-congress-to-act

Rost, J. C. (1991). *Leadership for the twenty-first century*. Praeger.

Semuels, A. (2018, March 28). Chicago's awful divide. *The Atlantic*. https://www.theatlantic.com/business/archive/2018/03/chicago-segregation-poverty/556649/

Shapiro, B. (2017, July 8). *How to debate "white privilege" with facts* [Video]. YouTube. https://youtu.be/l5lnZeAGd3g

Shugerman, E. (2017, October 17). Me too: Why are women sharing stories of sexual assault and how did it start? *The Independent*. https://www.independent.co.uk/news/world/americas/me-too-facebook-hashtag-why-when-meaning-sexual-harassment-rape-stories-explained-a8005936.html

Spears, L. C. (2002). Introduction: Tracing the past, present and future of servant-leadership. In L. C. Spears & M. Lawrence (Eds.), *Focus on leadership: Servant-leadership for the twenty-first century* (pp. 1–16). Wiley.

Stohlberg, S. G., & Rosenthal, B. M. (2017, August 12). Man charged after white nationalist rally in Charlottesville ends in deadly violence. *The New York Times*. https://www.nytimes.com/2017/08/12/us/charlottesville-protest-white-nationalist.html

Thompson, C., Schaefer, E., & Brod, H. (2003). *White men challenging racism: 35 personal stories*. Duke University Press.

Thorbecke, C. (2016, October 28). Timeline of the Dakota access pipeline protests. *ABC News*. http://abcnews.go.com/US/timeline-dakota-access-pipeline-protests/story?id=43131355

Van Dierendonck, D., & Patterson, K. (2015). Compassionate love as a cornerstone of servant leadership: An integration of previous theorizing and research. *Journal of Business Ethics, 128*(1), 119–131. https://doi.org/10.1007/s10551-014-2085-z

Vetter, L. (2010). Overview: Feminist theories of leadership. In K. O'Connor (Ed.), *Gender and women's leadership: A reference handbook* (pp. 3–10). Sage Reference.

Walumbwa, F. O., Avolio, B. J., Gardner, W. L., Wernsing, T. S., & Peterson, S. J. (2008). Authentic leadership: Development and validation of a theory-based measure. *Journal of Management, 34*(1), 89–126.

Word of the Year. (2017). Dictionary.com. http://www.dictionary.com/e/word-of-the-year-2017/

Wren, J. T., & Faier, E. (2006). Contemplating context. In G. Goethals & G. Sorenson (Eds.), *The quest for a general theory of leadership* (pp. 205–220). Edward Elgar.

THE COURAGEOUS WHOLENESS
OF SERVANT-LEADERSHIP

Chapter 8

Do Women Stand Back to Move Forward?

Gender Differences in Top US Business Leaders'
Messages of Servant-Leadership

KAE REYNOLDS

The persistent absence of women in the upper echelons of management is
an issue that continues to occupy the concern of governments, businesses,
and leadership researchers. Despite a plethora of research to understand
the reasons behind the persistent gender leadership gap, actual progress
in practice remains minimal, with only 5.1% of Fortune 1000 executives
being women (Catalyst, 2016). One potential reason behind the perpetual
systemic bias against women may be the rigid underlying androcentric
philosophies of leadership (Eicher-Catt, 2005; Morales, 2019). Servant-
leadership presents an alternative approach to the concept of leading that
is gender-integrative (Lehrke & Sowden, 2017; Reynolds, 2011; Reynolds,
2016). Yet this contemporary leadership model has been criticized for being
too soft and inadequate in a fast-paced, profit- and performance-driven neoliberal society (Laub, 2018; Smith et al., 2004). Moreover, the presumably
"feminine" aspects of servant-leadership are another reason for hard business
to reject servant-leadership (Lehrke & Sowden, 2017; Reynolds, 2016).
Despite a growing body of literature on the effectiveness of executive female
leaders (Adams, 2016; Conyon & He, 2017; Dezső & Ross, 2012; Eagly,
2007; Moreno-Gomez et al., 2018) and of servant-leadership (Choudhary

et al., 2013; de Waal & Sivro, 2012; Sousa & van Dierendonck, 2017), there remains a need to clarify the impact of gender on servant-leadership practice in a business context (Lehrke & Sowden, 2017; Sims & Morris, 2018; Washington et al., 2006). This study aims to explore the viability of servant-leadership for top business executives and for women seeking to break through the glass ceiling.

Business leaders in the United States generally enjoy exceptional status and power (Seider, 1974). With the ascent of a successful businessperson to the office of the president, the public has recently become acutely aware of how communication reveals leaders' attitudes. Public gatherings such as university graduation ceremonies represent one way in which society celebrates leaders and develops concepts of leadership (Condit, 1985). Commencement speeches are often delivered by recognized leaders and are cultural artifacts that can reveal a great deal about the priorities of the speakers (Hargrove et al., 2011; LaWare, 2009). As a performance of leadership (Condit, 1985), ceremonial speaking has the purpose of clarifying, negotiating, and reifying shared values (Agnew, 2008). Traditionally, commencement speeches offer graduates wisdom about the state of the world and advice for the future through the experiences of the speakers (Agnew, 2008; Bordelon, 2010; LaWare, 2009). As such, the commencement addresses of prominent business leaders can illuminate their espoused leadership theories and practices.

This study takes an exploratory approach to analyzing gender differences in servant-leadership by analyzing the rhetorical constructions of leadership of top US business executives in ceremonial speech. Employing a mixed method of content analysis, the chapter explores whether and how top business leaders convey messages of leadership in their rhetoric. The espoused leadership attitudes of Fortune 1000 leaders (women and men) and Power 50 women are examined to provide further insight into gendered aspects of servant-leadership, as well as the potential of servant-leadership as a viable gender-integrative option for high-performing organizations and as a gender-equalizer for women business leaders.

Servant-Leadership and Gender

Gendered Conceptualization of Servant-Leadership

Most servant-leadership literature does not adequately address the roles of women in leadership or issues of gender. A surge in empirical research on servant-leadership over the past 20 years (Eva et al., 2019) has contributed a deeper understanding of Greenleaf's (2003) philosophy of leadership, yet attention to gender is still limited to a small body of studies and theoretical commentaries. Numerous conceptual models and survey instruments have been developed in an effort to operationalize servant-leadership, advance theory in the academic circuit, and enhance understanding (Eva et al., 2019; Parris & Peachey, 2013; van Dierendonck 2011; VanMeter et al., 2016). Many of the conceptual models differentiate servant-leadership from other leadership perspectives through constructs such as communal behaviors (Hogue, 2016), compassionate love (van Dierendonck & Patterson, 2015), *agapáo* (Ayers, 2008; Patterson, 2004), altruistic motives (Barbuto & Wheeler, 2006), or self-sacrifice (Matteson & Irving, 2006). Within the patriarchal understanding of leadership, these distinguishing aspects of servant-leadership are characterized by their association with traditional feminine behaviors or traits (Eicher-Catt, 2005; Lehrke & Sowden, 2017; Reynolds, 2011). Yet many other authors studying servant-leadership fail to acknowledge the gendered assumptions underpinning these constructs. Although interpretations diverge and converge as to which leadership aspects constitute servant-leadership definitively, the existing gendered interpretations within the field tend to agree that its differentiating factors of servant-leadership are associated with feminine-gendered notions of communion as opposed to masculine-gendered notions of agency.

Leadership in general, and particularly in business contexts, continues to be predominantly masculinized (Bierema, 2016; Lehrke & Sowden, 2017), and masculine ways of leading are still consciously and subconsciously regarded as superior (Madsen & Adrade, 2018). Gender socialization perpetuates the notion that leadership is a masculine role and culturally incongruent with communal and nurturing behaviors expected and perceived of women. Such deeply rooted gender expectations continue to hinder women's ability to successfully navigate the labyrinth to the C-suite proportional to women's representation in the workforce and society (Adams, 2016). Due to the systematic nature of gender bias in leadership (Eagly & Karau, 2002; Madsen & Andrade, 2018) operating within a patriarchal matrix, the feminization of servant-leadership might be expected to perpetuate the disadvantaging of women in achieving leadership status (Brescoll, 2016; Lammers & Gast, 2017). Therefore, understanding gender differences in leaders who espouse servant-leadership attitudes can contribute to better understanding servant-leadership and its impact on women's attainment of leadership roles.

Gender Differences in Servant-Leadership

Despite the growing theoretical and empirical research based on servant-leadership, there is still little understanding of the role gender differences (or the lack thereof) may play in servant-leadership and in women's attainment of leadership. Within the broader field of leadership, extensive research has been conducted on gender differences, however, findings remain inconclusive. Some evidence has shown that gender differences in leadership style and effectiveness are not significant (Eagly & Johnson, 1990; Eagly et al., 2003; Eagly et al., 1995), yet further research continues to provide evidence that gender bias is the main contributor to the glass ceiling (Brescoll, 2016; Eagly & Karau, 2002; Eagly & Sczesny, 2009). Dominant themes in the field underscore the belief that women's leadership is characterized by aspects of communion and relationality, for example, emotionality, collaborative approaches, inclusive communication, and participative decision making (Brescoll, 2016; Fine, 2007; Madden, 2007; Parker, 2005). Social role and gender congruency theories suggest that the gendered expectations and perceptions of women's leadership perpetuate the double bind that prevents women from rising to executive ranks. The assumption here is that relational, collaborative, supportive, and inclusive approaches to leadership are perceived as ineffective for business leadership.

As such, it is not surprising that skepticism prevails about employing a servant-leadership approach in masculinized business contexts when considering gender. Women may be more likely than men to adopt attitudes of servant-leadership (de Rubio & Kiser, 2015; Duff, 2013; Hogue, 2016; Washington et al. 2006) and as servant-leaders may be better suited to leadership roles in specific contexts (Duff, 2013; Politis & Politis, 2018; Sims & Morris, 2018). Previous studies suggest that servant-leadership is a viable option for women to be successful as leaders (Ngunjiri, 2010; Politis & Politis, 2018). Female leaders may demonstrate the communal servant-leader behaviors such as altruistic calling, emotional healing, and organizational stewardship more than men (Beck, 2014). Some female business owners felt their leadership was more authentic when adopting communal servant-leadership attitudes (Sims & Morris, 2018). However, lack of gender differences in agentic and communal servant-leader behaviors would suggest that servant-leadership creates a possibility for leaders to "step out of gender roles" (Barbuto & Gifford, 2010, p. 10), allowing women to integrate gender-congruent communal and gender-incongruent agentic behavior in their leadership. In patriarchal systems, however, traits and behaviors associated with femininity are valued less. Trends in servant-leadership theorizing on gendering and gender differences support the notion that servant-leadership successfully combines feminine (communal) and masculine (agentic) attributes and behaviors, and assert that this integration of gendered attribution may be beneficial for women leaders. Nevertheless, there is still the issue that servant-leadership in and of itself is perceived as predominantly feminine and in the larger context of gender bias would still be disadvantaged.

The Present Study

To determine the servant-leadership attitudes of top US business executives and explore gender differences therein, this study analyzes messages of servant-leadership in the rhetoric of their commencement addresses. The study follows a mixed-methods content analysis design conducted in three stages. Although gaining in popularity in the field of leadership, content analysis is not yet widely applied in servant-leadership research. Because communication is one of the most important aspects of leadership behavior, content analysis has the potential to extend empirical research in leadership meaningfully and enrich leadership studies through contextually rich data (Insch et al., 1997). Mixed-methods designs are also not very common in dominant leadership publications (Stentz et al., 2012). Although qualitative and mixed-methods studies are also becoming more common, they are still largely marginalized in terms of publication in high-ranking journals (Gardner et al., 2020).

Method

The first stage consisted of a quantitative content analysis procedure modeled after Hargrove (2009), and applying analytical constructs at word level using content matrices of predefined terms associated with the main constructs servant-leadership (SL) and non-servant-leadership (NSL), and their subconstructs. The second stage comprised a structured qualitative content analysis applying predefined coding schemes modeled after the format used by Oliver (2004). The third stage was a semistructured thematic analysis also guided by the predefined analytical constructs.

The content matrices and coding schemes for SL and NSL developed by Reynolds (2013) were used. The schemes adapted subconstructs of the Servant Leadership Survey (SLS) (van Dierendonck & Nuijten, 2011) for

SL: accountability, authenticity, courage, forgiveness, empowerment, humility, standing back, and stewardship, and modified subconstructs from Hargrove's (2009) content matrix with dimensions from Bass's (1999) and Kouzes and Posner's (2010) leadership models for NSL: forward-looking, motivation, credibility, inspiration, influence, and idealization. These subconstructs also formed the basis for thematic analysis. Coding schemes guided coders in rating the speeches as individual units and in tagging phrases and sentences within the text. Content validation ensured that the words assigned to each construct/subconstruct in the content matrices were distinct and the definitions provided in the coding schemes discrete. In Stage 3 rhetorical devices (sentence strings stories, appeals, arguments) in constructing messages were coded using the predefined analytical (sub)constructs.

The traditional gender binary is applied within the gender-integrative perspective. A comprehensive and inclusive gender spectrum analysis is beyond the scope of this chapter. The contributions of more expansive critical theory perspectives that problematize social inequalities of gender, gender identity, sexual orientation, and other categories are highly valuable and pertinent; nevertheless, this chapter is limited in its approach by binary gender differences in servant-leadership.

Commencement addresses delivered by prominent US business executives between 2005 and 2012 provided the data. The sample was drawn from the Fortune 1000 (F1000) and Top 50 Women in Business lists—also known as the Power 50 (P50), with 25 different female and 25 different male leaders. Transcripts, manuscripts, and video recordings of speeches were matched to the speakers and collected from the Internet. If more than one speech per speaker occurred within the study's time span, the speech with the highest word count was included. Only addresses held at commencement ceremonies of four-year institutions of higher education in the United States were included.

Stage 1

To begin, word counts were noted, and tallies compared by the main constructs, subconstructs, and by gender. Correlation of word frequencies at the main construct level was carried out, then means and standard deviations were calculated and compared. The average word count was between 2,194 and 2,278 words, and the highest and lowest range of words between 944 and 4,334; men tended to have average higher word counts. Female leaders used words related to both SL and NSL more frequently than males at both main and subconstruct levels, with the exception that male speakers had higher word frequencies for the SL subconstructs accountability and forgiveness. Results of Pearson's correlation (table 8.1) showed that SL language usage was significantly and positively correlated with NSL language usage (p = 0.00, r = 0.53).

Means comparisons showed the frequency of words associated with NSL (M = 93.57) had a higher mean total than those associated with SL (M = 34.22) and that female speakers displayed a higher total frequency of both main constructs SL (M = 37.36) and NSL (M = 100.32) (table 8.2). At the subconstruct level, female speakers' means comparisons also showed a

Table 8.1. Pearson's Correlation of Word Frequencies: Servant-Leadership and Non-Servant-Leadership

		Servant-Leadership	Non-Servant Leadership
Servant-Leadership	Pearson Correlation	1	0.53*
	Sig. (2-tailed)		0.00
	N	50	50
Non-Servant Leadership	Pearson Correlation		1
	Sig. (2-tailed)		
	N		50

*Correlation is significant at the 0.05 level (2-tailed)

Table 8.2. Mean and Standard Deviation of Frequencies: Servant-Leadership and Non-Servant-Leadership

	Gender	Mean	Std. Deviation	N
Non-Servant-Leadership	Female	100.32	35.39	25
	Male	86.72	3373	25
	Total	93.57	34.82	50
Servant-Leadership	Female	37.36	14.26	25
	Male	31.08	19.64	25
	Total	34.22	17.28	50

higher frequency of words associated with six of the eight SL subconstructs (table 8.3). The male speakers had a slightly higher mean total frequency of SL subconstructs accountability (M = 4.44) and forgiveness (M = 0.28) as compared to the female speakers, thus reinforcing the results of the tallies.

A multivariate analysis using MANOVA (table 8.4) showed that gender did not have a significant effect on the use of the words associated with SL (F (1, 48) = 1.67; p = 0.20) or NSL (F (1, 48) = 1.93; p = 0.17). However,

Table 8.3. Mean and Standard Deviation Frequencies: Servant-Leadership Subconstructs

	Gender	Mean	Std. Deviation	N
Accountability	Female	2.80	1.98	25
	Male	4.44	5.98	25
	Total	3.62	4.49	50
Authenticity	Female	4.84	5.22	25
	Male	3.88	3.15	25
	Total	4.36	4.29	50
Courage	Female	4.40	3.82	25
	Male	3.92	5.45	25
	Total	4.16	4.66	50
Forgiveness	Female	0.16	0.37	25
	Male	0.28	0.54	25
	Total	0.22	0.47	50
Empowerment	Female	5.40	3.03	25
	Male	5.00	4.59	25
	Total	5.20	3.85	50
Humility	Female	7.40	6.80	25
	Male	5.40	4.68	25
	Total	6.40	5.87	50
Standing Back	Female	5.84	3.73	25
	Male	3.96	2.86	25
	Total	4.90	3.42	50
Stewardship	Female	6.52	6.56	25
	Male	4.20	4.65	25
	Total	5.36	5.75	50

Table 8.4. MANOVA Gender Effects: Servant-Leadership and Non-Servant-Leadership

Source	Dependent Variable	Type III Sum of Squares	df	Mean Square	F	Sig.
Corrected Model	Servant-Leadership	492.980a	1	492.98	1.67	0.20
	Non-Servant-Leadership	2312.00	1	2312.00	1.93	0.17
Intercept	Servant-Leadership	58550.42	1	58550.42	198.82	0.00
	Non-Servant-Leadership	437299.52	1	437299.52	365.89	0.00
Gender	Servant-Leadership	492.98	1	492.98	1.67	0.20
	Non-Servant-Leadership	2312.00	1	2310.00	1.93	0.17
Error	Servant-Leadership	14135.60	48	294.49		
	Non-Servant-Leadership	57368.48	48	1195.18		
Total	Servant-Leadership	73179.00	50			
	Non-Servant-Leadership	496980.00	50			
Corrected Total	Servant-Leadership	14628.58	49			
	Non-Servant-Leadership	59680.48	49			

a. R Squared = 0.03 (Adjusted R Squared = 0.01)

at the subconstruct level (table 8.5) the results showed that gender had a significant effect on only one SL subconstruct, standing back ($F_{(1, 48)} = 4.00$; $p = 0.05$).

Table 8.5. MANOVA Results for Tests of Between-Subjects Effects for SL Subconstructs

Source	Dependent Variable	Type III Sum of Squares	df	Mean Square	F	Sig.
Corrected Model	Accountability	33.62a	1	33.62	1.70	0.20
	Authenticity	11.52b	1	11.52	0.62	0.44
	Courage	2.88c	1	2.88	0.13	0.72
	Forgiveness	0.18d	1	0.18	0.83	0.37
	Empowerment	2.00e	1	2.00	0.13	0.72
	Humility	50.00f	1	50.00	1.47	0.23
	Standing Back	44.18g	1	44.18	4.00	0.05
	Stewardship	67.28h	1	67.28	2.08	0.16
Intercept	Accountability	655.22	1	655.22	33.03	0.00
	Authenticity	655.22	1	655.22	51.15	0.00
	Courage	865.28	1	865.28	39.12	0.00
	Forgiveness	2.42	1	2.42	11.17	0.00
	Empowerment	1352.00	1	1352.00	89.39	0.00
	Humility	2048.00	1	2048.00	60.09	0.00
	Standing Back	1200.50	1	1200.50	108.66	0.00
	Stewardship	1436.48	1	1436.48	44.48	0.00
Gender	Accountability	33.62	1	33.62	1.70	0.20
	Authenticity	11.52	1	11.52	0.62	0.44
	Courage	2.88	1	2.88	0.13	0.72
	Forgiveness	0.18	1	0.18	0.83	0.37
	Empowerment	2.00	1	2.00	0.13	0.72
	Humility	50.00	1	50.00	1.47	0.23
	Standing Back	44.18	1	44.18	4.00	0.05*
	Stewardship	67.28	1	67.28	2.08	0.16
Error	Accountability	952.16	48	19.84		
	Authenticity	892.00	48	18.58		
	Courage	1061.84	48	22.12		
	Forgiveness	10.40	48	0.22		
	Empowerment	726.00	48	15.13		
	Humility	1636.00	48	34.08		
	Standing Back	530.32	48	11.05		
	Stewardship	1550.24	48	32.30		
Total	Accountability	1641.00	50			
	Authenticity	1854.00	50			
	Courage	1930.00	50			
	Forgiveness	13.00	50			
	Empowerment	3734.00	50			
	Humility	1775.00	50			
	Standing Back	3054.00	50			

Source	Dependent Variable	Type III Sum of Squares	df	Mean Square	F	Sig.
Corrected	Accountability	985.78	49			
Total	Authenticity	903.52	49			
	Courage	1064.72	49			
	Forgiveness	10.58	49			
	Empowerment	728.00	49			
	Humility	1686.00	49			
	Standing Back	574.50	49			
	Stewardship	1617.52	49			

a. R Squared = 0.02 (Adjusted R Squared = –0.01)
b. R Squared = 0.01 (Adjusted R Squared = –0.01)
c. R Squared = 0.05 (Adjusted R Squared = 0.03)
d. R Squared = 0.03 (Adjusted R Squared = 0.01)
e. R Squared = 0.03 (Adjusted R Squared = 0.01)
f. R Squared = 0.04 (Adjusted R Squared = 0.02)
g. R Squared = 0.09 (Adjusted R Squared = 0.07)
h. R Squared = 0.07 (Adjusted R Squared = 0.05)

Discussion of Stage 1

The findings of Stage 1 suggested that the business leaders in the Fortune 1000 and Power 50 would tend to espouse more generalized attitudes of leadership rather than attitudes of servant-leadership. Word frequency tallies showed that words associated with NSL as a main construct occurred more often than words assigned to the SL construct. The mean differences analysis supported the finding that NSL language was the most salient among the two main constructs within the speeches of both women and men. This is not surprising considering that the content matrix had a higher number of entries (NSL=144:SL=70) many of the words related to a generalized concept of leadership, for example, NSL are much more common in general language usage (e.g., world, making, great, change). The correlation between NSL and SL suggests that the more leaders constructed messages conveying leadership in general, the more they tended to integrate messages of servant-leadership attitudes. The correlation may also be an indication that distinguishing between the two main constructs is difficult at word level due to the fact that SL is inherently a leadership attitude and thus becomes confounded. The range of word count indicated that some speeches may have utilized much more space (e.g., words) to convey messages. Volumes of words and the minimal frequency required to indicate a theme (e.g., one mention of a word) could explain the high standard deviations observed. Despite lower average word counts, the more frequent use of words associated with leadership in the females speeches suggests that in general the women leaders in this sample tended to highlight messages related to leadership in their commencement addresses more than the men. Although no significant gender differences in the leadership messages at the main construct level were found, women's speeches had a significantly higher use of words associated with the SL construct standing back as compared to the men's. Men's speeches showed higher use of words associated with accountability and forgiveness, but the difference was not significant. To explore these results further, Stages 2 and 3 of the study focused on qualitatively assessing the thematic occurrence of the main constructs and subconstructs and comparing thematic constructions.

Stage 2

A structured qualitative analysis was carried out using coding schemes with specific focus on differentiating between expressions of leadership at the main construct level. The 50 speeches were analyzed at phrase and sentence levels to gain a general impression of messages conveying leadership. The construction of SL and NSL themes was analyzed and grouped according to occurrence (only SL, mostly SL, mostly NSL, only NSL, neither SL nor NSL) and then compared by gender. The two largest groupings were of speeches that contained messages expressing mostly SL and only SL. Women's speeches were coded with SL more often, with 22 out of 25 speeches having at least one SL-coded unit, whereas then men's speeches were slightly more balanced, with 16 out of 25 obtaining an SL-coded unit. SL was coded much more frequently in female speakers' passages (149 passages compared to 83) by a few more speakers (22 compared to 16 male speakers).

The speeches were then analyzed for coding density. For this analysis, the coding coverage for each speech was calculated on the two main constructs, plotted within each speech then compared by gender (figures 8.1 and 8.2). The SL-coded passages reached an overall higher density among the female speakers and a wider range than among the male speakers (figure 8.1). The range for NSL was narrower for both female and male speakers, and the density for NSL messages in the women's speeches (14.54%) was lower than the density for SL (23.59%), but higher than the density in the men's speeches on both SL (12.02%) and NSL (8.63%) (figures 8.1 and figure 8.2).

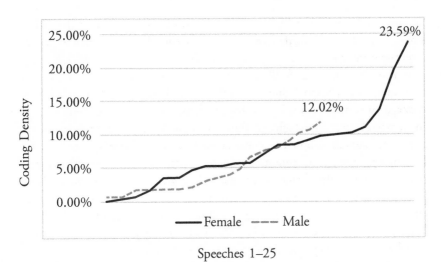

Figure 8.1. Servant-Leadership Coding Density by Gender.

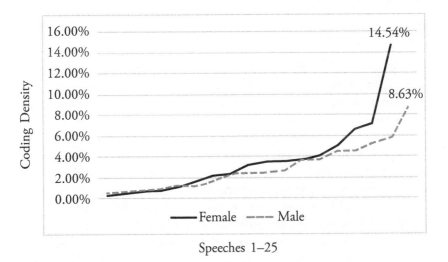

Figure 8.2. Non-Servant-Leadership Coding Density by Gender.

Discussion of Stage 2

The results of Stage 2 contradict and supplement Stage 1 findings. Coding analysis reveals that SL messages were much more prevalent in the leaders' rhetoric than Stage 1 statistical analysis suggested. When taken in context,

SL and combinations of SL and NSL were observed more often than NSL alone. Stage 2 reveals further that when leadership became a theme, deeper interpretation showed that speakers leaned more toward expressions of servant-leadership. This finding supports the correlation between SL and NSL messages in Stage 1 due the result that a higher density of coded NSL messages was accompanied by a higher density of coded SL messages. As such, Stage 2 analysis, which accounted for richer interpretation of contextualized messages as opposed to constrained word-level analysis, demonstrates how messages of SL became more salient in context. These findings suggest that the stronger the theme of leadership in a given speech, the more likely a speaker is to convey messages of SL rather than NSL attitudes. Further contradictions to Stage 1 findings are also observed for gender differences. Stage 2 findings support the comparison of the means, as coding resulted in a higher frequency and density of SL messages in female speakers' texts than in the male speakers' texts. Stage 3 analysis takes the qualitative interpretation of the speeches a step further to explore constructions and messages in more depth.

Stage 3

In Stage 3 thematic analysis considered the broader use of rhetorical devices in conveying messages of SL and NSL through coding of their subconstructs. As a comprehensive discussion of the Stage 3 results is beyond the scope of this chapter, those findings that best inform Stages 1 and 2 are reported in brief. Using the coded passages, the speeches were analyzed according to subconstructs at the phrase, sentence, and strings-of-sentences level, with attention to rhetorical devices (stories, appeals, statements) and how these devices create meaning in the construction of leadership. The overall thematic strength of individual subconstructs was noted and then illustrated and interpreted through exemplary extracts. The first part of the thematic analysis focused on messages to illustrate SL and NSL both as individual constructs and as combined constructs. In the second part, a more in-depth interpretation of subconstructs of SL is provided to understand the different ways in which women and men construct messages conveying servant-leadership.

In the speeches that were coded in as communicating NSL exclusively, the most salient ideas communicated by the speakers included the need for initiating transformation to effect positive changes and the importance of achieving excellence. Speeches coded exclusively with SL messages focused strongly on stewardship through serving the community and giving back to society. Most of the speeches communicated some combination of expressions of NSL and SL. When NSL remained the predominant message present in the speech, the focus of the speech was congruent with themes of NSL but contained a few statements expressing SL-related concepts. Examples below demonstrate how these themes can be interpreted separately or become intertwined.

- Indra K. Nooyi highlighted the importance of always striving for excellence and setting the high standards necessary to be successful, and noted further that people who achieve the greatest success are those who recognize the value of others.

- George S. Barrett commented on the importance of empowerment and being humble but emphasized the significance of innovation and progress.

- Janet L. Robinson discussed the importance of leaders being role models and taking risks but also stressed the importance of empowering others and giving back to community.

- Kenneth I. Chenault expressed his belief in the crucial roles of initiating change and taking action but emphasized that this should be done to solidify diversity and stewardship as moral values.

Themes within the Analytical Subconstructs

The structured thematic analysis showed that SL had stronger coding density for women than for men in their speeches. In this section, differences in the ways that women and men constructed SL messages are presented. Overall, four of the eight SL constructs were the most prevalent for women in the coded passages. These constructs were stewardship, courage, humility, and standing back. Two themes, humility and standing back, showed the strongest differences in coding density for the female speakers as compared to the male speakers. These themes associated with the women's speeches are discussed in brief to illustrate differences in how the female and male speakers constructed their messages.

Stewardship and courage were the most salient themes in all of the speeches, and the female speakers showing a stronger tendency to highlight stewardship. Among the women, stewardship was characterized by messages around social responsibility and giving back to society. For example, Patricia Woertz encouraged graduates to make their choices such that they can best contribute to society. Sabrina Simmons called for graduates to look beyond the limits of their work context and seek to contribute to their families and communities. Barbara Desoer emphasized bringing one's full value to every task to bring value to society. Some thematic constructions by male speakers included stewardship as having a social conscience and a deeper purpose, addressing wider global needs, and viewing the responsibility of an organization to serve the community and to protect and enhance the world.

Courage was also a strong theme throughout the speeches. The female speakers conveyed messages related to courage more than men. A common theme between the genders was courage as a form of questioning the status quo. Women's constructions of courage included messages highlighting aspects such as challenging authority both as a leader and as a follower. Sheryl Sandberg emphasized that leaders have the responsibility to encourage questioning authority. Other women, such as Amy Woods Brinkley and Barbara Desoer, discussed the need to seek unconventional solutions and be critical in one's thinking. In contrast, the male speakers constructed courage more in terms of risk taking, being a catalyst for change, and shaping the future.

Humility is one of two themes, humility and standing back, that showed the strongest tendencies in coding density for the female speakers. The women executives' messages tended to highlight self-knowledge and interdependence as core aspects of humility in their practice. Carly Fiorina commented on how achievement and success cannot be achieved by heroics or without the support of others. Sabrina Simmons commented about the way humility allows people to see beyond their own ambitions and view the bigger picture. Sheryl Sandberg also noted the facilitating capacity of humility toward achieving broader societal goals. Within this theme, the men tended to highlight the need to acknowledge others and translate recognition of others into organizational practice.

Finally, the SL construct standing back emerged as one of the themes with the strongest coding density among the women business leaders compared to the men in this study. The female executives constructed messages of standing back with themes related to the development of self and others. Lifelong learning and mentorship were strong themes within this subconstruct. Kay Krill emphasized how facilitating others' growth can strengthen the community. She described her passion for mentoring and empowering women that she has channeled into a girls' leadership-mentoring program.

Patricia Woertz made a compelling case for how a drive for self-development and unquenchable curiosity can be a differentiating factor for success.

Discussion of Stage 3

Stage 3 results further confirm the correlation between NSL and SL messages with themes of general leadership underpinning attitudes of servant-leadership. The thematic analysis indicated that most speakers, female and male, tended to communicate a combination of SL and NSL principles. Overarching SL messages that were articulated in the speeches included an emphasis on serving the community and giving back to the community, and overarching messages of NSL messages highlighted initiating transformational change and setting high standards for achieving ambitious goals and excellence. Although both women and men constructed messages conveying servant-leadership attitudes of stewardship, courage, humility, and standing back, the ways in which they made meaning out of these subconstructs differed slightly. The subtlety of word usage to highlight different aspects of SL could explain how the quantitative analysis yielded some contradictory results to the thematic analysis, as the thematic interpretation in context revealed the intertwined meanings of non-servant and servant-leadership. The richer interpretation revealing the subtle differences in language usage can explain how their meaning could not be fully captured by the statistical analysis and why they did not reach statistical significance. Stage 3 did, however, confirm the statistically significant gender difference observed in Stage 1 showing that the females speakers conveyed messages aligned with the subconstruct standing back more frequently than males.

General Discussion

This study sought to address the leadership gender gap by exploring the viability of servant-leadership as a gender-integrative model of leadership for top business executives. Because the feminization of servant-leadership might be expected to perpetuate gender bias and have a negative impact on women's leadership role attainment, the design attempted to clarify the presence of servant-leadership practice in a high-performing business context and provide insight into gender differences. Findings showed that most of the US business executives of Fortune 1000 companies and Power 50 women conveyed messages of leadership that espoused attitudes of servant-leadership in their commencement speeches. Women business executives made leadership a theme more frequently and with greater density than the men. At least some of the results in all three stages suggest that women in this sample tended to espouse servant-leadership more than the men. The female and male business leaders constructed messages conveying servant-leadership attitudes aligned with and integrating both communal and agentic aspects, with women displaying a higher density of messages with gender congruency. Furthermore, findings showed that gender differences in the constructions of messages through which servant-leadership attitudes were conveyed were minimal and subtle. In all three stages, standing back showed the greatest salience as an aspect of servant-leadership that differentiated the leadership messages among the female and male speakers.

As the first study to explore servant-leadership and gender differences in the rhetoric of Fortune 1000 and Power 50 executives, this study contributes to understanding servant-leadership in a high-performing business context. Although some skepticism exists about servant-leadership's effectiveness in highly competitive business contexts, many of the Fortune 1000 and Power 50 leaders in this study displayed attitudes that included characteristics of servant-leadership. Hence the findings contribute to the literature suggesting that servant-leadership is viable for high-performing business contexts (de Waal & Sivro, 2012; Laub, 2018; Sims & Morris, 2018). This contribution may have implications for strategic leadership that have not been previously considered. Upper echelons theory asserts that executive leaders' characteristics and attitudes are reflected in organizational outcomes (Hambrick, 2018). The gender of CEOs and the gender composition of executive teams may influence the impact of executive behaviors on firm outcomes (Adams, 2016; Neely et al., 2020). The experiences, values, and personalities of executive leaders have a strong influence on the way they perceive and interpret their circumstances and act on their decisions (Hambrick, 2007). If the Fortune 1000 and Power 50 leaders practice the leadership attitudes conveyed in their speeches, then the results of this study could provide some evidence of the business success of servant-leadership in upper echelons.

A further contribution of this study is new evidence that top US female and male business leaders espouse gender-integrative approaches to leadership. Most of the speakers, both women and men, tended to display at least some attitudes that aligned with both communal and agentic sub-constructs of servant-leadership. It has been asserted in the literature that the integration of feminine and masculine qualities of servant-leadership may promote gender equity (Oner, 2009; Reynolds, 2011), and that women leaders, by leveraging the communal aspects of servant-leadership, may be more able to access leadership roles (Hogue, 2016; Lehrke & Sowden, 2017). The gender-integrative nature of servant-leadership allows women to create an authentic leader identity that is congruent with gender expectations (Sims & Morris, 2018). Although the results presented here suggest that gender-integrative and servant-leadership attitudes do not hinder the attainment of executive leadership roles, they do not provide a causal link between espousal of gender-integrative servant-leadership and increased entry for women into the C-suite.

This was the first study to employ mixed-methods content analysis to explore the leadership communication of top US business leaders in terms of gendered aspects of servant-leadership. Although the findings in this study indicated that traditional gender socialization continues to shape leadership and servant-leadership attitudes, it also supports evidence that gender differences are minimal (Gipson et al. 2017). The tendency for women in this sample to espouse servant-leadership more than the men aligns with literature suggesting that women in practice are expected and perceived to display servant-leadership more than men (Duff, 2013). Social role theory (Wood & Eagly, 2015) supports the claim that communal aspects of servant-leadership are more aligned with female gender socialization. However, considering that nearly all the differences observed in the interpretive analysis were not statistically significant, this study may provide new evidence that the double-bind effects of gender congruency in leadership practice may be diminishing. This result is supported in discourse around the gender-integrative impact of servant-leadership (Lehrke & Sowden, 2017; Reynolds, 2016). Insight into the subtlety of gender differences has not been addressed to a great extent in the literature, particularly those studies using statistical measures.

A final contribution of this study is the interpretive insight it provides into the gendered construction of servant-leadership dimensions. Although the Fortune 1000 and Power 50 leaders constructed messages conveying similar servant-leadership aspects, the subtle differences in how they made sense of their servant-leadership demonstrates the elusive nature of gendering in communication. Despite gender differences being subtle, a deeper understanding of one specific difference pertained to certain aspects of servant-leadership that women highlighted in their speeches. In all three stages, the women conveyed messages aligned with attitudes and behaviors of standing back, as this subconstruct showed the greatest salience both interpretively and statistically. These results are partially in line with the assessment of Sousa and van Dierendonck (2017) in their clustering of humility with standing back as other-oriented (communal) dimensions of servant-leadership, which would in turn align with gender congruous expectations.

Standing back is understood as a moderated stance of self-awareness and awareness of others; leaders put the needs and interests of others above their own, support the personal growth of others while pursuing with care and intent their own self-improvement (Verdorfer, 2016). It includes an appropriate estimation of one's merits and achievements, and the ability to find the appropriate middle ground between self-promotion and self-protection (Sousa & van Dierendonck, 2017), self-absorption and self-sacrifice, self-aggrandizement and self-deprecation. Standing back is also displayed through an ability to shift focus away from oneself, recognize and promote the contributions of others, and stay in the background when success is achieved (de Waal & Sivro, 2012). The emphasis among the women executives of fostering personal growth in others and pursuing their own lifelong learning is supported in the literature: Sims and Morris's (2018) account of women business owners showed a strong tendency for meeting the self-actualization needs of both their followers and themselves. It also reinforces the claim that the mutual fostering of personal growth is a key aspect not only of servant-leadership (van Dierendonck & Patterson, 2015) but also of business success (Sims & Morris, 2018). Nevertheless, the question remains whether women engaging in behaviors associated with standing back fosters their attainment of executive roles or whether this differentiating factor might indeed contribute to the persistent gender leadership gap in the upper echelons of business.

Implications

The insights that this study contributes—in particular regarding the subtle differences in the constructions of servant-leadership experienced, perceived, and conveyed by women executives—have theoretical and practical implications. As the first mixed-methods content analysis of executive leader communication in servant-leadership, it provides an example of means by which interpretive approaches can aid in distinguishing subtle differences in the construction of leadership meaning. However, further research is needed to clarify disagreement within the literature as to the gendered nature of servant-leadership constructs in order to better differentiate them. Theoretical implications concern primarily further expansion of research design to explore servant-leadership and gender and further development of existing research models. The exploration of gender provides insights for reevaluating existing instruments and models and refining these through more rigorous gender analysis of constructs with heightened awareness of gender bias. Further development of research to clarify gendered and gender-integrative aspects of measurement could prove useful in better understanding gender differences (or lack thereof). For example, there is still some disagreement as to the clustering of the subconstructs according to gendered aspects of communion and agency. Sousa and van Dierendonck (2017) described stewardship as an action-oriented (agentic) dimension related to "giving direction," whereas Reynolds (2011), Barbuto et al. (2014), and Sims and Morris (2018) described stewardship more as a communal concept in terms of altruism, trust, and "giving back" to the community.

This study also contributes to claims that attitudes and the practice of servant-leadership may play a role in the leadership success and attainment of executive roles for women. Although several studies assert that promoting gender-congruent yet gender-integrative ways of leading would be beneficial to women business leaders (Lehrke & Sowden, 2017; Sims & Morris, 2018), a word of caution remains. Some evidence suggests that promoting supposedly more feminine behaviors can also prove detrimental to women's attainment of leadership (Adams, 2016; Brescoll, 2016; Lammers & Gast, 2017). It is worth noting that then men in this sample were all ranked highly in the Fortune 1000 (all in the top 400 firms), whereas only about half of the women ranked as highly, and that there were so few women represented in the F1000 that the study was extended to include the Power 50 women in order to balance the sample. Do women stand back to move forward and upward in business leadership, or could standing back be a factor that *holds them back*? The results of this study cannot conclusively offer a causal link. Therefore, further research in needed to ascertain whether gender congruency promotes or hinders women's attainment of leadership roles.

Awareness of the reduction of gender bias may increase opportunities for women to become leaders and the desirability of leadership roles for women (Hogue, 2016). Not only do leaders on executive boards need to become more aware and accepting of a gender-integrative paradigm of leadership, but so do followers in order for servant-leadership practice to be more widely accepted and for women to be provided more access to executive leadership roles (Brescoll, 2016: Lehrke & Sowden, 2017). The practical implications of this study address a need for human resource development (HRD) practitioners and business leaders to promote and reward servant-leadership and gender competency. Strategic HRD can work with executives and HR business partners to develop recruitment, selection, and promotion criteria, as well as interventions aligned with and highlighting the communal and agentic aspects of servant-leadership while ensuring the equal development of these in both genders. As an example, specific development of the attitude of standing back could be targeted. Women seeking to develop their leadership practice can leverage servant-leadership and be encouraged to choose to lead and create further social change; men can be encouraged to lead in more gender-integrative ways through servant-leadership and pave a path to increased gender integration in the upper echelons of the business world.

Limitations and Future Research

The sample in this study represented a small elite population consisting of business leaders from predominantly nonmarginalized groups of the largest, most financially successful companies in the United States. Although results have the potential to be representative of this limited population, conclusions are not generalizable to wider contexts transnationally or transculturally. This study was also constrained by the scope of the data sampling, for example, its focus on a specific form of rhetoric generated within a specific genre (as opposed to data generated by human subjects in response to surveys, experiments, or interviews). The structured, unobtrusive content analysis further limits the study. This method does not consider more contextualized versions of experience, nor does it give voice to the audience or the speakers by unveiling their personal interpretations of their own messages, which could be achieved through interviews or other forms of more interactive data collection. Finally, this research is limited by the constraining gender binary categories.

Future studies should attempt to include interviews with the leaders about their speeches and with audience members. Comments posted online that refer to commencement speeches could be included in future inquires for an audience perspective. Accessing a wider range of genres for data sampling of leader communication, such as autobiographies, speeches in other contexts, and communications with shareholders, could enrich further research. Facebook broadcasts or tweets could help assess gender differences in servant-leadership attitudes and practices. Case studies with explorations of communication and including financial information about the leaders' companies could also provide interesting insight into the viability of servant-leadership organizational effectiveness. Intersectional research could enhance concepts of servant-leadership through an exploration of the experiences of marginalized groups highlighting race, ethnicity, religion, gender identity, sexual orientation, socioeconomic status, and relevant effects. Experimental and quasiexperimental studies could also further examine the extent to which gender-congruent behavior promotes or hinders women's leadership attainment.

Conclusion

The results of this study offer a glimpse into the shared attitudes and subtle differences in attitudes constructed by some of the most powerful business leaders in the United States. Gender integration requires a fundamental transformation of the way we experience humanity. The irony of conducting research on gendered aspects of servant-leadership lies in the need to invoke gender binaries for analysis to dismantle them. If organizations are to become more gender competent, a revaluation of our expectations of women and men must shift so that our concepts of leadership can shift from constraining binaries of masculine or feminine to simply "human" and "effective." This study provides a small window to a possible world in which ideals of servant-leadership are espoused by the most powerful leaders. As women's leadership experience continues to gain legitimacy, and women's ways of leading, such as servant-leadership, become more widely recognized, there is potential for servant-leadership to transform androcentric systems of organizing into gender-integrative systems.

Based on the attitudes observed in the speeches of the Fortune 1000 and Power 50 leaders, espousing servant-leadership can be considered a viable and desirable leadership option for top executives of high-performing businesses in a competitive corporate environment. Although some differences in framing their servant-leadership approaches can be observed, overall, these differences are subtle, and in the larger picture the servant-leadership practices and attitudes are present in women and men. Both successful female and male executives espoused some aspects of servant-leadership and integrated both communal and agentic gendered aspects of servant-leadership. By virtue of this gender-integrative potential, any person, male, female, or other-gendered, may be successful with a servant-leadership attitude and practice. Much more research still needs to be done to understand which aspects of leadership (if any) give women the edge and whether women executives' leadership contributes something unique to business outcomes.

The female executives of the Fortune 1000 and Power 50 broke through the glass ceiling, and in this study many of them did so while espousing aspects of servant-leadership. Although there may be a business case for promoting women to executive positions, the social justice case should be more compelling (Reynolds, 2016). There is more at stake than the immediate benefits to women of having more female top executives and to the business world of embracing servant-leadership. Simply promoting women and adopting servant-leadership-driven development programs will not necessarily remedy the deeply rooted underlying gender bias that infuses society or the androcentric matrix of profit-driven organizational cultures. The first step toward transformation is awareness: a call to action for explicit discussion of gendered reality. It remains the task of servant-leadership scholars to provide foresight and initiate an intentionally gender-integrative discourse of leading through serving, to create and foster a gender-holistic model of leadership with the potential to forge gender-integrative organizations, and to open up the matrix for more representation of women in executive positions.

References

Adams, R. B. (2016). Women on boards: The superheroes of tomorrow? *The Leadership Quarterly, 27*, 371–386. https://doi.org/10.1016/j.leaqua.2015.11.001

Agnew, L. (2008). "The day belongs to the students": Expanding epideictic's civic function. *Rhetoric Review, 27*(2), 147–164. https://doi.org/10.108/073 50190801921768

Ayers, M. R. (2008, August). *Agapáo in servant-leadership* [Paper presentation]. Servant Leadership Roundtable, Regent University, Virginia Beach, VA, USA.

Barbuto, J. E., & Gifford, G. T. (2010). Examining sex differences of the servant leadership dimensions: An analysis of the agentic and communal properties of the Servant Leadership Questionnaire. *Journal of Leadership Education 9*(2), 4–21. https://www.leadershipeducators.org/page-1014283

Barbuto, J. E., Gottfredson, R. K., & Searle, T. P. (2014). An examination of emotional intelligence as an antecedent of servant leadership. *Journal of Leadership & Organizational Studies, 21*(3) 315–323. https://doi.org/10.1177/1548051814531826

Barbuto, J. E., & Wheeler, G. T. (2006). Scale development and construct clarification of servant leadership. *Group & Organization Management, 31*(3), 300–326. https://doi.org/10.1177/1059601106287091

Bass, B. M. (1999). Two decades of research and development in transformational leadership. *European Journal of Work and Organizational Psychology, 8*(1), 9–32. https://doi.org/10.1080/135943299398410

Beck, C. D. (2014). Antecedents of servant leadership: A mixed methods study. *Journal of Leadership & Organizational Studies, 21,* 299–314. https://doi.org/10.1177/1548051814529993

Bierema, L. L. (2016). Women's leadership: Troubling notions of the "ideal" (male) leader. *Advances in Developing Human Resources, 18*(2), 119–136. https://doi.org/10.1177/1523422316641398

Bordelon, S. (2010). Composing women's civic identities during the progressive era: College commencement addresses as overlooked rhetorical sites. *College Composition and Communication, 61*(3), 510–533. https://www.jstor.org/stable/40593338

Brescoll, V. (2016). Leading with their hearts? How gender stereotypes of emotion lead to biased evaluations of female leaders. *The Leadership Quarterly, 27*(3), 415–428. https://doi.org/10.1016/j.leaqua.2016.02.005

Catalyst. (2016). *Knowledge center: Statistical overview of women in the workforce* (Data file). http://www.catalyst.org/knowledge/statistical-overview-women-workforce

Choudhary, A. I., Akhtar, S. A., & Zaheer, A. (2013). Impact of transformational and servant leadership on organizational performance: A comparative analysis. *Journal of Business Ethics, 116*(2), 433–440. https://doi.org/10.1007/s10551-012-1470-8

Condit, C. M. (1985). The functions of epideictic: The Boston Massacre Orations as exemplar. *Communication Quarterly, 33*(4), 284–299. https://doi.org/10.1080/01463378509369608

Conyon, M. J., & He, L. (2017). Firm performance and boardroom gender diversity: A quantile regression approach. *Journal of Business Research, 79,* 198–211. http://dx.doi.org/10.1016/j.jbusres.2017.02.006

de Rubio, A., & Kiser, A. I. T. (2015). Gender and age differences in servant leadership. *Academy of Business Research Journal, 1,* 49–63.

de Waal, A., & Sivro, M. (2012). The relation between servant leadership, organizational performance, and the high-performance organization framework. *Journal of Leadership & Organizational Studies, 19,* 173–190. https://doi.org/10.1177/1548051812439892

Dezső, C., & Ross, D. G. (2012). Does female representation in top management improve firm performance? A panel data investigation. *Strategic Management Journal, 33,* 1072–1089. https://doi.org/10.1002/smj.1955

Duff, A. (2013). Performance management coaching: Servant leadership and gender implications. *Leadership & Organization Development Journal, 34*(3), 204–221. https://doi.org/10.1108/01437731311326657

Eagly, A. H. (2007). Female leadership advantage and disadvantage: Resolving the contradictions. *Psychology of Women Quarterly, 31*, 1–12. https://doi.org/10.1111/j.1471-6402.2007.00326.x

Eagly, A. H., Johannesen-Schmidt, M. C., & van Engen, M. L. (2003). Transformational, transactional, and laissez-faire leadership styles: A meta-analysis comparing women and men. *Psychological Bulletin, 129*(4), 569–591. https://doi.org/10.1037/0033-2909.129.4.569

Eagly, A. H., & Johnson, B. T. (1990). Gender and leadership style: A meta-analysis. *Psychological Bulletin, 108*(2), 233–256. https://doi.org/10.1037/0033-2909.108.2.233

Eagly, A. H., & Karau, S. J. (2002). Role congruity theory of prejudice toward female leaders. *Psychological Review, 109*(3), 573–598. https://doi.org/10.1037//0033-295X.109.3.573

Eagly, A. H., Karau, S. J., & Makhijani, M. G. (1995). Gender and the effectiveness of leaders: A meta-analysis. *Psychological Bulletin, 117*(1), 125–145. https://doi.org/10.1037//0033-2909.117.1.125

Eagly, A. H., & Sczesny, S. (2009). Stereotypes about women, men, and leaders: Have times changed? In M. Barretto, M. K. Ryan, & M. T. Schmitt (Eds.), *The glass ceiling in the 21st century: Understanding barriers to gender equality* (pp. 21–47). American Psychology Association.

Eicher-Catt, D. (2005). The myth of servant leadership: A feminist perspective. *Women and Language, 27*(1), 17–25. https://www.academia.edu/14264417/The_Myth_of_Servant_Leadership

Eva, N., Robin, M., Sendjaya, S., van Dierendonck, D., & Liden, R. C. (2019). Servant Leadership: A systematic review and call for future research. *The Leadership Quarterly, 30*(1), 111–132. https://doi.org/10.1016/j.leaqua.2018.07.004

Fine, M. G. (2007). Women, collaboration, and social change: An ethics-based model of leadership. In J. L. Chin, B. Lott, J. K. Rice, & J. Sanchez-Hucles (Eds.), *Women and leadership: Transforming visions and diverse voices* (pp. 177–191). Blackwell. https://doi.org/10.1002/9780470692332.ch8

Gardner, W. L., Lowe, K. B., Meuser, J. D., Noghani, F., Gullifor, D. P., & Cogliser, C. C. (2020). The leadership trilogy: A review of the third decade of the leadership quarterly. *The Leadership Quarterly, 31*(1), 1–26. https://doi.org/10.1016/j.leaqua.2019.101379

Gipson, A. N., Pfaff, D. L., Mendelsohn, D. B., Catenacci, L. T., & Burke, W. W. (2017). Women and leadership selection, development, leadership style, and performance. *The Journal of Applied Behavioral Science, 53*(1), 32–65. https://doi.org/10.1177/0021886316687247

Greenleaf, R. K. (2003). *The servant-leader within: A transformative path* (H. Beazley, J. Beggs, & L. C. Spears, Eds.). Paulist Press.

Hambrick D. C. (2007). Upper echelons theory: An update. *The Academy of Management Review, 32*(2), 334–343. http://www.jstor.com/stable/20159303

Hambrick, D. C. (2018). Upper echelons theory. In M. Augier & D. J. Teece (Eds.), *The Palgrave Encyclopedia of Strategic Management* (pp. 1782–1785). Palgrave Macmillan.

Hargrove, D. (2009). *A content analysis of leadership language in campaign speeches communicated by senators Hillary Rodham Clinton and Barack Hussein Obama* [Unpublished doctoral dissertation]. Our Lady of the Lake University.

Hargrove, D., Duncan, P. A., Green, M. T., Salter, C., & Trayhan, J. M. (2011). Obama vs. Clinton: A study exploring the impact of leadership language. *Current Topics in Management, 15*, 95–116. https://doi.org/10.4324/9780203793084

Hogue, M. (2016), Gender bias in communal leadership: Examining servant leadership. *Journal of Managerial Psychology, 31*(4), 837–849. https://doi.org/10.1108/JMP-10-2014-0292

Insch, G. S., Moore, J. E., & Murphy, L. D. (1997). Content analysis in leadership research: Examples, procedures, and suggestions for future use. *The Leadership Quarterly 8*(1), 1–26. https://doi.org/10.1016/S1048-9843(97)90028-X

Kouzes, J. M., & Posner, B. Z. (2010). *The truth about leadership: The no-fads, heart-of-the-matter facts you need to know.* Jossey-Bass.

Lammers, J., & Gast, A. (2017). Stressing the advantages of female leadership can place women at a disadvantage. *Social Psychology, 48*(1), 28–39. https://doi.org/10.1027/1864-9335/a000292

Laub, J. (2018). *Leveraging the power of servant leadership: Building high-performing organizations.* Palgrave Macmillan. https://doi.org/10.1007/978-3-319-77143-4

LaWare, M. (2009, November). *Redefining the good life: Life lessons and virtues in commencement speeches by women at women's colleges* [Paper presentation]. National Communication Association (NCA) 95th Annual Convention 2009, Chicago, IL, USA.

Lehrke, A. S., & Sowden, K. (2017). Servant leadership and gender. In C. J. Davis (Ed.), *Servant leadership and followership: Examining the impact on workplace behavior* (pp. 25–50). Palgrave. https://doi.org/10.1007/978-3-319-59366-1_2

Madden, M. (2007). Strategic planning: Gender, collaborative leadership, and organizational change. In J. L. Chin, B. Lott, J. K. Rice, & J. Sanchez-Hucles (Eds.), *Women and leadership: Transforming visions and diverse voices* (pp. 192–208). Blackwell. https://doi.org/10.1002/9780470692332.ch9

Madsen, S., & Andrade, M. (2018). Unconscious gender bias: Implications for women's leadership development. *Journal of Leadership Studies, 12*(1), 62–67. https://doi.org/10.1002/jls.21566

Matteson, J. A., & Irving, J. A. (2006). Servant versus self-sacrificial leadership: A behavioral comparison of two follower-oriented leadership theories. *International Journal of Leadership Studies, 2*(1), 36–51. https://regentparents.regent.edu/acad/global/publications/ijls/new/vol2iss1/matteson/mair.pdf

Morales, C. J. (2019). *Intersectionality: Engaging the epistemology of leadership theory* [Doctoral dissertation, Antioch University]. AURA. https://aura.antioch.edu/etds/517

Moreno-Gomez, J., Lafuente, E., & Vaillant, Y. (2018). Gender diversity in the board, women's leadership and business performance. *Gender in Management: An International Journal, 33*(2), 104–122. https://doi.org/10.1108/GM-05-2017-0058

Neely, B. H., Lovelace, J. B., Cowen, A. P., & Hiller N. J. (2020). Metacritiques of upper echelons theory: Verdicts and recommendations for future research. *Journal of Management, 46*(6), 1029–1062. https://doi.org/10.1177/014920 6320908640

Ngunjiri, F. W. (2010). *Women's spiritual leadership in Africa: Tempered radicals and critical servant leaders.* SUNY Press.

Oliver, C. R. (2004). *Impact of catastrophe on pivotal national leaders' vision statements: Correspondences and discrepancies in moral reasoning, explanatory style, and rumination* [Unpublished doctoral dissertation, Fielding Institute]. https://web.archive.org/web/20160303174802/http://dareassociation.org/Carl.Oliver_Dissertation_2004.pdf

Oner, H. (2009, April). *Is servant leadership gender bound in the political arena?* [Paper presentation]. Midwest Political Science Association 67th Annual National Conference 2009, Chicago, IL, USA. http://www.allacademic.com/meta/p364186_index.html

Parker, P. S. (2005). *Race, gender, and leadership: Re-envisioning organizational leadership from the perspectives of African American women executives.* Lawrence Erlbaum.

Parris, D. L. & Peachey, J. W. (2013). A systematic literature review of servant leadership theory in organizational contexts. *Journal of Business Ethics, 113*(3), 377–393. https://doi.org/10.1007/s10551-012-1322-6

Patterson, K. A. (2004, August). *Servant leadership: A theoretical model* [Paper presentation]. Servant Leadership Research Roundtable, Regent University, Virginia Beach, VA, USA. https://www.semanticscholar.org/paper/Servant-leadership%3A-A-theoretical-model-Patterson/ed70d23a13185ab032df4e135 32d5a92d7f657eb

Politis, J. D., & Politis, D. J. (2018). Examination of the relationship between servant leadership and agency problems: Gender matters. *Leadership & Organization Development Journal, 39*(2), 170–185. https://doi.org/10.1108/LODJ-01-2016-0020

Reynolds, K. (2011). Servant leadership as gender-integrative leadership: Paving a path for more gender-integrative organizations through leadership education. *Journal of Leadership Education, 10*(2), 155–171. https://journalofleadershiped.org/jole_articles/servant-leadership-as-gender-integrative-leadership-paving-a-path-for-more-gender-integrative-organizations-through-leadership-education/

Reynolds, K. (2013). *Gender differences in messages of commencement addresses delivered by Fortune 1000 business leaders: A mixed-methods content analysis informed by servant-leadership and the feminist ethic of care* [Doctoral dissertation, Gonzaga University].

Reynolds, K. (2016). Servant leadership: A feminist perspective. *International Journal of Servant Leadership*, *10*, 35–63. https://www.gonzaga.edu/school-of-leadership-studies/departments/ph-d-leadership-studies/international-journal-of-servant-leadership/ijsl-issues/ijsl-volume-10

Seider, M. S. (1974). American big business ideology: A content analysis of executive speeches. *American Sociological Review*, *36*(6), 802–815.

Sims, C. M., & Morris, L. R. (2018). Are women business owners authentic servant leaders? *Gender in Management: An International Journal*, *33*(5), 405–427. https://doi.org/10.1108/GM-01-2018-0003

Smith, B. M., Montagno, R. V., & Kuzmenko, T. N. (2004). Transformational and servant leadership: Content and contextual comparisons. *Journal of Leadership & Organizational Studies*, *10*(4), 80–91. https://doi.org/10.1177/107179190401000406

Sousa, M., & Van Dierendonck, D. (2017). Servant leadership and the effect of the interaction between humility, action, and hierarchical power on follower engagement. *Journal of Business Ethics*, *141*, 13–25. https://doi.org/10.1007/s10551-015-2725-y

Stentz, J. E., Plano Clark, V. L., & Matkin, G. S. (2012). Applying mixed methods to leadership research: A review of current practices. *The Leadership Quarterly*, *23*(6), 1173–1183. https://doi.org/10.1016/j.leaqua.2012.10.001

van Dierendonck, D. (2011). Servant leadership: A review and synthesis. *Journal of Management*, *37*, 1228–1261. https://doi.org/10.1177/0149206310380462

van Dierendonck, D., & Nuijten, I. (2011). The servant leadership survey: Development and validation of a multidimensional measure. *Journal of Business and Psychology*, *26*, 249–267. https://doi.org/10.1007/s10869-010-9194-1

van Dierendonck, D., & Patterson, K. (2015). Compassionate love as a cornerstone of servant leadership: An integration of previous theorizing and research. *Journal of Business Ethics*, *128*, 119–131. https://doi.org/10.1007/s10551-014-2085-z

VanMeter, R., Chonko, L. B., Grisaffe, D. B., & Goad, E. A. (2016). In search of clarity on servant leadership: Domain specification and reconceptualization. *Academy of Marketing Science Review*, *6*, 59–78. https://doi.org/10.1007/s13162-016-0075-2

Verdorfer, A. P. (2016). Examining mindfulness and its relations to humility, motivation to lead, and actual servant leadership behaviors. *Mindfulness*, *7*, 950–961. https://doi.org/10.1007/s12671-016-0534-8

Washington, R. R., Sutton, C. D., & Field, H. S. (2006). Individual differences in servant leadership: The roles of values and personality. *Leadership & Organization Development Journal*, *27*(8), 700–716. https://doi.org/10.1108/01437730610709309

Wood, W., & Eagly, A. H. (2015). Two traditions of research on gender identity. *Sex Roles*, *73*, 461–473. https://doi.org/10.1007/s11199-015-0480-2

Chapter 9

A Poetics of Servant-Leadership

Nadine Chapman

One day somebody "identified" me. Beside me, in the queue, there was a woman with blue lips. She had, of course, never heard of me; but she suddenly came out of that trance so common to us all and whispered in my ear (everybody spoke in whispers there): "Can you describe this?" And I said: "Yes, I can." And then something like the shadow of a smile crossed what had once been her face.

—Akhmatova, 1985, p. 87

Anna Akhmatova places her great elegiac poem "Requiem" in the years of the Yezhov terror, during Stalin's purges, when she spent seventeen months in prison queues, trying to see her son, Lev. Out of great fear, which relegates people to suspicion of one another and a depraved anonymity, comes this face-to-face expression, the giving of oneself in relationship to another. The openness expressed here in speech is not yet a conceptual act based on the will but an attitude in response to the other person. Akhmatova responds to the woman's turn to her with the word, spoken and poetic. In so doing, she takes responsibility for her own presence and acknowledges the other, as well as the vulnerability of the woman before her. She then moves to the knowing, moral act of using the word in a particular form. She leads through her poetic response, as a voice for human dignity in the midst of mass terror. As a poet, she fuses this need to speak out with the fullness of language.

Many leadership models address the importance of language and value various creative language forms, especially storytelling, on some practical level. Recognizing that human beings understand their relationship to the cosmos and one another through narrative, Wheatley (1998) emphasizes the importance of storytellers. She writes of servant-leadership and changes in organizations as a new story, a tale of life beginning with a dream that creates a world image (pp. 340, 344, 348). Greenleaf (1977/2002) cites Alfred North Whitehead's call for understanding language's link to imagination, seeing it as a critical facility for the leader (p. 18). In "Bearing Witness," Autry (1998) finds the language of everyday work and lives inadequate for the expression of feeling and meaning. He explains the need for a more metaphorical view (p. 311). Greenleaf (1977/2002) offers a poem by Robert Frost, "Directive," as a way of sharing the leadership journey. He assigns the poem's power to the use of symbol, for "all symbols are potential sources of new meaning" (p. 316). He continues to acknowledge creative language's impact on his thinking in "My Debt to E. B. White," noting White's ability to see the whole (Greenleaf, 1998, p. 235).

In the essay "An Inward Journey," reprinted in the second volume of *The International Journal of Servant-Leadership,* Greenleaf (1977/2002) writes that reading "Directive" with understanding involves awareness, "letting something significant and disturbing develop between oneself and a symbol" (p. 329). He encourages us to risk being moved by symbols that "cry out to speak to us" (p. 329), for interacting with them offers meaning and the possibility of new creation. It is often the underlying symbol that allows the poet to express something as abstract as the meeting place between human feelings and the universe. Inspiration does come from the impact of the natural world as symbol. Even a tree stump gives something beyond itself in meaning, in transcendence through poetry.

For Greenleaf (1977/2002), the inward journey of "Directive" involves "radical, searing losses," symbolized in the poem as that which is "burned, dissolved, broken off" (p. 330). It also means, according to Frost, following a guide "who only has at heart your getting lost" (p. 331). Yet this is the path of great religious traditions, the path of seekers. Encountering the unknown seems a necessary step to finding oneself. Rather than marking tragedy, such painful losses "are seen as opening the way for new creative acts" (p. 339). Greenleaf believes that the willingness to grasp the opportunities loss presents requires faith, humanity, and spiritual growth. It can lead to the greatest gift possible: love. Society's rejected—the misfits and the undesirable—may move ahead on this road to spiritual growth with more ease than those lauded as upright citizens of good works. Awareness, for Greenleaf, "is infinite and therefore equal in every human being," but it requires consciousness of uncompensated personal losses and the errors of cultural inheritance (p. 340).

> Your destination and your destiny's
> A brook that was the water of the house,
> Cold as a spring as yet so near its force
> Too lofty and original to rage. (as cited in Greenleaf, 1977/2002,
>   p. 335)

Within Frost's use of the water, "the great symbol of wholeness," Greenleaf identifies the need to look at the past, but not for security and comfort (p. 335). Instead, the seeker also risks drinking from the cup of new and fresh ideas.

> Here are your waters and your watering place.
> Drink and be whole again beyond confusion. (as cited in
>   Greenleaf, 1977/2002, p. 339)

Robert Pinsky (1999), US poet laureate (1997–2000), focuses on a past presented in "Directive" as "mysterious spiritual reality" attained through a journey (p. 70). Pinsky believes that, moving beyond the individual, Frost's poem suggests that the destiny of a people rests on "the fragile, heroic enterprise of remembering," the act of historical recovery (p. 70). Here memory serves as the source of wholeness, and Frost challenges us to engage in this cultural work of recovery that helps shape us as a people.

> The height of the adventure is the height
> Of country where two village cultures faded
> Into each other. Both of them are lost. (as cited in Greenleaf,
>   1977/2002, p. 333)

Greenleaf and Pinsky see this memory quest as challenging but critical to knowing ourselves. Beyond our personal journeys of growth, as responsible people, is the grace of sharing our symbolic experiences with others and receiving their understanding and guidance.

In exploring poetry's role in leadership theory, Wheatley (1998) and Greenleaf (1977/2002) provide an important doorway. The phenomenological investigations of Levinas (1989, 1993) and Ricoeur (1976, 1991) further open the view by connecting poetry to ethical response. Meaning level (an aspect of our understanding and our ability to grant it symbolic function) becomes paramount and is accessed through poetry, lyric fiction, metaphor, and imaginative narrative fiction. Ricoeur (1991) understands poetry "not only in the sense of rhythmic and rhymed forms of language, in the broad sense of the word lyric fiction," but also as narrative fiction "in the sense that the plot of narrative is a creation of productive imagination which projects a world of its own" (p. 452). The poetic preserves and enlarges language's capacity for meaningfulness often through the power of figurative speech. Original metaphors the poet creates bring to language the implicit semantics of the symbol and help lead us to symbolic understanding (Ricoeur, 1976, p. 59). Ricoeur (1991) demonstrates that there is not just an epistemological and political imagination but also a more fundamental linguistic imagination that generates meaning, especially through the power of metaphor (pp. 448–462). As a poet, I am called by the face of the other, by the vulnerability and need shown in the other's face, to respond from this linguistic depth. Such an ethical relation, the one-for-the-other, comprises the central movement of Levinas's (1993) philosophy, and it is the ground from which this essay proceeds. Levinas even prefers the word *sanctity* or *apres vous* to *ethics*, where sanctity "is the principle of an ethics whose foundations rest on the priority of the other and on 'my' finite responsibility" for her or him (as cited in Hansel, 1999, p. 169). In this essay, servant-leadership is explored by describing the initial ethical movement in the poetic response to others found in the work of each of four poets.

Dangerous Vitality

Greenleaf (1977/2002) views the servant-leader as one willing to "create dangerously," a phrase taken from Nobel Prize winner Albert Camus's last lecture (p. 61). Such a person has some foresight or intuition for the unknowable that comes of listening to others and putting their priorities first. Wheatley (1998) finds that the servant-leader gives voice to a story of life that serves the human spirit and nurtures it. It is relational, based on "the nature of life to move toward one another" (p. 349). Servant-leaders "act in service to the great creative desires that each of us carries" and possess the courage to tell the story (pp. 349–350). Servant-leadership begins with the movement toward service, and "then conscious choice brings one to aspire to lead" (Greenleaf, 1977/2002, p. 13). But Greenleaf sees one "limitation on language": the need for the hearer to make "that leap of imagination that connects the verbal concept to the hearer's own experience" (p. 18). The leader's generous and creative response proves critical to the hearer's leap of imagination and to leadership theory in that it serves "as an indication of the way" (*Compact Edition of the Oxford English Dictionary,* 1971, p. 1588). Such an indication, forged of reflection, awareness, discernment, and inspiration, occurs prior to any model.

The ability to lead entails going in advance—taking a risk for the other person, with the willingness to speak out in the fullness of language. Such a position suggests a foundational role for poetry, including lyric fiction, in theories of leadership, especially servant-leadership. This role deserves study for many reasons, notably poetry's expressions of ethical response and responsibility, transcendence, and semantic innovation as important for new possibilities of thought. The leader often relies on the poet's figurative language ability to project a sense of vision and moral imagination, to speak and write in depth of a fresh approach, or to propose an altered path. To appreciate these dynamic connections involves unmasking the interrelated nature of ethical movement, poetic language, and thought as they find expression in responsive, responsible leadership.

Connections between servant-leadership theory, Levinas's transcendental ethical philosophy, and Ricoeur's hermeneutic phenomenology, as well as poetry and literary theory, can form an important nexus of life philosophy, contemplation, and action. In the following section, key terms that appear in the essay are defined, showing how terms traditionally associated with specific disciplines are used in the present context.

Groundwork

A phenomenological starting point, where phenomenological inquiry begins and philosophical orientation occurs, is "the conviction that a radical interrogation of meaning requires us to penetrate beneath the established concepts of empirical, logical or scientific 'objectification' (what Husserl called the 'natural attitude') to that concretely 'lived experience' of . . . temporal and historical *being-in-the-world*" (Kearney, 1984, p. 7).

Hermeneutics. In a general philosophical sense this term implies a theory, method, or approach to interpretation. As Ricoeur (1974) notes,

> Hermeneutics involves the general problem of comprehension. And, moreover, no noteworthy interpretation has been formulated which does not borrow from the modes of comprehension available to a given epoch: myth, allegory, metaphor analogy, etc. . . . in Aristotle, *hermeneia* is not limited to allegory but concerns every meaningful discourse. (p. 4)

Ricoeur also insists that "every hermeneutics is thus, explicitly or implicitly, self-understanding by means of understanding others" (p. 17). By overcoming the distance between the person and the text or signs, the person can "appropriate meaning" to herself or himself (p. 16).

Meaning. In phenomenological approaches to understanding, one aims to explore meanings. Poetic images allow us to read meaning into images, though "we *see* some images only to the extent that we first *hear* them" (Ricoeur, 1991, p. 128). Expressive meaning, such as that derived from poetry, is "meaning obtained from contexts that express, and thus elicit, such things as mood, feeling, emotion, values. . . . Expressive meaning may also have cognitive or other kinds of meaning associated with it" (Angeles, 1992, p. 180). For Levinas (1993), the other person gives sense to expression, and it is only by her or him that a phenomenon as a meaning is, of itself, introduced into being (p. 95).

The face. Levinas's description of "the face" and his references to its "appearance" refer to a dimension of the other person. This term is fundamental to Levinas's philosophy. With an allusion to Plato's idea of the Good, Levinas characterizes the face as coming from on high. Some other metaphors he uses characterize "the other as a stranger, as naked (not clothed in the cultural paraphernalia that make us similar), as destitute or marginal, as an orphan or widow" (Peperzak, 1998, pp. 114–115). The focus is not on representation but on vulnerability. Peperzak notes that aside from these negative qualifications,

> the only way to express the impact made by the other [the face] in positive terms is to use ethical language: the other reveals a command; to address me (in looking at or speaking to me) is to reveal my being-for-the-other in the sense of serving, respecting, and honoring the other's "height." As other—not through any deed or wish or will—the other deserves my devotion or dedication to or responsibility for him or her. . . . Here a kind

of ought is the only possible correlate of the manifestation of the "being." My obligation to serve the other coincides with my being what I am as revealed by the other's presence before me. (p. 115)

Many connections exist between poetry, philosophy, ethics, and leadership, and the ethical movement of language, which knows no boundaries, precedes all such demarcations. Boundaries tend to preserve influence and authority through spheres of power. Drawing from the metaethical philosophy of Levinas, psychologist George Kunz (1998) argues that such a Darwinian approach or thesis "is challenged by the thesis that is beyond any thesis: *ethical responsibility*" (p. 23). The idealistic myth of individual freedoms over individual responsibility falls to the call from the weak for "the strong, especially as a community, to protect them," for "conscience is not a private whisper; it is knowing together" (p. 23).

As a writer of poetry, in a heightened way, I may respond to the face of the other person in need. I can never live in some hiding place of inwardness. My words express not only content as knowledge but also the interhuman debt, our vulnerability to one another. I am concerned with language that sees, hears, and touches the particular person. Such concrete, sensory detail avoids abstraction and fights against dehumanization. Of special interest is my unique opportunity for an expressive response that accepts the call for an ethical answer. This is not a disembodied moment but requires movement of one human being toward another within the contingencies of daily life.

As a fine art, creative writing is *praxis*. Freire (2001) finds that a "true word" is not only reflection but also *praxis*, capable of transforming reality (p. 87). Without this dimension, language becomes empty. The oppression of voice eventually leads to resentment, depression, and even rage. The poet's voice and relations with the world become an invaluable force in society as ethical leadership (Guare, 2001, pp. 82–87). Wheatley's (1998) new tale for servant-leadership moves from the old mechanistic story of domination and control, which engenders fear, to "autopoiesis—self-creation—from the same root as poetry" (p. 346). Leadership as the author's voice crying out through poetry in the literal face of injustice participates in this critical movement.

Poets consistently lead through their art without organizational authority, and Heifetz (1994) finds certain benefits in this type of leadership, including the ability to

a) deviate from the norms of authoritative decision making,

b) more readily raise questions that disturb,

c) [have] more *latitude for creative deviance,*

d) [live] closer to the detailed experiences of some stakeholders in the situation. (p. 188)

Again, the echo of Camus's voice is heard: create dangerously! In this context, several examples of how the poet's ethical response and the language of poetry may prove integral to leadership theory can illuminate the process of poetic leadership and its global range.

Four Poets

The world is not a horse you can bridle,
To be mounted and ridden at your pleasure.

—da Todi, 1982, p. 181

Italian poet Jacopone da Todi sent this warning to Pope Boniface VIII while imprisoned from 1278 to 1303 (Peck, 1980, pp. 125–131). Jacopone's religious poetry is marked by its lack of moderation and by an intemperance of language that scandalized conventional critics. He made sport of the corruption around him and railed against the flagrant abuse of ecclesiastical power, especially that of Pope Boniface VIII, who excommunicated Jacopone and sent him to a subterranean cell, where he suffered solitary confinement for almost five years. In his prison poems, "without rival in the literature of his time for their mocking self-scrutiny, an astounding variant of Franciscan humility, Jacopone marked the beginning of a *vita nova* and a new poetry" (Hughes, 1982, p. 57). In his first letter to Boniface, *Lauda LVI,* he says two shields protect him against the Pope's anathema and excommunication:

For I have two shields, and unless I lay them aside
No steel can pierce my flesh, per secula infinita
The first shield is on the left, the other on the right.
The one on the left has been proven as hard as diamond,
No weapon can penetrate it:
This shield is my self-hatred, bonded to God's honor.

The shield on the right is of ruby;
It blazes like fire, flames leaping high:
It is made of ardent love of neighbor.
Step closer and you'll feel its heat with a rush.
Do what you will, this love will overcome you.
(da Todi, 1982, p. 178)

As poet and mystic, Jacopone da Todi leads by offering a poetic response to those of his time. Composing his poetry in the familiar Umbrian dialect, considered coarse by the elite of his day, rather than Latin, immediately connected Jacopone to the common people, and this linguistic affinity for them was rewarded with their deep affection (Peck, 1980, pp. 180–181). One prison poem, marked by an ironic realism that voices the poet's resolve, so captured his near contemporaries that he is pictured in the prison on a fifteenth-century manuscript, and a fifteenth-century mural shows him with a book open to the poem's first line. His poetry was known widely before the first printed edition appeared in 1490 (Lawrence, 2003, p. 237). He is also a poet of the present age in many ways. As a well-educated young businessman, Jacopone (1230–1306) would have shared in the economic boom that swept through north and central Italy in the last half of the thirteenth century. According to Peck (1980), this period saw a revolution in food processing and marketing, clothing, trade, and public works, such as paved streets and squares, and water and sewer systems (pp. 19–23). In the midst of new wealth and commercial progress, with its intense interest in law, money became "the complicated and fascinating new toy of the urban classes" (p. 46). But Jacopone turned away from all this and became a "fool" for God, willing to suffer ridicule and jest, willing to say or do anything as long as he could live in Christ's love.

As an itinerant preacher and a Friar Minor, his poverty acted as a symbol or pledge for an emptying of self. By discussing the soteriological implications of Jacopone's radical Franciscan poverty, McKenna (1997) helps the modern reader understand why this poet was willing to suffer ecclesiastical persecution rather than abandon a life of economic destitution. As north and central Italy rapidly moved from a gift economy to a profit economy, with "increased reliance on money, which set a more universal and less personal value upon goods and services rendered" (p. 273), Jacopone's life and poetry cried out for the intensely personal value and allegiance of the gift. Radical Franciscans identified the gift's value with Christ's generosity. The economic dilemma of separating the person from the product is no less critical today, and the need for the poetic response as a true voice of leadership appears no less urgent.

Sor Juana Inés de la Cruz, a seventeenth-century Colonial Spanish nun of the Order of Saint Jerome, Mexico, wrote secular and religious poetry, plays, essays, scholarly research, and religious treatises. Her intellectual biography, *Response,* written in 1691, is a major statement of women's intellectual freedom. The danger the male clergy perceived in a woman so skilled in logic and poetry pervaded her life. In "Primera Sueno," or "First Dream," Sor Juana (1997) used the Baroque Latin American style as a poetic challenge to traditional concepts of the Catholic Church and women. Merrim (1999) notes that "from the first lines onward," the poem "associates knowledge with the feminine" (p. 237) and voices Sor Juana's response to her own persecution and the injustices done to the women around her. With its indomitable will to know, the Soul treasures

> the Spark of the Divine she hears within,
> judging that she is nearly free of all
> that bind her, keeps her from liberty,
> the corporeal chains
> that vulgarly restrain and clumsily
> impede the soaring intellect that now,
> unchecked, measures the vastness of the Sphere.
> (de la Cruz, 1997, p. 93)

Sor Juana suffered enclosure and silencing for assuming roles that challenged traditional gender systems, but her response to injustice often confused her contemporaries because she fought for women's rights through the subtlety of poetry (Stavans, 1997, p. xli). Despite the forces against her, this autodidact, writing from within a convent, brilliantly defended women's learning and intellectual freedom in the New World's patriarchal, misogynist culture. Sor Juana's work reveals the important link between creative expression and philosophical inquiry as evidence of developing an activist consciousness within a leadership that serves and heals the world. Many of the goals Sor Juana sought mirror the still unmet desires of women at the beginning of the twenty-first century, making her dream and its world image changes for women a still unfolding story of leadership.

Twentieth-century Russian poet Anna Akhmatova lived in poverty and peril throughout the Stalinist period. The government expelled her from the Soviet Writers' Union because of her belief in the power of poetry to move from ethical address to justice. A premiere example of what Levinas calls the ethical moment occurs in the beginning of "Requiem" when Akhmatova (1985) describes waiting in a queue outside the prison to see her son. A woman turns to her and asks if she can describe this (p. 87). "Requiem" is that famous poetic response. The poem's narrator later describes the horror of the situation:

> Someone should have shown you—little jester,
> Little teaser, blue-veined charm-
> er, laughing-eyed, lionized, sylvan-princessly
> Sinner—to what point you would come:
> How, the three hundredth in a queue,
> You'd stand at the prison gate
> And with your hot tears
> Burn through the New-Year ice.
> How many lives are ending there! Yet it's
> Mute, even the prison-poplar's
> Tongue's in its cheek as it's swaying. (p. 90)

In the end, the poet bears witness not just for the one woman but for the many silenced by totalitarian force:

> I have woven for them a great shroud
> Out of the poor words I heard them speak. (p. 95)

Akhmatova does not turn away from the danger in this form of servant-leadership. By connecting the horror of the concrete experience in the here and now with the symbolism of evil through her metaphors, the poet manages to express what remains buried in ordinary language. In the process, Akhmatova reinterprets the symbolism of evil for the twentieth century. Her creative language of integrity becomes a moral act of resistance.

Chilean poet Gabriela Mistral, the first Latin American to be awarded the Nobel Prize for Literature, helped organize Mexico's entire rural education system after the revolution. She accepted the 1945 prize as "the candidate for women and children" (Tapscott, 2002, p. 236). In her introduction to *Poemas de las Madres,* or *The Mothers' Poems,* Mistral (1996) writes about walking on a street in Temuco and seeing a passing man make a crude remark to a poor pregnant woman sitting in the doorway of a shack. At that moment she felt profound solidarity, "the infinite pity of woman for woman," and posed this question: "If the purpose of art is to make every-thing beautiful, with an immense mercy, why haven't we purified, for the eyes of the impure, *this?*" (p. 3). Writing with what she described as almost religious intention, she gave the world *The Mothers' Poems*. One of these, "My Prayer," says,

> Like the women who place jars
> outside to gather the evening dew, I
> place my breasts before God; I give
> Him a new name. I call Him The One
> Who Fills, and ask Him for the liqueur
> of life. My child will arrive thirsty,
> looking for this. (p. 13)

Gabriela Mistral's words give poetic expression to women whose voices gender and poverty severely blunt or deny. Through a new set of metaphors or other types of imaginative language, the poet leads us to an altered experience of the world by making visible what was not seen. The role of mother, a central motif in Mistral's writing, highlights a vision of women in the public sphere, bonding nature to nation (Marchant, 1999, p. 50). She becomes the voice of the disempowered—indigenous poor women and children—and their desires. Mistral's view of the poet as servant of the people is reflected by the inscription on her tomb: "What the soul does for the body so does the poet for her people" (Agosin, 1997, p. 19).

The poet's role in serving the other person by first responding to the call of the face, and then using language to bear witness, constitutes a critical act of ethical leadership. Leadership that moves from ethical response to a responsive and responsible moral imagination has struck some as being so attuned to unspoken longings and the provocation of thought that those who exercise it do so at a risk. Totalitarian societies strive to silence their great poetic voices, for the poet's vision, expressed in metaphors and images, has the power to suggest new ways of knowing and feeling. In a counterpoint form of despair, democracies based on capitalism marginalize poetry by trivializing poetic expression. Is there any reason to think that the techno-logical world of power would respond more graciously to a challenge than the world of secular and ecclesiastical greed did in Jacopone da Todi's time?

Many political entities have considered poetry dangerous or subversive because of its strong resistance to the mere functional or utilitarian use of language (Ricoeur, 1991, p. 449). The poet who cannot turn away from injustice or from attempts to falsify the original intention of the discourse cries out in the fullness of language. The face of injustice is a specific human face. Servant-leadership theory is founded on such responses.

Poetry as Central to Leadership Theory

Ethical leadership and language begin with openness to the other. Peperzak (1991), writing on Levinasian ethics and the turn to hermeneutics, describes how the author presents herself and espouses herself "to the benevolence or violence of readers" over whom she has no power (p. 59). By offering a word, the poet opens herself. This openness does not constitute a message, but an appeal, a call or provocation to which the reader may respond with words of his or her own. Poetry moves out of this exposed, expressive voice, childlike in its lack of self-defense, as it has not yet learned to dissemble or deceive to protect itself. In its orientation toward the other person, a work of art, such as poetry, may constitute an impulse without guaranteed remuneration. Levinas (1993) describes this generous impulse, moving beyond the same or self in time, as "liturgy" in the Greek sense, for it "designates the exercise of a function which is not totally gratuitous, but requires on the part of him who exercises it a putting out of funds at a loss" (pp. 92–93). Being more attached to the life of the other than one's own life and giving voice to that relationship is the first value. By offering a word, one "in a sense prays" (Levinas, 1989, p. 149). Ethical movement dwells in this initial poetic impulse.

This position honors the subject over the object and orients Levinas's philosophy, which rests on the ethical appeal and responsibility of the human voice. Levinas's (1989) call for ethics as first philosophy offers a new depth, orientation, and language perspective to leadership theory. For Levinas, ethics precedes freedom. Responsibility as an obligation to respond to and for the other person "is prior to my own liberty" (Hansel, 1999, p. 171). This is radical servant-leadership, based not on a moral quality, value system, or the highest point in a hierarchy of virtues but upon speaking out.

The transcendence practiced in poetry, as an initial generous impulse that goes beyond the self in response to the face of the other, is not full of grand plans or actions. It realizes itself as endurance and patience, despite rejection, for "instead of an ascension by means of elitism and originality, it demands a descent to service and devotion" (Peperzak, 1991, p. 63). Such a movement does not preclude the idea of moral freedom and choice, however.

As Reinhold Niebuhr observed, moral imagination is necessarily a responsive and responsible imagination, constituted in dialogue, capable of answering (Daloz et al., 1996, p. 151). While moral leadership is cited as a key issue in leadership studies, Mangan (2002) says scholars do not agree on how to define terms such as *morals* and *values,* which they, nevertheless, find crucial to understanding leaders (p. A10). Polley (2002) argues that servant-leadership as a model "cuts across various leadership theories and provides a foundational philosophy for theories that emphasize principles congruent with human growth" (p. 125). Sendjaya and Sarros (2002) address differences between servant-leadership and other charismatic, transformational models, and review literature suggesting that servant-leadership exceeds such models by "its recognition of the leader's social responsibilities to serve those people who are marginalized by a system" (p. 62). Spears (1998) identifies deep awareness as one characteristic of the servant-leader. He notes the servant-leader's place in understanding issues involving ethics and taking the risk of response (p. 6). Greenleaf (1977/2002) states, "Awareness is not a giver of solace—it is just the opposite. It is a disturber and an awakener" (p. 28). Ethical leadership as the author's or leader's voice crying out through speaking and writing in the literal face of injustice actively participates in this critical movement.

The risk of figurative language the poet uses is real. Metaphor revels in polysemy, giving words multiple meanings that refuse containment. Thompson (2000) finds a leader's ability to communicate vision is not a matter of "charisma . . . or a way with words" but "is the capacity to use *symbol and metaphor* to convey layers of meaning beyond that accessible to mere rationality and its word-forms" (p. 191). No researcher should deny the troubling, even volatile nature of such disparate interpretive potential. When Greenleaf (1977/2002) honors Camus and admonishes servant-leaders to create dangerously, he acknowledges such factors. But taking this risk with language seems essential for leadership theory, in part, because "the first danger to our present culture is a kind of reduction of language to communication at the lowest level or to manipulate things and people," for then language becomes merely instrumental (Ricoeur, 1991, p. 448). Poetry can challenge the status quo because it has the capacity to create new worlds, new ways of thinking.

Some caution in the linking of language and leadership theory is warranted here. The call for a universal language as a means of cross-cultural communication remains potent in scientific-technological society (Senge et al., 1994, p. 88). Newman (1982) dispenses all notions of one language serving as well as another. If languages are not even equal in adapting scientific symbols, how can they be equal in metaphorical richness, force, musicality, precision of thought? Revelations of objective truth do not cease being subjective, precisely because they are written by a person. Wyschogrod (2000) notes that language itself "already refers to the one who hears and the one who speaks" (p. 153). But the one who speaks does so against a *lifeworld*, "so one can never summarize all the contexts of language and all the positions in which interlocutors could find themselves" (p. 154). For Ricoeur (1998), the polysemic nature of language, specifically poetic language, rules out all absolute interpretations. He also notes that while scientific language operates more or less directly, literary or poetic language "operates in a more subtle, more indirect manner, inasmuch as the chasm between language and reality has reached much greater depths" (p. 86). The images of poetry lead us farther than we know. In saying the image or hearing it, the listener participates in the sound which carries her or him away. In this moment, there is no longer a oneself, but rather a passage beyond self. For Levinas (1989), such is the captivation or incantation of poetry (p. 133).

While some important thinkers in servant-leadership studies address poetry's contribution to leadership theory through works of literature and specific creative writers, the foundational role creative language can play in leadership's conceptual and expressive range, including its vitality, is most often neglected. Therefore, samples of poetry that express a poet's ethical response to others serve as primary documents for future study. Secondary sources include literary analysis of the historical periods and poetry types by literary scholars.

Key questions emerge from these considerations. How do the poet's voice and response to another person or persons in oral and/or written creative expression prove valuable, even critical, for servant-leadership theory? What meaning does this reveal? How does poetry take leadership theory beyond the mere functional or utilitarian use of language to make ethical vision and linguistic imagination possible?

Conclusion

This essay attempts to describe the meanings the poet and poetry have for leadership theory, especially servant-leadership theory. Such an investigation can add to the field of leadership studies by articulating important links between poetry, ethics, and leadership. From the convergence of Greenleaf, Wheatley, Ricoeur, and Levinas, we begin to build an awareness of servant-leadership theory's rich and powerful connection with language studies, especially creative language and ethics. This points leadership theory away from the economic profit model and toward a creative synthesis that elevates personal and collective vulnerability, sincerity, authenticity, and responsibility. Many more studies of language and leadership theory are needed.

The profound notion of poetic voice suggests an ethical response to others and demands a radical role and vision of service. Just as the congregation gives meaning to the cantor's voice through their answering verse, and audience response to the author becomes an integral part of the poem, so the servant-leader relies on the voices and journeys of those he or she serves for vision and guidance. Poetry's unique ability to speak metaphorically, to point toward the symbolic depth of meaning between people and between people and the natural world, suggests a subtle, important, even dangerous role for the poet's voice in servant-leadership studies and for the servant-leader's voice in society.

Knowledge as rational thought will never capture the movement of love, for love begins in faith, believing that love without reward is valuable. Semantic innovation, transcendence and responsibility for the other reside together in the world of the poetic word. But first comes the response to the stranger, the lost one, the disenfranchised person as gift. And this is love, giving oneself in physical and verbal, then written, sound and form. Poet Elizabeth Jennings (1989) writes:

> Love is the argument, the lyric moment,
> The care for ritual, the need for growth
> And cities rise above the misty mountains
> Before the sunlight loves them with its gold. (p. 49)

Greenleaf (1997/2002) tells us love can fill the vacuum of loss, every loss we can imagine, but he does not discount suffering on the servant-leadership journey (p. 327). There is a cost for ethical response and for interaction with a symbol that creates new meaning and requires responsibility for the suffering of others. That cost may lead us into *the harsh realities of* loss, leaving us dissolved, burned, broken off. Yet the cost of servant-leadership inherently also leads us to meaning touched with elegance and loveliness, as well as legitimate power and greatness. In that meaning, in the face of every loss, we discover that not only are we well-loved, we become love.

References

Agosin, M. (1997). Introduction: Gabriela Mistral, the restless soul. In G. Mistral, *Gabriela Mistral: A reader* (pp. 17–24). White Pine Press.

Akhmatova, A. (1985). *You will hear thunder* (D. M. Thomas, Trans.). Ohio University Press.

Angeles, P. A. (1992). *The HarperCollins dictionary of philosophy* (2nd ed). HarperCollins Publishers.

Autry, J. (1998). Bearing witness. In L. C. Spears (Ed.), *Insights in leadership* (pp. 308–313). John Wiley & Sons.

Compact edition of the Oxford English Dictionary (1971). (Vols. 1–2). Oxford University Press.

da Todi, J. (1982). *The Lauds* (E. Hughes & S. Hughes, Trans.). Paulist Press.

Daloz, L. A. P., Keen, C. H., Keen, J. P., & Parks, S. D. (1996). *Common fire: Leading lives of commitment in a complex world.* Beacon Press.

de la Cruz, S. J. (1997). *Poems, protest, and a dream* (M. S. Peden, Trans.). Penguin.

Freire, P. (2001). *Pedagogy of the oppressed.* Continuum Publishing.

Greenleaf, R. K. (1998). My debt to E. B. White. In L. C. Spears (Ed.), *The power of servant-leadership* (pp. 235–261). Berrett-Koehler Publishers.

Greenleaf, R. K. (2002). *Servant leadership: A journey into the nature of legitimate power and greatness* (L. C. Spears, Ed.; 25th anniversary ed.). Paulist Press. (Original work published 1977)

Guare, R. (2001). Educating in the ways of the spirit: Teaching and leading poetically, prophetically, powerfully. *Religious Education, 96(1),* 65–87.

Hansel, J. (1999). Utopia and reality: The concept of sanctity in Kant and Levinas. *Philosophy Today, 43(2),* 168–175.

Heifetz, R. A. (1994). *Leadership without easy answers.* Belknap Press.

Hughes, S. (1982). Introduction: Toward a first reading of the *Lauds.* In J. da Todi, *The Lauds* (pp. 1–65). Paulist Press.

Jennings, E. (1989). *Tributes.* Carcanet PL.

Kearney, R. (Ed.). (1984). *Dialogues with contemporary continental thinkers.* Manchester University Press.

Kunz, G. (1998). *The paradox of power and weakness.* SUNY.

Lawrence, V. (2003). Translating Jacopone da Todi: Archaic poetries and modern audiences. *Translation & Literature* 12(2), 231–251.

Levinas, E. (1989). *The Levinas reader* (S. Hand, Ed.). Basil Blackwell.

Levinas, E. (1993). *Collected philosophical papers* (A. Lingis, Trans.). Kluwer Academic Publishers.

Mangan, K. (2002). Leading the way in leadership. *The Chronicle of Higher Education,* 48(38), A10.

Marchant, E. A. (1999). The professional outsider: Gabriela Mistral on motherhood and nation. *Latin American Library Review,* 27(53), 49–66.

McKenna, T. (1997). Jacopone of Todi and the soteriological implications of poverty. *Downside Review, 115,* 271–279.

Merrim, S. M. (1999). *Early modem women's writings and Sor Juana Ines de la Cruz.* Vanderbilt University Press.

Mistral, G. (1996). *The mothers' poems* (C. J. Kyle, Trans.). Eastern Washington University Press.

Newman, J. H. (1982). *The idea of a university.* Notre Dame.

Peck, G. (1980). *The fool of God, Jacopone da Todi.* The University of Alabama Press.

Peperzak, A. (1991). Presentation. In R. Bernasconi & S. Critchley (Eds.), *Rereading Levinas* (pp. 51–66). Indiana University Press.

Peperzak, A. (1998). Levinas' method. *Research in Phenomenology, 28,* 110–125.

Pinsky, R. (1999, October). Poetry and American memory. *The Atlantic Monthly, 284,* 60–70.

Polley, M. (2002). One university's response to the anti-leadership vaccine: Developing servant-leaders. *Journal of Leadership Studies, 8*(3), 117–130.

Ricoeur, P. (1974). Existence and hermeneutics (K. McLaughlin, Trans.). In D. Ihde (Ed.), *The conflict of interpretations* (pp. 3–24). Northwestern University Press. (Original work published 1969)

Ricoeur, P. (1976). *Interpretations theory: Discourse and the surplus of meaning.* The Texas Christian University Press.

Ricoeur, P. (1991). *A Ricoeur reader: Reflection and imagination* (M. Valdes, Ed.). University of Toronto Press.

Ricoeur, P. (1998). *Critique and conviction* (K. Blarney, Trans.). Columbia University Press.

Sendjaya, S., & Sarros, J. C. (2002). Servant-leadership: Its origin, development, and application in organizations. *Journal of Leadership & Organizational Studies,* 9(2), 57–64. https://doi.org/10.1177/107179190200900205

Senge, P. M., Kleiner, A., Roberts, C., Ross, R. B., & Smith, B. J. (1994). *The fifth discipline fieldbook: Strategies and tools for building a learning organization.* Currency Doubleday.

Spears, L. C. (1998). Introduction. In L. C. Spears (Ed.), *Insights on leadership* (pp. 1–14). John Wiley & Sons.

Stavans, I. (1997). Introduction. In *Sor Juana Ines de la Cruz: Poems, protest, and a dream* (pp. xi–xliii). Penguin Group.

Tapscott, S. (2002). Translator's remarks. In G. Mistral, *Selected prose and prosepoems* (pp. 235–246). University of Texas Press.

Thompson, C. M. (2000). *The congruent life: Following the inward path to fulfilling work and inspired leadership.* Jossey-Bass Publishers.

Wheatley, M. (1998). What is our work? In L. C. Spears (Ed.), *Insights on leadership* (pp. 340–351). John Wiley & Sons.

Wyschogrod, E. (2000). *Emmanuel Levinas: Revisioning moral philosophy.* University of Chicago Press.

Chapter 10

He Named Me Malala

Malala's Voice, Vision, and Leadership

CARLA PENHA-VASCONCELOS

One child, one teacher, one book, one pen can change the world.

—Yousafzai, 2013

The Universal Declaration of Human Rights says that "everyone has the right to education" (United Nations, 1948, art. 26). According to the United Nations Educational, Scientific and Cultural Organization (2016), education is "a fundamental human right and essential for the exercise of all other human rights. It promotes individual freedom and empowerment and yields important development benefits" (p. 1). Girls' education is part of the second- and third-millennium goals of achieving universal primary education and promoting gender equality and empowering women that are being revised in the frame of the 2030 Agenda for Sustainable Development.[1] Even though education is a human right, the United Nations Children's Emergency Fund estimated that more than 60 million girls are out of school

---

1. For information about the Millennium Goals and the 2030 Agenda for Sustainable Development, see the United Nations website available at http://www.un.org/millenniumgoals/.

(UNICEF, 2015). Most of these girls are denied this basic human right to education for the simple fact that they were born female.

Even though we identify progress toward the achievement of universal girls' education, today millions of girls still experience exclusion and discrimination from the educational system, especially in developing countries. Many organizations and governments are creating and implementing policies, programs, and practices toward reducing the number of girls who are not in school. They know that girls' education is a powerful means that will permit the achievements of other goals, such as the combat of poverty around the world. UNICEF (2015) affirms that "providing girls with an education helps break the cycle of poverty. . . . When all children have access to a quality education rooted in human rights and gender equality, it creates a ripple effect of opportunity that influences generations to come" (p. 1).

Millions of girls do not have the opportunity to attend school because of different barriers that derive from culture, religion, political, and economic reasons. Many communities believe that a girl is less valued in society and must be responsible for the household and families (some prioritizing marriage and pregnancy at early ages). Also, because of poverty, many families do not have access to enough food or water, giving priority to nourish exclusively boys instead of both boys and girls. And many communities around the world are suffering multiple oppressions by abusive regimes and terrorist groups.

When girls have access to education, they have a remarkably positive effect on their own lives and on their families and communities. They acquire the ability to remove multiple barriers and pursue other rights that will help society toward the achievement of social, cultural, political, and economic development. One example of a girl who discovered the beauty, magic, and importance of learning and developing knowledge is Malala Yousafzai. Malala is a girl that since her childhood has valued education, but when the Taliban started closing and bombing schools in Pakistan's Swat Valley, she experienced the real oppression of being threatened by a patriarchal and terroristic system that denies millions of girls access to education.

The objective of this chapter is to dive into Malala Yousafzai's life while analyzing her film, *He Named Me Malala,* from a film technique perspective. Moreover, we will look at her story, identifying how she finds her voice and creates her vision while giving leadership lessons during her tireless fight for the education rights of the millions of girls, first in Pakistan and later all around the world.

Film Analysis

When I was little, many people would say, "Change Malala's name. It's a bad name. It means 'sad.' " But my father would always say, "No, it has another meaning—'bravery.' "

—Yousafzai, as cited in Guggenheim, 2015

He Named Me Malala by David Guggenheim is a persuasive documentary with the purpose of addressing an extremely important social justice issue (Barsam & Monahan, 2016, p. 74): girls' right to education. The film depicts Malala Yousafzai's life story before and after she was attacked by a Taliban insurgent on her way to school. At the beginning of the film we are immersed in the story of Ziauddin's decision to name his daughter Malala after a Malalai of Maiwand, a female warrior from Afghanistan that encouraged her people to fight in a war in the nineteenth century. The story of this great female warrior is illustrated by the technique of animation, a type of motion picture that will help the audience dive into the story of Malala's family and her magic childhood (p. 111). The narrative of the film consists of a storytelling technique that contrasts images of animation, life action, old videos, and photographs that explain and delineate Malala's life. While using hand-drawn animation, the movie presents a beautiful mise-en-scène of the Swat Valley, with its rivers, mountains, and city, and concludes by influencing the audience's emotional response to Malala's life in Pakistan (p. 165). The multiple colorful scenes show the happiness of Malala's birth, then Malala as a baby living at her father's school, and later as a child that discovers her love for education. The film creates a magical environment around Malala's life, as if she had been born with a special objective and destiny around education.

The director, David Guggenheim, opts to present a story that is mainly focused on the relationship of daughter and father, and how this relationship creates a powerful value system in their family. In order to explain how Malala found her voice, the documentary begins by illustrating how Malala's father was capable of finding his voice, first as a child, later as teacher, and finally as an educational activist. In Ziauddin's words, "If you keep silent, you lose the right to exist" (as cited in Guggenheim, 2015). Ziauddin found himself to be an educator that believed and practiced equality. He explains, "Education is power. It is just a light in complete darkness" (*Daily Mail,*

2014). Malala's father truly believed that girls had the right to education, and he raised his daughter Malala according to this value.

To illustrate how Malala finds her voice, the film gracefully illustrates the environment and the family culture in which she was raised. Her father's school is the place where she discovered her love for education, even before being able to say her first words. A dynamic narrative cuts from the present to the past in a flashback (Barsam & Monahan, 2016, p. 497). The film presents Malala's story as a child and a teenager who becomes an educational activist that denounces Taliban terrorism in Pakistan. In continuously contrasting timelines, the film uses parallel techniques that encourage the audience to consider the similarities and the differences of the narrative and the scenes at different times in Malala's life (Pramaggiore & Wallis, 2011, p. 16). Through these techniques, Malala's past and present lives are constantly merging throughout the documentary.

In the present narrative of the film, we identify two parts of Malala's life. In one part, at home, we see Malala as a teenager living a happy life with her family, playing with her brothers, and studying for her tests. In the other part, we see the public figure of Malala as an international activist that visits girls around the world with the objective of inspiring them to study and raise their voices against injustice. She uses her powerful image to bring to the attention of the international community and global leaders the reality of millions of children around the world. Her image helps to fundraise for the Malala Fund, an organization that works for girls' education, to empower and unlock their potential, while raising their voices (Malala Fund, 2016).

The editing is the basic creative force in the film (Barsam & Monahan, 2016, p. 496), illustrating Malala's past and present lives in a very emotional way. Among the images of Malala's different realities we find scenarios of warfare illustrated by the editing of multiple videos, photos, and audios from that time. One of the most emotional parts of the film is when her father is narrating the time that Malala got shot. The director decided to use photos of the actual bus in which Malala was attacked, followed by images of a flashback reconstruction of Malala being taken to the hospital, first in Pakistan, and later in England. The scenes are presented with short shots that give close-ups and extreme close-ups of the hospital equipment and the intravenous tubes, followed by images in fast motion that accelerate the action during the scenes (p. 497). The fast motion also causes blurs in some frame transitions scenes in the hospital room, expressing the confusion and uncertainty of the time when Malala was in coma (p. 505).

Finally, during the film we can see how, from beginning to end, the director has decided to show images of Malala's present life, expressing the idea of her constant movement around the world. In many of the scenes in which she is traveling by car, we see multiple close-up shots of Malala looking out the window. These scenes are constantly communicating her pure and true emotions and feelings while creating proximity and connection with the audience.

Malala's Leadership Lessons

> This is where I will begin, but it is not where I will stop. I will continue this fight until I see every child in school.
>
> —Yousafzai, 2014

Looking at Malala's story, we identify how at the age of only 11 she was able to find her voice while identifying the injustice of an oppressive terrorist system. Following her love for education and her true belief that inequality should not be acceptable, and with the support of her father, Malala decided to denounce the Taliban organization. Burns (2003) explains that "the key distinctive role of leadership at the outset is that leaders take the initiative" (p. 172). Taking initiative and being willing to speak when others were afraid was what both Ziauddin and Malala decided to do, following their belief in freedom and human rights.

In Malala's practice of supporting girls' rights, she said, "In my heart was the belief that God would protect me. If I am speaking for my rights, for the rights of girls, I am not doing anything wrong. It's my duty to do so" (Yousafzai & Lamb, 2006, p. 141). In doing so, she showed bravery, commitment, and a great spirit of sacrifice. She knew that people were listening, and she decided to reprehend and challenge oppression. On national Pakistani radio, she questioned, "How dare the Taliban take away my basic right to education?" (p. 142). She knew that she was a target, but she also knew that showing her face and voice would inspire others to follow the path of denouncing the Taliban terror. Malala said, "I think of it often and imagine the scene clearly. Even if they come to kill me, I will tell them what they are trying to do is wrong, that education is our basic right" (Peer, 2012). Malala was afraid, but she refused to accept fear as a condition for her life. She embraced her call to leadership and decided to lead not from fear but from hope, faith, and love (Palmer, 2000).

Malala was exercising a real leadership practice. Amanda Sinclair (2007) once said, "Leadership should be aimed at helping to free people from oppressive structures, practices and habits encountered in societies and institutions, as well as within the shady recess of ourselves" (as cited in Jackson & Parry, 2008, p. xv). Sinclair recognized that she had a voice and a duty to society, and that she did not have to accept tradition or misuse of religion that justified an unjust system. She was already practicing a critical consciousness and a revolutionary leadership (Freire, 2000). Thus, she decided to use her words to remind others that they could and should also stand up in order to change things. About this idea Malala later says,

> We should not wait for someone else to come and raise our voice. We should do it by ourselves. We should believe in ourselves. Yes, we can do it. One day you will see that all the girls will be powerful; all the girls will be going to school. And it is possible only by our struggle; only when we raise our voice. (as cited in Nelson, 2013)

In 2011, when Malala was awarded with Pakistan's First National Youth Peace Prize in recognition of her peaceful activist work, the death threats increased, but even then she refused to keep silent. Malala said, "My feeling was nobody can stop death . . . so I should do whatever I want to do" (Yousafzai & Lamb, 2006, p. 224). On the 9th of October 2012, Malala was shot on her way to school. She fought to survive, and again showed her determination and persistence, now to be alive, and to continue to speak out for girls' right to education. Once Malala had recovered, she said, "It feels like this life is a second life. People prayed to God to spare me, and I was spared for a reason—to use my life for helping people" (p. 301). Her image as a miraculous survivor and a young hero who faced death in order to keep following her values and sense of justice traveled around the world. At the United Nations, Malala said,

> So here I stand, one girl among many. I speak not for myself, but for all girls and boys. I raise up my voice—not so that I can shout, but so that those without a voice can be heard. . . . They [the Taliban] thought that the bullets would silence us. But they failed. And then, out of that silence came, thousands of voices. The terrorists thought that they would change our aims and stop our ambitions[,] but nothing changed in my life except

this: Weakness, fear and hopelessness died. Strength, power and courage were born. I am the same Malala. My ambitions are the same. My hopes are the same. My dreams are the same. (Yousafzai, 2013)

Malala's dedication and devotion to others' needs shows that she is truly a servant-leader. Greenleaf (1977) says, "The servant leader is servant first. . . . It begins with the natural feeling that one wants to serve first" (p. 13). When she took the initiative to fight for the rights of the millions of girls, Malala was not only leading the way but also creating a vision, compelling millions of people to listen her message of a world without war, poverty, or injustice, where people would be more wise, more free, more autonomous, more healthy, and better able themselves to become servants (Greenleaf, 1977).

Malala's international advocacy creates a network that works in cooperation with local communities and activists. She uses her image to communicate different realities and needs, such as raising money to build schools, to pay teachers, and to create educational opportunities for girls around the world. Malala is creating a global movement to empower girls. Her leadership is based on her vision of empowering girls so that they can to stand up and speak for themselves, demanding their rights and not accepting oppression and violence. In her work visiting girls, especially in developing countries, Malala talks and listens to their dreams and needs, always hearing directly from the girls themselves. She does not assume she knows what they need; rather, she respects their differences and perspectives. Her relationship with people communicates empathy, simplicity, humility, and the recognition of her own and others' multiple vulnerabilities. Malala's practice of leadership is in the dynamics of listening, dialoguing, and guiding. It is dialogue that "does not impose [and] does not manipulate" (Freire, 2000, p. 168).

Conclusion

Malala shows ideals and practices that remind me of the circular power dynamics of leadership relations. She knows that she represents the voice and the power of millions of people around the world, people that also risk their lives in the fight for human rights. This is what the social justice movement is about. About a recognition that we, together, in a communion of values, can unite our power in this fight against oppression. Malala's love of education and people shows a unique authenticity that in today's world is not easy to find while looking at a single image. Watching the movie, I felt touched not only by her story but also by her incredible personality and the peaceful emotions that she is capable of communicating. For me, Malala is a genuine powerful and transversal example to us all. She is inspiring us all, from girls in developing countries to citizens listening to her speech to the political leaders that set our global goals and define our destinies.

In my experience working with women and for women, the most powerful leadership process in the fight for social justice is the one based on the idea of the collective way of leading in community. This is what I see in Malala's practice. She proposes an educational empowering process in which everybody is included, especially those that have always been excluded and oppressed. It is a collective work that looks to balance different perceptions and needs in a leadership that facilitates and coordinates, working together, not with one voice but with many, in cooperation and dialogue. As Malala said, "It is so hard to get things done in this world. You try and too often it doesn't work. But you have to continue. And you never give up" (as cited in Guggenheim, 2015). This is what Malala is inspiring us to do, to never give up.

References

Barsam, R., & Monahan, D. (2016). *Looking at movies: An introduction to film* (5th ed.). W. W. Norton & Company.

Burns, J. M. (2003). *Transforming leadership: A new pursuit of leadership*. Atlantic Monthly Press.

Freire, P. (2000). *Pedagogy of the oppressed*. Bloomsbury.

Greenleaf, R. (1977). *Servant leadership: A journey into the nature of legitimate power and greatness*. Paulist Press.

Guggenheim, D. (Director). (2015). *He named me Malala* [Film]. Fox Century.

Jackson, B., & Parry, K. (2008). *A very short, fairly interesting, and reasonably cheap book about studying leadership*. Sage.

London, B. (2014, June 12). My father Bill always made sure he was home for dinner every night: Chelsea Clinton, Richard Branson and Ziauddin Yousafzai—Malala's father—open up about their families ahead of Father's Day. *The Daily Mail United Kingdom*. http://www.dailymail.co.uk/femail/article-2656211/My-father-Bill-sure-home-dinner-night-Chelsea-Clinton-Richard-Branson-Ziauddin-Yousafzai-Malalas-father-open-families-ahead-Fathers-Day.html#ixzz44F84c32j

Malala Fund. (2016). About the fund. https://www.malala.org/about

Nelson, A. (2013, October). Malala reminds us that leadership comes in all shapes and sizes. *Forbes*. http://www.forbes.com/sites/skollworldforum/2013/10/11/malala-reminds-us-that-leadership-comes-in-all-shapes-and-sizes/#1a0809532ee5

Palmer, P. (2000). *Let your life speak: Listening for the voice of vocation*. Jossey-Bass.

Peer, B. (2012, October 10). The girl who wanted to go to school. *The New Yorker*. http://www.newyorker.com/news/news-desk/the-girl-who-wanted-to-go-to-school

Pramaggiore, M., & Wallis, T. (2011). *Film: A critical introduction*. Pearson.

United Nations. (1948). Universal declaration of human rights. http://www.un.org/en/universal-declaration-human-rights/index.html

The United Nations Children's Fund (UNICEF). (2015). Girls' education and gender equality. http://www.unicef.org/education/bege_70640.html

United Nations Educational, Scientific and Cultural Organization. (2016). The right to education. http://www.unesco.org/new/en/education/themes/leading-the-international-agenda/right-to-education/

Yousafzai, M. (July 12, 2013). Sixteenth birthday speech at the United Nations. https://malala.org/newsroom/archive/malala-un-speech

Yousafzai, M. (December 10, 2014). Nobel Peace Prize acceptance speech. https://malala.org/newsroom/archive/malala-nobel-speech

Yousafzai, M., & Lamb, C. (2006). *I am Malala. The girl who stood up for education and was shot by the Taliban*. Little, Brown & Company.

Chapter 11

An Evaluation of *Moonlight*'s Intersectional Pedagogy

How Does Identity Affect Leadership?

Matthew Williams

I grew up as a white, catholic, American, heterosexual male in a top 5% income household in a safe neighborhood, with some life-altering yet not terminal medical issues. Because of this privilege, I was able to focus on my unlimited education to the near exclusion of all else for the first two decades of my life, allowing me to fall in love with learning, with challenging intellectual discussions, with *magis,* and with *cura personalis.* Yet as my undergraduate career draws to a close, I find myself questioning how those circumstances affected what I learned, questioning if and how the self-awareness I thought I had gathered may have been misinformed. What obscured history, even from the past 100 years, have I been allowed to neglect through unconsciously following a dominant narrative educational system? The rioting response to the deaths of George Floyd, Ahmaud Arbery, and Breonna Taylor, among many other black people, at the hands of the police gives urgency to my search for stories and perspectives forced down by the dominant narrative's will to standardize and suppress (Sabur et al., 2020). Yet even as this critical moment in the fight for racial equality passes, I notice a failure of empathy, a failure to listen, a failure of self-awareness, a failure of servant-leadership among my white friends and family, myself included.

My social media feed fills with opinions and instructions of white people on how to best respond and be supportive of those struggling, while almost no one publicly admits to a lack of knowledge and even fewer openly show dedication to learning the perspectives hidden behind the media. Perhaps this seeming failure of the values of servant-leadership (which include listening, empathy, and awareness), and by extension servant-leadership itself (Greenleaf, 1977/2002), drives my interest in evaluating its limitations and capacity for effecting social change in situations of oppression through the 2016 film *Moonlight* (Jenkins).

A History of Race, Gender, and Sexuality in Hollywood

Moonlight (Jenkins, 2016) centers on the story of a queer black boy/man at three crucial, different stages in his lifetime (Little, Chiron, and Black), as he grapples with his sexuality growing up in a lower-class Miami neighborhood. Since its release, many have lauded the film as groundbreaking, but in order to understand how it dismantles the dominant narrative, we must explore the history of depictions of intersectionality on the silver screen. While constructions of gender, sexuality, and race have reflected and informed the opinions of the general public since the invention of film itself, the major stereotypical constructions of each facet of identity trace back to different time periods. As Bogle (1997) outlines, the most common representations of black people in film can be simplified down to five major stereotypes (a few with variations) that can be identified in film as early as Edwin S. Porter's 1903 *Uncle Tom's Cabin*. The tom is the persecuted yet faithful and submissive middle- to old-aged black man, most clearly identified by its namesake (Bogle, 1997), the Uncle Tom of *Uncle Tom's Cabin* (Porter, 1903), but also traceable in some of the roles of Sidney Poitier, such as John Prentice in *Guess Who's Coming to Dinner* (Kramer, 1967), and Danny Glover, such as Langston in *Sorry to Bother You* (Riley, 2018), where the stereotype is undermined quite effectively. The coon is the simple-minded, cowardly, buffoonish, amusing black person, often seen as either a pickaninny (i.e., the kid version; Bogle, 1997), in roles such as Prissy from *Gone with the Wind* (Fleming, 1939) and Topsy from *Uncle Tom's Cabin* (Porter, 1903), or the harmless, naïve, comical philosopher Uncle Remus (Bogle, 1997), undermined in Danny Glover's role in *To Sleep with Anger* (Burnett, 1990), but never more degrading than as the unreliable, crazy, good-for-nothing pure coon (Bogle, 1997), most clearly portrayed in Rastus from *How Rastus*

Got His Turkey (Wharton, 1910). The tragic mulatto was often featured as a young woman on her way to marriage with a white man but diverted at the last minute by the knowledge of her blackness (Bogle, 1997), seen most clearly in Peola from *Imitation of Life* (Stahl, 1934). The mammy comes in the form of the big, asexual, fiercely independent, middle-aged woman, most famously associated with the roles of Hattie McDaniel (Bogle, 1997), especially Mammy from *Gone with the Wind* (Fleming, 1939), yet also found in roles such as Delilah from *Imitation of Life* (Stahl, 1934). Lastly, but perhaps most pertinent to America's current political turmoil, the hypersexual, savage, violent, brutal black buck lusts exclusively and extremely for white women (Bogle, 1997), found most clearly in Gus and Silas Lynch from *The Birth of a Nation* (Griffith, 1915), which originated the stereotype. While some may be inclined to call the actors who engaged with such stereotypes sellouts for only going after roles that perpetuated stereotypes about them, it is important to acknowledge that the alternative of fighting the stereotyping often resulted in their Hollywood careers being destroyed, such as in the case of Butterfly McQueen. These stereotypes were not just a few of the available roles for Black people; they were the only roles available to black actors for the better part of the first century of narrative filmmaking and continue to pose difficulties to black actors and filmmakers looking for more complex representation (Bogle, 1997).

In contrast, queerness did not appear as a particular negative stereotype until the days of the Motion Picture Production Code, which expressly forbid "sex perversion or any inference to it" (Quigley & Lord, 1929, p. 595). While the earliest depictions of queerness on film are found in the Dickson Experimental Sound Film (Dickson, 1894), portraying two men dancing together, and in the pansy, sissy men and butch femme of silent comedies, films of precode Hollywood offered little in the way of progressive depictions of queer people, often opting to make fun of queers rather than openly attack or degrade them (Benshoff & Griffin, 2006; Ellis, 2019; Russo, 1987). However, after Quigley and Lord labeled depictions of homosexuality as contributory to the degradation of moral standards in society, Hollywood began to portray queers with much more subtle and open hostility. Throughout the years of the Production Code, filmmakers developed the technique of (queer)coding, in which filmmakers would use stereotypes of queer people to evoke queerness, which could slip past the Production Code Administration (Benshoff & Griffin, 2006; Ellis, 2019; Russo, 1987). Often filmmakers would specifically code their villains, so as to reinforce public association of queerness with villainy, evil, disgust, and so on, a practice seen quite blatantly in Disney films such as *One Hundred and One Dalmatians* (Reitherman et al., 1961) with Cruella de Vil, *Sleeping Beauty* (Geronimi et al., 1959) with Maleficent, and *Peter Pan* (Geronimi et al., 1953) with Captain Hook, as well as in Hitchcock films such as in *Rebecca* (Hitchcock, 1940), *Rope* (Hitchcock, 1948), *North by Northwest* (Hitchcock, 1959), and *Psycho* (Hitchcock, 1960) with Mrs. Danvers, Philip Morgan and Brandon Shaw, Philip Vandamm, and Norman Bates, respectively. Since the code's dismantling, stereotypes of queer people still exist in mainstream cinema but have taken on other forms, such as queerbaiting practices, where queer representation is hinted at but never explicitly confirmed, so as to not alienate more conservative audiences (Ellis, 2019), such as with Sherlock and Watson in *Sherlock* (Gatiss et al., 2010–2017) and Captain Marvel in *Avengers: Endgame* (Russo & Russo, 2019), and queercatching marketing techniques where queer characters are "confirmed" or "promoted" in marketing for films and books, only for the character in the text to lack any sort of meaningfully depicted queerness (Ellis, 2019), such as Dumbledore in the *Harry Potter* (Rowling, 1997–2007) franchise, Lefou in *Beauty and the Beast* (Condon, 2017), and Valkyrie in *Thor: Ragnarok* (Waititi, 2017). That said, the past 40 years have also shown new progress through the development of the indie film scene, in which many queer filmmakers have been able to portray their experiences more openly.

By contrast, the 20th and 21st centuries have shown more progression of LGBTQ and racial minority rights, more widespread acceptance of people who identify as LGBTQ or as a racial minority, and more openness around discussing such topics such as the legalization of gay marriage (Levy, 2019) or the civil rights movements and the current movement against police brutality (Sabur et al., 2020).

Intersectionality and Leadership Theory

Unfortunately, though, it appears that the inquest into leadership differences as a result of identity has been rather limited and misguided, as most theories tend to push for the universal approach and view of leadership over a specific approach and view. As of Jackson & Parry (2011), identity had primarily been used to refer to the characteristics or traits of a leader, and discussions about identity in the context of societal power relations seem to have extended only to gender difference. Watson & Johnson (2013) place leadership of people who identify as LGBTQ under the category of authentic leadership, suggesting that leading as a LGBTQ person is intrinsically tied to "knowing one's true self and acting in accord with that true self" (Jackson & Parry, 2011, p. 117). Parker (2005) presents a more promising construction of leadership that acknowledges the impact of intersectionality and calls for more inclusive frameworks and more diverse authors for leadership studies, yet her move to reenvision "21st Century leadership as meaning-centered" (p. xxiii) still pushes back toward a universal theory of leadership, gives more benefits to people who rank higher in the societal matrix of privilege by allowing them to reap knowledge from the less-privileged, and fails to acknowledge the dangers of cultural appropriation to less-privileged populations. Recent sociological studies on intersectionality, such as Kimball et al. (2018), provide more empirical insight into how less-privileged identities can coconstruct within people and how dangers that may apply to one identity or another can multiply in intensity alongside the coconstruction.

Servant-leadership is one of these models that is hailed as "universal," largely due to the perceived benefit it offers to practitioners through enacting its core values of listening, empathy, awareness, healing, love, commitment to the growth of people, and building community (Greenleaf, 1977/2002; Reynolds, 2014; Tilghman-Havens, 2018). While such practices may indeed prove beneficial to people of all backgrounds, the essence of how these theories teach people how to lead ultimately gives privileged people more to benefit from than those who live outside of the world of privilege, as "depending on the gender, race and social identity of the leader, servant-leadership may or may not be experienced as Greenleaf intended" (Tilghman-Havens, 2018, p. 104). Intriguingly though, while each provides solutions to this issue, both neglect to take into account the positionality of us, the authors of leadership theory, myself included, within the system of privilege, and how our positionality might make us rather unsuited to appreciate the dangers of our ideas, actions, and leadership theories for those whose intersectional identity places them outside of the dominant narrative (Tilghman-Havens, 2018; Reynolds, 2014). In "fixing" servant-leadership, both authors have failed to fully engage one of its core values, awareness. In other words, the picture of leadership of/for less privileged members of our society constructed by more privileged members of our society is not wrong but incomplete in its appreciation of the complex effects identity can have on leadership. Hence, by engaging the intersectionality of race, queerness, and disability in *Moonlight* (Jenkins, 2016), I hope to broaden the perspective on leadership of those outside our societal matrix of privilege.

A Quick Theoretical and Personal Note on Intersectionality

To address my concern for the intersectional identity of the author, I must elucidate my current place in our societal matrix of privilege and my own experiences of struggling with identity before I can effectively engage with *Moonlight* (Jenkins, 2016) as an intersectional text, fully recognizing that a white man's struggles is one of the last personal narratives the world needs to hear. For clarification on how to understand my intersectionality, the intersectionality of *Moonlight*'s characters, and the intersectionality of leadership itself, I offer the definition of *intersectionality* from Collins and Bilge (2020):

> Intersectionality investigates how intersecting power relations influence social relations across diverse societies as well as individual experiences in everyday life. As an analytic tool, intersectionality views categories of race, class, gender, sexuality, . . . , nation, ability, ethnicity, and age—among others—as interrelated and mutually shaping one another. Intersectionality is a way of understanding and explaining complexity in the world, in people, and in human experiences. (p. 4)

As I leave Gonzaga, one of the realizations I have come to is that my overcommitted lifestyle (math, film, ministry/spirituality, service, tutoring) has left a rather indelible mark on my body. While my own choices greatly affected the severity of this invisible mark, one of the few relatively unprivileged areas of my life, health/ability, offers a reason for concern. Around age four, my body became the host to a condition known as panhypopituitarism, a rare disorder according to the National Institute of Health, which affects people in rather subtle ways, fatigue being the most significant byproduct in my lifetime (Gounden & Jialal, 2020). I don't like to think of myself as *disabled* out of a combination of pride and not wanting to discredit the comparative impact other more severe conditions may have on the people who carry them, but I still recognize that when my friends respond to my statements of exhaustion by saying they "know the feeling," it is as ableist and empathetic as their lack of education on my condition allows them to muster. However, by ignoring my body's response to my overcommitted lifestyle and only affording it relief by taking shortcuts, I've found myself somewhere with uncertain roads backward or forward, a moment that may afford another climactic experience of finding myself through losing myself in a manner resonant with how Greenleaf (2013) interprets following the "guide . . . who only has at heart your getting lost" from Robert Frost's *Directive* (p. 24). This experience with my own body affords a personal interest in discussions of bodies in film and social justice.

However, if I am to give a more complete framework of my fascination with the film and social justice in question, I must also acknowledge the impact of my own queerness. While I have been fully aware of my bisexuality for the past 18 months and out for arguably 12 months, I have not yet fully unpacked the circumstances that led to the realization of my sexuality. I do, however, recognize that the most interesting part of my realization was that the initial feelings of attraction toward men that I had were primarily physical, almost animal, in spite of my body's inability to produce testosterone on its own (aka, one of the more significant hormones necessary in having a sex drive). Since my realization and coming out, I have also recognized that my "sexual awakening" brought about a fundamental change in the way I see the world, others, and myself. Furthermore, I find this perspective and confidence ever-changing as my attraction melds from person to person, and I continue to explore other gender- and sexuality-nonconforming aspects of myself.[1] Because of this limited experience with unprivileged identities, the primary foci of my analysis will be queerness and disability, yet I will attempt to engage with race as well. Importantly, as there are no white characters in the film, this will leave my analysis of the film incomplete, in accordance with my lack of experience of racial otherness and limited understanding of critical race theory and intersectionality.

Moonlight: The Call of Queerness

As many will recognize, one of *Moonlight*'s (Jenkins, 2016) most revolutionary moves is its engagement with the experience of black queerness. Van Leer (1997) comments that "African American culture [is] usually assumed to be heterosexual, and gay culture [is] usually thought to be white" (p. 158), assumptions informed by the stereotypes of race and queerness depicted on the silver screen, implying that to exist as both queer and black is a breach of social taboo. While *Moonlight* (Jenkins, 2016) combats this social taboo

---

1. While I no longer identify as Catholic or Christian, my belief system still carries heavy influences from such religions. However, *Moonlight*'s interaction with religion is rather minimal, so I will not go into detail on my intersectionality with religion.

through an assortment of choices, it is not the first nor the only film to do so (Walcott, 2019). Rather it is among the first to receive widespread acclaim and acceptance through a theater run that raked in $65.3 million at the box office, making back its $1.5 million budget nearly 45 times over (Box Office Mojo, 2017). The clearest and most centralized manner in which *Moonlight* (Jenkins, 2016) combats the social taboo of black queerness is through the identities of its main characters, Chiron and Kevin, both of whom are given a rather fluid and unlabeled sexuality by way of the film's three-act structure delineated across moments in their lives. Imbued with a hyperfocus on the characters through comprising 90% of the film's shots with close-ups and medium close-ups, Jenkins intentionally avoids the voyeurism to which such a narrative film might lend itself by focusing just as much on the specificity of the "cruelly beautiful" world Chiron lives in, ascribing to, in Jenkins words, "the theory that in order to be universal, you have to be specific" (as cited in Ventrella, 2016a). One might say that by avoiding such voyeurism, Jenkins has engaged the servant-leadership values of aware-ness and listening (Greenleaf, 1977/2002), as such cinematographic choices acknowledge a rise in voyeurism of police violence against black bodies and the greater negative impact it has upon people of color (Duong, 2020; Reign, 2016). While these broad strokes paint an identity-independent gateway to empathy for the audience, edging on a call for servant-leadership (Greenleaf, 1977/2002), a functional understanding of intersectionality clarifies that the film's leadership is not completely the work of empathy but the work of people whose experiences mirror those depicted in the film.

Moonlight's (Jenkins, 2016) call for empathy extends through many more subtle moments and references in the film, yet as we consider these filmmaking choices, we find the call also embeds itself within the intersec-tional identities of our characters. For example, the color blue pervades the film, and while one could understand and analyze the film on colors alone, at its most generic level, this blue is a baptism (Barsam & Monahan, 2019; Sasso, 2017). This baptism is visually appealed to most directly in the image that has come to epitomize the film, Juan teaching Little how to swim, both in water and in life (Jenkins, 2016; Ventrella, 2016b). We see the theme of baptism reappear in moments that highlight Little's solitude, such as when Chiron and Black wash their faces in two slightly different-toned blue-lit bathrooms and Little bathes himself, and in moments that highlight risk, such as when Kevin and Chiron first explore their sexuality on a beach under the moonlight, many of the costume choices of the second act, and the color of Chiron's school (Jenkins, 2016). Furthermore, the last shot of the film, in which Little looks back at us, bathed in moonlight, evokes the name of the source material (Ventrella, 2016b) and a story in which Juan told Little "In Moonlight, Black Boys Look Blue," suggesting that Chiron has found himself at last (Jenkins, 2016; Ventrella, 2016b). What turns this baptism into a call is the soundscape of the film. The sound of waves appears in many of the scenes mentioned above, as the opening to the film, when Black chooses whether to follow Kevin into his apartment, and is evoked in some of the more disorienting moments of the film for Chiron and the viewer, such as when the other kids pound on the doors of Little's hiding place and when Chiron runs into Paula trying to get back into the house to find money for drugs (Jenkins, 2016). Also, the main musical theme of the film becomes closely associated with Chiron finding himself, as it often plays over moments when Chiron is in a liminal or physically moving space, such as trains or cars, symbolizing Chiron's internal movements, as well as when he gets beat up on the high school grounds (Jenkins, 2016; Ventrella, 2016c). However, as we experience Chiron's baptism with full knowledge of his feelings at each evocation, it also baptizes us into queerness. By leading his audience into an experience of queerness, Barry Jenkins opens a vacuum in which the audience is asked to explore their own sexuality and gender, as opposed to just experiencing Chiron's sexuality. Similarly, entering into a relationship or leadership dynamic with a person who identifies as LGBTQ may cause us to find new aspects of our own sexuality and gender, not unlike how Greenleaf (1977/2002) calls us to self-awareness, but more specific.

Chiron's wandering nature, always trapped between who he is and who he needs to be to survive in his world, however, makes it clear that he knows himself even less than the audience does. Furthermore, while Chiron may practice more empathy and love than he thinks he does, particularly with regard to his mother's drug addictions, he lacks any coherent commitment to many other values of servant-leadership, such as building community, growth in people, and healing (Greenleaf, 1977/2002). In fact, throughout the entire film, only Juan, Kevin, and Teresa show some conception of servant-leadership, and the characteristics of servant-leadership are only shown when Chiron needs their guidance. Since Chiron is the only person in the world of the film who experiences love, empathy, and healing from those characters, we know that the term *servant-leader* would not be an appropriate way to label Juan, Kevin, or Teresa. While *Moonlight* (Jenkins, 2016) itself may be practicing and advocating some characteristics of servant-leadership through inviting its audience into an experience of empathy with characters who practice some characteristics of servant-leadership, the infrequent use of these characteristics and the complexity of its characters makes it clear that servant-leadership is too narrow a lens to describe the leadership with which *Moonlight* and its characters engage, necessitating another view of leadership that can encapsulate the complexity that can be imbued by queerness, race, and disability, namely a more intersectional view of leadership.

Perhaps even more significantly, *Moonlight's* (Jenkins, 2016) call stems from its characters' racial identities while minimizing the significance of race in the film's ability to connect with a "universal" audience. One could even argue that race is a defining aspect of the world, as the diner sequence is the only part of the film in which white people make an appearance. Additionally, throughout the film, Jenkins minimizes even the mention of race by constraining commentary on possible experiences of racism to one-liners, such as when Paula mentions that she "ain't seen [Teresa] since the funeral," implying that it was Juan's funeral and raising the question of how he died. Essentially, Jenkins is interested in presenting an experience of queerness within a world that is black rather than examining blackness within a world that is queer (see *The Watermelon Woman* for an examination of the latter; Dunye, 1996), normalizing race in a manner rarely seen on film. This normalization of race affords Jenkins an escape from the racial stereotypes of old Hollywood because many of the racial stereotypes observed by Bogle (1997) are defined by the character's relationship to white people. While race is not as centralized as queerness in *Moonlight* (Jenkins, 2016), the film still executes leadership affected by black skin through treating it similarly to how almost all films have treated white skin, a move made radical by the lack of critically and commercially acclaimed films preceding it that have done so and made possible by the work put into color toning the film so that people may appreciate the nuances and beauty of black skin in a previously unseen way (Barsam & Monahan, 2019). This move can also clue us into how servant-leadership is/can be *universal*, namely that it functions so more in its effect than its use. In the case of *Moonlight*, Jenkins (2016) has created characters with which anyone can empathize, yet it was his own blackness and access to friends who identify as queer and black that allowed him to create such a specific world, and it may be that people who identify with one or more of Chiron's identities find something more specific to empathize with or critique (Walcott, 2019). Though the film is undoubtedly self-aware in a manner befitting servant-leadership (Greenleaf, 1977/2002), the self-awareness is intrinsically tied to its interest in telling a story about black queerness, the identity of our characters. Hence, servant-leadership is broad enough to describe the leadership *Moonlight* engages and advocates yet not specific enough to capture the nuance of Jenkins's work.

By all appearances, Chiron as a teenager is not a leader. As Sasso (2017) notes, the frequent yellow lighting in this section and plaid yellow shirts Chiron wears emphasize his lack of courage, his cowardice, something most people would not list among the traits of a leader. He does not stand up to his bullies for most of the second act, and makes no effort to act on any of his potential queer desires until at least the climax of the act in the scene with Kevin on the beach (Jenkins, 2016). On the beach, Kevin controls the entire interaction. When Chiron says something truthful, Kevin's always one step ahead of him with his retorts, and when they move in for a more erotic invitation, Kevin clearly remains in control by cradling Chiron's head in his hand and arm, and giving Chiron a hand job with his other hand. Many people interpret this scene as confirmation of Chiron's gayness, when in fact all this scene confirms is Kevin's interest in guys, as Chiron is just following his lead. When we get the haunting line from Black toward the end of the film, "You're the only one who's ever touched me," it mainly serves to confirm that their previous sexual encounter was significant for Chiron, yet one can also read the line as one of Chiron's few acts of true leadership, opening up in a self-aware, love-driven way. Both moments are certainly directed and acted well enough to give no indication of whether Chiron ever even thought of the moment on the beach as consensual.

In contrast, both the second act beach scene and the sequence in the diner and Kevin's apartment feature Kevin listening, empathizing, loving, and serving Chiron in prime form (Greenleaf, 1977/2002). His forward snipes are playful and loving, clearly trying to get Chiron to open up, and when he offers comments such as "that breeze feel good as hell, man" or "feels so good it make me want to cry" (Jenkins, 2016), it's clear that he's trying to help Chiron open up, to help Chiron heal, to help Chiron make himself whole. Kevin also knows enough of Chiron to know when to press hard, such as his comments in the diner and in his apartment of "Who is you, Chiron?" and "That ain't you, Chiron," and when to be softer and more open, such as the beach scene and after Chiron confesses, "You're the only one who's ever touched me" (Jenkins, 2016). Even Kevin beating Chiron up on the school grounds could be seen as teaching Chiron to stand up for himself, in a manner not quite congruent with servant-leadership. Importantly, though, Jenkins never shows us inside Kevin's house, so we never really know what makes him tougher and Chiron softer, but nonetheless, it's clear that Kevin shows up when Chiron needs him in a manner that can be largely understood through servant-leadership. With servant-leadership, one can understand how Kevin is a leader for Chiron, but with intersectionality, one can understand why Kevin is such an effective leader for Chiron. Kevin serves Chiron with empathy made effective because they are both black queer guys in a poor neighborhood, which tells Chiron that Kevin knows what he goes through as much as anyone. Kevin's own self-awareness and confidence effectively help Chiron to become more self-aware because Kevin is already sure of himself as a black queer guy. Kevin heals Chiron effectively through their sexual encounters because his knowledge of the difficulties of being a queer black guy also tells him what Chiron needs. Thus Kevin's leadership shows us another way in which intersectionality can fill out a picture that servant-leadership might be able to start.

Furthermore, by requiring Chiron to open up in order to complete his journey of self-discovery, the film provides an equally significant opportunity to see intersectional experiences become an even more relevant measure for leadership than servant-leadership. While Kevin is a leader for Chiron, the emphasis on Chiron's point of view throughout these events makes Chiron a leader for the audience. The lack of confirmation around Chiron's sexuality gives the audience a vacuum to imprint onto and examine their own sexual and gender identity within the context of the film, evoking once more the awareness of a servant-leader (Greenleaf, 1977/2002; Tilghman-Havens, 2018). We find this style of leadership tied to sexuality perhaps most often during adolescence and college, when people start to reach sexual awareness (Zhu & Chan, 2017). When this happens, those who physically and sexually mature more slowly can become social outsiders due to a physically different appearance or lack of sexual interest, which, especially in smaller communities, can lead to others around them imprinting a sexual identity onto them and using the sexually unmatured to explore their own sexuality, either mentally or physically. Think of the people whose love interests everyone supposedly "knew" before they did. Did that attraction ever genuinely come from the person himself, herself, or themselves, or was there a component of everyone wanting to see what it would be like (i.e., if and how the sexually unmatured would fail) if the sexually unmatured person was attracted to such a person? This complicates the leadership dynamic because the sexually unmatured person is the one affecting others, yet they may not be doing so of their own volition. While they are leading others to awareness and healing (Greenleaf, 1977/2002; Jackson & Parry, 2011; Reynolds, 2014; Tilghman-Havens, 2018), the sexually unmatured person can often end up more confused and hurt than they were before the interaction, not to mention the dangers of nonconsensual sexual interactions, which increase with intensity of the sexual imprinting. If the interaction is not bringing healing to all, can we truly call it servant-leadership on the part of the sexually unmatured person?

This concept of the sexually unmatured allows us to enter a discussion of the co-construction of disability and queerness in leadership, as delayed physical sexual maturity can often become a disability, in either a medical or functional sense. The classic film joke to prove someone's gay, since at least the time of *Midnight Cowboy* (Schlesinger, 1969), is a failed sexual encounter/arousal by a member of the opposite sex, giving us the history/basis for viewing sexual immaturity as a functional disability when portrayed on the silver screen. While I commend Jenkins for his avoidance of a very clichéd and outdated joke, disability remains one of the relatively unexplored categories in *Moonlight* (Jenkins, 2016), only really ever being hinted at a few times throughout the movie. One could argue Chiron has an implicit functional disability in his lack of sexual activity and lack of control when he finally engages sexually, but the evidence is less compelling for us to think of any lack of sexual maturity in Chiron as a disability. To the exceedingly sexually mature person, manipulating the vacuum I described previously can be an easy process. Thus, the only way we can truly think of sexual immaturity as a functional disability is if there is some psychological or physical impedance to engaging in sexually mature interactions, which does not apply to Chiron, as we are given no reason to think his lack of sexual activity amounts to anything more than cowardice in the second act. However, we are given enough evidence to think of Little and Black as functionally disabled in this way. Little is made functionally disabled in a very physical manner in the locker room scene of the first act, which implies that Little has smaller sex organs than the other boys in the room, that he has not started puberty yet. However, Black's functional disability is clearly more mental, brought on by trauma through the lasting effects of being sexually aroused, then attacked by Kevin in high school. Rather than make his own identity and name for himself, Black has taken on the nickname Kevin gave him in high school, and we also learn that he has never been with anyone else. Exacerbated slightly from what medical studies have concluded to be the impact of late sexual maturity (Zhu & Chan, 2017), the reappearance of the color yellow in gradually less subtle ways clarifies the mental block Black has constructed around his traumatic interactions with Kevin in high school specifically, but more widely in the chance for any sexual interaction to be successful. Because of this mental block in conjunction with his traumatic memories of Kevin, Black continues to fear that any sexual interaction he has will result in physical pain for him; hence his functional disability of being mentally impeded from sexual interactions. Considering the whole film, the amount of exploration of sexuality and disability coconstructing one another may be lacking, but where it does appear, Jenkins (2016) gives a fairly accurate, functional exploration.

Where disability affects queerness within an intersectional construction of leadership can be mapped across four continua proposed by Kimball et al. (2018) of queer ideals, queer performativity, punishment, and intersectionality. Their description of the four continua follows as such:

> First, students expressed *queer ideals* which reflected diverse thinking about, and rejection/adoption of, restrictive gender and sexual norms, binaries, and labels. For some students, this continuum was theoretical, while for others, it was personal. The second *queer performativity* continuum encompassed the different ways students enacted their gender and sexuality *queer ideals* through everyday language and behavior. The third continuum represents varying levels of concern regarding *punishment* when adopting *queer ideals* and engaging in *queer performativity*. The fourth *intersectionality* continuum explicates variations in student propensity to discuss and/or reflect upon their single and/or intersecting gender, sexual, and disability identities as intersectional (e.g., mutually constituting, reinforcing). (Kimball et al., 2018, para 18; emphasis in source)

Depending on the person, placement along and engagement with each continua can vary, which further clarifies the need to specify a theory of intersectional leadership beyond the umbrellas of authentic leadership or servant-leadership, as the first two continua (and arguably the fourth) are the only areas in which we see the constructive ideals of such leadership theories embodied. In fact, the third continuum regarding *punishment* gives reason to question the extent to which authentic leadership or servant-leadership alone are viable leadership methods for people who identify as LGBTQ and disabled, as it suggests that many queer and disabled people have reason to not strive for self-awareness and that self-advocacy may not always bring healing, to name a few examples of how "servant-leadership may or may not be experienced as Greenleaf intended" (Tilghman-Havens, 2018, p. 104). When someone's very identity can destroy their efficacy and reputation as a leader, can you really blame them for ignoring or not emphasizing those parts of their personality to be able to sustain their ability to lead others? Solomon (2017) takes this one step further to frame this sense of hiding for self-protection as the central thematic concern of *Moonlight*'s title, suggesting that "to moonlight is to pretend to be something [one] is not" (para 28). By the spectra across each of the four categories, we find that disability enhances the complexity of queer experiences and increases the subtlety in evaluating intersectional leadership, as it removes the need for a person to act in a queer manner or to universally publicly identify as queer in order to practice leadership pertaining to their identity as queer.

Furthermore, we can map many of the categories proposed by Kimball et al. (2018) as generated by the intersection of disability and queerness onto the intersection of race and queerness and observe Chiron act in ways that intersect with each category. After Little asks Juan about the f-slur, we can feel that the question of how he identifies is always on his mind, which would be significant under any circumstances, but is made much more pressing by living within a largely heterosexual black world (Jenkins, 2016). In Chiron and Black, we get a couple of instances of the characters engaging in queer behavior, but for the most part, fear of getting beaten up or hurt by his black schoolmates or drug dealers due to engaging his queer side causes him to suppress his queerness. Furthermore, we can recognize these as a result of the intersection between Little/Chiron/Black's queerness and race because the type of disability he has is very functional and temporary, whereas the primary manner in which disability and queerness coconstruct each other is when the disability is more permanent and life controlling. In *Moonlight*, Little/Chiron/Black's race is the permanent and life-controlling aspect of his identity, so it is the primary part of his identity that coconstructs with his queerness. However, because race is more a part of the setting of the film rather than specific to Chiron, most of the race-affected leadership is occurring across the film, rather than just in Chiron's character. Obviously, much more nuance exists around the impact of race on leadership, but given my personal lack of experience with race as a social barrier, I find myself unqualified to comment further on lessons of queer leadership intersected with race as found in *Moonlight*.

Conclusion

In the introduction to his inaugural book on servant-leadership, Greenleaf (1977/2002) offers several concerns about servant-leadership, of which the most pertinent to my concerns is "for the individual in society and his or her seeming bent to deal with the massive problems of our times wholly in terms of systems, ideologies, and movements" (p. 19). While his recognition that systems, ideologies, and movements are made by and up of people, and that personal improvement is at least as important as and often a predecessor for societal change, are certainly true, his concern remains embedded in an one-way understanding of the leadership dynamic wherein the leader affects society, ignoring the effects that society may have on the leader. Intersectionality complicates this one-dimensional view of leadership by asserting that one's identity affects one's place in society, which impacts the person in a unique manner, even if that person is a leader (Parker, 2005). While it has not entered discussions of intersectionality yet as having a significant impact on one's experience of the world and justice system, geopolitical location could be considered as another aspect of intersectionality, especially in the world of today's protests, where we see a wide variety of police response to protests.

One can find many insights about servant-leadership and intersectional leadership in *Moonlight's* (Jenkins, 2016) exploration of queerness, race, functional disability, and, beyond the scope of this paper, class and masculinity. By evoking an intersectional, coconstructed queerness through a well-balanced flow between vacuums and baptisms of fluid sexuality pertaining so many different identities, *Moonlight* calls out for us to search for the "queer within us all," just as any effective, intersectional leader identifying as queer would do. While the experience of queerness is the primary focus of *Moonlight*, ignoring the impact of racial identity of *Moonlight's* characters in their experience of queerness oversimplifies the levels of fear, loneliness, and discrimination in the lives of its main characters. Indeed, the chapter is limited in addressing the impact of race in *Moonlight* by the knowledge and identity of its author. Furthermore, to leaders or scholars of leadership who engage with the text, *Moonlight* offers the opportunity to examine their own practices and assumptions about leadership, to see if there may be virtue to viewing and learning from intersectional leadership as its own style.

References

Barsam, R., & Monahan, D. (2019). *Looking at movies: An introduction to film* (6th ed.). W. W. Norton & Company, Inc.

Benshoff, H. M., & Griffin, S. (2006). *Queer images: A history of gay and lesbian film in America*. Rowman & Littlefield Publishers, Inc.

Bogle, D. (1997). Black beginnings: From *Uncle Tom's Cabin* to *The Birth of a Nation*. In V. Smith (Ed.), *Representing blackness: Issues in film and video* (pp. 13–24). Rutgers University Press.

Box Office Mojo. (2017, July 13). *Moonlight*. https://www.boxofficemojo.com/title/tt 4975722/?ref_=bo_se_r_1

Burnett, C. (Director). (1990). *To sleep with anger* [Film]. The Samuel Goldwyn Company.

Collins, P. H., & Bilge, S. (2020). *Intersectionality*. Polity Press.

Condon, B. (Director). (2017). *Beauty and the beast*. Walt Disney Pictures; Mandeville Films.

Dickson, W. (Director). (1894). *The Dickson experimental sound film* [Film]. Thomas A. Edison, Inc.

Dunye, C. (Director). (1996). *The watermelon woman* [Film]. First Run Features.

Duong, D. (2020, June 12,). Videos of shootings are a "sick sort of voyeurism," can cause PTSD. *Healthing.Ca*. https://www.healthing.ca/mental-health/somatics-how-watching-trauma-manifests-in-your-body

Ellis, R. (2019, Jan 30). *The evolution of queerbaiting: From queercoding to queercatching* [Video]. YouTube. https://www.youtube.com/watch?v=riKVQjZK1z8&t=1775s

Fleming, V. (Director). (1939). *Gone with the wind* [Film]. Selznick International Pictures; Metro Goldwyn-Mayer.

Gatiss, M., Moffat, S., Vertue, B., Eaton, R., Jones, B., & Vertue, S. (Executive producers). (2010–2017). *Sherlock*. Hartswood Films; BBC Wales; WGBH.

Geronimi, C., Jackson, W., & Luske, H. (Directors). (1953). *Peter Pan* [Film]. Walt Disney Productions.

Geronimi, C., Larson, E., Reitherman, W., & Clark, L. (Directors). (1959). *Sleeping beauty* [Film]. Walt Disney Productions.

Gounden, V., & Jialal, I. (2020, February 24). Hypopituitarism (panhypopituitarism). In StatPearls Publishing (Ed.), *StatPearls*. StatPearls Publishing. https://www.ncbi.nlm.nih.gov/books/NBK470414/

Greenleaf, R. K. (2002). *Servant leadership: A journey into the nature of legitimate power and greatness* (L. C. Spears, Ed.; 25th anniversary ed.). Paulist Press. (Original work published 1977)

Greenleaf, R. K. (2013). An inward journey. *International Journal of Servant Leadership, 8/9*(1), 23–36.

Griffith, D. W. (Director). (1915). *The birth of a nation* [Film]. David W. Griffith Corp.

Hitchcock, A. (Director). (1940). *Rebecca* [Film]. Selznick International Pictures.

Hitchcock, A. (Director). (1948). *Rope* [Film]. Transatlantic Pictures.

Hitchcock, A. (Director). (1959). *North by northwest* [Film]. Metro-Goldwyn-Mayer.

Hitchcock, A. (Director). (1960). *Psycho* [Film]. Shamley Productions.

Jackson, B., & Parry, K. (2011). *A very short, fairly interesting and reasonably cheap book about studying leadership* (2nd ed.). Sage Publications.

222 | Matthew Williams

Jenkins, B. (Director). (2016). Moonlight [Film]. A24; Plan B Entertainment; Pastel Productions.

Kimball, E., Vaccaro, A., Tissi-Gassoway, N., Bobot, S. D., Newman, B. M., Moore, A., & Troiano, P. F. (2018). Gender, sexuality & (dis)ability: Queer perspectives on the experiences of students with disabilities. Disability Studies Quarterly, 38(2). https://dsq-sds.org/article/view/5937/4907

Kramer, S. (Director). (1967). Guess who's coming to dinner [Film]. Columbia Pictures.

Levy, M. (2019, June 20). Gay rights movement. Encyclopædia Britannica. https://www.britannica.com/topic/gay-rights-movement

Parker, P. S. (2005). Race, gender, and leadership: Re-envisioning organizational leadership from the perspectives of African American women executives. Lawrence Erlbaum Associates.

Porter, E. S. (Director). (1903). Uncle Tom's cabin [Film]. Edison Manufacturing Company.

Quigley, M., & Lord, D. A., S. J. (1929). The motion picture production code. https://www.asu.edu/courses/fms200s/total-readings/MotionPictureProductionCode.pdf

Reign, A. (2016, July 6). Why I will not share the video of Alton Sterling's death. The Washington Post. https://www.washingtonpost.com/posteverything/wp/2016/07/06/why-i-will-not-share-the-video-of-alton-sterlings-death/

Reitherman, W., Luske, H., & Geronimi, C. (Directors). (1961). One hundred and one dalmatians [Film]. Walt Disney Productions.

Reynolds, K. (2014). Servant-leadership: A feminist perspective. The International Journal of Servant-Leadership, 10(1), 35–63.

Riley, B. (Director). (2018). Sorry to bother you [Film]. Significant Productions; MNM Creative; MACRO; Cinereach; The Space Program; Annapurna Pictures.

Rowling, J. K. (1997–2007). Harry potter (Vols. 1–7). Bloomsbury Publishing; Scholastic Press; Pottermore.

Russo, A., & Russo, J. (Directors). (2019). Avengers: Endgame. Marvel Studios.

Russo, V. (1987). The celluloid closet: Homosexuality in the movies (Revised ed.). Harper & Row Publishers, Inc.

Sabur, R., Sawer, P., & Milward, D. (2020, June 8). Why are there protests over the death of George Floyd? The Telegraph. https://www.telegraph.co.uk/news/0/us-america-riots-george-floyd-death-protests/

Sasso, A. T. (2017, April 14). "Moonlight": A story told with color. ReelRundown. https://reelrundown.com/movies/Moonlight-A-Story-Told-with-Color

Schlesinger, J. (Director). (1969). Midnight cowboy [Film]. Jerome Hellman Productions.

Solomon, E. (2017, April 26). Loving-moonlight(ing): Cinema in the breach. Southern Spaces. https://doi.org/10.18737/M75M3F

Stahl, J. M. (Director). (1934). Imitation of Life [Film]. Universal Pictures.

Tilghman-Havens, J. (2018). The will to (share) power: Privilege, positionality, and the servant-leader. *International Journal of Servant Leadership, 12*(1), 87–128.

Van Leer, D. (1997). Spectatorship in black gay and lesbian film. In V. Smith (Ed.), *Representing blackness: Issues in film and video* (pp. 157–181). Rutgers University Press.

Ventrella, P. (Producer). (2016a). *Cruel beauty: Filming in Miami* [Video/DVD]. A24.

Ventrella, P. (Producer). (2016b). *Ensemble of emotion: The making of moonlight* [Video/DVD]. A24.

Ventrella, P. (Producer). (2016c). *Poetry through collaboration: The music of moonlight* [Video/DVD]. A24.

Waititi, T. (Director). (2017). *Thor: Ragnarok*. Marvel Studios.

Walcott, R. (2019). Moonlight's necessary company. *GLQ, 25*(2), 337–341. https://doi.org/10.1215/10642684-7367792

Watson, L. W., & Johnson, J. M. (2013). *Authentic leadership: An engaged discussion of LGBTQ work as culturally relevant*. IAP.

Wharton, T. (Director). (1910). *How Rastus got his turkey* [Film]. Pathé Frères.

Zhu, J., & Chan, Y. (2017). Adult consequences of self-limited delayed puberty. *Pediatrics, 139*(6), Article e20163177. https://doi.org/10.1542/peds.2016-3177

Chapter 12

The Leadership Philosophy of Mary Parker Follett (1868–1933)

JUDY I. CALDWELL AND CAROLYN CRIPPEN

Who ever has struck fire out of me, aroused me to action which I should not otherwise have taken, he has been my leader.

—Follett, 1918/1998, p. 230

The current study used qualitative historical analysis methodology to investigate systematically whether there was evidence of servant-leadership competencies in Mary Parker Follett's work and life. Although Follett conducted her work approximately 100 years ago, many of her ideas, such as win-win, power-over versus power-with, and conflict resolution, would be considered leading edge today. In fact, Bennis (2003) argued, "Just about everything written today about leadership and organizations comes from Mary Parker Follett's writings and lectures" (p. 178), and Drucker (2003) referred to her as the "prophet of management" (p. 9). Despite the importance of Follett's work to the study of leadership, management theory, business, and education, no one has yet formally investigated her leadership philosophy. This was the purpose of the present study. To this end, a biographical profile of Follett was created using primary and secondary sources. This profile was then examined for evidence of the seven pillars and 21 core competencies of servant-leadership as outlined by Sipe and Frick (2009).

A Brief Overview of Mary Parker Follett's Life

Follett was born in 1868 in Quincy, Massachusetts, to a middle-class family (Tonn, 2003). As her parents had the resources, she was able to attend elite schools that many of her peers were not. At the age of 24 years, she enrolled in Radcliffe College, the women's branch of Harvard University. At Radcliffe, she received instruction from notable Harvard scholars, including William James and Albert Bushnell Hart. Her areas of study were economics, law, government, and philosophy. In 1898 she graduated from Radcliffe with the highest distinction. Her undergraduate paper, titled "The Speaker of the House of Representatives," earned her considerable acclaim and established her as a scholar (P. Graham, 2003).

From 1900 to 1908, Follett devoted her energies to social work in Roxbury, a poor neighbourhood of Boston. Realizing that people in the community needed a place to socialize, she introduced the idea of leaving schools open in the evening to serve as social gathering places. Eventually, the community centers began to include programs in vocational counseling and placement. The project became national, and Follett was viewed as a leader in the movement.

It was this work in the community that helped form her views on politics (P. Graham, 2003). In 1918, she published her second book, titled *The New State: Group Organization the Solution of Popular Government* (republished in 1998), which critically examined government, democracy, and the role of the community.

In 1924, Follett published her third book, *Creative Experience* (republished in 2013), which focused on group process and interaction. Follett believed that by working in groups, the inherent talents of every individual are tapped; that group dynamics release the full potential of the individual. According to Follett, the purpose of working in groups is to uncover the collective thought, and so the outcome of group processes is something "new" that would not have otherwise been created.

During the 1920s, some of Follett's greatest followers were in the world of business. She was often asked to give lectures to businessmen and to serve as a business consultant. These lectures became some of her best-known works. In 1942, Metcalf and Urwick published a collection of her speeches posthumously in a book titled *Dynamic Administration: The Collected Papers of Mary Parker Follett* (republished in 2013).

In 1926, Follett's long-time companion, Isobel Briggs, died. Follett was devastated and moved to London for both work and companionship.

In December 1933, while visiting Boston, she became ill and died there in the hospital. She was 65 (P. Graham, 2003).

Servant-Leadership

Robert Greenleaf (1904–1990) coined the term *servant-leadership* in his 1970 essay titled *The Servant as Leader*. Greenleaf (1970/1991) defined *servant-leadership* as follows:

> The servant-leader is servant first. . . . It begins with the natural feeling that one wants to serve, to serve first. Then conscious choice brings one to aspire to lead. . . . The difference manifests itself in the care taken by the servant first to make sure that other people's highest priority needs are being served. The best test, and difficult to administer, is: do those served grow as persons; do they, while being served, become healthier, wiser, freer, more autonomous, more likely themselves to become servants? And, what is the effect on the least privileged in society; will they benefit, or, at least, not be further deprived? (p. 15)

Although Greenleaf first introduced the philosophy of servant-leadership, it was Larry Spears that continued Greenleaf's legacy by editing and coediting numerous books on servant-leadership, and writing countless articles, essays, and reviews on the topic (Spears & Lawrence, 2004). Spears (1998, 2004) identified in Greenleaf's writings 10 characteristics of servant-leadership: listening, empathy, awareness, healing, persuasion, conceptualization, foresight, stewardship, commitment to the growth of others, and building community.

More recently, Sipe and Frick (2009) introduced seven pillars (and 21 core competencies) of servant-leadership. They define a servant-leader as "a *person of character* who *puts people first*. He or she is a *skilled communicator*, a *compassionate collaborator* who has *foresight*, is a *systems thinker*, and *leads with moral authority*" (p. 4; emphasis in source). The seven italicized characteristics in the definition above refer to the seven pillars of servant-leadership, and they are, with their corresponding core competencies, presented below.

Pillar I. A Person of Character—A Servant-Leader makes insightful, ethical, and principled decisions.

1. Maintains Integrity

2. Demonstrates Humility

3. Serves a Higher Purpose (Sipe & Frick, 2009, p. 15)

Pillar II. Puts People First—A Servant-Leader helps others meet their highest priority development needs.

1. Display a Servant's Heart

2. Is Mentor-Minded

3. Shows Care & Concern (p. 34)

Pillar III. Skilled Communicator—A Servant-Leader listens earnestly and speaks effectively.

1. Demonstrates Empathy

2. Invites Feedback

3. Communicates Persuasively (p. 45)

Pillar IV. Compassionate Collaborator—A Servant-Leader strengthens relationships, supports diversity, and creates a culture of collaboration.

1. Expresses Appreciation

2. Builds Teams & Communities

3. Negotiates Conflict (p. 77)

Pillar V. Foresight—A Servant-Leader imagines possibilities, anticipates the future, and proceeds with clarity of purpose.

1. Visionary

2. Displays Creativity

3. Takes Courageous, Decisive Action (p. 104)

Pillar VI. Systems Thinker—A Servant-Leader thinks and acts strategically, leads change effectively, and balances the whole with the sum of its parts.

1. Comfortable with Complexity

2. Demonstrates Adaptability

3. Considers the "Greater Good" (p. 130)

Pillar VII. Moral Authority—A Servant-Leader is worthy of respect, manages change effectively, and establishes quality standards for performance.

1. Accepts and Delegates Responsibility

2. Shares Power and Control

3. Creates a Culture of Accountability (p. 155)

Recently, numerous researchers have been investigating servant-leadership characteristics to see if they are evident in the work and lives of prominent individuals. For example, Crippen and Nagel (2013) used the case study method to investigate whether there was evidence of servant-leadership in sport. The research participants were two elite NHL hockey players, Henrik and Daniel Sedin of the Vancouver Canucks. The researchers collected their data using face-to-face interviews. The participants' responses were then compared to Sipe and Frick's (2009) seven pillars of servant-leadership. Based on their analysis, Crippen and Nagel (2013) concluded that the Sedin brothers did indeed demonstrate the seven pillars of servant-leadership.

Negron (2012), using the case-study method, examined whether servant-leadership characteristics were applicable in a for-profit setting, that is, in a proprietary institution of higher education. Negron (2012) conducted the study as an interpretive biography. To this end, he carried out in-depth interviews with the research subject and 13 of his colleagues, peers, and employees. He also examined secondary sources, including the research subject's curriculum vitae, records, and articles. In examining the themes that emerged from the data, Negron (2012) concluded that servant-leadership can be effective in a proprietary institution of higher education, but that more evidence was required to determine whether "servant leadership can address needs in for-profit organizations related to competitiveness and firm decision-making" (p. iv).

Crippen (2004) used qualitative methods to conduct historical analyses of biographical profiles of three pioneer women in Winnipeg, Manitoba. Using various primary and secondary sources, profiles of the lives of the women were created. These profiles were then compared to the 10 characteristics of servant-leadership identified by Spears (1998). Crippen (2004) found evidence of servant-leadership characteristics in the lives of all three women, that the call to leadership came early in their lives, and that they "served their communities first, and it was through their service they became recognized as leaders" (p. xi).

It is interesting that despite the importance of Follett's ideas for contemporary thought on leadership, and her clear contributions to leadership study, no one has yet investigated the type of leader that she was. The current study thus fills an important gap in the literature on leadership theory. First, it adds to a growing number of recent publications involving Mary Parker Follett that are beginning to give a voice to an important female scholar who was all but forgotten in leadership circles only a couple of decades ago. Second, it adds to the growing field of servant-leadership by investigating the servant-leadership characteristics of an important scholar who did her work a century ago. In doing so, it contributes to those studies that have analyzed servant-leadership competencies in individuals in various leadership roles, such as those discussed above (i.e., Crippen, 2004; Crippen & Nagel, 2013; Negron, 2012).

Methodology

Qualitative Historical Analysis

As an individual's behaviors are shaped throughout life by cultural, historical, and personal forces, an examination of Follett's servant-leadership characteristics required an in-depth analysis of her life experiences. Thus, following Crippen (2004), the current study used the qualitative historical analysis method to build a biographical sketch of Mary Parker Follett, in the aim of answering the following research question: is there evidence of servant-leadership characteristics in the work and life of Mary Parker Follett?

According to Maykut and Morehouse (1994), "The goal of qualitative research is to discover patterns which emerge after close observation, careful documentation, and thoughtful analysis of the research topic" (p. 21). Qualitative methods should be employed if the researcher is searching for patterns in the aim of understanding a given person, situation, or phenomenon, and the following assumptions are made: multiple realities exist and they are sociopsychologically constructed, events are mutually and simultaneously shaped, and the goal of the research is discovery (Maykut & Morehouse, 1994).

Other researchers have conducted similar analyses of servant-leadership characteristics in prominent leaders but have instead used the case study method (for example, see Crippen & Nagel, 2013; Haitt, 2010; Negron, 2012; Omoh, 2007). A case study is a qualitative research strategy "in which the researcher develops an in-depth analysis of a case, often a program, event activity, process, or one or more individuals" (Creswell, 2014, p. 14). According to Yin (2009), case studies are used to

> contribute to our knowledge of individual, group, organization, social, political and related phenomena . . . the distinctive need for case studies arises out of the desire to understand complex social phenomena. In brief, the case study method allows investigators to retain the holistic and meaningful characteristics of real-life events. (p. 4)

Unlike previous studies that have used the case study method to investigate servant-leadership characteristics in prominent leaders, the current study used a historical analysis to investigate whether there are servant-leadership competencies evident in Follett's work and life. Yin (2009) discussed the difference between these two types of methodology. Specifically, the historical method is used "when no relevant persons are alive to report, even retrospectively, what occurred and when an investigator must rely on primary documents, secondary documents, and cultural and physical artifacts as the main source of evidence" (p. 11). Case studies, in contrast, can use a variety of evidence, including "documents, artifacts, interviews and observations—beyond what might be available in a conventional historical study" (p. 11).

In the current study, with the primary investigator's own background and beliefs directing the analysis, an interpretation of Follett's leadership philosophy was uncovered from primary and secondary sources. The primary sources used were Follett's major writings, including *The New State: Group Organization the Solution of Popular Government*, *Creative Experience*, and *Dynamic Administration: The Collected Papers of Mary Parker Follett*, edited by Metcalf and Urwick and published posthumously, and the secondary source used was the comprehensive biography of Mary Follett, written by Joan Tonn (2003) and titled *Follett P. Follett: Creating Democracy, Transforming Management*.

The biographical analysis consisted of a two-step process. First, the biographical sketch of Follett's work and life was examined for:

    a. The most significant personal, social, and political events that shaped her leadership philosophy.

    b. Comments, behaviour, and/or events that indicated either directly or indirectly servant-leadership characteristics. The information gathered was then compared to the seven pillars and 21 competencies of servant-leadership put forward by Sipe and Frick (2009).

Second, Follett's writings were divided into key themes, and these themes were examined for evidence of Sipe and Frick's (2009) seven pillars and 21 competencies of servant-leadership. Finally, conclusions relating to Follett's leadership philosophy were presented.

The reason for using Sipe and Frick's (2009) framework in this analysis, as opposed to Spears's (1998, 2004) 10 characteristics, was twofold. First, in 2004, Frick authored Greenleaf's comprehensive biography and was therefore given access to all of Greenleaf's writings and other related documents (Crippen & Nagel, 2013). Second, following Crippen and Nagel (2013), it was decided that Sipe and Frick's framework was not only more recent than Spears's framework but was also "deeper and broader in scope" (p. 5).

It is important to note that for ethical considerations, it was essential that the authors avoid reporting only results that were consistent with the hypothesis under investigation (Creswell, 2013). Thus, results that were both consistent and inconsistent with evidence of servant-leadership competencies in Mary Parker Follett's work were sought and reported.

Findings

Themes in Follett's Writings

As Follett's ideas held amazingly constant over time, it was easy to see major themes in her writing throughout her entire career. Some of the themes that emerged included group process, power-with versus power-over, conflict resolution/constructive conflict, control/authority, the role of the individual in the community, circular response, and the law of the situation. The themes that emerged were examined for evidence of servant-leadership as defined by the seven pillars and 21 competencies of servant-leadership put forward by Sipe and Frick (2009). The findings, divided by pillar, are presented below.

Pillar I: A Person of Character

> All that I am, all that life has made me, every past experience that
> I have had—woven into the tissue of my life—I must give to the
> new experience.
>
> —Follett, 1924/2013a, p. 136

In Follett's writings it is evident that she placed a great deal of importance on character and integrity in business. For example, she stated,

> I see no reason why business men should have lower ideals than
> artists or professional men. . . . I think that we may feel that
> business men can make as large a contribution to professional
> ideals as the so-called learned professions. I think, indeed, that
> the business man has opportunities to lead the world in an
> enlarged conception of the expressions "professional honour,"
> "professional integrity." That phrase which we hear so often,
> "business integrity," is already being extended to mean far more
> than a square deal in a trade. (Follett, 1942/2013b, p. 143)

Follett (1942/2013b) also spoke of loyalty to one's work. She argued that in business, "the ideal is loyalty to the work rather than to the company," and that the businessman "may change his firm; but he remains permanently bound to the standards of his profession" (p. 136). She argued that loyalty was about "sticking to professional standards instead of merely giving the public what it wants" (p. 137). She also addressed corporate responsibility, arguing that businesses have a responsibility "for maintenance of standards, for the education of the public, and for the development of professional standards" (p. 136).

Also falling under Pillar I, Follett (1942/2013b) spoke of leaders serving a higher purpose. For example, she argued that business, through management style, could contribute to overall culture: "You need not . . . give your daytime hours to a low thing called business, and in the evening pursue culture. Through your business itself, if you manage it with style, you are making a contribution to the culture of the world" (p. 140), and further, that "leaders of the highest type do not conceive their task merely as that of *fulfilling* purpose, but also that of finding ever larger purposes to fulfill, more fundamental values to be reached" (p. 288).

Moreover, Follett's views on influencing others clearly demonstrated an ethical approach, with her arguing that power should be shared (power-with) rather than coercive (power-over): "Coercive power is the curse of the universe; coactive power, the enrichment and advancement of every human soul" (Follett, 1924/2013a, p. xiii). Follett's views on power will be further elaborated upon in the section discussing Pillar VII, moral authority.

Follett was also clearly serving a higher purpose in her work in the community, such as in her contribution to the community centers movement and her work with vocational counseling and placement. A specific example is seen in her arguments for safety in the workplace:

> In our attempts at social legislation we have been appealing chiefly to the altruism of people: women and children ought not to be overworked, it is cruel not to have machinery safeguarded, etc. But our growing sense of unity is fast bringing us to a realization that all these things are for the good of ourselves too, for the entire community. (as cited in Tonn, 2003, p. 276)

Pillar II: Puts People First

> The person who influences me most is not he who does great deeds but he who makes me feel I can do great deeds.
>
> —Follett, 1918/1998, p. 230

There is a great deal of evidence in Follett's writings demonstrating the competencies described by Sipe and Frick (2009) under Pillar II. For example, she clearly saw the need to put people first: "What we care about is the *productive* life, and the first test of the productive power of the collective life is its nourishment of the individual" (Follett, 1924/2013a, p. xiii). Follett (1942/2013b) acknowledged the importance of treating employees fairly, and argued that such fair treatment was an essential part of a successful organization: "Business management includes: (1) on the technical side, as it is usually called, a knowledge of production and distribution, and (2) on the personnel side, a knowledge of how to deal fairly and fruitfully with one's fellows" (pp. 122–123). Follett was a humanist writing at a time when the prevailing view of business and organization was increasingly mechanistic in nature. Counter to Frederick Taylor and the dehumanizing goals of scientific management, Follett (1942/2013b) argued "that we can never wholly separate the human and the mechanical problem . . . the study of human relations in business and the study of the technique of operating are bound up together" (p. 124). She further stated that people are central to any organization, and that we should

> un-departmentalize our thinking in regard to every problem that comes to us. . . . I do not think we have psychological and ethical and economic problems. We have human problems with psychological, ethical, and economic aspects, and as many more as you like. (p. 184)

Under Taylor's scientific management theory, employee empowerment was not a priority, which caused issue for Follett. She argued that institutions of the time were founded on a philosophy that "did not mean the development of individuals but the crushing of individuals—all but a few" (Follett, 1918/1998, p. 170). Instead, Follett (1942/2013b) was concerned about the education and empowerment of employees:

> It is one of the leader's chief duties to draw out from each his fullest possibilities. The foreman should feel responsible for the education and training of those under him, the heads of departments should feel the same, and so all along up the line to the chief executive. (p. 267)

She further argued,

> The best type of leader to-day does not want men who are subservient to him, those who render him a passive obedience. He is trying to develop men exactly the opposite of this, men themselves with mastery, and such men will give his own leadership worth and power. (p. 267)

Evidence of her view of leader as servant can also be found in her writings:

> The test of a foreman now is not how good he is at bossing, but how little bossing he has to do because of the training of his

men and the organization of their work. The job of a foreman thus conceived, we have . . . a leader not ordering his men, but serving his man. (p. 274)

Follett not only wrote about leader as servant but also demonstrated it in the way she ran the community centers. Specifically, she realized that for the long-term success of the centers, self-governance was essential, and so the best individuals for the task would be those that could teach young people about self-management. These leaders would be able to teach young people

how to win self-government, to train them in the ways of self-direction. . . . He is not the best manager who imposes the most progressive ideas on his district—he is the best manager who guides the people of his district to express and develop the best in themselves. (Follett, as cited in Tonn, 2003, pp. 240–241)

Once management was in place in any of her projects, she stepped away and allowed the program to run itself: "Each project, no matter how dear to her heart, was eventually turned over to a capable colleague. If a crisis arose, Follett could be counted on to help . . . but Follett most often restricted her involvement to offering praise and encouragement" (Tonn, 2003, p. 228).

Follett was also an inspiring mentor: "Follett honed her formidable entrepreneurial, political, managerial, and fundraising skills and became an inspiring mentor to a new generation of Boston civic leaders" (Tonn, 2003, p. 5). Tonn (2003) also stated that "many who listened to Follett found themselves coaxed to a larger vision of their role in society—and then inspired by her passion to a program of action" (p. 2). It is evident here that Follett exemplified many of the core competencies of Pillar II: she clearly demonstrated a servant heart, was mentor minded, and showed care and concern.

Follett, however, made comments on service that may at first seem contrary to Greenleaf's (1970/1991) philosophy of servant-leadership and thus inconsistent with the current hypothesis under investigation. In *The New State*, Follett (1918/1998) stated,

I do not believe that man should "serve his fellow-men"; if we started on that task what awful prigs we should become. Moreover, as we see that the only efficient people are the servers, much of the connotation of humility has gone out of the word service! Moreover, if service is such a very desirable thing, then every one must have an equal opportunity for service. (pp. 84–85)

Greenleaf (1970/1991) argued that the best test of servant-leadership was to ask the question,

Do those served grow as persons; do they, while being served, become healthier, wiser, freer, more autonomous, more likely themselves to become servants? And what is the effect on the least privileged in society; will they benefit, or, at least, not be further deprived? (p. 15)

Follett surely believed in service in this regard, as witnessed throughout her biography and in her writings. She believed in empowering others so that they could become their best possible selves and, in turn, become servants who empower others. It is evident that what Follett meant by the above comment was that leaders should not simply relinquish whom they are in order to serve others. Instead, every individual, both leader and follower, should bring what they have to offer to the situation, that subordination does not mean "subordination of the individual to 'others' . . . it means the subordination of the individual to the whole of which he himself is a part" (Follett, 1918/1998, p. 82).

Pillar III: Skilled Communicator

Discussion is to be the sharpest, most effective political tool of the future.

—Follett, 1918/1998, p. 212

Greenleaf (1970/1991) argued that "only a true natural servant automatically responds to any problem by listening *first*" (p. 18). There is evidence in Follett's biography that she was a true listener. Tonn (2003) shared a comment from a colleague of Follett's who stated that Follett "would talk to anyone who cared to talk to her and she would really listen. She was continuously testing her ideas against the facts brought to light as the results of these countless conversations" (p. 2).

Follett was also effective in clearly sharing her ideas. In terms of her communication skills in action, Tonn (2003) wrote, "Her plainness faded as soon as she spoke. The warmth of her voice, the elegant gestures of her hands, her stylish wit, and her attentive listening were irresistible" (p. 2). Tonn (2003) further stated that Follett "could illuminate for any audience the most complex concepts with homely, unforgettable metaphors drawn from the minutiae of daily life" (p. 2):

> Even as a young woman, Follett had been able to captivate an audience. Not only was she bright and articulate, but she also found ways to make both her message and her presentation compelling. She challenged her listeners to see the larger significance of day-to-day issues—placing them in philosophical, political, economic, and social context—and, at the same time, she was remarkably adept at illustrating difficult concepts or principles in anecdotes that her audience could easily grasp and appreciate. (p. 243)

Follett was also said to be very persuasive in her writing. For instance, a colleague argued that Follett

> reasons with such strength and clearness, and fortifies her position with so many illustrative facts, that a large part of her readers will accept her statements as the whole of the case and her conclusions as the end of the whole matter. (as cited in Tonn, 2003, p. 86)

The importance she put on communication can also be seen in her writings. Follett (1918/1998) referred to the idea of discussion as "truth-seeking." She stated that in true discussion, you can see how others' ideas can enrich your own, "In a discussion you can be flexible, you can try experiments, you can grow as the group grows" (p. 210).

Follett (1918/1998) suggested that one of the advantages of genuine discussion "is that it tends to make us think and to seek accurate information in order to be able to think and to think clearly" and that it also helps us to "overcome misunderstanding and conquer prejudice" (pp. 210–211). According to Follett, true discussion

> will always and should always bring out difference, but at the same time it teaches us what to do with difference. The formative process which takes place in discussion is that unceasing reciprocal adjustment which brings out and gives form to truth. (p. 212)

Pillar IV: Compassionate Collaborator

> The potentialities of the individual remain potentialities until they are
> released by group life.
>
> —Follett, 1918/1998, p. 6

Follett (1918/1998) saw the individual as a social being. She argued that through group life the individual finds identity, meaning, and purpose. She disagreed with many of her colleagues at the time who believed that "individuals are more rational, more innovative, and more productive working alone than when joined with others in a group" (Tonn, 2003, p. 274). Follett instead argued that people tend to bring their best when working in a group, anticipating the psychological concept of social facilitation (Tonn, 2003).

Follett's (1918/1998) passion for unity and the building of communities was evident in her work with the community centers. It was through these centers that she felt communities could be built and the political landscape could be changed:

> Political progress must be by local communities. Our municipal
> life will be just as strong as the strength of its parts. We shall
> never know how to be one of a nation until we are one of a
> neighborhood. And what better training for world organization
> can each man receive than for neighbors to live together not as
> detached individuals but as a true community? (p. 202)

According to Greenleaf (1977/2002), in order to build communities what was needed was "enough servant-leaders to show the way, not by mass movements, but by each servant-leader demonstrating his or her own unlimited liability for a quite specific community-related group" (p. 53). It is clear from Follett's life's work that she did her part in this regard.

In terms of negotiating conflict, many of the current views on conflict resolution can be traced to Follett. Follett (1942/2013b) did not shy away from conflict and, in fact, believed that it could lead "to invention" and "to the emergence of new values" (p. 36). She discussed three ways of dealing with conflict: domination, compromise, and integration. In the case of domination, no one wins; there is "non-freedom for both sides, the defeated bound to the victor, the victor bound to the false situation thus created—both bound" (Follett, 1924/2013a, pp. 301–302).

In the case of compromise, both sides give up some aspect of their desire, leading to the conflict not being fully resolved and thus resurfacing at some later point in time:

> If we only get compromise, the conflict will come up again and again in some other form, for in compromise we give up part of our desire, and because we shall not be content to rest there, sometime we shall try to get the whole of our desire. (Follett, 1942/2013b, p. 35)

The most desirable way of dealing with conflict, according to Follett, is integration, which involves the weaving into the solution the desires and interests of all parties involved. Here, a solution is found at the expense of no one. Follett (1942/2013b) stated that in order to achieve integration, all pertinent information needs to be brought into the open; the desires of both sides need to be fully uncovered. That is, full opportunity "needs to be given in any conflict, in any coming together of different desire, for the whole field of desire to be viewed" (p. 39). However, she acknowledged the complexity in achieving integration in conflict situations. Specifically, she stated that the main obstacle to integration is that it "requires a high order of intelligence, keen perception and discrimination, more than all, a brilliant inventiveness" (p. 45).

Follett (1942/2013b) further argued that we should not feel limited by an either-or approach:

> Our outlook is narrowed, our activity is restricted, our chances of business success largely diminished when our thinking is con-strained within the limits of what has been called an either-or situation. We should never allow ourselves to be bullied by an "either-or." There is often the possibility of something better than either of two given alternatives. (p. 49)

Instead, we need to be directed by the situation:

> My solution is to depersonalize the giving of orders, to unite all concerned in a study of the situation, to discover the law of the situation and obey that. Until we do this I do not think we shall have the most successful business administration. (p. 58)

Moreover,

> One person should not give orders to another person, but both should agree to take their orders from the situation. If orders are simply part of the situation, the question of someone giving and someone receiving does not come up. Both accept the orders given by the situation. (p. 59)

This, she stated, is "the best preparation for integration in the matter of orders or in anything else . . . a joint study of the situation" (p. 61). To Follett, integrative unity was key:

> I think on every board, in every committee, the same effort should be made, namely, to substitute conferring for fighting, to recognize that there are two kinds of difference, the difference which disrupts and the differences which may, if properly handled, more firmly unite, and to realize that if unity is the aim of conference, it is not because unity in the sense of peace is our primary object— you can get peace at any moment if your sledge hammer is big enough—but because we are seeking an integrative unity as the foundation of business development. (pp. 76–77)

Follett's view on the sharing of power will be continued below in the in the section covering Pillar VII, moral authority.

Also relevant to Pillar IV is the fact that Follett (1924/2013a) was a great supporter of diversity and considered it life's "most essential feature" (p. 301). In fact, she argued that "fear of difference is dread of life itself" (p. 301). Follett believed that diversity in times of conflict was the root of great ideas, "Our 'opponents' are our co-creators, for they have something to give which we have not. The basis of all cooperative activity is integrated diversity" (p. 174), she wrote, and we should "seek a richly diversified experience where every difference strengthens and reinforces the other" (p. 302). It is through diversity that Follett (1918/1998) believed unity would be attained: "Unity, not uniformity, must be our aim. We attain unity only through variety. Differences must be integrated, not annihilated, nor absorbed" (p. 39) and so, "instead of shutting out what is different, we should welcome it because it is different and through its difference will make a richer content of life" (p. 40).

Pillar V: Foresight

> The lamp of experience is both to illumine our way and to guide us
> further into new paths.
>
> —Follett, 1924/2013a, p. 230

Greenleaf (1977/2002) wrote,

> Leaders know some things and foresee some things that those
> they are presuming to lead do not know or foresee as clearly.
> This is partly what gives leaders their "lead," what puts them
> out ahead and qualifies them to show the way. (p. 35)

Follett was clearly a leader in this regard; she had clear views on what needed
to be done to change government, and she shared many of these ideas in *The
New State*. Specifically, Follett (1918/1998) imagined a unified government
that was concerned about every individual and not just the majority. She
did not believe that unity could be attained until the government moved
beyond a focus on votes:

> Democracy is not brute numbers; it is a genuine union of true
> individuals. The question before the American people to-day
> is—How is that genuine union to be attained, how is the true
> individual to be discovered? The party has always ignored him;
> it wants merely a crowd, a preponderance of votes. (pp. 5–6)

Also, in *The New State*, Follett (1918/1998) voiced her opinion on
how the political landscape could be changed through group association,
that is, through the community center movement:

> Our proposal is that people should organize themselves into
> neighborhood groups to express their daily life, to bring to the
> surface the needs, desires and aspirations of that life, that these
> needs should become the substance of politics, and that these
> neighborhood groups should become the recognized political
> unit. (p. 192)

She also stated,

Representation is not the main fact of political life; the main concern of politics is modes of association. We do not want the rule of the many or the few; we must find that method of political procedure by which majority and minority ideas may be so closely interwoven that we are truly ruled by the will of the whole. We shall have democracy only when we learn to produce this will through group organization—when young men are no longer lectured to on democracy, but when they are made into the stuff of democracy. (p. 147)

Like Greenleaf (1970/1991, 1977/2002), Follett (1942/2013b) was also aware of the importance of vision in leadership. She stated that the

most successful leader of all is one who sees another picture not yet actualized. He sees the things which belong in his present picture but which are not yet there. Indeed, the kind of insight which is also foresight is essential to leadership. (pp. 279–280)

She further argued that we should look to a leader to "open up new paths, new opportunities for the development of individuals, of groups, of the whole plant" and that great leaders "see not only larger situations, but situations of greater value to all concerned" (p. 265).

Also relevant to Pillar V is the fact that Follett knew how to take clear and decisive action when problems arose. According to Tonn (2003), "When a problem presented itself, she was eager to develop an action plan and was resolute about getting things accomplished" (p. 3). This decisive action can be seen in her service work in the community.

Follett was clearly visionary. This is most evident in the fact that many of her ideas, which were leading edge at the time, are still relevant today, including her ideas of power-with versus power-over (discussed below in the in the section covering Pillar VII, moral authority) and conflict resolution (which was discussed above under Pillar IV, compassionate collaborator).

There is also no question that Follett was a courageous woman, moving against traditional female roles by writing and speaking about politics and other social matters at a time in history when women were not even permitted to vote. What is even more incredible is that the ideas that she shared were very highly regarded in circles, such as business, that were dominated by men.

Pillar VI: Systems Thinker

> To live gloriously is to change undauntedly.
>
> —Follett, 1918/1998, p. 99

Follett was clearly comfortable with complexity. In forming her ideas, Follett drew from various systems of thought that were gaining popularity at the time, including behaviorism, Gestalt psychology and psychoanalysis. This ability likely grew from her academic years with such powerful mentors as A. B. Hart. However, according to Tonn (2003), she "did not ally herself with a single school but freely borrowed from the various systems those ideas that seemed most relevant to her concern with the constructive uses of conflict" (p. 364).

Follett (1924/2013a) could also see the complexity in human relations. Her concept of the circular response is a powerful one:

> I never react to you but to you-plus-me; or to be more accurate, it is I-plus-you reacting to you-plus-me. "I" can never influence "you" because you have already influenced me; that is, in the very process of meeting, by the very process of meeting, we both become something different. It begins even before we meet, in the anticipation of meeting. (pp. 62–63)

Further, Follett (1942/2013b), being influenced by the Gestalt school, saw the importance of balancing the whole with the sum of its parts, which she combined with her idea of the circular response:

> I have been saying that the whole is determined not only by its constituents, but by their relation to one another. I now say that the whole is determined also by the relation of whole and parts. Nowhere do we see this principle more clearly at work than in business administration. Production policy, sales policy, financial policy, personnel policy, influence one another, but the general business policy which is being created by the interweaving of these policies is all the time, even while it is in the making, influencing production, sales financial, and personnel policies. Or put it the other way round—the various departmental policies

are being influenced by general policy while they are making general policy. (p. 195)

In fact, Parker (1984) argued that Follett's ideas contributed to the founding of the systems theory of organization. Her ideas relating to the systems school of thought are summarized nicely in the following:

> She accepted the need for organisms to exercise self-control and hence advocated that executives should manage with their fellow workers, should be allowed to self-adjust, and that organizations should allow collective, self-control. In addition, she saw the organizations as being pluralistic (rather than stressing authoritarian, hierarchical control) and stressed two-way feedback of information as well as both lateral and vertical coordination of controls. . . . She recognized control as a continuous process rather than as a static function, and she emphasized her belief in focusing primarily on the operation of the whole system (e.g., the organization) rather than on its parts in isolation from one another. Furthermore, she stressed the interaction of individuals and groups with their environment. (pp. 743–744)

Follett's (1918/1998) complexity of thinking can also be seen in her views on how true democracy should be achieved:

> We do not want the rule of the many or the few; we must find that method of political procedure by which majority and minority ideas may be so closely interwoven that we are truly ruled by the whole. We shall have democracy only when we learn to produce this will through group organization. (p. 147)

She argued that democracy is found through the group; that people need to move away from individualism and toward group process, what she called "the new principle of association" (p. 3):

> The group process contains the secret of collective life, it is the key to democracy, it is the master lesson for every individual to learn, it is our chief hope for the political, the social, the internal life of our future. (p. 23)

Pillar VII: Moral Authority

> The best leader knows how to make his followers actually feel power themselves, not merely acknowledge his power.
>
> —Follett, 1942/2013b, p. 290

As with the first six pillars, Follett demonstrated the core competencies listed under Pillar VII. Follett (1918/1998) believed that everyone has a responsibility to their community, their city, and their country; that everyone fails to benefit when someone is not doing their part:

> The taking of responsibility, each according to his capacity, each according to his function in the whole . . . this taking of responsibility is usually the most vital matter in the life of every human being, just as the allotting of responsibility is the most important part of business administration. (Follett, 1942/2013b, p. 64)

She further argued that through neighborhood organization, responsibility could be developed, that "men will learn that they are not to *influence* politics through their local groups, they are to *be* politics" (Follett, 1918/1998, p. 240), and, further, that by performing their humblest duties, they are "creating the soul of this great democracy" (p. 242).

Also relevant to Pillar VII, Follett (1942/2013b) argued that we should be accountable for our own mistakes:

> The one who made the mistake should certainly be the one to rectify it, not as a matter of strategy, but because it is better for him too. It is better for all of us not only to acknowledge our mistakes, but to do something about them. (p. 68)

In terms of sharing power, Follett was an early voice emphasizing the idea of power-with rather than power-over. She introduced these terms in *Creative Experience* when stating that "genuine power is power-with, pseudo power, power-over" (Follett, 1924/2013a, p. 189). In fact, Follett argued that "the power of the strong is not to be used to conquer the weaker: this means for the conquerors activity which is not legitimately based, which will therefore have disastrous consequences later; and for the conquered, repression" (p. 189). Consistent with Follett's views on power, Greenleaf

(1977/2002) argued that the efficacy of coercive power lasts only as long as the coercion is strong and, further, that coercion will ultimately diminish an individual's autonomy.

Instead of coercive power, Follett (1942/2013b) argued for the decentralization of authority; that "authority is inherent in the situation" (p. 150) and not attached to any official position. That is,

> authority should go with knowledge and experience; that that is where obedience is due, no matter whether it is up the line or down the line. Where knowledge and experience are located, there . . . you have the key man to the situation. (p. 148)

In other words, "Authority belongs to the job and stays with the job" (p. 149). The idea of total authority was foreign to her. Instead, she argued in favor of functional authority, where each person has the final authority for his or her own tasks. She further stated,

> This conception of authority and responsibility should do away . . . with the idea almost universally held that the president delegates authority and responsibility. . . . I do not think that the president or general manager should have any more authority than goes with his function. (pp. 148–149)

As discussed above under Pillar IV, Follett (1924/2013a) argued in favor of a nonhierarchical authority; that true power comes not from authority but from integration:

> The only possible way of getting rid of the greed and scramble of our present world is for all of us to realize that the power we are snatching at is not really power, not that which we are really seeking, that the way to gain genuine power, even that which we ourselves really want, is by an integrative process. (p. 188)

Further, that because integration is

> the basic law of life, orders should be the composite conclusion of those who give and those who receive them; more than this, that they should be the integration of the people concerned and the situation; more even than this, that they should be the

integrations involved in the evolving situation. If you accept my three fundamental statements on this subject; (1) that the order should be the law of the situation; (2) that the situation is always evolving; (3) that orders should involve circular not linear behavior—then we see that our old conception of orders has somewhat changed, and that there should therefore follow definite changes in business practice. (Follett, 1942/2013b, pp. 65–66)

Under Pillar VII, Sipe and Frick (2009) also stated the importance of managing change. Follett wrote extensively about change; specifically, she believed that the true leader is the situation, and that this situation is constantly evolving. This can be seen in the previous quote as well as in the following: "The best type of leader does not seek *his* ends, but the ends disclosed by an evolving process in which each has his special part" (Follett, 1942/2013b, p. 288).

Follett and Transformational versus Servant-Leadership

Some may, in reading Follett's work and biography, argue that instead of demonstrating servant-leadership, she embodied transformational leadership. In fact, Follett did allude to the concept of transformational leadership long before Burns (1978) formulated, and Bass (1985) expanded upon, the model. In both transformational and servant-leadership the needs, values, and empowerment of followers is essential. However, an important difference between transformational and servant-leaders is what each considers to be the highest priority. In transformational leadership, the leader serves himself/herself and/or the organization first: "The primary allegiance of the transformational leader is clearly to the organization (or to themselves) rather than to follower autonomy or to universal moral principles" (J. Graham, 1991, p. 110). In this case, the "individualized consideration and intellectual stimulation of the followers . . . help tap the creativity of followers for solving organizational problems and serving organizational purposes" (p. 111). In the case of servant-leadership, the primary allegiance is to the employee, as "the leader humbly serves the led, rather than expecting to be served by them" (p. 111); the servant-leader's highest priority is seeing that the needs of others are being met. Follett's (1942/2013b) transformational views can be seen in the following:

When you have made your employees feel that they are in some sense partners in the business, they do not improve the quality of their work, save waste in time and material, because of the Golden Rule, but because their interests are the same as yours. . . . We find, however, that when there is some feeling in a plant, more or less developed, that the business is a working unit, we find then that the workman is more careful of material, that he saves time in lost motions, in talking over annoyances, that he helps the new hand by explaining things to him, that he helps the fellow working at his side by calling attention to the end of a roll on the machine, etc. (p. 82)

However, we are going to argue that there is evidence in Follett's writing suggesting that her leadership philosophy moved beyond transformational leadership and into the realm of servant-leadership. As discussed above, an important difference between transformational and servant-leadership is that with the former, the primary allegiance is to the company, with the empowerment of employees serving the needs of the organization. With servant-leadership, the primary allegiance is to the employee; a servant-leader's highest priority is seeing that the needs of followers are being met (J. Graham, 1991). The importance that Follett (1942/2013b) places on fulfilling the needs of the individual can be seen in the following:

Group activity, organized group activity, should aim: to incorporate and express the desires, the experience, the ideals of the individual members of the group: also to raise the ideals, broaden the experience, deepen the desires of the individual members of the group. Obedience in relation to leadership can be discussed only in terms of these two aspects of the group process. From a study of this process we see that leadership rightly understood increases freedom as it heightens individuality. (p. 275)

Furthermore, it is not only individual growth that Follett (1942/2013b) viewed as central to leadership; she also considered human relations a higher priority than the needs of the organization:

They may be making useful products; in addition to that they may be helping the individuals in their employ to further development; but even beyond all these things, by helping in solving the problems of organization, they are helping to solve the problems of human relations, and that is certainly the greatest task man has been given on this planet. (p. 269)

She further stated, "To me the chief function, the real service, of business [is] to give an opportunity for individual development through the better organization of human relationships" (pp. 140–141).

Summary

As discussed at length in the findings section of this chapter, there is significant evidence of Sipe and Frick's (2009) seven pillars and 21 core competencies of servant-leadership in Follett's work and life. Specifically, in examining both her biographical profile and the themes in her writing it is evident that Follett was a woman of character, put people first, was a skilled communicator, was a compassionate collaborator, had foresight, was a systems thinker, and demonstrated moral authority.

What is interesting is that Follett demonstrated these competencies at a time prior to the formulation of the model of servant-leadership by Greenleaf (1970/1991). In fact, Greenleaf's essay outlining the philosophy of servant-leadership was published almost four decades after Follett's passing. This demonstrates that a woman living and working during the turn of the twentieth century was able to embody the characteristics of a model of leadership that had not yet been formally recognized.

Concluding Remarks

In 1977, Greenleaf (1977/2002) was optimistic when he wrote that people were beginning to "relate to one another in less coercive and more creatively supporting ways" (p. 23); or, in other words, that people were learning to interact in a more constructive manner, a manner described by Follett in 1924 when she wrote *Creative Experience*. Like many great leaders, Follett had a dream, "and for something great to happen, there must be a great dream. Behind every great achievement is a dreamer of great dreams" (Greenleaf, 1970/1991, p. 18). Follett dreamed of a unified government that was built from the ground up; a government that was not simply concerned about votes or the majority but was sincerely concerned about the welfare of every individual. She believed that such a government could be obtained through group association, by the building of communities, and she worked tirelessly to do so through her hands-on work in the community and through her writings and speeches. Despite the importance of Follett's work and the fact that many of her ideas on leadership are still pertinent today, she is not widely known in leadership circles. By formally investigating Follett's leadership philosophy, it is hoped that attention will be drawn to her important contributions, giving her the recognition she so rightfully deserves.

References

Bass, B. M. (1985). *Leadership and performance beyond expectations.* Free Press.

Bennis, W. (2003). Thoughts on "The Essentials of Leadership." In P. Graham (Ed.), *Mary Parker Follett: Prophet of management* (pp. 177–181). Beard Books.

Burns, J. M. (1978). *Leadership.* Harper & Row.

Creswell, J. W. (2013). *Qualitative inquiry and research design: Choosing among five approaches* (3rd ed.). Sage.

Creswell, J. W. (2014). *Research design: Qualitative, quantitative, and mixed methods approaches* (4th ed.). Sage.

Crippen, C. (2004). *Three women pioneers in Manitoba: Evidence of servant-leadership* [Doctoral dissertation]. Retrieved from ProQuest. 3143999.

Crippen, C., & Nagel, D. (2013). Exemplars of servant leadership in sport: Henrik and Daniel Sedin. *PHEnex Journal, 5*(2), 1–17.

Drucker, P. (2003). Introduction to Mary Parker Follett: Prophet of management. In P. Graham (Ed.), *Mary Parker Follett: Prophet of management* (pp. 1–9). Beard Books.

Follett, M. P. (1998). *The new state: Group organization the solution of popular government.* The Pennsylvania State University Press. (Original work published 1918)

Follett, M. P. (2013a). *Creative experience.* Martino Publishing. (Original work published 1924)

Follett, M. P. (2013b). *Dynamic administration: The collected papers of Mary Parker Follett* (H. C. Metcalf & L. Urwick, Eds.). Martino Publishing. (Original work published 1942)

Frick, D. M. (2004). *Robert K. Greenleaf: A life of servant leadership.* Berrett-Koehler Publishers.

Graham, J. W. (1991). Servant-leadership in organization: Inspirational and moral. *Leadership Quarterly, 2*(2), 105–119.

Graham, P. (Ed.). (2003). *Mary Parker Follett: Prophet of management.* Beard Books.

Greenleaf, R. K. (1991). *The servant as leader.* Robert K. Greenleaf Center. (Original work published 1970)

Greenleaf, R. K. (2002). *Servant leadership: A journey into the nature of legitimate power and greatness* (L. C. Spears, Ed.; 25th anniversary ed.). Paulist Press. (Original work published 1977)

Haitt, E. M. (2010). *Analysis of servant-leadership characteristics: Case study of a for-profit career school president* [Doctoral dissertation]. Retrieved from ProQuest.

Maykut, P., & Morehouse, R. (1994). *Beginning qualitative research: A philosophic and practical guide.* Falmer Press.

Negron, M. (2012). *Analysis of servant leadership: An interpretive biography of a prominent leader in proprietary higher education* [Doctoral dissertation]. Retrieved from ProQuest.

Omoh, D. A. O. (2007). *Analysis of servant leadership characteristics: A case study of a community college president* [Doctoral dissertation]. Retrieved from ProQuest.

Parker, L. D. (1984). Control in organizational life: The contribution of Mary Parker Follett. *Academy of Management Review, 9*(4), 736–745.

Sipe, J., & Frick, D. (2009). *Seven pillars of servant leadership: Practicing the wisdom of leading by serving.* Paulist Press.

Spears, L. C. (1998). Introduction: Tracing the growing impact of servant-leadership. In L. C. Spears (Ed.), *Insights on leadership: Service, stewardship, spirit, and servant-leadership* (pp. 1–14). Wiley.

Spears, L. C. (2004). The understanding and practice of servant-leadership. In L. C. Spears & M. Lawrence (Eds.), *Practicing servant leadership: Succeeding through trust, bravery, and forgiveness* (pp. 9–24). Jossey-Bass.

Spears, L. C., & Lawrence, M. (Eds.). (2004). *Practicing servant leadership: Succeeding through trust, bravery, and forgiveness.* Jossey-Bass.

Tonn, J. C. (2003). *Mary P. Follett: Creating democracy, transforming management.* Yale University Press.

Yin, R. (2009). *Case study research: Design and methods* (4th ed.). Sage.

Chapter 13

Can I Be Fearless?

Margaret Wheatley

Fear is the cheapest room in the house. I would like to see you living
in better conditions.

—Hafiz, 1999, p. 39

Human history is filled with stories of countless people who have been fearless.
If we look at our own families, perhaps going back several generations, we'll
find among our own ancestors those who also have been fearless. They may
have been immigrants who bravely left the safety of home, veterans who
courageously fought in wars, or families who endured economic hardships,
war, persecution, slavery, oppression, or dislocation. We all carry within us
this lineage of fearlessness.

But what is fearlessness? It's *not* being free of fear, for fear is part of
our human journey. Parker Palmer (1998/2007), an extraordinary educator
and writer, notes,

> Fear is so fundamental to the human condition that all the great
> spiritual traditions originate in an effort to overcome its effects
> on our lives. With different words, they all proclaim the same
> core message: "Be not afraid." . . .

It is important to note with care what that core teaching does and does not say. "Be not afraid" does not say that we should not *have* fears—and if it did, we could dismiss it as an impossible counsel of perfection. Instead, it says that we do not need to *be* our fears, quite a different proposition. (p. 58)

If fear is this fundamental to being human, we can expect that we'll feel afraid at times, perhaps even frequently. Yet when fear appears, we don't have to worry that we've failed, that we're not as good as other people. In fact, we're just like other people! What's important is to notice what we *do* with our fear. We can withdraw or distract or numb ourselves. Or we can recognize the fear, and then step forward anyway. Fearlessness simply means that we do not give fear the power to silence or stop us.

In my own experience, I think there's an important difference between courage and fearlessness. Courage emerges in the moment, without time for thought. Our heart opens and we immediately move into action. Someone jumps into an icy lake to save a child, or speaks up at a meeting, or puts themselves in danger to help another human being. These sudden actions, even if they put us at risk, arise from clear, spontaneous love.

Fearlessness, too, has love at its core, but it requires much more of us than instant action. If we react too quickly when we feel afraid, we either flee or act aggressively. True fearlessness is wise action, not false bravado or blind reactivity. It requires that we take time and exercise discernment. Zen teacher Joan Halifax speaks about the *practice of nondenial*. When we feel afraid, we don't deny the fear. Instead, we acknowledge that we're scared. But we don't flee. We stay where we are and bravely encounter our fear. We turn toward it, we become curious about it, its causes, its dimensions. We keep moving closer, until we're in relationship with it. And then, fear changes. Most often, it disappears.

I've heard many quotes from different traditions that speak to this wonder of fear dissolving. "If you can't get out of it, get into it." "The only way out is through." "Put your head in the mouth of the demon, and the demon disappears." Some of my best teachers about fearlessness are part of a global network of younger leaders (in their teens, twenties, and thirties) with whom I've worked for several years. They call themselves "walkouts." They walk out of work and careers that prevent them from contributing as much as they can, they walk out of relationships where they don't feel respected, they walk out of ideas that are limiting, they walk out of institutions that make them feel small and worthless. But they don't walk out to disappear—they *walk out to walk on*. They *walk on* to places where they can make a real contribution, to relationships where they're respected, to ideas that call on their strengths, to work where they can discover and use their potential.

From these younger leaders, I've learned the importance of asking periodically, "What might I need to walk out of?" It's a big question, and it demands a lot of bravery to even ask it. By posing this question, we're being brave enough to notice our fears and see them clearly. We're being brave enough to recognize where we're called to be fearless in our own lives. This powerful question helps us discover the places, the work, and the relationships that we need to *walk on to* in order to realize and offer our gifts.

I hold a vision of what's possible if more of us are willing to practice nondenial, if we look clearly at what frightens us in our personal lives and in our society. With clearer vision, we could walk through our fear and say "no" to what disturbs us. We could walk on and take a stand. We could refuse to be cowed or silenced. We could stop waiting for approval or support. We could stop feeling tired and overwhelmed. We could trust the energy of "Yes!" and begin to act for what we care about.

Fearlessness offers us a great blessing—the strength to endure and persevere. In late 2004, the Ukrainian people protested a fraudulent election that had denied them the president they knew they had elected, Viktor Yushchenko. They wore orange scarves and waved orange banners, becoming known as the "Orange Revolution." Their tactic was simple: Go into the streets and stay there until you get what you need. Refuse to give in, don't stop protesting until you accomplish your goal. Their example of persevering protest inspired citizens in many different countries (as far away as Ecuador and Nepal) to take to the streets and stay there until they got what they needed.

Today, in this troubled world, we need all the gifts that fearlessness offers us—love, clear seeing, bravery, intelligent action, perseverance. Fearless, we can face our fear and move through it. Fearless, we can reclaim our vocation to be fully human. Fearless, we can bring into being the world that Paulo Freire (2018) dreamed for us all: "A world in which it will be easier to love" (p. 40).

I Want to Be a Ukrainian

Margaret Wheatley

When I come of age,
When I get over being a teen-ager
When I take my life seriously
When I grow up
        I want to be a Ukrainian.

When I come of age
I want to stand happily in the cold
for days beyond number,
no longer numb to what I need.

I want to hear my voice
rise loud and clear above
the icy fog, claiming myself.

It was day fifteen of the protest, and a woman standing next to her car was being interviewed. Her car had a rooster sitting on top of it. She said "We've woken up and we're not leaving till this rotten government is out." It is not recorded if the rooster crowed.

When I get over being a teen-ager
when I no longer complain or accuse
when I stop blaming everybody else
when I take responsibility
        I will have become a Ukrainian.

The Yushchenko supporters carried bright orange banners which they waved vigorously on slim poles. Soon after the protests began, the government sent in thugs hoping to create violence. They also carried banners, but theirs were hung on heavy clubs that could double as weapons.

When I take my life seriously
when I look directly at what's going on

when I know that the future doesn't change itself
that I must act
      I will be a Ukrainian.

"Protest that endures," Wendell Berry said, "is moved by a hope far more modest than that of public success: namely, the hope of preserving qualities in one's own heart and spirit that would be destroyed by acquiescence."

When I grow up and am known as a Ukrainian
I will move easily onto the streets
confident, insistent, happy to preserve the qualities
of my own heart and spirit.

In my maturity, 1 will be glad to teach you
the cost of acquiescence
the price of silence
the peril of retreat.

"Hope," said Vaclev Havel, "is not the conviction that something will turn out well, but the certainty that something makes sense regardless of how it turns out."

I will teach you all that I have learned
the strength of fearlessness
the peace of conviction
the strange source of hope
      and I will die well, having been a Ukrainian.

References

Freire, P. (2018). *Pedagogy of the oppressed* (M. B. Ramos, Trans.; 50th anniversary ed.). Bloomsbury.

Hafiz. (1999). *The gift: Poems by Hafiz the great Sufi master* (D. Ladinsky, Trans.). Penguin.

Palmer, P. J. (2007). *The courage to teach: Exploring the inner landscape of a teacher's life.* Jossey-Bass. (Original work published 1998).

Chapter 14

Prophetic Story Weaving and Truth Telling

On the Road to Servant-Leadership in *Smoke Signals*

ERIN DAVIS

When the sins of our fathers visit us, we do not have to play host.
We can banish them with forgiveness. As God, in his Largeness and
    His Laws.

—August Wilson, *Fences*

North Dakota
At my grandfather's 95th birthday party, I visit his table.
Spread out in front of him are photographs from his childhood.
Each shot taken from far away, as if faces weren't important
on the North Dakota plains, ancient family members
dotting the flat landscape like tiny shrubs.

I point to a picture with no people, only tents on the grass.
He explains that the local tribe would set up camp
on his family's land and trade in town. He found it exciting,
but he worried about their horses because they were hobbled.
Even after his father explained why, he remained

uneasy. I thought they might trip over their own legs
and get hurt, he says. I wanted to untie them.

Later my dad tells me that he'd never seen that picture,
never knew about the tribe and the tents. And I wonder
if it might have cushioned what was hard between them—
the cowering under the kitchen table if dishes weren't done,
the fist to the face after a broken curfew—if just once
my dad had heard the story of the hobbled horses,
animals conditioned to accept pressure and restrictions,
and how a long time ago
his father had wanted
to free them. (Davis, 2018, p. 18)

Ever since I watched the film *Smoke Signals* (Eyre, 1998), I have been struck
by the depth with which its exploration of intergenerational trauma and
forgiveness moves me and resonates with me. The above poem illustrates
why I am so drawn to its theme of reconciliation between father and
sons. My grandfather is now ninety-nine, in good health, and living in an
assisted living home in California. Unlike Victor, the film's protagonist, who
must wrestle with the emotional legacy of his dead father's abandonment
and abuse, my father has had a lifetime to negotiate his relationship with
his father and reconcile with the dysfunctional example of masculinity
he grew up with. He not only avoided repeating his father's violent patterns, but he committed himself to a life of nonviolence and has been a
loving, gentle presence in the lives of his children and grandchildren. As
for my grandfather, he learned to say the words *I love you* to his children
and grandchildren forty years ago, and for the last eleven years, since my
grandmother died, has faithfully remembered to send us all birthday cards
with kind, handwritten notes in them. I know, however, that his anger
lurks below the surface, and he does not acknowledge that his parenting
was problematic. For that reason, my father has found that the best way
to have a loving and respectful relationship with him is, for the most part,
from a distance.

Palmer (2000) wrote that if we are to become whole, we must embrace
our shadows and our light. I am grateful to my father for speaking honestly
with me about the shadows in his relationship with my grandfather while at
the same time teaching me to see the light in him. The man who punched

my father in the face for violating his curfew is the same man who would read Shelley and Keats before I came to visit so that he could talk about his love of language with me, his English major granddaughter. My father has been a true servant-leader to his children and grandchildren. I am grateful to the prophetic voices and servant-leaders in his life, my mother among them, who helped him to grapple in a healthy way with his father's legacy so that he could embrace a more life-giving vision of masculinity and fatherhood. It is with that gratitude that I approach my analysis of Thomas's servant-leadership role in Victor's journey to forgive his father in the film *Smoke Signals*.

Shadow, Light, and the Cracks in the Lens

I am mindful of the shadow of sexual harassment allegations against screen-writer Sherman Alexie that were brought to light two years ago (Neary, 2018), and I acknowledge that my analysis of Thomas as a servant-leader who helps Victor embrace a more healthy vision of masculinity coexists with that shadow. In "Understanding Patriarchy," bell hooks (2004) defined patriarchy as "the single most life-threatening social disease assaulting the male body and spirit in our nation" (p. 17) and pointed to feminist think-ing and practice as the only way that threat can be addressed. She insisted that men must let go of the will to dominate in order for patriarchy to be dismantled, and called for an understanding that all of us have been social-ized to accept sexist thought and action (hooks, 2004) because patriarchy is systemic (Remnick, 2017).

In her introduction to *Outlaw Culture*, hooks (2015) pointed to cul-tural criticism as an important arena "for the exchange of knowledge, or the formation of new [feminist] epistemologies" (p. 7). In particular, she found film criticism to be a place in which the personal meets the academic, valuable not because it allows us an escape from the oppression of patriarchy but because it creates a space "of confrontation and collectivity" (Humm, 1997, p. 34). The critical lens with which she approaches cultural and film criticism is one that is unflinchingly committed to ending sexist oppression and to creating context for constructive conflict (hooks, 2015). It is through this lens that she recognized both the sexism of Paulo Freire's language and the liberatory power of his work (hooks, 2014), and the patriarchal nature of Thich Nhat Hanh's views on marriage and family and the wisdom of his teachings on work and other social issues (Tworkov, 1992). It is also through this lens that she took issue with Spike Lee's cinematic portrayal of black masculinity and femininity while also praising the political art of his films (Humm, 1997). hooks (2015) saw cultural criticism in general and film criticism in particular as a space for liberatory discussion informed by a love ethic.

The #MeToo movement confronts us on both an individual and collective level with the question of how to approach the artistic work of men who have acted out of the patriarchal will to dominate and hurt women. Critics have noted that Alexie's status as the best-known Native American writer, his power within the publishing industry (Keeler, 2018), and his ability to write so movingly about racial injustice (Laban, 2018) make it particularly painful to grapple with his behavior. Yin (2018) called for Alexie's works to be recontextualized so that they engender discussion not only about racial justice issues but also about the systematic sexism faced by women in male-dominated industries and the extent to which artists should be separated from their art. Bayers (2018) pointed out that *Smoke Signals* is a collaborative creation between screenwriter, director, and actors and contended that it should not be judged in the same way as work produced by Alexie alone. Finding value in the way the film undermines the buddy movie trope to show that Native women are "important to the formation of a Native masculinity" (p. 249), he argued that the film "raises powerful questions about Native masculinity that contribute to undermining the very distorted masculinity exhibited by Alexie's actions" and concluded that one can study this film without redeeming its writer (p. 242). In a thoughtful pondering of the value of teaching Alexie's work in the wake of the accusations against him, Spanke (2018) suggested that if Alexie's works are to be taught, they should be taught "with an eye toward the cracks in the lens, as opposed to simply through it" (p. 106).

I write my analysis of Thomas's servant-leadership in *Smoke Signals* with an eye toward the cracks in the lens. In "Feminist Manhood," hooks (2004) called for a "wise and loving politics" (p. 123) that holds space for critique and contention as we work to dismantle patriarchy. Believing that "there is a creative, life-sustaining, life-enhancing place for the masculine in a nondominator culture" (p. 115), she pointed to the need for an ethic of love in which men let go of the will to dominate and "choose life over death" (p. 134). This ethic of love, she explained, is rooted in service. Servant-leadership, in its disruption of the hierarchical notions of long-established power structures (Reynolds, 2016), has the potential to help us move toward a nonpatriarchal culture that values a more life-sustaining, life-affirming vision of masculinity. In the character of Thomas in *Smoke Signals*, we see that potential unfold.

Thomas and Victor

In a small trailer in the middle of the Arizona desert, Thomas Builds-the-Fire asks Suzy Song for a story. "Do you want lies, or do you want truth?" Suzy asks him. "I want both," he replies. In the film *Smoke Signals*, written by Sherman Alexie and directed by Chris Eyre (1998), Thomas is both truth teller and story weaver. He speaks his truth and weaves his stories for Victor Joseph, with whom he has traveled from the Coeur d'Alene Indian reservation in Idaho to retrieve the ashes of Victor's father, Arnold. Throughout the film, Thomas devotes himself to both Victor and the memory of Victor's father, even in the face of Victor's angry efforts to push him away. Thomas's truth telling and story weaving, along with his acts of generosity and presence, are all based on a sense of *connectedness* that he feels for Victor and his father. That sense of connectedness, a key concept in both spiritual and servant-leadership (Jackson & Parry, 2011), is a gift that allows Victor to begin the process of forgiving his father. Paulo Freire (2000) explained that "hope is rooted in men's incompletion, from which they move out in constant search—a search which can be carried out only in communion with others" (p. 91). It is just this kind of communion that Thomas provides for Victor.

One of the underlying precepts of servant-leadership is that of nourishing one's followers to become more whole (Jackson & Parry, 2011). Thomas's perpetually hopeful stance toward Victor and the memory of Victor's father, as well as his presence with Victor on the journey to bring Arnold Joseph's ashes home, create space for the kind of healing that Victor needs to forgive his father and become more whole. Alexie and Eyre use the trope of a buddy road trip movie as a vehicle for Victor and Thomas's spiritual journey (Slethaug, 2003), exploring the theme of forgiveness and reconciliation in father-son relationships against the backdrop of the historical trauma of Native American displacement and oppression brought about by colonialism. At different points in the film, Thomas is a prophetic voice for Victor. As their journey progresses, Thomas exhibits four of the characteristics identified by Spears (2010) as fundamental to the development of servant-leaders: empathy, healing, awareness, and commitment to growth.

Servant-Leadership

Robert K. Greenleaf (1977/2002) developed his concept of servant-leadership after reading Herman Hesse's (1956/2003) *A Journey to the East* and being inspired by the character of Leo, who first makes himself known as a servant to the protagonist and his companions as they travel on a mythical pilgrimage to the east in search of collective and individual truths, and is later revealed to be the leader of their organization. Greenleaf (2011) defined the servant-leader as "servant first—as Leo was portrayed. Becoming a servant-leader begins with the natural feeling that one wants to serve, to serve first. Then, conscious choice brings one to aspire to lead" (p. 25). This vision of a leader as servant first reimagines power, reinventing it "from its highly pervasive, coercive nature" (San Juan, 2005, p. 188) to a "two-way influence between leaders and followers" (Jackson & Parry, 2011, p. 63). According to Greenleaf (2011), the best test of the effectiveness of a servant-leader is this: "Do those served grow as persons? Do they, while being served, become healthier, wiser, freer, more autonomous, more likely themselves to be servants?" (p. 25).

Thomas's primary impulse in his relationship with Victor is one of service. By the end of his journey with Thomas, we see Victor becoming healthier and freer because he is able to release much of the anger he had toward his father, approach his father's memory from a more forgiving stance, and begin to take emotional responsibility for his own life. Allan (2006) pointed out that "to describe and interpret justice and forgiveness from a personal perspective is not only foreign to our modern way of life, but often also brings about an intense nexus of fear, anxiety, and lack of hope" (p. 142). Throughout their journey together, Victor's irritated and often hostile reactions to Thomas's service demonstrate that Victor is caught in this nexus. It is Thomas's gifts of presence, truth telling, and story weaving that create the emotional and psychological space Victor needs to face the fear, anxiety, and lack of hope that stem from his father's abandonment.

Servant-Leadership Revealed in
Smoke Signals' Cinematic Devices

The recurring motifs in *Smoke Signals* offer insights into Thomas's servant-leader nature and into the development of Victor's journey to forgive his father. The motifs of fire and ash are central to the film's mise-en-scène. In one of the film's first scenes, Alexie and Eyre use these motifs to establish Thomas and Victor as two young men connected by intertwining losses. Thomas, whose parents died in a fire when he was an infant, is rescued from that same fire by Victor's father. Victor twice loses his father: once as a child when Arnold Joseph abandons him and his mother, and again as a young adult when he learns that his father has died in Arizona. Eyre establishes Thomas as the story weaver through Thomas's voiceover in the very first scene narrating the events of the Fourth of July fire that took the life of his parents. As Thomas explains that "there are children who aren't really children at all. They're just pillars of flames that burn everything they touch," the flames from the house fire take up the entire frame. When Thomas continues, "There are some children who are just pillars of ash that fall apart as you touch 'em," the camera cuts to the smoldering aftermath of the fire. "Me and Victor," Thomas explains, "we were children born of flame and ash."

The title of the film itself, *Smoke Signals*, underscores the theme that the destructive energy of fire can be harnessed to create communication that facilitates healing—between friends, between sons and fathers, and between the past and present (Slethaug, 2003). It is Thomas who insists on communication with Victor from childhood onward, often asking Victor questions about his dad that Victor would rather not have to think about: "Hey Victor, heard your dad left. Why did he leave? Does he hate you?" "Hey, Victor, heard your dad was living in Phoenix, Arizona, now?" "Hey, Victor. What do you remember about your dad?" These ever-present questions serve to keep Arnold Joseph at the forefront of Victor's consciousness. Thomas, the servant-leader, demonstrates an *awareness* (Spears, 2010) of Arnold Joseph's role in Victor's pain that refuses to let Victor deny or bury that pain.

Because of the fire that kills Thomas's parents and forever changes Arnold Joseph, the concept of *home* is intertwined with personal loss and pain for Thomas and Victor, losses that are layered on top of the historical trauma of oppression and displacement experienced by the Coeur d'Alene tribe (Bayers, 2018). The fire happens on Independence Day, a day that represents freedom for most European Americans, but one that can be tinged with painful irony for Native Americans. Slethaug (2003) noted that the Fourth of July fire "brings home the fact that blame and guilt of personal and cultural tragedies must be accepted and shared before improvements can be made," and that the key to healing and preventing the further erosion of both relationships and culture is the concept of shared responsibility (p. 4). From childhood onward, Thomas feels a connection to, and responsibility for, Victor and the memory of Arnold Joseph. This connection and sense of responsibility fuels Thomas's *commitment to Victor's growth* (Spears 2010) as he accompanies him on his journey to retrieve the ashes of Arnold Joseph's body, a journey that culminates in Victor releasing Arnold Joseph's ashes into the Spokane River and releasing the anger that he holds toward his father.

Because Alexie and Eyre use the trope of the buddy/road trip movie as a vehicle for Thomas and Victor's spiritual journey, vehicles of transportation are important motifs in the film's mise-en-scène, revealing both the chaotic social problems caused by the historic displacement of Native Americans, and the ways in which healthy patterns can arise from both personal and communal chaos (Slethaug, 2003). The first vehicle we see in the film is the broken-down KREZ traffic van, from which Lester Falls-Apart reports the comings and goings of reservation life. We see Lester cheerfully offering his report from this broken-down van in 1976 and again in 1988, signaling to the audience that though the underlying social problems of the reservation may remain unchanged, there is also an underlying hopefulness present as well. This underlying hopefulness is also represented in the car that only goes backward, driven by the two women on the reservation who give Victor and Thomas a ride on the first leg of their journey. Slethaug (2003) points out that this vehicle that only goes backward is a fitting symbol for a mode of transportation that carries Victor and Thomas off the reservation and into "a headlong pursuit into American values and commodification" (p. 4).

It is important to notice, however, that these two women who provide Victor and Thomas the transportation needed for the first leg of their journey have joyful dispositions, even as they tease them about needing a passport because they are "leavin' the res and going to a whole different country, cousin." Thomas trades them a story for the ride, and he tells them an epic tale about Arnold Joseph in the sixties, saying that "he was a perfect hippie because all the hippies were tryin' to be Indians anyway." When one of the women playfully proclaims that the story Thomas tells them as payment for the ride is "a fine example of the oral tradition," she is signaling that Thomas's epic portrayal of Arnold Joseph, one that differs sharply from Victor's image of him, is rooted in the traditions of the Coeur d'Alene community. According to Greenleaf (1970), community is central to servant-leadership, allowing individuals to experience connection and interdependence, thereby fostering *individual growth* (Spears 2010).

The bus that carries Victor and Thomas from Spokane to Phoenix on their journey to Arnold Joseph's trailer in Arizona also represents the movement from chaotic patterns to more healthy ones. The protagonists in road trip movies are typically males experiencing some kind of crisis with masculinity (Bayers, 2018). Victor's crisis with masculinity is intertwined with his Native American identity, both of which are affected by the emotional scars left by Arnold Joseph's abandonment of him, and he experiences this crisis in more acute ways once he is on the bus taking him from Spokane to Phoenix, away from his culture and community. Their encounters with nonnatives on the bus spark a conversation between Victor and Thomas about what being a "real Indian" means. After once again becoming irritated with Thomas's asking him what he remembers about his dad, Victor lectures him about "real" Indian identity, advising him to "quit grinnin' like an idiot . . . you gotta look like a warrior," and telling him to free his hair from his braids and get rid of the suit that he wears all of the time. Thomas, rather than reacting defensively or taking offense, is open to Victor's advice and delights in it. He is truly happy to be receiving Victor's attention, but he is also demonstrating an *awareness* (Spears 2010) of a shift in the power dynamic between them, as Victor goes from being annoyed with Thomas to truly wanting to help him. Thomas's openness to Victor's advice makes space for Victor to articulate his understanding of Indian masculinity, and the bus taking them both to Phoenix is a vehicle for the "spiritual homecoming" that awaits Victor at Arnold Joseph's trailer (Slethaug, 2003, p. 4).

Eyre juxtaposes the internal and communal pain Victor and Thomas experience on their journey with the natural beauty of the Idaho and Arizona landscapes, often framing tense, emotional character interactions within the doorways of houses, the windows of cars, or the mirrors of bedrooms, and cutting away to wide or aerial shots of the rolling green hills and tall pines of Idaho or the stark beauty of the Arizona desert. The shots that are framed within doorways, windows, and mirrors often connect Victor's memories of his painful past with his current journey. When Victor initially refuses Thomas's offer of money to help him get to Arizona to retrieve his father's ashes, Victor walks out of the convenience store door, and for a moment, we see the adult Victor in the doorway looking out at the child Victor standing outside. Eyre uses this shot to transition to a memory from Victor's childhood that reveals both the pain and love inherent in his relationship with his father. Later, when Thomas and Victor are in a diner together and Thomas is telling Victor the story of the time Arnold Joseph found him alone at Spokane Falls and took him to Denny's, Victor gets up and goes into the restroom. Eyre cuts to a scene of young Victor walking into his parent's bedroom and finding them passed out drunk on the bed. Victor's parents are framed within the reflection of their bedroom mirror.

Eyre then cuts back to a medium close-up shot (Barsam & Monahan, 2019) of adult Victor staring into the diner bathroom mirror, and back to still another shot framed through the window of his parents' bedroom of young Victor throwing beer bottles at his father's truck. Yet another painful scene in which Victor's father hits him for spilling his beer is framed within the windows of Arnold Joseph's truck, the same truck he drives away in when he leaves Victor and his mother.

These tight shots show the audience how close and immediate Victor's pain is, but Eyre also uses them to show us hope in key points in the film. For example, when Thomas tells his epic tale about Arnold Joseph to the two young women driving the backward car, Eyre frames the shots from the interior of the car through the passenger window, and they alternate between medium close-up shots of Thomas and Victor with a bright blue sky and fluffy white clouds in the background and close-up shots (Barsam & Monahan, 2019) of Thomas's face. These shots allow the audience to see the love and attention with which Thomas delivers his story, and the irritation that registers on Victor's face as he tells it. After Thomas and Victor hop in the car, Eyre cuts to an extreme long shot of the car driving backward across the reservation, taking Thomas and Victor on the first leg of their journey. Eyre often uses extreme long shots or aerial shots to represent movement in *Smoke Signals*—movement toward Arizona and back home, and movement toward healing and forgiveness. Thomas's stories—which paint Victor's father in often epic, mythic strokes—demonstrate his *empathy* (Spears, 2010) for both Arnold Joseph and Victor, and create space for that movement.

The Prophetic Power of Thomas's Story Weaving and Truth Telling

The servant-leader is sensitive to the concerns and well-being of others. Beyond their ability to recognize the problems of those they seek to serve, servant-leaders must commit themselves to the time necessary to address those concerns in order to help those they serve reach their full potential (Northouse, 2019). Greenleaf (2011) believed that the servant-leaders among us are often "prophetic voices of great clarity . . . addressing the problems of the day and pointing to a better way to live fully and serenely in these times" (p. 22) as they focus on the well-being of people in their communities (Greenleaf, 1970). The stories Thomas tells Victor about his father may not be strictly factual, but they place Arnold Joseph and Victor's struggles within the broader context of the struggles of their Native American community. Indeed, he places their journey within that context as he and Victor walk through the Arizona desert to find Suzy Song and Arnold Joseph's trailer:

> We've been travelin' a long time, ain't it? I mean Columbus shows up, and we start walkin' away from that beach, tryin' to get away, and then Custer moves into the neighborhood drivin' down all the property values. Then old Harry Truman drops the bomb, and we gotta keep on walkin' somewhere.

Armbruster-Sandoval (2008) notes that this bit of story weaving also critiques the "hidden addiction" of US militarism (p. 131). And while Thomas's mythic, humorous, not-always-factual stories frustrate Victor, they serve the prophetic purpose of holding Victor's father up in a different light for him, and create an opening for him to eventually hear important truths about both Arnold Joseph and himself.

We see the influence of Thomas's prophetic story weaving in Victor's realization that Arnold Joseph told Suzy Song a false ending to the story about their basketball game with some Jesuits in order to make Victor look good. In that moment in his journey, after arriving at his father's and Suzy Song's trailers in the middle of the desert, Victor is able to see the truth of the love behind his father's lie. However, painful memories can be debilitating in their power to generate resentment and block an individual's ability to let go and heal (Armbruster-Sandoval, 2008). Victor still has much healing to do as he and Thomas journey back home in his father's truck, the same truck Arnold Joseph used to drive away from Victor and his mother when Victor was a boy. As a weary Victor tells Thomas that he's tired of his stories and that his dad was nothing more than a drunk who beat him and his mom, Thomas shifts from mythic story weaving to unflinching truth telling as he explodes at Victor: "Your dad was more than that! You've got it all wrong, Victor! Maybe you don't know who *you* are!" When Victor lashes out and says, "I wish he would have let you burn in that fire, you know? Then he wouldn't have left me," Thomas returns with, "He was always leaving, Victor!" This argument with Thomas, which culminates in Victor crashing into a car stopped on the highway, is the final catalyst for Victor to make peace with his past and forgive his father. Paulo Freire (2000) described those who are committed to human liberation as "not afraid to confront, to listen, to see the world unveiled" and to commit themselves "within history" to fight on the side of the oppressed (p. 39). While Thomas commits himself to Victor's struggle first by offering him financial support, and then by accompanying him on his journey, he is unafraid to enter into crucial dialogue with Victor, placing Victor's struggle to reconcile with the memory of his father within the context of the larger struggles of their people, and offering Victor difficult but liberating truth about his father.

San Juan (2005) noted that applying a psychoanalytical lens to leadership can help us understand the way leaders deal with power, noting that a leader's feeling of personal power "is nurtured through childhood experiences" (p. 199). One's early experience with family relationships influences the way one understands power dynamics. Victor's earliest childhood experiences were with alcoholic parents. His father abandoned him after being unable to give up alcohol as Victor's mother did. Thomas was raised by his grandmother because his parents died in the same fire that Arnold Joseph both started and saved him from. Neither Victor nor Thomas have fathers who can shape their identities in positive ways, but their relationship with the women who raised them provide them with a "gender complementarity" that allows them to successfully journey together toward wholeness (Bayers, 2018, p. 252). This gender complementarity is evident in two back-to-back scenes that take place before Victor and Thomas leave together for Arizona. When Victor's mother Arlene drops a piece of fry bread on the floor and says "Damn arthritis," Victor responds by rubbing her hands and saying soothingly, "Hurting bad today, ain't it?" Eyre cuts directly from this to a scene of Thomas kneading bread for his grandmother in their kitchen. We see Thomas's servant-leader nature as he stands in the kitchen and works while his grandmother sits and looks up at him. Victor's scene with his mother demonstrates his *potential* for servant-leadership as well. The positions of Victor and his mother are inverted from Thomas and his grandmother's positions, with Victor seated, looking up with love and compassion at his mother. While Victor may not have the impulse to be a servant *first* (Greenleaf, 2011), he has the potential to develop that impulse, and the prophetic power of Thomas's story weaving and truth telling will help him do that.

Conclusion

One of the underlying precepts of servant-leadership is nourishing others to become whole (Jackson & Parry, 2011). In offering Victor his money, his presence, and, most importantly, his stories, Thomas provides Victor with the nourishment he needs to forgive his father and to begin the process of becoming whole. Freire (2000) taught that humanization is "the people's vocation," a vocation that is "affirmed by the yearning of the oppressed for freedom and justice, and by their struggle to recover their lost humanity" (pp. 43–44). In *Smoke Signals*, Thomas Builds-the-Fire helps Victor recognize his yearning to be free of his anger toward his father, allowing him to recover the humanity that anger and pain had cost him. Thomas's sense of connectedness to Victor and Arnold Joseph, his commitment to Victor's growth, and his servant-leader characteristics of empathy, healing, and awareness allow Victor to begin the process of forgiving his father and becoming more whole. Through his story weaving and truth telling, Thomas is a prophetic voice pointing Victor to "a better way" that will allow him "to live more fully and serenely" (Greenleaf, 2011, p. 22).

At the end of the film, Victor gives Thomas some of his father's ashes. Both of these children of fire and ash, whose identities have been intertwined since infancy, have the same idea: to release Arnold Joseph's ashes at Spokane Falls. "Your father will rise like a salmon, Victor! He will rise!" Thomas exclaims. Victor, rather than show irritation, simply replies that while he had the same idea, he never thought of his dad rising like a salmon, only that "it would be more like throwing something away when it is no use." In the final scene of the film, Thomas's grandmother, upon welcoming him home, says, "Tell me what happened, Thomas. Tell me what's going to happen." Thomas closes his eyes, and Eyre cuts to an aerial shot of the Spokane River winding its way to Spokane Falls, where Victor releases his father's ashes with a loud, cleansing cry. In a voiceover, Thomas asks a series of questions about forgiving fathers: "How do we forgive our fathers? Do we forgive our fathers in our age, or in theirs? . . . If we forgive our fathers, what's left?" Due in no small part to Thomas's prophetic story weaving and truth telling, Victor will have the chance to find out.

References

Allan, K. (2006). Servant-leadership, forgiveness, and unlimited liability: Fathers and sons. *The International Journal of Servant-Leadership, (2)*1, 141–146.

Armbruster-Sandoval, R. (2008). Teaching smoke signals: Fatherhood, forgiveness, and "freedom." *Wicazo Sa Review, (23)*1, 123–146. https://doi.org/10.1353/wic.2008.0008

Barsam, R., & Monahan, D. (2019) *Looking at movies: An introduction to film.* W. W. Norton.

Bayers, P. L. (2018). Native women and the regeneration of Coeur d'Alene masculinity in Chris Eyre's *Smoke Signals*. *Rocky Mountain Review, (72)*2, 240–261.

Davis, E. (2018). North Dakota. *Trestle Creek Review, 32*, 18.

Eyre, C. (Director). (1998). *Smoke signals* [Film]. Miramax.

Freire, P. (2000). *Pedagogy of the oppressed*. Bloomsbury.

Greenleaf, R. K. (1970). *The servant as leader*. The Greenleaf Center for Servant Leadership.

Greenleaf, R. K. (2002). *Servant leadership: A journey into the nature of legitimate power and greatness* (L. C. Spears, Ed.; 25th anniversary ed.). Paulist Press. (Original work published 1977)

Greenleaf, R. K. (2011). Who is the servant-leader? *The International Journal of Servant-Leadership, (7)*1, 21–26.

Hesse, H. (2003). *The journey to the East* (H. Rosner, Trans.). Picador. (Original work published 1956)

hooks, b. (2004). *The will to change: Men, masculinity, and love*. Atria Books.

hooks, b. (2014). *Teaching to transgress: Education as the practice of freedom*. Routledge. https://www.amazon.com/dp/B00J4JH351

hooks, b. (2015). *Outlaw culture*. Routledge. https://www.amazon.com/dp/B009E1NH7Y

Humm, M. (1997). *Feminism in film*. Indiana University Press.

Jackson, B., & Parry, K. (2011). *A very short, fairly interesting, and reasonably cheap book about studying leadership*. Sage.

Keeler, J. (2018, March 12). Why reading Sherman Alexie was never enough. *Yes!* https://www.yesmagazine.org/social-justice/2018/03/12/why-reading-sherman-alexie-was-never-enough/

Laban, M. (2018, March 20). Why Sherman Alexie's sexual misconduct feels like a betrayal. *Electric Lit*. https://electricliterature.com/why-sherman-alexies-sexual-misconduct-feels-like-a-betrayal-fe3055e035e7

Neary, L. (2018, March 5). "It just felt so wrong": Sherman Alexie's accusers go on the record. *NPR*. https://www.npr.org/2018/03/05/589909379/it-just-felt-very-wrong-sherman-alexies-accusers-go-on-the-record

Northouse, P. G. (2019). *Leadership* (8th ed.). Sage.

Palmer, P. (2000). *Let your life speak: Listening for the voice of vocation*. Jossey-Bass.

Remnick, D. (Host). (2017, November 16). America after Weinstein [Audio podcast episode]. In *The New Yorker Radio Hour*. https://www.newyorker.com/podcast/the-new-yorker-radio-hour/america-after-weinstein

Reynolds, K. (2016). Servant-leadership: A feminist perspective. *International Journal of Servant-Leadership, 10*(1), 35–63.

San Juan, K. S. (2005). Re-imagining power in leadership: Reflection, integration, and servant-leadership. *The International Journal of Servant-Leadership, (1)*1, 187–209.

Slethaug, G. E. (2003). Hurricanes and fires: Chaotics in Sherman Alexie's *Smoke Signals* and *The Lone Ranger and Tonto Fistfight in Heaven. Literature/Film Quarterly, (31)*2, 130–140.

Spanke, J. (2018). Magnificent things and terrible men: Teaching Sherman Alexie in the age of #MeToo. *English Education, 51*(1), 101–107.

Spears, L. (2010). Character and servant leadership: Ten characteristics of effective, caring leaders. *The Journal of Virtues & Leadership, (1)*1, 25–30.

Tworkov, H. (1992). Agent of change: An interview with bell hooks. *Tricycle.* https://tricycle.org/magazine/bell-hooks-buddhism/

Yin, A. (2018). In the wake of #MeToo, how do we teach problematic pieces in the classroom? *The Weekender: The Daily Californian.* https://www.dailycal.org/2018/04/29/revisiting-sherman-alexie-in-school-amidst-the-metoo-movement/

SECTION III

THE SPIRITUAL BEAUTY OF SERVANT-LEADERSHIP

Chapter 15

Selma

An Exploration of the Womanist Lens
and the Servant-Leader

CARMEN DELA CRUZ

Most of the Black community remember where they were the day the
news broke that Barack Obama would be the 44th president of the United
States. In 2008, I was living in the historic city of Atlanta, where I had left
behind the dust of an unpaved country road in Russellville, Arkansas. I had
wondered then if any of the inhabitants of the predominately White town
were somewhere celebrating too. I stared at the screen in the hip Inman
Park area with my brother and mixture of folks of different races, and we
took to the streets and started shouting and laughing with strangers in the
street, "Yes we can! Yes, we can!" I was so hopeful. I had not lived through
what our parents had experienced as children in the Jim Crow South, or
fully understood what our grandmother who was born in 1918 had seen
in her day, but I'd had my own taste of racism. I had received a unique
education from the time our parents moved us from our hometown of Pine
Bluff, Arkansas, to Russellville. My father had accepted a nuclear chemist
position at AP&L, now Entergy, and I'm sure my parents too were filled
with hope as they moved into a new home in our all-White neighborhood.
My mother was an educator and took it upon herself to visit schools and
talk to teachers. I was with her as one teacher gave us strange looks and

said, "We don't have many of y'all here." At five years old, I don't think I really understood who the "y'all" was that she was referring to. My mother decided to enroll us in St. John's Catholic School at the advice of a neighbor whose two girls were half Mexican. My parents, who had both attended Catholic school, decided that paying the tuition was worth it if it meant a better education; as my mother said, "The nuns would be mean to everyone." My brother and I made up two of the three Black kids at the school, and there were three Hispanics, including the neighbor's two kids. The real education happened outside the schoolyard in our all-White neighborhood. We did what kids do, which is to find other kids to play with. One day the older White boys that my seven-year-old brother had played with several times before had a few new friends join in. These new friends were not as keen to allow my brother to play baseball with them. I sat watching as the boys who we had thought were friends stood by as one of their friends laughed, pushed my brother, and said, "Oh let the little nigg** play." We were able to make a quick escape as some of the boys laughed and some stood silent. We ran the mile or so home, fighting back tears. This was one of the moments that I became acutely aware that I was different. There would be several other moments like riding the school bus in the third grade and having a White boy of five or six say, "Hey, what would you do if I called you a nigg**?" In middle school, another White boy got on our bus a few times, wearing a homemade shirt that read, "KKK I'm a Member," without any repercussions from the bus driver or school officials. These devastating occurrences awakened me to the fact that my very presence, my color, incited this behavior in some people. However, I had parents who also taught me that those people were just ignorant and that there were also good people in the world. I made friends in that rural town who had probably never truly known a Black person, and I was definitely the first Black person in their home for sleepovers or parties. So, I carried with me this duality of humanity's love and hate. I was also fortunate that my mother moved us to Atlanta when I started high school, which gave us an entirely new perspective on the wealth of opportunity for Blacks in all fields. There, I worked in media at Turner Broadcasting and found that it was not unusual to have Black managers or a Black vice president of operations. After Obama's election, I was hopeful, along with so many people of color in the world, that change was not just a campaign slogan but that real change in the minds and hearts of people was under way. However, with the recent civil unrest surrounding the protests to honor the lives of George Floyd, Breonna Taylor, Ahmaud Arbery, and others affected by senseless violence, it seems necessary to ask, where are we now? Where is the leadership that the country needs?

In the present climate, films such as Ava DuVernay's (2014) *Selma* now feel more relevant than ever. I can remember watching the film for the first time and thinking how powerful and disturbing it was. I felt connected but at the same time I felt distant from the events happening on-screen. Growing up, I had sat through television specials about Dr. King that often rushed through his life and death and usually ended with some reading of the "I Have a Dream" speech. While these specials did not necessarily make any negative statements, and served to celebrate the life of King, there was no depth to these projects to tell audiences who he was behind the podium. Film is an art form that can give shape to characters and reimagine history in new ways, having an almost transportive quality. Yet biopics about historical leaders can fall into the trap of regurgitating similar well-known facts about historical figures without giving new insight into their motivations. In DuVernay's (2014) *Selma*, King is a central character, but *Selma* is not a biopic. *Selma* is an artistic look at the events that shaped the historic 1965 march to Selma, Alabama, and an examination of King's character as a leader and as a man. *Selma* addresses the question of who King was and what type of leadership allowed him to unite so many people under one cause. Through DuVernay's womanist lens, the events leading up to the march on Selma and the signing of the Voting Rights Act of 1965 can be viewed in a powerful new light, and King is shown not as a sainted figure who was a central part of the civil rights movement but as a servant-leader with human flaws.

When *Selma* (DuVernay, 2014) begins, the camera takes audiences inside King's home, giving us a more intimate portrait of him. You see him fretting about a tie that his wife, Coretta Scott King, has picked out for him. Quickly, the audience realizes that he is dressing for an important event, and the conversation between husband and wife seems innocent but hints at issues within their family life. The dialogue about King's not wanting to seem like they are "living high on the hog" shows that he is very conscious about his image and how he wants to look as a minister and leader in the Black community. As the scene shifts to the Nobel Peace Prize ceremony for King, it is juxtaposed with the scene of the four little girls who are bombed in the church in Birmingham. This scene shows the girls giggling in the church, which is filled with a golden light. The choice to have the girls discussing how to get Coretta's hairstyle both shows how enamored Black women at the time were with her and makes the scene more heartbreaking. As the sudden explosion hits, DuVernay chooses to play with the depth of field, blurring the images of the little girls, with only pieces of fabric from their dresses moving slowly in the air. Then we see their legs in the air, and the camera closes in on their little black patent leather shoes and white socks. The image of these little girls all dressed up for church reminded me of summers spent in my grandmother's Black Baptist church in Pine Bluff, Arkansas. It was not as casual as the Catholic masses we attended. You were expected to be well dressed and stylish every Sunday, and I had also owned a pair of little black patent leather shoes for going to church with my grandma. These added layers give a more human element that might not have been realized by a White or male director.

The Womanist Lens

It seems clear that similar to Black female filmmakers such as Kasi Lemmons, who directed films such as *Eve's Bayou* (Lemmons, 1997) and *Harriet* (Lemmons, 2019), that DuVernay's point of view may be influenced by a womanist perceptive (Barron, 2016, p. 208). The term *womanist*, coined by writer and activist Alice Walker, speaks specifically to a branch of feminism for Black women or women of color. "A womanist, according to Walker, loves other women and prefers women's culture, a very antipatriarchal orientation. However, womanists also evince a commitment, 'to survival and wholeness of entire people, male and female'" (Gilkes, 2009, p. 286). In essence, the initial scene in *Selma* also points to DuVernay's (2014) careful portrayal of both King and his wife, Coretta. DuVernay, like Walker, is passionate about issues that affect both women and the entire Black community. In the wake of George Floyd's death, a recent *Harper's Bazaar* article (Gonzales, 2020) asks DuVernay and other cast members to reflect on the timing of *Selma*'s release. The 2014 film debuted five months after a video surfaced showing another Black man, Eric Garner, being choked as he pleaded, "I can't breathe." The entire *Selma* cast showed up to an event to promote a film about the civil rights movement, wearing black T-shirts with the white letters spelling, "I Can't Breathe." David Oyelowo, who plays King, recounts the calls that came in from members of the Academy Award voting board:

> Members of the Academy called in to the studio and our producers saying, "How dare they do that? Why are they stirring S-H-I-T?"

and "We are not going to vote for that film because we do not think it is their place to being doing that." (Gonzales, 2020)

This glimpse behind the scenes of the film industry suggests that people of color in the industry are not imagining larger issues of systemic racism. DuVernay, who was the first Black woman to receive a Golden Globe nomination for best director, decided to use her platform for social activism despite the displeasure of some in the film industry with the power to vote. *Selma* went on to receive only one Oscar, for best original song, for "Glory," written by Common and John Legend, but despite not winning an Oscar for best picture or being snubbed for the Oscar's best director nomination, DuVernay's unique voice in *Selma* speaks for itself.

In an interview with NPR, DuVernay discusses what makes her voice different from that of a male director, revealing her thoughts on the re-creation of the 1963 Birmingham church bombing that killed four young Black girls:

I was much more interested in reverence for the girls. It was important to me that you hear their voices. You hear what their concerns are at that moment as four little Black girls walking down a staircase in what should be a safe place, in their sanctuary, in their church. They're talking about Coretta Scott King's hairstyle. They're talking about what little Black girls talk about—getting your hair wet and keeping it pressed and doing all that kind of kind of thing. You start to come into their world just as they are taken out of the world. (Gross, 2015)

This interview also highlights the sanctity of the Black church, as she DuVernay out the sanctuary that such buildings should represent. The repeated motif of the golden light that you see in the churches seemed to convey that feeling of sanctity and hope about the Black church (Barsam & Monahan, 2016, p. 15). DuVernay sets the stage for a very different kind of film about the civil rights movement and King's life, showing her vision of the leadership that must take place in the short time in 1964 when King wins the Nobel Peace Prize and President Lyndon Johnson signs the Voting Rights Act in 1965. The obstacles that unfold tell us a great deal about the mammoth task that the Southern Christian Leadership Conference (SLC) undertakes, along with the volunteers to the cause, and it also sets the perfect stage to show a more up-close view of King as a servant-leader.

Defining Servant-Leadership

In discussing King as a servant-leader, it's important to define what servant-leadership entails and to look at the work of Robert Greenleaf, who first coined the term *servant-leadership*. In Greenleaf's (1977/2002) book *Servant Leadership*, he discusses his source of inspiration behind the theory of servant-leadership:

> The idea of the servant as leader came out of reading Hermann Hesse's *Journey to the East*. In this story we see a band of men on a mythical journey, probably also Hesse's own journey. The central figure of the story is Leo, who accompanies the party as the servant who does the menial chores, but who also sustains them with song. He is a person of extraordinary presence. All goes well until Leo disappears. (p. 21)

Greenleaf illustrates how the character Leo from Hesse's (1956) *Journey to the East* is seemingly a lowly servant but somehow he is also the force that ultimately gives the crew direction on their journey. Once Leo, who is actually head of the order, is gone, the crew lose focus and everything unravels. As Greenleaf (1977/2002) further describes what makes Leo a great leader, one can see that service is an essential element of servant-leadership:

> But to me, this story clearly says that *the great leader is seen as servant first*, and that simple fact is the key to his greatness. Leo was actually the leader all of the time, but he was servant first because that was what he was, *deep down inside*. Leadership was bestowed upon a person who was by nature a servant. It was something given, or assumed, that could be taken away. His servant nature was the real man, not bestowed, not assumed, and not to be taken away. He was servant first. (pp. 21–22)

This idea of the servant as the leader resonates in *Selma* as you see King revealed in layers as a minister who first is the servant to God, the servant to his followers, and the servant to the Black community in his capacity as the leader of the SCLC. Early in the film, we see King take the issue of voting rights for Blacks to President Johnson before he leaves for Selma. Prior to King's arrival, Johnson has discussed with his advisor that he has other seemingly more important initiatives to pursue and seems frustrated that the signing of the 1964 Civil Rights Act six months earlier was not enough to resolve racial conflict or pacify King. King is direct about what is needed to assist Negroes in the south:

> Well Mr. President, I'm here to speak with you about the denial of the basic American right for the Negro, the right to vote. Technically, I know we already have it. Yes, Mr. President, we both know in the South, Black voters are kept off the rolls and out of the voting booth by systematic intimidation and fear. Now, you asked how you could help. We want federal legislation granting Negroes the right to vote unencumbered, and we want federal protocol eliminating the decades long dismissal and illegal denial of Blacks seeking the vote. And we want robust enforcement of that protocol. (DuVernay, 2014)

Despite President Johnson's praise of King as a statesmen and the one to lead the movement as the safe Negro, "not one of these militant Malcom X types," Johnson denies King's request, saying that he needs to address "the war on poverty." King persists in telling him that voting rights cannot wait due the thousands of racially motivated murders in the South that include the four little girls in the church bombing:

> And you know the astounding fact that not one of these criminals who murder us when and why they want has ever been convicted. Not one has been convicted because they are protected by White officials chosen by an all-White electorate. On the rare occasion that they face trial they are freed by an all-White jury. White because you can't serve on a jury unless you are registered to vote. (DuVernay, 2014)

When he leaves the president's office announcing, "Selma it is," it is clear King has made his best effort to articulate to Johnson the urgent need for Blacks to have voting rights in the United States, and he is unwavering in his decision to pursue justice for Blacks despite the danger in which this puts him. He must be a servant to the cause. The president alludes to the fact that King has turned down offers to have a position in the White House, which again emphasizes King's desire to be in the best position to serve, caring little for titles or honors.

While King's leadership aligns with the characteristics of servant-leadership, it is also arguable that he also shows characteristics of transformational leadership, which shares commonalities with servant-leadership.

Transformational leadership, known for its four key behaviors, "idealized influence (or charismatic influence), inspirational motivation, intellectual stimulation, and individualized consideration" (Stone et al., 2004, p. 350), bears a strong resemblance to servant-leadership, especially in its relationship to followers. Researchers have analyzed whether one is possibly a subset of the other: "Both transformational leadership and servant leadership emphasize the importance of appreciating and valuing people, listening, mentoring or teaching, and empowering followers. In fact, the theories are probably most similar in their emphasis upon individualized consideration and appreciation of followers" (Stone et al., 2004, p. 354). Seemingly, the achievements of the civils rights movement are closely aligned to this symbiotic relationship between leader and follower that is attributed to both transformational leadership and servant-leadership. The followers must trust the vision and foresight of King and other leaders in the SCLC, and similarly there must be a level of trust from leader to follower. Although King is driven by service to others, he exudes an extraordinary amount of charisma that appears transformative to the lives of his followers. As the character Annie Cooper is introduced as an older Black woman who is trying to register to vote, one can assume that she has been inspired by King's work with the SCLC. Through DuVernay's (2014) womanist lens, Cooper has real agency. DuVernay makes a point of showing the grace and dignity that Cooper possesses even in the face of the racist White man who asks her to recite the preamble to the constitution when she attempts to register to vote. After she recites the preamble to a man who obviously doesn't think that a Black woman would possess such knowledge, she is also able to meet the challenge of telling him how many county judges there are in Alabama. She is then asked to name all 67 judges and denied the right to vote when she does not know them. As a big red "DENIED" stamp is marked on her form, Cooper still walks out with her head held high. This moment does not appear to deter Cooper from wanting to vote, because the next time you see her on-screen, she is sitting in the church along with many others who have come to hear King speak in all his golden light of glory. The speech ends with a call to action:

> Those that have gone before us say no more. That means protest, that means march, that means disturb the peace, that means jail, that means risk, and that is hard. We will not wait any longer. Give us the vote. We are not asking. We are demanding. Give us the vote. (DuVernay, 2014)

As the camera pans across the room, a close-up of Cooper reveals that she is chanting right along with the crowd, "Give us the vote!" The camera also focuses on another character, Jimmie Lee Jackson, along with his mother and grandfather, who also are moved to join the protest. This scene illustrates the unique ability King has to get followers to answer the call to serve. This may be the distinction between the transformational leader and the servant-leader:

> Transformational leadership and servant leadership do have points of variation. There is a much greater emphasis upon service to followers in the servant leadership paradigm. Furthermore, while both transformational leaders and servant leaders are influential, servant leaders gain influence in a nontraditional manner that derives from servanthood itself (Russell and Stone, 2002). In so doing, they allow extraordinary freedom for followers to excise their own abilities. (Stone et al., 2004, p. 354)

The idea of servanthood drawing people in seems to explain part of King's magnetic appeal. It is not just about giving speeches like a politician. In the film, we see the depth of King's work behind the scenes as he rolls up his sleeves to strategize and goes out to protest hand in hand with his followers.

Charismatic Influence and Prophetic Voice

Yet King's charisma is also marked by the element of speaking in a way that is awe inspiring. Perhaps it is his educational background, his experience as a Baptist preacher, or his love of gospel music that gives him this unquantifiable element of leadership:

> Jay Conger (1991) drafted probably the best explanation ever written about the inspirational leadership impact of the "I have a dream" speech and other rhetorical techniques that leaders use. The rhythm and harmony of a song, and not just the lyrics, can also generate a following. Usually it is the rhythm or the "riff" that draws our attention to a song. It is only when we are following the sound of the music that we can then understand the lyrics. All too often these will have a powerful message, one that can

generate sensemaking and commitment to a cause. However, it is the music that we follow. It is the music that is a form of leadership. (Jackson & Parry, 2011, p. 129)

This comparison of King's delivery of the "I have a dream speech" to music is fitting. If you watch any one of King's speeches, you can hear the beautiful cadence to his voice and see his dynamic ability to draw people in. He is perhaps an example of the prophetic voice that Greenleaf (1977/2002) refers to:

> The variable is not in the presence or absence or the relative quality and force of the prophetic voices. Prophets grow in stature as people respond to their message. If their early attempts are ignored or spurned, their talent may wither away. It is *seekers*, then, who make prophets, and the initiative of any one of us in searching for and responding to the voice of contemporary prophets may mark the turning point in their growth and service. (p. 22)

Greenleaf's reflections on prophetic voices refer back to this connected relationship with the seeker or follower, which means that King's followers, inspired by his voice, are also the key to propelling him and his message forward. So how does one even begin to tackle the seemingly insurmountable task of emulating the prophetic voice of Dr. Martin Luther King, Jr.?

While *Selma* (DuVernay, 2014) has an ensemble cast of talented actors, the British Nigerian actor David Oyelowo is the one that must face the impossible task of playing King. Oyelowo is the glue that must hold the film together, and he manages to succeed where some have failed to tap into the rhythm and power of King's voice. It is almost eerie watching how much he achieves the feeling and sound of one of King's speeches. In a behind-the-scenes interview with *O, The Oprah Magazine*, the actor discusses the shooting of the epic speech scenes:

> I knew I'd have to throw down an epic speech, which was terrifying because King was one of the greatest orators of all time. So before filming two speeches in a church in Atlanta—in front of 500 extras—all of us prayed together. And then an unforecast thunderstorm hit, and the lights went. Afterwards, the sky turned

an incredible purple, and not one but two rainbows appeared. (Davis, 2015)

It seems that the actor needed to experience a spiritual and divine moment to help him channel King's voice. Additionally, DuVernay's (2014) choice to film in an actual church in Atlanta is an essential ingredient to recreating the feeling of attending a Southern Baptist church. While I have attended a few good sermons in Southern Baptist churches, I have never witnessed the kind of preaching that King epitomized or that the actor David Oyelowo embodies in the film. I can only imagine what it must have been like to sit in those pews and listen to King's sermons during that oppressive time for Black folks in the United States and receive that uplifting call to action from King. It is also important to note that DuVernay did not own the intellectual property rights to King's speeches, which were licensed by King's estate exclusively to Stephen Spielberg. Therefore, she took on the daunting task of rewriting his speeches while also trying to maintain both the rhythm of King's delivery and the spirit of his intention (Suskind, 2014). The incredible and moving words that the actor speaks are also attributed to the writing talent of DuVernay, who is not credited for any of her writing contributions to the script due to a prior contract with the original screen writer, Paul Webb.

After the stirring performance in the church scene, it is not surprising to see that Cooper and others, such as Jimmie Lee Jackson, join the cause. First, you see that Jackson and his grandfather are calling to King after his speech, "Dr. King! Dr. King!" King reaches out his hand in greeting as he continues to talk to a reporter. This scene shows King not only as a respected minister and activist but as a celebrity within in the Black community. It shows again this charismatic element of idealized influence associated with transformational leadership. In the eyes of those Black folks watching in the church or on TV, Dr. King and the SCLC are part of a distinctive group to be admired. For Cooper and Jackson, it seems logical that they feel a connection to King, with his being a Black Christian man with a goals of equality; consequently, the speech spurs them on to join King's mission.

However, not everyone is thrilled to see King arrive in Selma. The leaders of the Student Nonviolent Coordinating Committee (SNCC), John Lewis and James Forman, who felt inspired and encouraged by King to form their group, are not happy to see King. The idea that Congressman Lewis, who played a pivotal role in the civils rights movement, was not onboard with the SCLC's plan to march on Selma paints a different picture of the challenges that King faced as a leader. In the film, King appears to realize that it would be better to have the support and involvement of the local SNCC group. A key component of transformational leadership is "a transformation in the attitudes and motivations, and consequently behaviors, of followers" (Jackson & Parry, 2011, p. 31), but servant-leaders also find ways to communicate with empathy even when someone's ideas or actions might not be in line with the overall goal of the organization. "The servant always accepts and empathizes, never rejects. The servant as a leader always empathizes, always accepts the person, but sometimes refuses to accept some of the person's effort or performance as good enough" (Greenleaf, 1977/2002, pp. 33–34). In the scene in which King and the SCLC face the two leaders of the SNCC, King must find a way to reason with them. King takes a diplomatic approach, complimenting them first on their grassroots efforts to raise Black consciousness, and then he explains how the SCLC works:

> But what we do is negotiate, demonstrate, resist, and a big part of that is raising White consciousness. In particular, the consciousness of whatever White man is sitting in the oval office. Right now, Johnson has other fish to fry. He'll ignore us if he can. The only way to stop him doing that is being on the front page of the national press every morning and by being on the TV news every night. (DuVernay, 2014)

King's tactic seems to be working, as you see the camera switch to a medium shot of the two young men. Lewis's demeanor is clearly different from that of Forman, who continues to look and respond in an angry fashion. Perhaps they are pondering King's point that it is important to raise White consciousness in order for real change to occur. When King asks Lewis and Forman if sheriff Jim Clark is like Laurie Pritchett, the sheriff in Albany who arrested protestors in a humane way, or if he is more like Bull Connor in Birmingham, it is Lewis who answers "Bull Connor" to confirm that Jim Clark is as treacherous and as brutal as they had heard. This means that Selma is an ideal place to stage their protest and get the attention of the media. From this small gesture, Lewis appears to be looking at the larger goal of voting rights for Blacks rather than whose territory it is. Thus, King's diplomacy has worked with Lewis, and both Lewis and Forman appear with other volunteers to march to the courthouse. King displays aspects of leadership that can be likened to both servant-leadership and transformational leadership because he uses his power of charismatic influence along with his empathy and desire to cultivate these future servant-leaders.

The Power of Images and Song

As the group of protesters march to the county courthouse, DuVernay gives audiences a great wide shot of the 100 or so Black men and women walking as a White woman standing in the street stares intently at them with disdain. King leads the group from the front with Andrew Young, Ralph David Abernathy, James Bevel, and with the leaders of SNCC, John Lewis and James Forman also at his side. We also see Cooper, along with three generations of the Jackson family: Jimmy Lee, his mother, and his grandfather. The big group walks on with the folky gospel song "I got the New World in My View" playing in the background. The gospel music positioned in this scene and other parts of the film seem to be a reminder of the resilience of Black people in difficult times. Similar to the Negro spirituals that soothed the souls of slaves in the field, helping them to keep thriving, the music is a reminder of this strength and also serves as their battle cry as they march to the front of the county voter registration office. As soon as the camera pans to show the formidable figure of sheriff Jim Clark lined up with other menacing-looking police officers holding billy clubs, there is a sense of foreboding that something will go wrong. King addresses Clark as a crowd of Whites shout out racial slurs. When Jackson's elderly grandfather has trouble sitting and is struck by the sheriff, it's not a complete shock. As Jackson goes to stand in front of the sheriff in a confrontational fashion, Cooper sacrifices herself for the young Black man. She hits Clark in the back of the head. Clark shouts out, "Get that nigg** woman" (DuVernay, 2014). Then the scene erupts in violence, and when several policeman grab Cooper to hold her down, the action starts to move in slow motion. In this pause in motion, it is almost as if viewers are transported back in time to Selma, and at the same time there is a moment that one can flash forward. You see rather than hear Cooper's screams as she is slammed to the ground. This silent scream echoes loudly for those watching today. Perhaps the images of the film blur with the current images of George Floyd on the ground as we hear the echoes of him pleading, "I can't breathe." There is power in this kind of moment that makes one pause to reflect on past and present events. This scene is juxtaposed with another startling scene of governor George Wallace making a declaration about "not tolerating a bunch of niggra agitators" (DuVernay, 2014). Governor Wallace, known for his disturbing speech that declared, "Segregation now, segregation tomorrow, and segregation forever," adds another level of emotion to the film. This drama captured by cameras is part of King's plan, and it reaches the front page of the newspaper in the hands of President Johnson. King and his followers stick to the battle plan to negotiate, demonstrate, and resist.

Paulo Freire (2010), Brazilian writer, educator, and philosopher, seemingly shared some of King's ideals on action:

> The revolutionary leader must realize that their own conviction of the necessity for struggle (an indispensable dimension of revolutionary wisdom) was not given to them by anyone else—if it is authentic. This conviction cannot be packaged and sold; it is reached, rather, by means of a totality of reflection and action. Only the leaders' own involvement in reality, within an historical situation, led them to criticize this situation and to wish to change it. (p. 67)

Freire echoes the notion that in order to be authentic and respected as a leader there must be direct involvement in the actions of the cause, and this is something that DuVernay (2014) articulates through King's character that despite the repeated reminders of "the closeness of death" that Coretta's character mentions, King persists in his mission to serve a greater purpose. He is sitting in a jail cell like everyone else after the incident with Cooper.

Shadow, Light, and Vulnerability

Despite King's jokes with his inner circle of the SCLC about Selma—"It's a good place to die" (DuVernay, 2014)—he has moments of doubt and weariness. In jail, King is away from his external support system of family and friends and cannot call upon the famous gospel singer Mahalia Jackson to sooth him with song. He, like other servant-leaders, may be motivated by his own search for healing:

> Perhaps, as with the minister and the doctor, the servant-leader might also acknowledge that his or her own healing is the motivation. There is something subtle communicated to one who is

being served and led if, implicit in the compact between the servant-leader and led, is the understanding that the search for wholeness is something they share. (Greenleaf, 1977/2002, p. 50)

King appears to have a close bond with Abernathy, whom he calls Ralphie. Abernathy must understand this servant-leader compact as both follower and friend to King. When King mentions to his friend Ralphie that he is tired, Ralphie reminds him, "Eyes on the prize, Martin." During the jail scene, DuVernay (2014) allows King to reveal vulnerability in the dialogue between these friends. King goes on to ask Abernathy,

How does it help a Black man to sit at a lunch counter if he doesn't own enough to buy the burger, or worse yet can't even read the menu 'cause there was no Negro school where he's from? What is that? Is that equality? What about in our minds? Equality in the Black psyche? Look at these men beaten down for generations.

King is contemplating real problems within the Black community that involve layered complexity. In his work, Freire (2010) makes a similar observation about the state of oppression: "One of the gravest obstacles to the achievement of liberation is that the oppressive reality absorbs those within it and thereby acts to submerge human beings' consciousness" (p. 51). Freire's statement, along with King's dialogue in the jail, is sobering in that it points to the enslavement of the mind that is so much harder to conquer, especially as it gets passed down from generation to generation.

The fact that King is contemplating the plight of all Black people shows that he is not just interested in helping a select few from his own educated class of Black folks, and it also shows that he is a human being who experiences dark moments of doubt. His role in bringing about change for Blacks and people of color in the United States and inspiring change in other places in the world such as South Africa is evident to those who know history, but as King talks privately with Ralphie, we are reminded that he is also just a man. In Parker Palmer's (2000) *Let Your Life Speak*, he explores the notion of the shadow and light in all of us:

But before we come to the center, full of light, we must travel in the dark. Darkness is the whole of the story—every pilgrimage has passages of loveliness and joy—but it is the part of the story most often left untold. When we finally escape the darkness and stumble into the light, it is tempting to tell others that our hope never flagged, to deny those long nights we spent cowering in fear. (p. 18)

Leaders like King are not supposed to show the darkness that Palmer speaks of, but when you carry a heaviness similar to that of a commander in the armed forces of being responsible for decisions that affect people's lives, how can you not feel weary at certain junctures? In his most vulnerable moments, King is able to share his thoughts with his friends in the inner circle of SCLC, who also ultimately take his lead. These also seem to be marks of a great leader, having a willingness to be vulnerable and being able to ask for help when needed.

Balancing Leadership and Legacy

When Jimmie Lee Jackson is killed by a state trooper after a peaceful protest, King must once again face the burden of what he is asking his followers to do. He cannot shirk his responsibility either as a spiritual leader or as the voice of the movement. DuVernay (2014) brings the camera into an intimate moment when King goes to console the Lee family, as you would expect a minister to do. He tells his grandfather honestly, "There are no words to soothe you, Mr. Lee. There are no words. I can tell you one thing for certain; God was the first to cry." After this heartbreaking exchange with the grandfather, we learn that Jackson, who had been only thirty-eight years old when he was killed, had also served in the army. King has no time to grieve because he deliveries a eulogy and another compelling call to action:

Who murdered Jimmy Lee Jackson? Every White law man who abuses the law to terrorize. Every White politician who feeds on prejudice and hatred. Every White preacher who preaches the bible and stays silent in front of his White congregation. (DuVernay, 2014)

King goes on to assert that Negro men and women who stand by and do not get involved as they watch their brothers and sisters get brutalized are also responsible, and the speech ends with a defiant declaration:

We are going back to Washington. We going to demand to see the president, and I'm going to tell him that Jimmy was murdered by an administration that spends millions of dollars every day to sacrifice life in the name of liberty in Vietnam that lacks the moral will and the moral courage to defend the lives of its own people here in America. We will not let go, and if he doesn't act, we will act. We will do it for all of our lost ones. All of those like Jimmy Lee Jackson gone too soon[,] taken by hate. (DuVernay, 2014)

From this passionate speech, it's clear that King will not accept from President Johnson that he has other agendas to address.

When King goes in for a personal conversation with President Johnson, the camera closes in tight and switches back and forth from one medium close-up of King with part of Johnson in the frame to a medium close-up shot of Johnson in the frame, and then a medium shot (Barsam & Monahan, 2016, p. 237). The camerawork shows both the close proximity that King has with the president and the intensity of the heated debate (DuVernay, 2014). When King divulges to President Johnson that he plans to march from Selma to Montgomery, Johnson appears concerned about the protection of the marchers, but he will not yield about proposing new legislation to help Blacks vote unencumbered in the South. King tells the president, "We need your involvement, we deserve your involvement as citizens of this country. Citizens under attack" (DuVernay, 2014). Johnson responds by telling him, "You're an activist[,] you got one issue, and I'm a politician[,] I got a 101" (DuVernay, 2014). After a less than fruitful exchange with King, Johnson is shown asking to speak to J. Edgar Hoover, who has been bugging King and offering to "dismantle the family" by using King's infidelity in marriage to their advantage. This is one of the scenes that may have caused debate with critics who thought that DuVernay made President Johnson more of a villain than he deserved. In a *Time* magazine article, it was suggested that Johnson did not encourage the bugging of King's home, and that this was already going on at the approval of Robert F. Kennedy (D'addario, 2015), and whether it was Lyndon B. Johnson or Robert Kennedy that ordered the surveillance, the evidence seems to point to the fact that Hoover continued to bug King and his followers, which DuVernay highlights in the FBI white type and reports that continuously appear on-screen throughout the film.

After the murder of a White priest who has joined King's cause, King and President Johnson have another heated exchange by phone. Johnson is infuriated that a group has come into the White House to stage a sit-in. King, who sees that President Johnson is still not ready to put forth a bill to give Blacks the right to vote, asks him to consider his legacy:

> I'm a preacher from Atlanta, and you are the man who won the presidency of the world's most powerful nation by the greatest landside in history four months ago, and you are also the man dismantling your legacy with each passing day. No one will remember the Civil Rights Act, but they will remember the standoff in Selma and that you never set foot in this state. They will remember you saying, wait, and I can't. (Duvernay, 2014)

These words must have haunted the president. Later in the film, Johnson does delay proposing a bill or getting involved in stopping the violence, but, ultimately, he does not want to be remembered in the same context as George Wallace. These parallels show us more about King's leadership. Johnson, by the nature of being a politician, acts in a manner that is more about transactional leadership as he mentions a "quid pro quo" to King. The questions King poses to President Johnson mirror some of the questions many may be asking now of Mr. Trump: "What kind of legacy will you leave behind?," "Will you be remembered as the president who do not speak out against racial injustice?," and "With Trump one must ask, will you be remembered as the president who instead of uniting the country during the time of a global pandemic and racial unrest, you continue to divide the country with actions such as using racial epithets like 'Kung Fu Virus' to describe a pandemic taking the lives of many in the United States and abroad?" Actions can tell us whether our leaders are acting to serve themselves or to serve the greater needs of the country. From *Selma* (DuVernay, 2014), one can see that King was committed to the fight of equality, and he was unwavering in his service to the cause that helped to get the Voting Rights Act of 1965 passed into law. King's service came at a very high cost, much like Medgar Evers or Malcom X, but in the eloquent words from *Selma* (DuVernay, 2014), "Our lives are not fully lived if we are not willing to die for those we love and what we believe."

Conclusion

Whether you believe, as actor Will Smith once said in a 2016 interview on the *Tonight Show* with Jimmy Fallon, that "racism isn't getting worse; it's getting filmed," or if you believe there has been a rise of overt acts of hate as a direct result of the current presidential administration, one can see the urgent need for more prophetic voices, more servant-leaders, like King to enact unity, change, and healing. It is also a reminder of the need for artists and filmmakers like DuVernay to paint historical moments in new ways. DuVernay's (2014) *Selma* takes on the heavy burden of making a film about the civil rights movement and about Dr. Martin Luther King, Jr. As a Black director, DuVernay also is faced with the burden of not damaging the Black legacy, and DuVernay artfully managed that delicate balance to create an admirable portrait of King that shows his imperfect nature as man without dwelling on the rumored infidelity in King's marriage. Instead, her lens seems to indicate a womanist perspective looking at things both as a woman and as a person of color. The camerawork, acting, editing, and writing give voice to the victims of violence who suffered in the civil rights movement and make us pause to reflect on the current civil unrest still sweeping the country. Despite being an imperfect man, King comes to life in DuVernay's (2014) *Selma* as a servant-leader whose leadership and method of peaceful nonviolent protest transformed freedoms for Blacks and people of color in the United States with the help of his SCLC members and volunteers from all races and walks of life. Recent events show us that his work is not yet done. In the words of Dr. King (1961), "Human progress is neither automatic nor inevitable. . . . Every step toward the goal of justice requires sacrifice, suffering, and struggle; the tireless exertions and passionate concern of dedicated individuals."

References

Barron, C. (2016). Not Just Indie: A look at films by Dee Rees, Ava DuVernay, and Kasi Lemmons. In L. Badley, C. Perkins, & M. Schreiber (Eds.), *Indie reframed: Women's filmmaking and contemporary American independent cinema* (pp. 204–220). Edinburgh University Press. http://www.jstor.org/stable/10.3366/j.ctt1g0529f.18

Barsam, R., & Monahan, D. (2016). *Looking at movies: An introduction to film* (5th ed.). W. W. Norton & Company.

Davis, A. (2015, January). Behind the scenes of the history: Making Selma movie. *O, The Oprah Magazine.* http://www.oprah.com/entertainment/behind-the-scenes-of-selma-ava-duvernay/all

D'addario, D. (2015, January 5). Selma: The Making of History. *Time, 185*(1), n.p.

DuVernay, A. (Director). (2014). *Selma* [Film]. Paramount Pictures.

Fallon, J. (2016, July 28). Will Smith marriage counsels America [Interview, TV series episode]. In *Tonight Show with Jimmy Fallon.* NBC.

Freire, P. (2010). *Pedagogy of the Oppressed* (30th ed.). Continuum.

Gilkes, C. (2009). Womanism. In N. Bercaw, T. Owner, & C. R. Wilson (Eds.), *The new encyclopedia of Southern culture: Gender* (Vol. 13, pp. 282–287). University of North Carolina Press. https://www-jstor-org.proxy.foley.gonzaga.edu/stable/10.5149/9781469616728_bercaw.72

Gonzales, E. (2020, June 5). Ava DuVernay recalls when Oscar voters disapproved of *Selma's* cast Eric Garner tribute. *Harper's Bazaar.* https://www.harpersbazaar.com/culture/film-tv/a32784470/ava-duvernay-selma-black-lives-matter/#

Greenleaf, R. K. (2002). *Servant leadership* (L. C. Spears, Ed.; 25th ed.). Paulist Press.

Gross, T. (2015, January 8). Sounds, spaces, and the spirit of Selma: A directors take [Interview transcript]. https://www.npr.org/2015/01/08/375756377/the-sounds-space-and-spirit-of-selma-a-director-s-take

Hesse, H. (1956). *Journey to the East.* Noonday Press.

Jackson, B., & Parry, K. (2011). *A very short, fairly interesting, and reasonably cheap book about studying leadership* (2nd ed.). Sage.

King, M. L., Jr. (Presenter). (1961, February 10). *Future of Integration.* Speech presented at New York University, New York, NY, United States.

Lemmons, K. (Director). (1997). *Eve's Bayou* [Film]. Trimark Pictures.

Lemmons, K. (Director). (2019). *Harriet* [Film]. Focus Features.

Palmer, P. (2000). *Let your life speak.* Jossey-Bass.

Stone, G. A., Russell, R. F., & Patterson, K. (2004). Transformational versus servant leadership: A difference in leader focus. *The Leadership & Organization Development Journal, 25*(4), 349–361. https://doi.org/10.1108/01437730410538671

Suskind, A. (2014, December 17). How Ava DuVernay struck a chord with Selma. *The Guardian.* https://www.theguardian.com/film/2014/dec/17/ava-duvernay-film-director-selma

Chapter 16

Servant-Leadership

A Brief Look at Love and the Organizational Perspective

KATHLEEN PATTERSON

According to Robert K. Greenleaf (1977/2002),

> Love is an indefinable term, and its manifestations are both
> subtle and infinite. But it begins, I believe, with one absolute
> condition: unlimited liability! As soon as one's liability for another
> is qualified to any degree, love is diminished by that much.
> Institutions, as we know them, are designed to limit liability
> for those who serve through them. (p. 52)

This is consistent with Winston (2002) and with a research model I proposed in 2003, both attempts to begin to name the connection between
love and servant-leadership. Winston admonishes leaders to begin to see
followers as hired hearts instead of hired hands, stating that this unique
call to servants-as-leaders begins with *agápao* love. *Agápao* love is moral
love, love that directs the servant-leader toward the right or the ultimate
good, at the right time and for the right reasons. The servant-leadership
model I proposed identified love as the cornerstone of the servant/follower
connection. To fully understand the important crucible where love meets
servant-leadership, a more thorough understanding of love is needed.

Love and Organizations

Love is a mysterious concept, a concept that has been of great importance to both scholars and leaders (Daft, 2002; Myers & Shurts, 2002).
Love has been acknowledged as having great importance by philosophers,
theologians, and all who are interested in ultimate concern and ultimate
meaning (Myers & Shurts, 2002). The various interpretations and understanding of the word *love* have been both perplexing (due to the concept
of being "in love") and complex, creating a constrained definition as well
as an assortment of typologies. According to Daft (2002), the day for love
in organizations has come, and gone should be the days of leading with
fear. Fear as a motivation tends to manifest in organizations as arrogance,
selfishness, deception, unfairness, and disrespect. In contrast, leading and
serving with love generates dignity, respect, and honor. Love, says Daft, is
a potent form of leadership—a way of living that can also open the door
for improved performance. Love has the power to create, and the result can
be emotionally connected employees, lives that are rich and balanced, and
an environment that allows members of the organizational community to
take risks, learn, grow, and move to better ground. Gunn (2002) calls love
in leadership a force, one that causes leaders to lead with understanding,
gratitude, kindness, forgiveness, and compassion.

Agápao Love

Love is considered the cornerstone of all virtues (Sanders et al., 2003),
providing a sense of meaning and fulfilling the higher needs of the community. Love creates legitimate discernment and presence (Yu, 1998). This
corresponds with what Winston (2002) has shown about love in the workplace setting: that *agápao*, or moral and social love, includes "embracing
the judgment and the deliberate assent of the will as a matter of principle,
duty, and propriety" (p. 5).

This perspective of love for leaders today is about actively considering
the needs of followers, along with a willingness to learn the gifts and talents
of each individual. The leader who leads with *agápao* love has a focus on
the employee first, then on the talents of the employee, and lastly on how
this benefits the organization.

Agápao love is a component of servant-leadership (Patterson, 2003;
Winston, 2002), a leadership in which the leader is emotionally, physically,
and spiritually present (Ferch & Mitchell, 2001). According to Autry (2001),

this presence takes the form of availability with responsibility. Servant-leaders are genuinely interested in the lives of followers (Crom, 1998), and consistently build people up and have a goal "to grow less and less as others grow more and more" (Turner, 2000, p. 85).

For the servant-leader, love is unconditional and fosters esteem and the excellence of the people, as well as a belief in humanity—specifically, that all humans have value in their own right (Russell, 2001; Russell & Stone, 2002; Wagner-Marsh & Conley, 1999). Leaders who lead with love exhibit feelings and foster understanding, gratitude, kindness, forgiveness, and compassion (Gunn, 2002). The servant-leader, invested in love, serves the best interests of others.

Love in Leadership

A recent article in the *MIT Sloan Management Review* (Ellis, 2004) states that there is new insight into emotion at the executive level, specifically circling around the concept of love. The language of love, as in "I love my people," has become an accepted paradigm of leadership; in fact, in some circles it is the preferred paradigm. A mature love, capable of forwarding social movement that is both enduring and complete, evokes in people their own life-giving and energized nature, and reflects Daft's (2002) leadership notion that it is "the heart rather than the mind that powers people forward" (p. 187).

But what does love looks like in the workplace? According to Gunn (2002), love makes people whole, opening the doors for faith and hope while liberating people from self-criticism, self-imposed limitations, isolation, and the ensuing diminishment of others. According to Gunn,

> When we lead with this power, we encourage without effort. We guide without rules. We direct without saying much. We see with our ears and listen with our hearts. We are confident without bluster. We are certain without worry. We can be firm without being mean. We can ask people to do much without feeling guilty. We can step aside so others can step up. (p. 12)

Love in Action

How a leader's maturity is manifested in the organization can be seen in the lives of those who lead with love. A look at William B. Turner of the

Synovus financial corporation provides valuable insights. Following this, I will briefly detail interviews I conducted with three organizational leaders on the connection between love and leadership. To give a miniature cross-section of leaders, I interviewed a minister, a military leader, and a business leader.

William B. Turner

William B. Turner is best known for his leadership in the financial industry, which some might consider a cold or uncaring field, and yet William B. Turner has led with love. In his book *The Learning of Love: A Journey toward Servant-leadership*, Turner (2000), a retired chairman of the Executive Committee of Synovus Financial Corporation and member of the board of directors for the Coca-Cola Corporation for eighteen years, spends a good deal of time talking about how he learned to love the people who worked for him. Turner credits his leadership training to his father and grandfather. Observing their leadership styles, he learned his most vital servant-leadership understanding: listening to others.

Turner (2000) recounts one life-defining circumstance about his grandfather, who owned a textile mill during the Great Depression. Textile mills were shutting their doors and calling it quits in this financial bust time; companies were unable to sell their products, causing pileups of useless inventory. Turner's grandfather decided to keep the mill running; in fact he had no money to pay employees and issued scrip to them enabling them to buy groceries. The decision to remain open, made from love, kept many people from starving during an extended and grueling time of economic hardship. Serendipitously, when the Depression ended Turner's grandfather was able to sell the large accumulation of stockpile.

What would cause a man to make a business decision that is seemingly illogical? Love for people was chosen over profits and losses. For Turner's (2000) grandfather, the decision was an extension of a life well lived. This had a tremendous impression on Turner, who made a conscious decision to lead by creating a culture where people could grow in three ways: materially, intellectually, and spiritually. He developed an organization that is a meaningful place to work. Turner proposes a love that is both a noun and a verb. From this elegant understanding, he furthers a persevering and artistic look at organizational life by showing that loving someone is more about asking how they want to be loved than about how you want to love them.

Initial Thoughts on Love and Leadership from Three Leaders

The first leader I interviewed was a minister. When asked about the connection between love and leadership, he commented, "One leader reflects on his own leadership by asking himself how much he really loves the people he leads—this reflection sets a new standard by which he views his leadership." He further proposed that a good leader should ask about motivations, and whether her or his motivations encompass both hidden and inner attitudes toward people, as well as overt actions. Giving an introductory look at the vulnerability love requires, he said,

> I've always known I want to love the people I lead, but I've never stretched the concept as far as to say that love is the way I lead them. I admit it frightens me a bit, because I have no idea where it might take me—or even what the next step might be.

The next leader interviewed was a military leader. He provided the following perspective on love in organizations:

> Love is evident in care people demonstrate for one another. When I walk through work areas—we call them duty sections—*agápao* love presents itself through the tones in the various conversations around me, offers for help, and inquiries about task and nontask challenges each is facing. People who really care for one another usually work for a leader who models such behavior. Naturally there are exceptions (loving workers in hostile environments and hostile workers in loving environments), but if an entire duty section demonstrates concern for one another both on task and off, the leader is likely influencing (encouraging, demonstrating, or at least allowing) such a climate.

He further stated that love can be boiled down to one word—*listen*. His manner of leadership seeks to listen rather than be heard, to understand rather than be understood. He reported that listening causes a leader to respect and genuinely care for each person:

> Five minutes of genuine attentive listening (with a desire to feel and understand) will expand our ability to relate and our desire to

help our followers. A desire to serve—to make others happy—is the essence of love. If we don't listen to those we lead, we will never understand them enough to love them.

The military leader provided insight into loving those with whom we work, postulating that love compels leaders to desire happiness, success, and rewards for others, and that this deep desire for the welfare of others can—and will—transcend animosity, disagreement, and contention. Furthermore, an environment of harmony can surface, and, notably, productivity increases, as well as efficiency. Another benefit is the realization of a more positive atmosphere in which people feel more confident and more creative. On a counter note, commenting on the potential drawbacks of love in the organization, he stated,

> Genuine care for others is hard work requiring a sustainable leader effort to love, care for, and support employees. In addition, *agápao* love is a love that demands action due to the desire to want to do for others in order to help them reach their goals and solve their problems. And sometimes this action will require a balance or a significant sacrifice from the leader—a high calling.

The third leader interviewed, a business leader, engaged a perspective on love and leadership that included an interior spirituality. Spirituality, he signified, is meant for the deep service of others:

> Because our company was shutting down a distribution center that I ran (back in the mid-1980s), I felt it was extremely important to help prepare all of the associates that I managed (mostly hourly and well over 100) to be as prepared as possible to transition into other jobs. With my management team, we (on our own . . . not the HR group) developed a series of seminars to share with the folks (a) what to wear to interviews, (b) how to interview, (c) how to prepare resumes, etc. During the process, because I was the building manager and had a fair degree of autonomy, I would pray openly for our entire workforce. This was an expression of . . . love toward and for them.

This business leader offered the following insight—he tried to set a thankful tone in the workplace by listening to and forming enduring relationships with employees. For those who desired, he led them in spiritual formation meant to deepen and enrich the interior of the person. Servant-leadership as a vocation, for him, meant creating a legacy in others that would in turn affect a future generation. He recounted a personal story of how an employee came to talk with him openly about a lifestyle choice, expecting rejection. The leader chose to love, spent a good deal of time with the employee, and deepened the relationship. Although the employee eventually left the organization, the dignity of the relationship endured. Leading with love, for this leader, is about time spent in service to others. He stated,

> Any time I know of employees who have had loved ones in the hospital, I make it a point to send notes of encouragement to them and their family, letting them know I'm praying for them and to be a support should they need anything from me or the company. The principle here is taking time for the little but very important things to express care and support for others.

Because of his understanding of love, he takes time to visit anyone who is in the hospital (on one occasion spending several hours visiting a new employee who was seriously ill). He stated that he takes time to pray with office staff that wish to and forms conversations in the organizational community that are vulnerable, transparent, and open; he is genuinely interested in the lives and the well-being of the employees and their families. He explained, "It is important to be sensitive to others and maintain flexibility to be sure that employees' families' needs are met." He reported, "Commitment and productivity is higher at work when a leader shows willingness to put others' needs over that of the business."

When asked about potential drawbacks to creating a culture of love in the organization, he offered the following insights:

> I'm not sure there are really any drawbacks when leaders love those with whom they work. Leaders, as responsible agents of an organization, are required to work with excellence for the company. This expectation in no way nullifies how we are to reflect and show love toward one another. Frankly, if we "love well" and continue to always pursue excellence as leaders, the best possible results will occur both for people *and* the organization. While we'll never do both of these perfectly—thank God for daily do-overs!

Love and the Organization

Servant-leadership offers a viable environment for love and leadership, a form of social and moral meeting place that is as powerful and transforming to the interior of the individual as it is to the culture of the organization. In the postmodern age the notion of death can take on an overly Western significance, one imbued with neglect, fears, regret, and isolation. Yet to those who love, love returns to them. Love in leadership can be a refreshing solvent to the acid that so often inhabits organizational life. The servant-leader, having developed a life of meaning and dignity, draws others toward meaning and dignity by loving well. In turn, the servant-leader is well-loved.

References

Autry, J. A. (2001). *The servant-leader: How to build a creative team, develop great morale, and improve bottom-line performance*. Crown Publishing Group.

Crom, M. (1998). The leader as servant. *Training, 35*(7), 6.

Daft, R. L. (2002). *The leadership experience*. South-Western.

Ellis, C. (2004). Leaders Who Inspire Commitment. Tapping traditional Asian values can instill cross-cultural capabilities. *MIT Sloan Management Review.* (Spring), p. 5.

Ferch, S. R., & Mitchell, M. W. (2001). Intentional forgiveness in relational leadership: A technique for enhancing effective leadership. *Journal of Leadership Studies, 7*(4), 70–83.

Greenleaf, R. K. (2002). *Servant leadership: A journey into the nature of legitimate power and greatness* (L. C. Spears, Ed.; 25th anniversary ed.). Paulist Press. (Original work published 1977)

Gunn, B. (2002). Leading with compassion. *Strategic Finance, 83*(12), 10–12.

Myers, J. E., & Shurts, W. M. (2002). Measuring positive emotionality: A review of instruments assessing love. *Measurement and Evaluation in Counseling and Development, 34*(4), 238–254.

Patterson, K. A. (2003). *Servant-leadership theory: A theoretical model*. Digital Dissertations, AAT 3082719.

Russell, R. F. (2001). The role of values in servant-leadership. *Leadership & Organization Development Journal, 22*(2), 76–83.

Russell, R. F., & Stone, A. G. (2002). A review of servant-leadership attributes: Developing a practical model. *Leadership and Organization Development Journal, 23*(3), 145–157.

Sanders, J. E., Hopkins, W. E., & Geory, G. D. (2003). From transactional to transcendental: Toward an integrated theory of leadership. *Journal of Leadership & Organizational Studies, 9*(4), 21–32.

Turner, W. B. (2000). *The learning of love: A journey toward servant-leadership.* Smyth & Helwys Publishing.

Wagner-Marsh, F., & Conley, J. (1999). The fourth wave: The spiritually-based firm. *Journal of Organizational Change Management, 12*(4), 292–302.

Winston, B. E. (2002). *Be a leader for God's sake.* Regent University-School of Leadership Studies.

Yu, J. (1998). Virtue: Confucius and Aristotle. *Philosophy East and West, 48*(2), 323–347.

Chapter 17

Clara Voce—The Greeting of Heart and Spirit

MARCIA NEWMAN

We began our lesson by envisioning her voice, where the voice was going, where she wanted to place it, where she intended the sound to flow, what she desired to express through the music, and what she wanted to feel after having sung the piece. We warmed up with vocal exercises and then I stopped and asked her, "Why sing? Why take time out of your hectic day at the bank to come here and sing?" "Because the gift of music should be used," she answered. "It gives me joy." *Clara voce*—clear voice—the greeting of heart and spirit.

The encounter with my student gave me pause. Because of my job with the Greenleaf Center and my life's work as a vocalist and voice teacher, I've been thinking about the elegant connections involved in the voice, vocal study, and servant-leadership. If art imitates life, then art and creative expression help us encounter new light, truth, and revelation. Certainly, learning to use the voice is tied to learning to be fully human.

Vocal singing, study, training, and execution draw pictorial allegories to some of the same issues people confront while growing in servant-leadership. Both are essentially about relationships with people, and growing people through those relationships.

It's a very ancient saying,
But a true and honest thought

That when you become a teacher,
By your pupils you'll be taught.
As a teacher I've been learning
(You'll forgive me if I boast)
But now I've become a pupil
Of the subject I like most:
Getting to know you.

—Anna in *The King and I*

The training of the voice stands apart from other types of instrumental instruction because many of the concepts must be communicated mainly through visual imagery, not by means of manual application. This often results in a close encounter between student and teacher on the level of human relationship. Vocal training, if done well, forms a growing relationship between people while they work and create together. A unique challenge for communication develops: the student must be able to see, hear, understand, and experience the concept on his or her own instrument, not one the teacher can access for personal demonstration. The outcome can mean deepened interpersonal communication, and a more transcendent way of relating to the physical world encountered every day. The experiences of servant-leadership are similarly aligned. The voices of both singer and leader are intrinsically connected to who we are, what engages our thought life, and what connects us to our spirit and innermost being.

In his essay "The Servant as Leader," Robert Greenleaf (1970) gives us a picture of the person who has found his or her voice:

> The central figure of the story is Leo, who accompanies the party as the servant who does their menial chores, but who also sustains them with his spirit and his song. He is a person of extraordinary presence. (Greenleaf, 1970, p. 1)

In Leo, the servant that accompanies a band of men on a mythical journey, we see someone wholly integrated and comfortable with the movement between serving and leading. He moves people through spirit, song, and presence.

In becoming more familiar with the model of the servant-leader in Greenleaf's (1970) writings, 10 personal characteristics stand out as noted by Larry Spears (1998), author, editor, and former executive director of the Greenleaf Center: listening, awareness, building community, commitment, conceptualization, empathy, foresight, healing, persuasion, and stewardship.

In the "art of the voice," used by both artist and servant-leader, the 10 characteristics become paramount.

For the leader and singer both, everything comes into play when we open our mouths to connect breath to expression and draw it forth into voice. As the singer engages mind, soul, and body to impart meaning and life through music, the need for personal knowledge is vital. The artist is immediately faced with his or her limitations for the task in terms of ability and experience. Is this piece at my level? Is it going to be a stretch? Will I be able to commit to practicing it and to the level of mastery needed to perform it? Where do I need to focus on technical aspects of the music, nuances, and emotional delivery? What fears am I facing in taking on this challenge? What stylistic changes that are new to me need to be made in the performance of this piece? What was the composer trying to communicate? Is this even suitable for my voice? Am I taking on something that is clearly beyond my ability?

And what of the leader when taking on a "new piece of music" in the organization? Is the staff ready for something like this? Will we be willing to stretch as needed to accomplish the task? Am I asking something of our organization that is outside our capabilities? If not, what technical issues do we need to practice and master in order to "perform" at our optimum? Will we "face our fears" in taking this on, in risking failure? Are we willing to be vulnerable?

Being self-aware includes being in touch with the physical self and how it is so intricately woven into our emotional and spiritual being. The voice is not just the "voice box" or house protecting the chords; it is the emergence of heart, mind, and inner strength connected to breath, which, sent through these minute pieces of tissue (a miracle of nature in themselves), becomes something larger than just a reflection of one or more parts. Likewise, a servant-leader, in artistically engaging "the song," becomes keenly aware of him or herself, and must be aware of how the individual presence is connected in a mysterious way to the body, spirit, heart, and breath of the collective voice that is making music in the organization. In their book *Spiritual Capital*, Danah Zohar and Ian Marshall (2004) share further insight into this notion of self-awareness and spirit:

> The word spiritual comes originally from the Latin spiritus, which means "that which gives life or vitality to a system." . . . For human beings, that which gives life—indeed that which gives unique definition—to our humanity is our need to place our

enterprises in a frame of wider meaning and purpose. The spiritual in human beings makes us ask why we are doing what we are doing and makes us seek some fundamentally better way of doing it. It makes us want our lives and enterprises to make a difference. (pp. 28–29)

When one embraces this mentality of abundance, then servant-leadership becomes a means to realizing that the whole is exquisitely greater than the sum of the parts.

What are the parts? For the singer, the parts are the possible limitations of a given body makeup, the resonating chamber, and the size and length of the vocal chords (which determine the voice range in which a person is able to sing). For the organization, it is the size of the group, the talents represented, and the potential of individual and communal leadership capacity. Both vocalist and organization, in facing and overcoming their given limitations, can "sing in a key" that is natural or built into their collective voices in order to "sing" and live and work in ways that are meaningful to the world. This ability to excel within the given gifts of a group is a characteristic that I believe sets the servant-leader apart from those who choose to lead by fear, authority, and control. The risking of self, knowing one's self-limitations, and being comfortable with those limitations in relationships reflect the artistic core of a servant-leader.

Unlike any other instrument, voice demands the willingness of the performer to engage in a level of openness and honesty that is inherently personal. The voice is not taken out of a case or tuned externally. It is an instrument connected to the wholeness of the human person. A singer cannot alter the weather or control humidity to keep the instrument in tune; unlike instruments protected by man-made cases, the voice is encased in the human body. When the body is ill, the person may be overwhelmed or stressed; when the body is bumped or damaged, no hardcover case protects it. Singers play on their instruments under varied circumstances with no insulation; singers are painfully aware of the internal and external influences of the nature of the day and where life hurts; it comes through in their singing, loud and clear. In Greenleaf's understanding of the singer-servant Leo, a complicated mystery is unveiled and we see what the singer is striving for in being aware—that the spirit, soul, and body are inseparable and are reflected in the presence of the whole person in performance. Strikingly, those who embark on the journey of love in their respective organizations find that their own voice is readable, discernible, and becoming light to others by listening empathically and deeply invoking others' true song:

> Most of us at one time or another, some of us a good deal of the time, would really like to communicate, really get through to a significant level of meaning in the hearer's experience. It can be terribly important. The best test of whether we are communicating at this depth is to ask ourselves, first, are we really listening? Are we listening to the one we want to communicate to? Is our basic attitude, as we approach the confrontation, one of wanting to understand? (Greenleaf, 1970, p. 11)

Singing often opens up emotional wounds "locked in our tissues"—wounds that require redressing or the voice will be hindered. The nature of bringing physical breath to art form often brings these areas in need of healing to the surface. I have been affected by this phenomenon as student and as a teacher. When it happens, a keen teacher, as a keen leader, sees that the need to embrace the interference is more pertinent to the moment than the study of vocal technique. The voice teacher and/or servant-leader becomes an instrument of healing for the student or follower.

Deep listening often unlocks the potential greatness of the singer to meet Greenleaf's (1970) best test of servant-leadership: becoming healthier, freer, wiser, more autonomous and more likely to serve! Empathy is one of the reasons good voice teachers are considered personal mentors or spiritual directors. They read between the lines of what is being said or not said, sung or not sung, discerning where the student is emotionally, physically and spiritually on a given day. How the teacher responds to what is being shared is crucial to uplifting the "hidden wholeness" (Palmer, 2004) in the student.

Rubenfeld (2000), trained as a conductor at the Juilliard School of Music, writes in her book *Listening Hand,*

> Soon I was able to hear the whole from the sum of its parts and then I learned to transmit this vision to the players, not through verbal commands but by using my face, my body and especially my hands. I could cradle the music, hold it in my hands and hold it out to the players. My hands could both listen and speak. . . . Like music, healing involves the capacity to listen to others and hear their inner song. Hearing silence as

> well as sounds is part of music, so the healer learns to listen to both sounds and silences. Impulses, needs, emotions and feelings in people are expressed through sounds and silences, words and wordless movements of the body. The healer listens to all these variations and helps the client achieve harmony. (p. 5)

There is something marvelous about teaching voice that nurtures and encourages the musical healer to read behind and between what the voice is saying. I once had a student who had a large gap between her head voice and her chest voice. After deep probing, it was apparent that her "little girl" voice and her "professional trainer's" voice were representative of two different styles of life manifested in her daily interactions. One voice she used for her family, illustrative of her desire to please and be a good girl. The other she used to reflect respect, authority, and responsibility. It became apparent that her voice fatigue and constant vocal cord irritation were the result of her not being able to bridge the two and bring forth her authentic self. Yet this meant spending time dealing with personal underlying issues and encouraging her to be courageous in looking inside herself to resolve the matter. I also encouraged her to play more, which she felt was an unexpected gift of the voice lesson! This scenario is similar to challenges presented to the leader who serves by listening. The deep work of love in an organization brings personal issues to the surface. The servant-leader doesn't attack or ignore but embraces and creates a space for healing. I have always valued my voice teachers as good healers who were there at critical junctures and later proved to be markers of wisdom and prophecy in my life.

When contemplating a given exercise, the singer asks questions that lie at the very heart of the use of the voice, such as, for what purpose am I going to share my gift? Who is my audience? How can I speak life to people, and what will be my medium? This is true for solo performing as well as choral exercise or dramatic singing in oratorio or opera. The concept of awareness is now coupled with conceptualization and foresight, and the desired end is realized in building community for the joy and well-being of others.

The Sound of Music, Rodgers and Hammerstein's (1959) delightful adaptation of the true story of the von Trapp Family Singers and their escape from Nazi-occupied Austria, weaves a wonderful tale of how the voice is instrumental in building community. Maria, a young Catholic postulant sent to the von Trapp home as temporary governess, shares the gift of communal singing and brings love, joy, healing, and life to seven children bereaved of a mother and under the control of an austere father who has lost his dreams.

In an especially poignant scene, Maria invites the children on an excursion to the Salzburg hills, where she, too, in loneliness and need, found joy through song and freedom of expression. Knowing the children are forbidden to sing by their father, Maria risks her position as governess by overriding his authority. Starting with total simplicity, "at the very beginning," she begins to teach them to "find their voices" by using the solfège method of singing, or "do-re-mi-fa-so-la-ti-do." From this base of technical simplicity, she weaves the notes into songs with skill, rhyme, imagination, balance, and teamwork. The songs demand give and take and contributions from all voices, both large and small. The children not only find pleasure but their wounded, fragile hearts also begin to heal of the rift generated by a lack of fatherly presence and spirit. Maria takes a major risk in addressing such wounds, knowing no further healing would take place should the wounds go uncared for. In the midst of the children's creativity, fun, and play, they aren't even really aware of what she has set out to do. Her next move of brilliance follows as she teaches them to test their newfound musical skills by working together on their native country song, "Edelweiss," to share with their father, in an act of love and forgiveness.

Maria, as teacher, has both led and served. She led the children to a place of beauty and risk and helped them find their heart's desire while at the same time serving them through her own vulnerability, honoring their places of fear, and sharing her own story of presence in order to encourage. This marked the beginning of their communal story as friends whose love grew to make them a family.

Fraulein Maria had an astonishing gift of conceptualization, an important keystone of servant-leadership, and one that many singers miss. Singing is in the body and outside the body at the same time, requiring the singer to take what he or she has and throw it into midair, and learn to use muscles and vibrations that cannot be directly touched and place them to maximize their effectiveness. The vocal chords are minute tissues residing in the larynx . . . the singer must visualize the making of the notes in the brain and then engage the brain to execute this to the larynx while concentrating on so many other things at the same time! Leadership often requires the same juggling of skills. Like Maria, the leader must be able to see the place where the group needs to go before getting there. The leader also visualizes what medium will be the most helpful in achieving that end, while at the same time "throwing" love and discipline into the mix and hoping they land where intended.

Barry Green (1986), author of several books relating to conceptualization, wrote in *The Inner Game of Music*,

> If you can't hear it in your head, you can't play it . . . when you can hold the sound and pitch of the music clearly in your head in this way, performing it accurately becomes easier. Your body has a sense of its goal. Effectively, you are playing a duet between the music in your head and the music you are performing. (p. 60)

Whether it is projecting the voice, sustaining a sequence of notes, climbing a scale, or "throwing your voice," the total exercise of music requires the mental visualization of execution or completion prior to delivery. Robert Greenleaf (1970) encouraged just such a precise understanding of foresight and conceptualization as key ingredients to a servant-leader's being able to draw followers into a compelling vision to accomplish a great dream.

What the singer receives as an "aha" in a voice lesson one day is easily lost before the body is trained to remember it, a commitment to something you can't put your fingers on and play again. Ask any vocalist who has had a bad practice or bad performance; he or she will tell you that it isn't uncommon to want to hide the instrument away for good where no one can hear it and be sure to never take it out again! Many of the principles of servant-leadership at their core sound noble, but in truth they require great discipline to master, and anyone who has ever embarked on a the journey of hard personal change knows that it is often long and exhausting. If one is motivated and willing, however, the price is minimal compared with the blessings found.

Indeed, this concept of commitment translates directly into vocal training as we consider the need to practice and refine the art as a "habit" and discipline. Prominent leadership expert Stephen Covey (2004) has written on this very subject, and named his book *The 8th Habit*. His book, though not written from the standpoint of a voice teacher, highlights the need for personal integration to be exercised as a habit that is then clearly reflected in the personality, character, and authenticity of the human being, which is then resonated through the human voice. And the voice, more than any other instrument, is a challenge to get a handle on, due to the fact that one doesn't play on it, like a cello or a flute. One plays "in it," so to speak, as we do the nitty-gritty of our character. If life is flowing, all is well, but deeper tests for the artist arise when life is degraded or immensely difficult. Servant-leaders cultivate the same perseverance during dark seasons and model honest and radiant resilience in the journey.

My first tenure with formal voice study in high school required that I drive to another town, pay for my own lessons, and work outside of school to pay for the gas and the lessons. It was definitely something I wanted to do—the crucial necessity of passion in pursing any given discipline, be it musical arts or servant-leadership. But the real first hurdle came in learning to sing the "e" vowel correctly. The goal of the classical singer is to get the voice into the resonant space high in the head so that the sound has room to vibrate. Choral music usually consists of "oohs" and "ahs" and "o" sounds, which make for a good blending of voices and are relatively easy to produce. The "e" vowel is one that takes immense visual and breath work. But once the singer achieves the feeling of the buzz or a tingle in the "mask," or resonating chamber, the sound can grow fuller and the singer can begin to sense some achievement. Tremendous physical core power is required to hold the air there. If not maintained, this core power is lost. Servant-leadership necessitates similar mastery and motivation. Servant-leadership evokes hard work, sacrifice, and a form of love that is as directly powerful as it is lovely and life-giving. Singers persevere toward the opportunity to find the mask's sweet spot, to feel that vibration and the coming together of artistic energy. The reward of servant-leadership is the same joy of accomplishing that that is immanently worthwhile, that which loves and serves the world:

> In my view of the world there are people whom I would call spirit carriers . . . those servants [who] find the resources and make the intensive effort to be an effective influence. The spirit is power, but only when the spirit carrier, the servant as nurturer of the human spirit, is a powerful and not a casual force. (Greenleaf, 1996, pp. 46, 48)

Once singers are comfortable in their skin, so to speak, they must find their center—their station of power from which to execute their voice. I think this is central to the admonition to "finding our voice." Ironically, for the singer, it has more to do with using the breath (the power), being totally grounded physically, and through complete relaxation of the voice box, releasing the sound to find its resonating chamber in the head. The less the neck and throat area are tight or strained, the better the flow of air and the greater the resonance potential for the sound to spin in the mask. This is true of leadership as well. A servant-leader can resonate presence more acutely after having found grounding in his or her personal core. In leadership as in singing, being wishy-washy, twisting and turning, can waste energy and keep life from being directed toward a place of resonance. The servant-leader, like the singer, must have the strength of technique and holistic discipline to hold the "well of energy" or breath so that it can go where intended. This, like all musical discipline, requires practice. But once discovered through the discipline of the art form, it gets easier and easier, and builds confidence. Ironically, more breath and core power are necessary to sing softly than to sing loudly. This is true of leadership as well. As a friend once said, "Vulnerability and control are really distant cousins juxtaposed on the opposite ends of the spectrum." Both the singer and the servant-leader discipline themselves to hold the tension between the two, whether executing a pianissimo or holding a relationship in balance.

Like good relational leadership, singing offers wonderful health benefits as well. Good vocal singing, using lots of breath, is a natural destressor, a detoxifier of the body and blood that helps the body produce natural endorphins, the hormones that give a good feeling after exercise. Great synergy in leading and serving can be a natural detoxifier of bad blood in a group, a source of joy and healing, and ultimately results in a great feeling of accomplishment. In both, when exercised regularly, we feel toned and joyful and we sleep well after a hard day's work. Irenaeus is known to have said, "The glory of God is the human being fully alive." Once the singer has found presence and has connected with breath and heart (spirit), the singer is ready to share the gift of song, his or her opus Dei. This is the culmination of the unique attributes that set each person apart from another and make each person's contribution in living so important and significant to the benefit of others.

My student said she knew she should sing, wanted to sing, and that it brought her joy. And using song, Leo served the men on their journey. Maria von Trapp found her place in the mountains, and her singing was a contribution that had profound effect on encouraging the joy, healing, and gifting of others. Ilana Rubenfeld (2000) uses her hands not only to read people's heart scores in music but as instruments of healing in physical therapy as well. Whatever our gifts are, I believe we are given them by God to use them. Stewardship is crucial. If we are given a gift or talent and withhold it, we suffer. Tom Paterson (1998) writes, "To a gifted musician, artist, writer, dancer, scientist, nurse, teacher, engineer—whatever the area of gift—there is no sense of living fully unless the person is doing her gift" (p. 140). He understood the correlation between doing work and making doing the work a joyful art. As people who need the mutual blessing of both sharing with and receiving from others, when we create opportunities to encourage stewardship of individual and collective giftings and resources, we treasure and further develop all humanity.

Like the legacy Robert Greenleaf left us through his understanding of human relationship, many of the best voice teachers today, who once had glorious careers as singers, are finding their greatest fulfillment pouring their musical wisdom into up-and-coming younger talent. Vocal training doesn't end when the voice loses tenor! If the mind is still active, a great singer can become a wonderful teacher. One of my first professors in college was Gerhard Hüsch, a famous lieder singer and performer in Germany, who was sharing his stewardship well into his eighties as a visiting professor at several universities. Imagine the voices he heard and sung with in that lifetime! Dr. Husch was free to share his expertise through images and visualizations, with the added bonus of years of experience. Not bound by ego and or career tenure, servant-leaders with years of life experience are free to share the joys of their journey and living a full life with those who are seeking the same:

> The ability to withdraw and reorient oneself, if only for a moment, presumes that one has learned the art of systematic neglect, to sort out the more important from the less important—and the important from the urgent[—]and to attend to the more important, even though there may be penalties and censure for the neglect of something else. . . . The servant-as-leader must constantly ask himself, how can I use myself to serve best? (Greenleaf, 1970, p. 12)

Today there is growing concern, and rightly so, about the potentially severe limits our very techno-savvy, noise-driven culture is placing on our lives. The exhortation to "find your voice" couldn't come at a more critical time. Finding the voice, the person, the spirit, the reason for being, if you will, may be seen as prophetic to the future leaders of our day. Whether one has a passion for Access Hollywood, decorating with Martha, cooking with Emeril, watching the stock market ticker tape, ESPN, CNN, Fox 24/7 cable news, the golf channel, or just net surfing, there is more information, and more to watch, listen to, and take in every day. Many of us have lost the ability to be at ease in silence and to take time for reflection.

Unencumbered, unstructured time for reflection is lessening as our work often demands more of the individual in terms of energy to process mass amounts of information. This carries with it the liability of spending more of oneself doing rather than being, and it is confirmed by the numbers of people who are drained, exhausted, overrun, angry, and out of breath. Many have little or nothing to say of lasting importance. The creative juices become dry, and many express a renewed hunger for a simpler lifestyle. Is there any correlation between finding our voice and finding our lives? If so, what questions do we need to begin asking?

> For when I hear a man discussing virtue or any wisdom who is a true man and worthy of the words he speaks, I am overjoyed; I put the speaker and the speech together to see how they fit and harmonize. And such a man seems to me properly musical, turned to the fairest harmony, not of the lyre or pleasant instruments, but actually tuned in his own life between words and deeds, not in the Ionian, nor yet in the Phrygian or Lydian; but in the Dorian, the only one of the harmonies truly Hellenic. Such a man makes me delight in his voice, and you would consider me a lover of talk, so eagerly do I take in what he says. (Plato, 1996)

To find our lives and "fine tune them to their fairest harmonies," we will need to listen acutely to hear our inner frequencies, our own heart strings, and honestly ask ourselves: to what are we being tuned? Putting aside the temptations of entertainment and noise, we do better by setting aside the time, as all serious musicians do, to practice and rehearse and envision the music to be played for the performance of our lives. In art and in life, it is the necessary and essential sacrifice:

> As a leader (including teacher, coach, and administrator) one must have facility in tempting the hearer into that leap of imagination that connects the verbal concept to the hearer's own experience . . . one of the arts of communicating is to say just enough to facilitate that leap. (Greenleaf, 1970, p. 11)

The road to personal growth and mastery can be taxing. It demands deep reflection, personal accountability, skills training, and great personal motivation to change. Commitment and dedication are required. The friendship of a good teacher/leader, then, becomes invaluable. The art of persuasion, encouraging the student/follower/coleader to stretch, grow and risk, is not only necessary, but also highly engaging, and will often make the difference in how a person looks back on his or her life. Mahatma Gandhi said, "My life is my message."

Finding one's voice is not merely an exercise in putting on a new outfit and being someone different. It certainly doesn't happen in a day, in a fortnight, or even a year. The struggle to come into life's graceful and beautiful tuning takes a lifetime—it is the journey. As Molly Fumia wrote,

> To be joyful in the universe is a brave and reckless act. The courage for joy springs not from the certainty of the human experience, but the surprise. Our astonishment at being loved, our bold willingness to love in return—these wonders promise the possibility of joyfulness, no matter how often and how harshly loves seems to be lost. (as cited in Klug, 1998, p. 127)

And to W. A. Mozart have been attributed the words, "Neither a lofty degree of intelligence, nor imagination, nor both together go to the making of a genius. Love, love, that is the soul of a genius."

The exhortation to find one's voice, though bold, need not be received with a sense of burden but rather with promise and joy. It is the gift of life, the promise of being fully alive, fully integrated, and sharing who we are without fear. Fearless, rather, we share who we are with *clara voce*—clear voice. Clear, shining voices, radiating the greeting of the heart and spirit to one another, are humanity's sweetest song. And, like Fraulein Maria with the children, in being our best selves, sharing from that deep well of love, we are full of fun, using our imaginations, risking, healing, and finding new joy while changing the lives of others.

May we fully enjoy each other's presence, spirit, and song!

References

Covey, S. R. (2004). *The 8th habit*. Free Press.

Green, B., & Gallway, T. W. (1986). *The inner game of music*. Doubleday.

Greenleaf, R. K. (1970). *The servant as leader*. The Robert K. Greenleaf Center.

Greenleaf, R. K. (1996). *Seeker and servant*. Jossey-Bass.

Klug, L. (Ed.) (1998). *All will be well: A gathering of healing prayers*. Augsburg.

Palmer, P. J. (2004). *A hidden wholeness: The journey toward an undivided life: welcoming the soul and weaving community in a wounded world.* Jossey-Bass.

Paterson, T. (1998). *Living the life you were meant to live.* Thomas Nelson.

Plato. (1996). *The collected dialogues of Plato, including the letters* (E. Hamilton & H. Cairns Eds.). Princeton University Press.

Rodgers, R., & Hammerstein, O., II (1959). *The sound of music* [Stage musical]. Broadway.

Rubenfeld, I. (2000). *Healing hands.* Bantam.

Spears, L. C. (1998). *Insights on leadership: Service, stewardship, spirit, and servant-leadership.* John Wiley & Sons.

Zohar, D., & Marshall, I. (2004). *Spiritual capital.* Berrett-Koehler.

Chapter 18

Spiritual Capital

Keynote Address, 2005 International
Servant-Leadership Conference

DANAH ZOHAR

Good morning, everybody. I'm as happy as you are to be at this conference again. I think it's my favorite conference. My second favorite is the
conference that Peter Senge runs, every November or December, the Soul
Conference or the Systems Theory Conference. What's nice about both of
these conferences is that they are more than conferences, they've built a
community around them and you see old friends and there's a great spirit
of community at the conferences, and that makes them both very special.
And the theme of servant-leadership brings out the nicest people.

I'm going to talk this morning about servant-leadership and spiritual
capital. I think that servant-leadership is a very profound and transformative
idea, and you must agree with me or you wouldn't be here. But I think it
could be more. I think it is the heart of what could be a whole overarching,
all-embracing new philosophy of organizations, and particularly business, a
philosophy that could help us do what has to be done, which is to reinvent
capitalism. Capitalism and servant-leadership just don't mix—capitalism as
we know it. And yet capitalism is a very, very powerful economic system,
and we all know that. So I want to turn capitalism on its head today, still
calling it capitalism but giving it a new philosophy to live by. And I call

321

this new philosophy *spiritual capital*. And I hope to make it clear to you as I talk this morning what that's all about.

I want to begin with a story from Ovid's tales of Greek mythology. These Greek myths have a power to them that our writers today just don't have. They always manage somehow to say more than the words in them. And I find the myth of a merchant called Aris Kythan, a larger-than-life story, very much to the point of what I want to say.

Aris Kythan was a very wealthy timber merchant. He owned thousands of acres of tree land. But he didn't have much of a soul. To him a tree was so many cubits of wood, and so many cubits of wood was so many dollars. (I don't think he called them dollars in those days, but that's what he would call them if he were around today.) There was on Aris Kythan's land one particularly special tree beloved by the gods. Birds nested in this tree, fairies and spirits nestled in the tree, and pilgrims came and tied their prayers to branches of the tree. But one day Aris Kythan came upon this tree, and having no soul, he looked at it and thought, "This is one of the best trees I've got on my land, this will give me x cubits of wood and it will make me even wealthier than I am today." So he took his ax and he chopped down the tree. Of course the tree withered, its branches fell, the tree died, the spirits had to fly away, the birds had to fly away, the prayers blew away in the wind. The gods were very angry with Aris Kythan. So they decided to put a curse on him. The curse was that Aris Kythan would become insatiably hungry. Nothing that he could eat would ever be enough to satisfy his hunger. Once he was afflicted by this curse, Aris Kythan began by eating all of his stores, but he was still hungry. So then he ate his wife and children, and he was still hungry. Left now with no possessions, no stores, no family, there was nothing left for Aris Kythan to eat but himself. I'll use Ovid's own words for this, because they have the power of the horror that overcame Aris Kythan: "Of a monster, no longer a man, and so at last the inevitable: he began to savage his own limbs. And there, at the final feast, devoured himself."

For me Aris Kythan is the ultimate symbol of capitalism and business as we know them today, a monster consuming itself. Capitalism in pursuit of profit is destroying natural resources on which it itself depends. Capitalism as we know it is destroying our global environment. Capitalism as we know it is chewing up the people within it. And it spits them out when it's finished with them. Capitalism as we know it all over the world is leading to social and political unrest because of the inequities that follow in its wake, because once again it thinks only of profit, and not of the consequences of its practices. And finally, which is why so many of you are here today, capitalism is causing a crisis of leadership for itself, because many of the best and brightest are leaving business for nonprofit organizations, or simply for farming, or crafts—more idealistic ways that they can earn their living and do something good for society.

It's difficult in today's capitalism and business as we know them to be a servant-leader. Not impossible, and there are wonderful cases that we hear about at this conference, but it is difficult. And those who are servant-leaders within our present system tend to be lonely and isolated, unless they come to Indianapolis the first week in June. The *Oxford English Dictionary* describes *capital* as wealth, power, advantage, and profit. But capitalism has taken all these words, wealth, power, advantage, and profit, and turned them into totally material terms. Wealth is how many bucks we can put in the bank, power is our power to accumulate more bucks, advantage is our advantage over our competitors, and profit, of course, is our material profit. It's all about money. In so many of the companies that I have worked for, I meet men and women who express tremendous stress and despair about this. They say that during the weekend, when I'm at home with my family, I go for walks in the country, I play with my kids, I care about the global situation, I worry about the state of American politics, I worry about the state of the world, but when I go into work on Monday morning I have to leave all that outside the door, because work is about making money for the shareholders of my company. This leads to a lot of the stress in business life, and the meaninglessness in business life, that are part of what is chewing up the people who work for business.

Capitalism and business as we know them, particularly capitalism, was conceived by the English philosopher Adam Smith. And Smith had a very narrow concept of what it means to be a human being. He said that there were two fundamental things that were true about human beings. First of all, we are economic creatures first and foremost. We are born to truck, barter, and trade. And secondly, we are selfish creatures. We will always look out for our own best interests. And these are the two primary philosophical assumptions that underlie the capitalist philosophy. And business has taken them up and practices them quite ruthlessly much of the time, again leaving very little space for the servant-leader who would serve higher motives and higher ideals.

Wherever I go in the world speaking, and I say that business shouldn't just be about money, people look at me, shocked, and say, "Well what else is business about? Of course it's about money." One conference I went to in Istanbul a few months ago broadened its base just a little bit, and it said that business is about getting customers. But why do you want to get customers? So you make more money. So it came to much the same thing. I have a very different philosophy, based on my commitment to servant-leadership: that business indeed is about wealth creation. Of course it is, it's about money and making money, but the question is for whom and for what should that money be made? For whom and for what should all those enormous skills and dynamism of the capitalist system be used? My answer to that is that I see business as society's instrument of wealth creation for the benefit of society as a whole. The taxes that businessmen often try not to pay in fact give us all that we've got in our very well-off Western societies. Those business taxes give us good health care systems, good education systems, and a wonderful infrastructure. The United States, well, we'll leave out the education and health because they're not the best in the world, or at least they're not freely accessible to everybody, but we certainly have the best infrastructure in this country.

I also see the purpose of business as job creation. It keeps the whole economy ticking over; it provides employees with a source of income; it provides all the stakeholders of business with the wealth they need to develop their higher aspirations and values. This is a very noble purpose for business, but one not actually articulated by businessmen themselves. And it's a pity, because they're missing the boat. Business is good for society, but we need to raise the motivations and the vision of business so that business becomes an instrument through which servant-leadership can permeate society. The stakeholders of business are not just the employees and the customers and the shareholders. The stakeholders are society as a whole, future generations, the planet, and life itself. What a noble profession to be in, if only businessmen could realize and aspire to achieving these goals with the wealth that they so successfully create!

I believe that the definition of *capital* interpreted from business and capitalism is too narrow. I believe very strongly that there are three kinds of capital that the wealth of business can amass. The first is, yes, material capital. Bucks, hard stuff. We need it, can't live without it, society can't develop without it. But the second kind of capital, which some people in business schools are beginning to talk about, is social capital. The notion of social capital was first introduced by Francis Fukuyama in his book *Trust,* and Fukuyama defines social capital as being measured by the extent to which crime is low in a society, trust is high in a society, illiteracy is low in a society, divorce rates are low in a society, and general sense of well-being is high in society. Fukuyama pointed out the obvious: many of our Western societies are not terribly high in social capital. Here in the United States there are millions of Americans without adequate healthcare, and our state education system is a bit of a disaster. The wealth that business is making has not gone into building social capital of the same high standard as the material capital that it is generating. But I'm here to talk about a third kind of a capital, that I call *spiritual capital*. Spiritual capital is reflected in what we believe in, what we exist for, what we aspire to, and what we take responsibility for. It's captured in the extent to which our business activities reflect our deepest meanings, our deepest values, our most profound purposes, and again, our most serious responsibilities. I argue in my work that spiritual capital is the bedrock of both social and material capital; that without meanings and values and profound purposes and a sense of responsibility, we cannot build a society high in trust, low in divorce, low in litigation, low in illiteracy, et cetera. And I argue further that without spiritual capital, even our material capital is going to be undermined. That monster will end up consuming itself.

I picture this like a wedding cake, if you want a visual image of it, where the spiritual capital is the big bottom tier of the cake, and social capital the middle tier, and then material capital the little bit at the top. The importance is on that foundational bottom layer; without it the cake collapses. I also believe that each of these kinds of capital is driven by one of three main kinds of intelligence that human beings have. Material capital uses our IQ, our rational, logical, problem-solving thinking. We're very good at that—it's what our education system stresses, it's what society has stressed since the seventeenth century in the Newtonian scientific revolution. Indeed it's been there in Western culture ever since Aristotle. "The right man is a rational man. Man is a rational animal," said Aristotle. And our IQ tests, as we know, have been used throughout the twentieth century to separate the winners from the losers, the high fliers from the guys who are just going to slug along in life. It's used to select those who will be officers in the army, go on to leadership training programs in management, become the heads of school systems instead of frontline teachers, and so on.

I'm sure that every one of you here knows that Daniel Goleman greatly widened this base of intelligence thinking when he introduced the concept of emotional intelligence in the mid-1990s. Goleman showed that emotions help us think, that without emotional intelligence we don't really effectively use our rational intelligence. Emotional intelligence is mirrored by things like trust, empathy with others, emotional self-awareness, emotional self-control, and an ability to notice and respond appropriately to the emotions of others. Many of you may work in companies or organizations that have taken on this emotional intelligence work. It's got really big-time throughout the corporate world and the educational world. There are pro-grams galore all over the globe in emotional intelligence. And emotional intelligence builds social capital.

I was very excited when Goleman's book came out in the mid-90s, because I had never been happy with the IQ paradigm. And I was thinking about this whole issue of wealth and wealth creation and the uses of wealth, and these three kinds of capital. But I couldn't quite at first put my finger on why it was that Goleman's work left me feeling just slightly dissatisfied. I felt there was more to say. This unease was crystallized for me one night, about a year or two after I'd read *Emotional Intelligence*, by my five-year-old son. I was putting my son to bed one evening, tucking him in, reading him his story, and out of the blue came the question, "Mommy, why do I have a life?" I was knocked back, as any parent would be by such a question, and was unable to give him an answer immediately. Within Ivan's ques-tion, "Why do I have a life?," I reflected, there were really four subsidiary questions. The child was asking me, in his own way, "What is a human life, Mommy," that is, "What is the meaning of life?" He was asking me, "Mommy, what is my life for?"—that is, "What is the purpose of my own life?" He was asking me, "Mommy, what should I do with my life?" This was about the vision he was going to have, the aspiration he was going to have as he grew up. And he was also asking me, "Mommy, what kind of a life should I lead, what kind of a man should I be when I grow up?" And that reflected a concern with what values he should adopt.

So in this question "Why do I have a life?" the child was asking about the meaning, the purpose, the vision, and the values that lie behind the human life. None of these were things that the *Emotional Intelligence* book on its own addressed, and I thought, this is the missing piece—meaning, purpose, vision, and values. I decided to call this, at the time, *spiritual intelligence*. Not spiritual in a sense having anything to do with religion; I don't think you have to believe in God, even, or belong to any religious group to be spiritually intelligent. Unfortunately all too many of us know people who *are* religious who are not very high in spiritual intelligence. There is no necessary correlation. *Spiritual intelligence*, as I define it, is our need for and access to those deeper meanings, those higher values, those more fundamental purposes in life, and the vision that inspires us to lead lives of greater meaning and value. Spiritual intelligence underlies spiritual capital. It's the intelligence we must use if we are to formulate and enact a new philosophy for business and capitalism.

I chose the word *spiritual* because it comes from the Latin word *spiritus*. *Spiritus* means the vitalizing principle, that which gives life to an organism, an organization, to any entity. It's what makes it live and breathe. And there has been a great deal of anthropological and psychological research in these last 25 to 30 years that has shown that what makes human life vital, living and breathing, is the fact that we have to have some sense of meaning, vision, purpose, and value to live our lives healthily and happily. It's what makes us definitively human. In short, I decided that the way to define the three intelligences is that IQ is about what I think, EQ is about what I feel, but SQ, as I call spiritual intelligence, is about what I am. And that's the same with servant-leadership. To be a servant-leader, you must *be* a kind of person. You *live* servant-leadership. Yes, you think it and you feel it, but it's no good thinking it and feeling it if you don't live it. We all know that the servant-leader communicates best to his potential followers by being a walking example of the kind of person he is asking others to be. It's not something you can fake.

I wrote my first book on spiritual intelligence to outline the basic idea. It was a struggle. People have asked me at this conference, "Which of your books do I buy?" Well, I think they're both pretty good. [Laughter.] But I think the second one is better. The reason is that in the first one I was wrestling with a new idea; I was stretching myself in every dimension of my being; and as one is doing when carving out a new idea, there wasn't always that crystal-clear clarity of everything falling into place. With the second book, which came four years later and took all of those four years to write, I got clearer about how spiritual intelligence relates to emotional intelligence, and I got clearer about the driving transformative principles of spiritual intelligence and how they relate to this concept of spiritual capital—the capital that, if business were to acquire it and build it, would transform society, business, and capitalism itself, and transform those who work within the large organizations of this world. I looked for the trans-formative principles. I found 12. I didn't just pick them out of the air.

My first passion in life was quantum physics, and I spent all my teenage years doing mad scientist experiments in my bedroom, and was inspired. I had lost my faith in Christianity by the age of 12, and quantum physics stepped in to fill the gap for a few years. I looked to quantum physics as a new language, a new set of metaphors, a new set of images, a new set of ideas that could help me answer the kinds of questions that my five-year-old son was asking: Why do I have a life? What does it mean to be here? What is a human life? Later, because of my passion for physics, I also got interested in chaos and complexity science. I don't know how sophisticated you people are about these new sciences, but the new sciences of the twentieth century give us a radically new paradigm for thinking about physical reality. Instead of thinking about discrete atoms that bump into each other and conflict with each other, it talks about patterns of dynamic energy being the basic building blocks of the universe. And these patterns of dynamic energy overlap and combine and self-organize and have power from within; they're in constant dynamic dialogue with the environment around them, as well as with each other; they thrive on mutations, difference; they have a sense of purpose about them; they are self-organizing in a particular direction that builds ever greater complexity.

I did a bit of research and found that, as a complexity scientist or a quantum scientist would define us, we are complex adaptive systems, biologically, without question. All of life is called a complex, adaptive system, because it has these properties of creating more order, more information, being self-organizing, holistic, thriving on mutation, et cetera. Totally different from the old bleak Newtonian picture that had inspired Adam Smith when he defined the principles of capitalism.

Recent neurological research has shown that there is both quantum and complex activity in the brain, particularly when we are thinking creatively. Complex systems are poised at what they call the edge of chaos. Not like the edge of this lectern, but the meeting points between order and disorder, between something being so boring that it loses us completely, or something being so chaotic that we can't deal with it. And as I said, they're the point in nature where new order and new information, that is, where creativity takes place. Ten principles define the behavior of these complex adaptive systems, which we in fact are walking versions of. I felt that these, because of the characteristics they have and the role they play in creativity, were the 10 principles that underlie spiritual intelligence. I added two more, drawing from the great spiritual traditions of all the peoples on this planet. I think that these 12 principles, which are conscious complex adaptive systems, are the driving forces that allow us to raise our motivations, to transform ourselves, our institutions, and our business lives, and to become creative in the way that is necessary in these times of ours, which are themselves poised at the edge of chaos. I want to run through these 12 principles for you as the building blocks of how you create spiritual capital.

I want to begin by saying that it is my opinion and that of others whom I have read, that our society, and business in particular, is driven at present by four negative principles: fear, greed, anger, and self-assertion. Fear, greed, anger, and self-assertion. There is a great deal of fear in business life. Fear of making mistakes, fear of losing money, fear of the anger of the boss, fear of losing one's job, fear of getting it wrong. There is, behind the entire capitalist system as we know it, nothing but craving, and it drives this whole consumer materialist society. Business is constantly trying not to meet our genuine needs with quality products but to create false needs in us where we will crave the products that it spews out. Our teenagers today dress themselves in Nike shoes and, oh, I don't know what all these various brands are, but someone has written a book, *Brandchildren* I believe, I mean a child these days, a teenager, goes around as a sort of mobile advertising unit. They define themselves in terms of products, spewed out by a consumer-driven, materialist system that has created in them the notion that to be a man today, you wear Nike shoes. And if we're to get beyond this, to raise our motivations to what I call the first four positive motivations, to move from fear to situational mastery, to move from craving and greed to integrity and self-mastery, to move from anger to cooperation, and to move from self-assertion to exploration, we've got to put some kind of energy into the system.

You can't change people's basic behavior if you don't change their underlying motivations. Motivations are kind of attracters of energy within the human system, and you can't change those attracters of energy unless you pump more energy into the system. In my book on spiritual capital I use the image of a pinball machine, where the holes in the pinball machine are the attracters that define particular motivational states: there's fear, there's anger, there's greed, there's self-assertion, and the balls are falling into them, and if we want to shift those balls out of those holes, we pull back the string and fire a new ball in and then all the balls go like this [makes wild gestures with hands] and they can fall into new and higher pockets. What is the energy that we shoot into a motivational system to shift those motivations? My answer is, these transformative principles of spiritual intelligence. So if we want to shift organizational culture, we do so by finding ways to embody these 12 principles.

The first transformative principle of spiritual intelligence is self-awareness. Not in the emotional sense—that's necessary, but it's not enough for what I'm talking about. I'm talking about awareness that I have a self in the first place, that there's more to me than my ego coping mechanisms and my ego strategies and my ego cravings and my ego games, that within me lie deeper levels of consciousness that aspire to and are in contact with higher things. So self-awareness is literally awareness of the self—not the ego but the self, which ultimately connects with the field of consciousness in the universe as a whole. It's what puts us in touch with the deep stuff. When you are self-aware at that level, you become authentic. You know who you are, and by *knowing who you are* I mean you know what you live for, what you would die for, what you fight for, what you want to achieve in life, what your values are, what gets you out of bed in the morning, what gets you through the pain that every one of us carries in our complex human lives. You cannot be real, you cannot be effective, if you are not authentic. We all ultimately pick up a fake. Now the fake is not always a nasty, conniving person who's trying to pull the wool over other people's eyes; the fake often, more tragically, is just someone who simply has not reached this level of self-awareness and authenticity, but it's available to every one of us.

The second principle of spiritual intelligence is spontaneity. Spontaneity has a bad reputation sometimes because it's been translated by many people to mean "do my own thing, let it all hang out, act on whim," which can be incredibly selfish and incredibly irresponsible, but it's almost the ethos of the times. All of psychotherapy is about this: learn to be me (by which they mean my ego); learn to express myself (by which they mean my ego); put my interests first, because that's what's authentic. It's all stuff that's got turned on its head.

Spontaneity comes from the same Latin word as the words *response* and *responsibility*. To be deeply spontaneous first of all requires a great deal of discipline and hard work. It isn't whim-like at all. It's more like the spontaneity of the martial arts warrior that requires incredible discipline that gives you a poise, like the poise of the Zen archer or the tightrope walker. And when you have that kind of poise, you are responsive to the moment. Think, later today, when you have a chance to digest today's session and reflect, how much baggage you bring to each moment and to each meeting in your life. There's your childhood experience, your prejudices, your assumptions, your fear, your fear of vulnerability, your fear of consequences if you show too much or respond too much. You don't really *meet* other people from here [gestures to belly] when you're carrying all that baggage, and therefore you're not truly being responsive. Children are. That's what's so special about children, or one of the many things that's special about children. They're just there, in the moment. They don't have any baggage, they just want to learn, they just want to meet people, they just want to see what you're like. And then they explode with these embarrassing comments when they see what people do.

The third word linked to spontaneity, *responsibility*, means to take responsibility for what I see in that moment. Make it mine, own it, and act on it. We live so much today in a victim society. It's somebody else's fault if I smoke cigarettes, so I should sue the tobacco company because those nasty men sell me this poisonous stuff. It's somebody else's fault if my gums bleed because I use a new toothbrush, so I sue the toothbrush manufacturer because he hasn't warned me. There are the most ridiculous examples in the American litigation system of people passing the buck of responsibility. We could go right up the ladder to the top in Washington, where we say, "It's Bush's fault that America's not on a healthy path today." Well, who is the American government? We elect them. You have to own your actions, and those actions need to happen spontaneously, from response to the moment, without the baggage.

The third quality of spiritual intelligence is to be vision- and value-led. This is the aspirational part: to live what you believe in. Which requires in the first instance to know what you believe in, and that's going to require a lot of reflection. But to live it, to aspire to it, to want to leave the world a better place than you found it, to want to make a difference—that was the answer I gave my poor five-year-old son a few weeks after he asked his question. I said, "Ivan, you're in this world to leave it a better place than you found it. You're in this world to make a difference." The poor child was probably expecting me to say something like, "Oh, we want you to grow up to be a doctor" or "We want you to grow up to be a scientist" or something like that, but this is what he got. But it is basically what human life is about: to make a difference. It's what servant-leadership is about. To leave the world, in whatever aspect of it you live, a better place than you found it. And you don't have to be Mother Teresa or Mahatma Gandhi to do this. You can be a taxi driver, a mother, a father, a cook, a shop floor manager, or a great leader. It's to make a difference in whatever sphere of the world you operate in. Consuela told so many inspiring stories yesterday of people making that difference for their own children or for their fellows. One human being who lives by vision and values to make a difference changes the world.

The fourth principle of spiritual intelligence is to be holistic. This is a buzz word—these days everything is holistic. I imagine Nike shoes are holistic in their advertising campaigns, but it does have a real meaning.

In quantum physics, which is where the sense of holism originally comes from, the great quantum physicist David Bohm said there is no such thing as separation in this universe. Everything is intertwined with, interwoven with, and has impacts upon everything else. I am defined in terms of you, you are defined in terms of me. We are in a field of consciousness, a field of meaning. And in energy fields, everything impinges upon, everything is defined in terms of, everything else in the field. What is the meaning of this *holism*? It means that I know that what I do matters. What I think matters. What I feel matters. If I want to change the world, I change myself first. Transformation begins right here. And there's nothing unimportant or useless about it, and no excuse for saying, "I can't make a difference in this world because those guys are in charge and they don't give me the chance . . ." One person can make one hell of a difference, at least to those around him. It's like dropping a stone in the water and watching that circle grow. Only in holism, it's all of a piece. We're one large system of meaning, consciousness, and value, so what I do can harm society or what I do can help society, but what I do does make a difference.

The fifth quality of spiritual intelligence is a celebration of diversity. We all talk about tolerance; tolerance is built into the American constitution. Tolerance is a mean concept, in a way, because when I tolerate you, I say, "That's okay with me, you be yourself, I'll let you do it, I'm generous, be different, be yourself." Celebration of diversity is so much stronger. Celebration of diversity is saying, "Thank God you're different from me, thank God you rattle my cage, thank God you challenge my assumptions, thank God you make me reconsider my values." Because when I meet you spontaneously in that moment, I meet your values, I meet your needs, I meet your difference, I respond to it, and it makes me question myself. My definition of a *human* is that a human is a questioning being. The ultimate questioning in this world is self-questioning. And a celebration of diversity is a celebration of the fact that people who are different from me make me question myself. That literally makes me grow new neurons in my brain. When I change my assumptions, when I shift my values, when I question myself, literally, the brain grows new neural connections to cope with the new information. If I don't, if I spend my time with people who agree with me, if I read newspapers that just ratify my point of view, if I go to business meetings expecting my subordinates to agree with me, my brain shrinks. It doesn't have anything to thrive on. There's nothing there to make new neurons develop. So the best companions are the companions that aren't like myself. The best fellow workers add richness to the mix by being different, by bringing in new ideas, new styles, new visions, new values.

One of the things that I loved about my country when I was a young American was its diversity. It's one of the things that we're somewhat losing touch with today, when there are people in America who want us all to believe the same thing and impose that on everybody. Diversity is one of the things that made this country great. Diversity is a fundamental cornerstone of freedom. Everybody has a point of view for a reason; you got it from somewhere. Everybody's point of view, again this comes from quantum physics in a way I don't have time to describe, but everybody's point of view has value. It's another stone in that pool with the ripples. So as many points of view as I can take in, the larger my brain gets and the more creative I become.

To celebrate diversity, I need another of the principles of spiritual intelligence, and that is the sixth principle, compassion. Emotional intelligence talks about empathy. Empathy is my ability to understand another's feelings. *Compassion* is a stronger word. *Compassion* comes from the Latin for "to feel with." When I am compassionate toward another who is different from me, I literally feel that person's feelings. That person may be my enemy. That person may belong to Al Qaeda. That person may be someone who took my wife or husband away. There can be awful things about this other person that I'm asking that we have compassion for. Because compassion doesn't mean giving in to. Doesn't mean being defeated by. Doesn't mean becoming weak in the face of. Compassion simply means being able to wear my neighbor's moccasins. To feel his or her feelings, to know where he or she is coming from, and to know that those feelings, from that person's point of view, have a validity, and I say this even about Al Qaeda, which is a very dangerous thing to say in this country. President Bush described those hijackers as cowards. Not many cowards give up their lives for something they believe in. They were wrong-headed. They did bad, evil things. But I don't myself believe there is such a thing in this world as an evil human being. There are men and women who do evil things. But there is goodness in every one of us, because there's a self in every one of us, and ultimately that self is in contact with the basic principles of the universe.

That's why I personally am against capital punishment. I saw this very profoundly a few years ago when as a journalist I went into a maximum-security prison and spent the morning with "ordinary" maximum-security criminals. These were people who had killed people, but only for money.

Then I spent the afternoon with sex offenders. These were men who had abused, raped, and in some cases killed children. I was frightened going into the second group. The "nice" prisoners in the morning who only killed people for money told me, "They're the scum of this establishment. You don't want to go spend your time with them."

I walked into this dialogue session in the prison, walked into a room of fifty sex offenders. I was the only woman, and there were four guards. I got a blinding headache; all my assumptions and prejudices came to the fore. I saw them as ugly, distorted men. Literally, they looked to me like they had distorted faces. I was terrified and I wanted to flee, but I knew I wouldn't get my story, so I stayed.

As the two hours of the dialogue session passed, I saw something that changed me profoundly and gave me this notion of compassion. Those men, though they could only express themselves through four-letter words, they hardly had language, all had a center. They said to me—they wanted this woman in the audience to understand them very much—"I've done bad things, but I'm not a monster, please understand that." They're called monsters. "I belong in here, I should be in here, but there's more to me than you think." They came up and wanted to be hugged, and I found by the end of the two hours I could hug them, men who had killed children, because, through compassion, I found myself able to relate to that deep kernel that is in every human being. I wouldn't let them out. God forbid. But I went away loving them. Not loving what they had done, and not feeling they should be anywhere but where they are, but loving them nonetheless, and they haunted me when I'd left the prison. There are no scum of the earth. There's scum in this world, without question, but there are no scum of the earth, and when we feel compassion we realize that.

The seventh quality of spiritual intelligence is to be field independent. This is a psychological term that means to stand against the crowd, be willing to be unpopular, be willing to stand up for what I believe in even if everybody else says you're wrong, you're crazy, we exclude you. It means to fight for what I do believe in. But this principle requires the next principle in combination.

The eighth principle is humility. There are a lot of people walking this earth who stand against the crowd, who make themselves unpopular, who fight for what they believe in and who do enormous harm. They're bullheaded, they're stubborn, they don't listen. In combination with humility the whole thing is very different. If I am humble, I question myself deeply. I listen to others. I listen to why they say I am wrong and I assess myself:

could I be wrong? And only when I have gone through the deepest process of gut-wrenching self-questioning do I then say, Yes, I'm right to fight for what I'm fighting for; yes, I stand by what I believe in. If I'm arrogant, I become a dictator, a monster, someone who doesn't listen, who causes a lot of harm. If I question myself, I become a woman of authenticity who stands by what I believe in and fights for it no matter what the consequences.

The ninth principle is a biggie, and that's asking fundamental questions. "Why?" My son's "Why do I have a life?" was a profoundly emotionally intelligent question, and perhaps the ultimate question. But this "Why?" goes through every aspect of our leadership. Why am I making this product rather than that product? Why am I using this design process rather than that process? Why am I treating my workers this way rather than that way? Why am I distributing my wealth this way rather than that way? Constantly undermining my own strategies and assumptions with questions. These questions are subversive. That's why senior management and senior politicians don't like them very much—they subvert authority. But I will remind you that this country was born of revolution and grew great on dissent. This country was the most subversive phenomenon to happen in the political world when it was founded. Subversion made America. Questioning authority, not just for the sake of questioning it, not just for the sake of raising banners and upsetting people and undermining people, but questioning because I deeply question the reason, the value, the vision behind everything, because I want to get to the real heart of things. It becomes a practice.

My definition of *man*, where Aristotle said "Man is a rational animal," I think a human being is a questioning animal. I think it is this questioning that has defined us, and this questioning that is driven by this need to understand, this need for meaning, this need for purpose. When we stop questioning, we stop living human lives. Children ask millions of questions, we know that, they drive us mad with it. Parents tell them, "Please stop barraging me with all these questions." Teachers tell them, "Stop asking questions, sit down and shut up and listen to what I'm trying to teach you." When Einstein was an old man he was asked what he most enjoyed about being a famous scientist, and he said, "Well, you know, when I was in school I was always in trouble because I was always asking what the teacher called 'foolish questions,' and the teacher was always saying, 'Albert, be quiet and listen.' But now that I'm a famous old scientist and everybody respects me I can ask all the foolish questions I want to." Foolish questions don't exist! There are no foolish questions! There are no inappropriate questions or wrong questions. Questions have a kind of integral value.

The tenth principle of spiritual intelligence is to reframe. That means just what it sounds like, to broaden the frame that you look at. I don't look at what's just under my nose, but I look at what impinges on it and what I impinge on. Look at the bigger picture, both in space and in time. One of the biggest problems of capitalism and business today—and it's affected life throughout society, as capitalism does—is short-termism. The idea that we look three months down the road when planning our activities—when those shareholder value accounts come in. Businesses don't take the long view. They aren't looking five years down the road, ten years down the road. Japanese companies look 200 years down the road when they run a transformation program. We look three months. You can't take care of the environment, you can't take care of your people, you can't take care of the planet and life and use your best resources and use your creativity if you live in a short segment of time. We've got to learn to take the long view.

And the same spatially. To realize what's outside the window. I addressed a group of executives from a power company in Britain. I got a little bit fed up with these people, the narrow things they were saying, and I sort of challenged them. I said, "Do you know what's going on outside the window?" You know what they said? They said, "We don't know what's going on outside the window and we don't care. Our job is to take care of our customers' needs now, our job is to look after our profits now, taking care of society and the environment is the government's business, it's not our business." They didn't reframe. They just thought of their own immediate needs, their own immediate profits, their shareholder value.

The positive use of adversity is the eleventh principle. We're all vulnerable; we all carry pain in our lives; every one of us has a story; every one of us has a history. Many of us will be ill, and many of us have lost loved ones to death. Every one of us has made a mistake, or many mistakes, in my case, and, I suspect yours. The positive use of adversity is to see these as growing points, to see them as opportunities. Doesn't make you feel any better at a funeral. But it's adversity in life that makes us strong. It's adversity in life that makes us grow. I had an Irish grandmother when I was a little girl; she raised me. And she used to say to me, "Danah, you must eat a peck of dirt a year," because I'd complain that the vegetables weren't very clean sometimes. She literally believed that I should eat this peck of dirt a year because it cleaned out my system. She had some other medical theories that were even wilder than that. But a peck of dirt does clean out the system. A peck of dirt makes us stronger. So that pain we bear in life, those mistakes we make in life, those setbacks, those losses, are there for a reason. We'd be such dull people if we didn't have them. To use them creatively is one of life's greatest challenges.

And finally, the twelfth principle of spiritual intelligence, which is the one closest to servant-leadership itself, is a sense of vocation. *Vocare,* the Latin word, means to be called, vocation, a sense of vocation, is to feel called to serve. To feel called to make a difference, to feel called to do something good, to feel called to cook that excellent meal for my family, or to make that quality product for my customers, or that new thing that nobody's ever had that's going to change people's lives. It's a sense of mission in life. It's like the sense of mission that monks used to have when they were called by God to serve. And I do think ultimately when we have a sense of vocation, it is by God whom we are called. Not necessarily the God of any religion, not necessarily a being in the sky—God is whatever I hold most sacred in myself, whatever I most value, whatever I most cherish. When I serve that, then I serve my people, my community, my products, my customers, the planet, and life itself. A sense of vocation, which is what drives the servant-leader, is the ultimate driving force to build spiritual capital. That's where our passion is, that's where our commitment is, that's where our engagement is. In the sense of "I have to. It has to happen. I dedicate myself to this. I'm going to make this happen."

There are two things I want to finish with.

I told you I see this as a new philosophy for business and capitalism, and in my book I call the servant-leader a knight. The reason I call them knights is that I have always been very inspired by the Knights Templar, those medieval monks who served their God through military activity. I'm not lauding the exact purpose of the Knights Templar but their style and their deep purpose. Unlike the knights who mostly fought in the Crusades who dressed themselves in rich garments and plumes and satin and fought for ladies and wealth, the Knights Templar took vows of chastity and poverty. Their cloaks were simple white cloaks with red crosses on them; they shaved their heads; and they eschewed all wealth, though their order was the wealthiest in Christendom. Their purpose was to guard Christian pilgrims wanting to visit the Holy Land. My admiration for the Knights Templar does not judge whether the Crusades were a good or bad thing, but acknowledges that men who were men of the world, fighting men, strong, capable men, could give all that up to serve their God—that's what I admire about them, and that's why in this book I call the servant-leaders knights.

I've written a credo for business knights that I would like to share with you. Indeed, I would like to challenge you to adopt this credo. I wish it would become the credo for business. If it did, business would join the professions. Business would become a vocation rather than a sleazy running after money. Business would become like practicing medicine, practicing teaching, practicing law. It would have codes and standards, ethics and values. I'll read you this and see what you think of it. It's called the Credo of the Business Knight.

> I believe that global business has the money and the power to make a significant difference in today's troubled world, and that by making that difference it can help itself as well as others. I envision business raising its sights above the bottom line. I envision business becoming a vocation, like the higher professions. To make this possible, I believe that business must add a moral dimension, becoming more service- and value-oriented, and largely eliminating the assumed natural distinction between private enterprise and public institutions. I envision business taking responsibility for the world in which it operates, and from which it creates its wealth, and I envisage myself becoming one of those business leaders who are servant-leaders—leaders who serve not just stockholders, colleagues, employees, products, and customers, but leaders who also serve the community, the planet, humanity, the future, and life itself.

I would love to see that credo on the wall of every institution of business in this country. I would love every one of you to be willing to take that vow of the knight. Some people say this kind of talk is naive. Some say, "It's hopeless, there are all those bad guys out there who want to carry on as they have been doing because the profits are so great, the opportunities so prevalent. People aren't going to change; I try to do this and I'm going to make a fool of myself, I'm going to get undermined, I may lose my job if I talk like this in the company."

I want to finish with something written by Kent M. Keith, and much loved by Mother Teresa. It's about doing something no matter what the consequences are. It's about doing something because you think it's right, and because you think it's worthwhile. It's called "Do It Anyway." He says,

> People are often unreasonable, illogical, and self-centered.
> Forgive them anyway.
> If you are kind, people may accuse you of selfish ulterior motives.

Be kind anyway.

If you are successful, you will win some false friends and some true enemies.

Succeed anyway.

If you are honest and frank, people may cheat you.

Be honest and frank anyway.

What you spend years building, someone may destroy overnight.

Build anyway.

If you find serenity and happiness, people may be jealous.

Be happy anyway.

The good you do today, people will often forget tomorrow.

Do good anyway.

Give the world the best you have and it may never be enough;

but give the world the best you have anyway.

You see, in the final analysis, it is all between you and God;

it was never between you and them, anyway.

Thank you very much.

Chapter 19

Modesty in Leadership

A Study of the Level-Five Leader

Lucia M. Hamilton and Charlotte M. Knoche

Human resource metrics and, in particular, the management practices that affect bottom-line performance have received increasing interest in recent years in the business community, as companies look to human capital rather than industrial capital to achieve success. A study that has garnered a great deal of attention in this area is the subject of Jim Collins's (2001) best-selling book *Good to Great*. In it, Collins reports on the findings of his research team in their analysis of companies who significantly outperformed their competitors over an extended period of time. The research team examined companies who had a 15-year cumulative stock return at or below the general stock market and then cumulative returns that were at least three times the market over the next 15 years. The researchers further stipulated that the firms had to perform exceptionally regardless of the performance of their industry. Of 1,435 companies studied, only 11 met their criteria. Although Collins specifically tried to avoid having his team examine the leadership style of the CEOs, the researchers persuaded him that a common leadership style was shared by the leaders of all 11 companies and should not be ignored. This leadership style, which Collins eventually termed the "level five leader" was characterized primarily by two things: modesty and an overwhelming sense of commitment to the organization above self. Collins admits in *Good to Great* that this finding did not fit the preconceptions of the research team.

These CEOs, described as "more Lincoln or Socrates than Patton or Caesar" (Collins, 2001, p. 3) were, according to the researchers, quiet, humble, shy, modest, and so forth. One individual is quoted as saying, "I never stopped trying to become qualified for the job" (p. 20). They were people with a "quiet, dogged nature" who conveyed an "awkward shyness and lack of pretense [that] was coupled with a fierce, even stoic, resolve" (p. 18). The researchers were clearly quite impressed by these people, as Collins states, "They have become models for us, something worthy to aspire toward" (p. 38).

Modesty or humility has received very little attention by researchers as a characteristic of leaders. In a metaanalysis of studies of leadership, there was not one mention of modesty cited in any study (Judge et al., 2002). A later study noted that modesty was not a typical characteristic of charismatic leaders (Bono & Judge, 2004), and a database search for articles using "modesty" or "humility" plus "leadership" turned up very little. One notable exception is Badaracco (2002), who coins the term *quiet leaders* to describe a person whose "modesty and restraint are in large measure responsible for their impressive achievements" (pp. 1–2). Certainly modesty is not a typical criterion when selecting for leaders. The fact that these highly successful firms were all led by people that were modest inspired this research.

Background

Why has modesty not emerged as a characteristic of leaders? There are many reasons for this. However, perhaps part of the issue may reside with the research focus on charisma and the traits of emergent leaders versus effective leaders. Over 400 studies on the topic of charisma were identified in a search in the PsychINFO database. Typical behaviors associated with charismatic leaders are "using inspirational language and delivery style" and engaging "in exemplary acts involving risk and sacrifice" (Kanungo, 1998). In a well-known study of US presidents, descriptors of charisma included "finds dealing with the press enjoyable," "enjoys the ceremonial aspects of the position," "is charismatic," and "is seen as a world figure" (House et al., 1991, p. 378). It is easy to see how modesty and charisma would appear to be incompatible qualities. Charismatic leaders appear very heroic and were especially appealing during the turnaround specialist era; their propensity for high drama captured the public's attention.

Traits such as dominance, capacity for status, sociability, social presence, and self-confidence have all been correlated with ratings for emergent leaders (Hogan et al., 1994; Judge et al., 2002). Modesty and kindness as traits for emergent leaders, however, have had mixed results (Bono & Judge, 2004). This emphasis on heroic traits encourages a mythology about what a leader should "look like" that is based on implicit leadership theory rather than data (Hogan et al., 1994). The search committees that generally select CEOs are quite likely to be subject to this bias. Consequently, we may be perpetuating a particular leadership style that appears heroic while under-valuing a quieter style that doesn't draw attention to itself.

There has been less research on effective leaders, although psychologists agree that this is a very important topic (Hogan et al., 1994). The difficulty has been to isolate such things as situational factors over which the leader has no control from the leaders themselves (Kanungo, 1998). Traits that have been linked to leader effectiveness are desire for advancement, energy, confidence, decisiveness, emotional stability, and conscientiousness (Hogan et al., 1994). However, many of these studies have been conducted in a laboratory setting, and Collins's (2001) is arguably one of the few studies to link business results with the personality characteristics of effective leaders.

It is important to state here that the researchers of this study are not saying that the level five leader is the only type of effective leadership style. However, research does indicate that the opposite of modesty—narcissism— is often a key derailer for managers, and narcissistic leaders are often seen as charismatic (Hogan & Kaiser, 2005; Tourigny et al., 2003). Arrogance, untrustworthiness, overambitiousness, and aloofness have been found to be common derailers (Hogan et al., 1994; Kanungo, 1998), but people with these characteristics often interview well and impress their supervisors. Large bureaucratic organizations that emphasize status and impression management are particularly vulnerable to these characteristics; the hiring process searches for the very characteristics that may contribute to those executives' ultimate failure (Hogan & Kaiser, 2005).

However, to characterize the level five leader as only modest would be inaccurate. These leaders are also individuals with a high degree of commitment to goals and a willingness to put the organization ahead of their personal interests. They take personal responsibility when things fail and are quick to credit others when things go well. As the researchers of this study considered what this meant, it seemed to imply that these leaders were conscientious people of good character and that there were underlying values that drove their behavior. Behaving consistently with one's values is a definition of integrity. It is interesting to note that Badaracco's (2002) book grew out of a course in moral leadership. And although the idea of leaders guided by a sense of internal principles is not new (Covey, 1990), again, it is not something that is given a high priority in the selection process. We are much more attuned to competencies than to character.

Research shows, however, that integrity is extremely important in gaining the support and trust of others. It may be, in fact, the most important factor in leadership effectiveness (Covey, 2004; Hogan et al., 1994; Hogan & Kaiser, 2005; Judge et al., 2002; Kanungo, 1998; Kouzes & Posner, 1987). As one author states, quoting Socrates, "The first key to greatness is to be in reality what one appears to be" (Maxwell, 1993, p. 36).

The closest theoretical orientation to the level-five leader seems to be the servant-leader concept developed by Robert Greenleaf (1991). Both concepts are outwardly focused rather than self-focused. Greenleaf said, "The great leader is servant first," and that the leader's first duty is to the employees. He stated that asking the question "Do those served grow as people?" is a means of assessing whether someone is a servant-leader (Greenleaf, 1991, p. 7). Collins's (2001) level-five leader is also outwardly focused, although he frames this as a focus on the organization rather than specifically on the employees. However, Collins also states that the level-five leader is concerned with succession and with the development of people. This seems very similar to Greenleaf's (1977/2002) concept. Both Greenleaf (1977/2002) and Collins (2001) mention Abraham Lincoln as a prototype for a leader that fits their respective concepts. Collins, in fact, says he considered calling the people in his study servant-leaders but rejected the idea because it seemed too soft. In addition, Collins (2001) suggested that Greenleaf's (1977/2002) concept did not include the commitment aspect. However, Greenleaf clearly states that the servant-leader is empathetic without sacrificing standards. He also notes that the servant-leader "elicits trust through competence . . . and values and a sustaining spirit . . . that will support the tenacious pursuit of a goal" (Greenleaf, 1991, p. 9). This certainly seems to indicate that commitment to high performance is important to the servant-leader. The difficulty with Greenleaf's (1977/2002) concept is that the servant-leader is, by his own admission, an intuitive concept based on his years assessing leaders at Bell Labs, and has not received analysis regarding its correlation with business performance. Perhaps that is why Collins's (2001) book has created such fervor in the business community, while Greenleaf's (1977/2002) ideas are arguably still not in the mainstream of corporate America practices.

For the purposes of comparison, the researchers have listed the attributes of each type of leader, based on a careful reading of Greenleaf (1977/2002) and Collins (2001) (see table 19.1).

Table 19.1. Greenleaf and Collins Leader Attributes

Greenleaf (1977/2002)	Level Five Leader (Collins, 2001)
Psychological self-insight, accurate self-appraisal	Modesty–credits others for success, accepts responsibilities for failures
Strong initiative	Fanatically driven to produce results
Inspirational goal setting	Inspired standards
Long-term sustained enthusiasm and commitment	Workmanlike diligence
Deep listening	Engage in debate and dialogue "Truth is heard" culture
Courageous	Determined pursuit of "best in world" strategies
Detached problem solving	Engage in debate and dialogue Questioning style, "truth is heard" culture
Other-centered communication	
Withdraws and reflects	
Accepting and empathetic	
Highly intuitive	Inferred from business results, hedgehog concept
High work standards	Inspired standards
Good judgment	Inferred from business results, hedgehog concept
Prescient regarding future events	Long-term perspective
Heightened awareness	Realistic confidence
Influences through gentle persuasion (questioning) and example	Questioning style
Motivations: (1) use talents for benefit of the common good, (2) shared wholeness, (3) growing people	Motivations: achieving long-term business success, using talents to benefit company
Love in community, demonstrated through unlimited liability for each other	"Love affair" on team, friends for life
Reference to Jesus as a servant-leader	May be spiritual, Select for character—rigorous process
First priority is to build a group of people who become healthier, stronger, and more autonomous	People first, strategy second; set up successors for the future
	Balance in lives
	Genius for simplicity
	Quiet, calm nature
	Focused, disciplined culture

As one can see from this chart, there appears to be quite a bit of overlap. In fact, only three attributes of the servant-leader and four of the level-five leader are unique to one type or the other. An important distinction might be made around communicating to be understood, and acceptance and empathy displayed by the servant-leader. These qualities suggest someone with high emotional intelligence. The servant-leader concept has been expanded over the years, and more recent interpretations include using encouragement and affirmation, building strong personal relationships, working collaboratively, valuing others' differences, sharing power, and releasing control (Laub, 2005); humility and emotional intelligence (van Dierendonck & Heeren, 2006); and willingness to teach and delegate (Russell & Stone as cited in Rennaker, 2006). As it has matured, it appears that the aspects of Greenleaf's (1991) original concept that relate to interpersonal capabilities have received most of the attention and have become deeper and richer—perhaps because this aspect is particularly appealing and found to be lacking in many leaders.

Interpersonal capabilities are largely ignored by Collins (2001). He does describe the cultures of the 11 companies as characterized by love, deep friendships, and respectful dialogue. Greenleaf (1977/2002) refers to communities characterized by love, and a more recent article asserts that servant-leaders create "cultures of trust" that validate and empower people rather than demeaning or alienating them (Fawell, 2006, p. 407).

Methodology

The purpose of this study was to better understand a leadership style shown to be effective in achieving business results, and to raise an awareness of alternative leadership characteristics that CEOs and managers may find beneficial for their organizations. As previously discussed, much leadership research has been conducted in laboratory settings. Because this leadership style struck the researchers as complex, involving multiple dimensions, a structured study focused on a few attributes seemed limiting. More importantly, the researchers were interested in understanding at a deep level the participants and how they came to be the people they were, a goal better suited to a collective case study (Stake, 2005, pp. 445–446). A case study in the form of naturalistic inquiry lends itself well to understanding complex phenomena and provides the researchers with vivid, rich, and dense descriptions in the natural language of the phenomena being studied (Eisner, 1991; Lincoln & Guba, 1985; Miles & Huberman, 1994; Polkinghome, 2005).

The researchers were initially drawn to an innovative study of master therapists (Skovholt & Jennings, 2004) that used a case study approach. This led to consensual qualitative research (CQR), an approach to understanding a small group of cases at a deep level. CQR has been used in the field of counseling psychology to understand therapists and those seeking counseling (Hill et al., 1997). CQR is closely linked to grounded theory (Strauss & Corbin, 1998). This strategy allows the data to emerge through a discovery process without preconceptions, yet "has a positivist concern for a systematic set of procedures" (Babbie, 2007, p. 296). Because the researchers hoped to find specific behaviors linked to typical managerial competencies, the idea that grounded theory is focused on understanding a "complex network of related constructs around a phenomenon" (Creswell, 2003, p. 15) seemed particularly apropos to the study. Knowing that they would be analyzing, organizing, and categorizing a significant amount of data, the researchers found that grounded theory offered both the structure and the flexibility they desired. Grounded theory also lends itself well to the incorporation of quantitative information (Babbie, 2007), something that was considered important to this study. However, it should be noted that the research evolved and was a blend of CQR and grounded theory protocols. More on this topic will be discussed later in this chapter.

The researchers also felt it was important to study the participants in their contexts. By understanding the cultures in which these individuals flourish, one might be able to both determine the likely fit of a level-five job candidate in a particular organization and identify those cultural elements that might be helpful in attracting this type of person. This is similar to the concept of transferability as identified by Lincoln and Guba (1985). Context seemed particularly important to this research because this type of leader is not usually seen as fitting the prevailing leadership image, and it seemed likely that the cultures that support this type of leader would be atypical as well. To summarize, the study can be seen as interpretative, incorporating both ethnographic and phenomenological elements into a primarily grounded theory orientation using a cross-case analysis.

A mixed-methods approach using concurrent procedures, incorporating both qualitative and quantitative elements, was chosen. Interviewing, a method commonly used in naturalistic inquiry, provided the main source of information. A strength of the interview process is that it facilitates the expression of various points of views and opinions; additionally, respondents are free to expound upon them as they see fit (Weller & Romney, 1988; Yin, 2003). Another advantage of interviewing is that it allows the researchers the freedom to clarify ambiguous responses or to pursue a particular train of thought. Psychological instruments intended for selection purposes were also incorporated; observations and documents provided helpful information as well.

Triangulation is important in naturalistic research, as it enhances the trustworthiness of the data (Lincoln & Guba, 1985), and it was an important part of this study's methodology. Interviews were conducted with both leaders and their direct reports. The leader-participants also took two personality instruments. Several of them provided additional unsolicited information, such as emails, videos, or annual reports, to help the researchers. TDIndustries provided information on its performance management plan and graciously invited one of the researchers to attend an introductory supervisory course to better understand how it operationalizes servant-leadership. Openness and an earnest interest on both sides characterized this experience. While they do not seek the limelight, the participants saw the value of bringing more understanding and attention to this leadership style, and were willing and equal colleagues in the research process. By gathering information from multiple sources, the researchers were able to draw "convergent conclusions from divergent data" beyond what the more typical qualitative study might reveal (Erlandson et al., 1993).

Selection of Participants

Participants were selected through a peer nomination process. A paragraph describing the leadership construct was written and offered to interested colleagues. The construct was based largely on the level-five leader. However, because two important elements of leadership—creating a vision and inspiring others to follow them—were not mentioned in Collins's (2001) work, concepts from Greenleaf's (1991) work were also included.

The Quiet Leader Construct

According to Collins (2001),

> The Quiet Leader has a strong sense of commitment to the long-term success of the organization and never wavers from this. He or she works hard and sets high standards for performance by self and others. The QL does not tolerate mediocrity in any form, yet will attribute bad results to self and good results to others. The QL has strategic thinking ability and sets a vision

for the company based on strong intuition and foresight—is able to think globally and grasp the implications of current actions at some later time. He or she has a modest nature, is quick to give credit to others and rarely credits self. He or she inspires trust through integrity and competence and is therefore able to persuade others to follow him/her. The QL is motivated to make the company the best it can be, not by personal ambition, and pursues this with quiet, calm determination. Rather than grand gestures, the QL moves in [a] steady and consistent manner toward the goal. Because of his/her commitment and modesty, the QL is seen as a "plow horse not a show horse." (p. 33)

When an individual was identified as someone who fit the construct, an inquiry was made to determine whether he or she would be interested in participating in the study. Since Collins (2001) notes that the people in his study resembled servant-leaders, and the researchers concurred, it was determined that some participants would be executives currently practicing servant-leadership. An organization well known in the field of servant-leadership, TDIndustries of Dallas, Texas, was approached and asked if they would participate. The human resources leader was interested in the study and agreed to the request. Four executives from the organization who fit the construct were then nominated. Two executives from a local Twin Cities credit union who had embraced both servant-leadership (Greenleaf, 1991) and the *Good to Great* (Collins, 2001) findings as part of their operating philosophy were also identified. It was determined that 6 to 10 participants would provide ample data for these initial case studies, and the nomination process was stopped when nine participants were confirmed.

In summary, all participants held leadership positions in their organizations. Eight of the nine had line responsibility. Three were CEOs, and a fourth was a former CEO. All had extensive work experience and their ages ranged from late 40s to early 60s. Organizations represented included a construction company, a bank, a credit union, a publishing company, and a food distributor. These organizations were primarily located in the Minneapolis–Saint Paul area, with the exception of TDindustries, which was headquartered in Texas. A limitation of this study was that some of the Texas-based interviews were conducted via conference call; another was that only one participant was female and no minority groups were represented.

Each selected participant was then asked to name three direct reports (DRs) who they believed knew them well enough and had worked with them long enough to provide meaningful insight into their leadership style, preferably a year or more. This study chose to interview direct reports because subordinates' perspectives have been linked with managerial job performance ratings, and it also provided a measure of triangulation (Hogan et al., 1994). It was important that the DRs had a depth of experience in the organization and that they could reflect on and articulate their experience in a meaningful way. A possible limitation of the study is that the leaders may have picked direct reports who they felt would provide more positive comments on their style, or who they thought might be willing to give the time, rather than identifying a broad spectrum of opinions.

Development of Questions

The development of the initial interview script was guided by the critical competencies of the level-five leader as identified by Collins (2001) plus basic managerial competencies such as decision making and communication. The competencies of the servant-leader were also researched, and questions regarding these were woven into the script. This approach is consistent with the findings of Strauss and Corbin (1998), who note that an examination of previous research and literature will also provide the necessary background information and will suggest a variety of theoretical and conceptual frameworks. Consistent with this method, the researchers drafted domains and then developed broadly based questions designed to access the basic behaviors unique to this personal leadership style. As the interviews were conducted and the relevant data was gathered and analyzed, investigation into some competencies was expanded while exploration of others was abridged or aborted.

A separate and different set of questions was developed for the direct reports; these addressed behaviors that they would have encountered and witnessed in various work situations. Both subjects and direct reports received their questions several days prior to the interview, consistent with CQR methodology (Hill et al., 1997).

Interviews

All participants were interviewed face-to-face in their environment, usually by both researchers. This enabled the researchers not only to interview the leader but also to observe the leader's facility, his or her interactions with other members of the organization, and interactions among other members of the organization, as well as the overall climate of the organization. Direct reports were primarily interviewed face-to-face, except for a few cases in which geographical distance or time constraints made it necessary to conduct the interview via phone.

Instruments

In addition to interviews, observations, and various documents, the study infused additional intentional triangulation by incorporating the Occupational Personality Questionnaire (OPQ) and Motivation Questionnaire (MQ). These were administered electronically to all participants. The OPQ and the MQ were developed and published by Saville-Holdsworth Limited (SHL, 1995, 2000) and have been used extensively for selection purposes in business. An ipsative version of the OPQ, recommended for selection purposes, was used. The OPQ measures personality characteristics important in the world of work in three domains: relationships, thinking styles, and feelings and emotions. It takes approximately 45 minutes to complete. The MQ examines motivating factors in work in four domains: energy and dynamism, synergy, intrinsic, and extrinsic. It takes approximately 20 minutes to complete. Both instruments were developed using subjects in professional or supervisory positions. Copies of both instruments were provided free of charge to the researchers in exchange for a copy of the study results.

Analysis of Data

To some degree, the analysis of the data began with the dialectic as the researchers discussed and categorized the data and checked and verified these categories with each other. The analysis then proceeded with the transcription of the 32 interviews. To protect the anonymity of the direct reports, participants were coded one through nine (e.g., SBJl), and the direct reports were listed by their respective participant and then identified by number (e.g., SBJl, DR2). Each interview transcription was identified only by this coding. These transcriptions totaled over 190 pages. All participants were sent their transcriptions to review and were able to make changes. They did not receive the transcripts of the DRs. At times, the transcription process generated more questions, which were sent to the participant with the transcription for his or her consideration. The responses of the participants were then incorporated into the transcription as a final version.

Following the CQR methodology, 16 domains were identified by the researchers after reading the transcripts. The comments of the interviewees in the transcriptions were then separated into clearly distinct thoughts, sometimes by breaking sentences, and categorized into the domains. In two instances subjects were contacted by phone or email to clarify an ambiguous point. On some occasions, comments were placed into more than one category. The researchers worked closely together to discuss and categorize the data. This method requires that the researchers maintain an honest, open dialogue; it values researchers' working collaboratively to "construct a shared understanding of the phenomena" (Hill et al., 1997, p. 522). This provides a check and balance for the researchers by not requiring that one person alone collect and code all the data. Nuances and shades of meaning were examined and discussed, context was considered, and an attempt was made to remain unbiased and objective. The consensual qualitative research model requires "mutual respect, equal involvement, and shared power" (p. 523), a process that worked well for the researchers. However, in its purest form, the CQR method would have required a team of researchers, a pool of judges trained to code, and auditors to judge and verify results. This was beyond the means of the researchers.

Comments were then paraphrased, with attention to simply rewording the interviewees' actual words in an objective manner, following the CQR methodology: "Our general rule is to make as few inferences as possible about the meaning of the data at this stage and to remain as close as possible to the participant's perspective of the experience" (Hill et al., 1997, p. 546). The researchers were careful not to add interpretations to the comments or otherwise change the meaning. A composite report for each participant was then developed, incorporating the paraphrased thoughts from both the leader and the direct reports into one document, along with representative quotes. After all individual case studies were analyzed, a cross-analysis was done to determine consistency across cases.

A bulleted list of 185 specific characteristics/behaviors shared by all nine participants was developed. Characteristics that were compelling or impressive yet not shared by all nine participants were eliminated at this juncture. Perhaps not surprisingly, the domain of leadership had the highest number of items. Thirty-four characteristics were included in more than one domain. For example, "admits gaps in knowledge" was seen as a behavior that fit both the decision-making and communication domains.

The direct reports were asked to "list five adjectives you would use to describe this person" during their interviews. A list of these adjectives was compiled separately from the transcriptions. An affinity diagram was then created, clustering related words and labeling each cluster. This will be discussed more in the "Results" section below.

The results of the OPQ and MQ were then analyzed, and descriptive statistics developed for illustrative purposes only, given the small sample size. The OPQ and MQ results are reported in standard scores called *stens*, with a mean of 5.5 and a standard deviation of 2. The means and standard deviations were computed for all the participants for 33 scales on the OPQ and 17 scales on the MQ. One participant did not complete the MQ.

Results

The study incorporated data from a variety of sources to develop a better understanding of a leader who is unassuming yet achieves strong results. The analysis paid particular attention to determining if there were characteristics that were common across all data sources to assess trustworthiness. The study revealed that, indeed, findings were consistent across the participant interviews, the interviews with the direct reports, and the results of the OPQ and MQ. In addition, the various approaches provided a complementary perspective. For example, several direct reports volunteered information about situations in which they themselves had failed to meet expectations, and how their supervisor had behaved. This information would not have been available to the study via the instruments.

As mentioned previously, 185 specific behaviors and motivators were identified in this study. Although these attributes may be useful in and of themselves for selection and development purposes, some summarization of key findings is also appropriate.

Qualitative Key Findings

A number of themes emerged from the analysis of the interviews, documents, and observations of the researchers. These themes consisted of the following qualities of leaders: a problem-solving approach, interpersonal capability, being motivators, a steadfast yet realistic pursuit of goals, humility and self-effacing humor, being highly principled, the importance of culture, an inquiring communication style, the judicious use of power, and commitment and modesty. Each of these will be discussed in more detail.

A Problem-Solving Approach

> He thinks about organizational wisdom, not just facts and fig-
> ures. (SBJ5, DR2)

Since this leadership style is shown to be highly effective in achieving business results, something that was also demonstrated by the participants in this study, how they achieve this was of particular interest to the researchers. A key element appears to be their problem-solving approach. All partici-pants saw complexity in situations. They further recognized the limits of their knowledge and were keenly aware of the need for a decision-making process that was respectful of diverse opinions, encouraged debate and open communication, and was focused on a quality outcome rather than an expedient one.

> I try to convey the idea that they are included, and I invite
> their ideas. I invite them to fully participate in whatever it is
> we are working on. And I listen and I give them feedback. And
> I try to make it very constructive. Feedback that is personal
> but helpful. So that they can come back and say "OK, well,
> this is my thinking and this is why I think the way I do."
> (SBJ9)

Whenever possible, decisions were openly discussed with employees and various options were put on the table. As one leader stated, "I involve the people closest to the issue to solve the problem. The people doing the work think it is their idea. And they are the quickest to change if it isn't working and try something else" (SBJ3).

They are also very reflective people and tend to contemplate before acting. They ask questions. This thoughtfulness is likely a factor in their growth as individuals. As one leader stated,

> I was fortunate to look at things differently, you know, to study
> things, to observe it. And I watched my manager, who was a
> manager of managers, and say, "What would I do in this situ-
> ation? Why is this working, why isn't it working?" And then as
> I became a manager, I was able to go back and say, "Here's the
> philosophy I am going to live by." (SBJ5)

Their decision-making process was thorough, though not hesitant. It would be unfair to characterize them as consensus makers. All were very aware of which decisions were solely theirs, and they did not shirk these tough decisions. It was very clear to the researchers that through this process, optimal decisions were made, and, importantly, employees felt a part of the decision-making process. For these leaders, decision quality and buy-in from employees are certainly success factors in achieving business results.

Interpersonal Capability

> I think your values and what you believe . . . that's going to determine your approach. And as complicated as relationships are, that's as complicated as one's approach to leadership and being the person you are. (SBJ6)

Although not specifically mentioned in the construct, all participants shared a strong interpersonal capability, an intriguing result for the researchers. Their ability to operate in a highly nuanced manner indicates strong emotional intelligence, keen recognition of their role, and the importance of a long-term perspective. They put a great deal of thought into important discussions with people and carefully considered the method of delivery and the message given. Compassion and a deep respect for people played a significant part in their interactions. One leader said, "If it's a people issue, I need to make time for it. I like to walk on the beach to work things through. I need time to process" (SBJ2). Direct reports repeatedly conveyed how much they appreciated this characteristic. One person offered the following:

> I talk to him about personal things. I feel I can trust him. He listens a lot. He may throw out scenarios. He doesn't tell me what to do. He asks questions. He doesn't give advice. He shares what he has been through. "Do it in a way you are comfortable with," he'll say. "This may help you." (SBJ4, DR1)

This is consistent with other research that indicates that the leader characteristic of having a humanistic approach is highly valued by staff (Wood & Vilkinas, 2004). There were numerous stories of how the supervisor had displayed a deep and genuine concern for the participant, sometimes retelling events that had transpired many years earlier. During several interviews the researchers observed moments when the participant was clearly disturbed, sometimes visibly emotional, regarding the impact of his or her actions on the employees. However, at other times, it became apparent that this type of leader may appear to delay performance discussions or at times may provide feedback in such a subtle manner that others may not "get the message."

Being Motivators

> Telling me I can't do something is . . . the best motivation you can give me, because I am going to try and come through and prove it. And not in a grandstanding kind of style, just let the track record see where it will take you. (SBJ8)

This type of leader strives to make an impact and leave a legacy through an organization that is financially healthy and composed of a capable team that can successfully address whatever business challenges they face. They are motivated not by status or personal advancement but by a sense of contribution. As one leader said,

> Maybe it's ambition to serve. I don't know. I can't say for sure what makes me aspire to leadership. I like making a difference. I like impacting things. I don't think it's an ego thing. It's a duty thing. I like helping. But I will say, being honest, that it feels good to be acknowledged for that. (SBJI)

These leaders tend to be risk takers who constantly strive for high quality, focusing on a cycle of continuous improvement rather than achieving a specific financial target. One leader described sending a 13-page memo to his boss, the president, providing a detailed argument for moving the business in a direction that was quite different from their current strategy. Oftentimes, this risk taking was a factor in the direct reports' enjoyment of their jobs. One DR, talking about a series of mergers the organization had gone through, told the researchers that he stayed in the organization because it was exciting and he wanted to see what would happen next.

Developing people was also perhaps as important as building a business. As one participant said, "The magic for me is when the passion builds in the group. It's not me" (SBJ3). Another said, "I like to help people find what is within themselves" (SBJ9). Yet another said, "The part I really get a kick out of is watching other people enjoy the challenge" (SBJ5). Not only did the researchers hear comments like these repeatedly from both the participants and the DRs, but the comments were emphatic. It was clearly an important aspect of their leadership style.

A Steadfast yet Realistic Pursuit of Goals

> I couldn't imagine *not* doing it. I just didn't even think about it. (SBJl)

The participants were all tenacious in pursuing ambitious goals. There were numerous stories of what appeared to be highly risky situations in which the leaders persevered because it was very clear to them that this was the right path, even though they were perhaps not able to see all the road signs leading to their destination. However, they also knew when another approach was clearly indicated, and they would adjust accordingly. They were able to be passionate yet objective. Their ability to remain somewhat detached appeared to be a good counterbalance to their strong sense of commitment.

Humility and Self-Effacing Humor

> We had a school play[,] and he was a bird in a gilded cage. (SBJ7, DR4)

Because modesty was an aspect of the construct, it is not surprising that the participants all exhibited a strong sense of humility. However, it also bears mentioning that this came through repeatedly in the interviews, particularly in the participants' tendency to employ a sense of humor that poked fun at themselves, and also in a distinct lack of comfort with official or prestigious titles. These leaders were anything but pompous.

Their self-effacing sense of humor enhanced their authenticity and likeability. In fact, it seemed to the researchers that the participants took pains to be authentic. The researchers found themselves immediately comfortable in their presence. Because they built rapport and conveyed a down-to-earth style, it was easy to have a conversation with them. this also likely supports an environment that gives people permission to admit to mistakes and lack of knowledge rather than placing energy on impression management. This style of using humor was interpreted by the researchers as an indication of the leaders' self-confidence and level of comfort with themselves; however, it is obvious that this view may not be shared by everyone. In some cultures this approach could, perhaps, work against them. Also, their sense of humor, combined with a driven, results-oriented style, may at times be confusing to people unaccustomed it.

Being Highly Principled

> [The CFO] was presenting some numbers on benefits changes. When we added it up, we realized we had more money than we needed. [He] was ignoring this. I thought it was important to give it back to the employees. I said, "We need to do this." He kept ignoring me. I said, "You aren't listening to me!" It felt like I was mean. In the end, though, we did decide to give it back. Others came up to me afterwards and said they were glad I pressed the issue. I feel I am the conscience of the group. I ask questions that others don't. (SBJ7)

It was anticipated that the participants would be people with integrity, as this was specifically mentioned in the construct. However, it was impressive to discover how highly principled they all were and how this guided their actions in a very central way. One of the leaders repeatedly used the phrase "What's the right thing to do?" (SBJ5). Several direct reports spoke of actions the participant had taken that were not easy or expedient but were chosen because they were clearly the best option from a values perspective. It also became apparent how the leader's strong sense of character engendered loyalty among employees and created deep emotional bonds. One DR said, "I've never liked a job as much as I like this one. It's like your dad. You want him to be proud of you" (SBJ5, DR3). Another said, "I admire him personally and professionally. So many people want to come work for him. We owe him what he gives us. We owe each other what he gives us" (SBJ3, DR2). The direct reports expressed a sense that they could trust their job to this person because they knew the leader would take actions that would be fair to the employee and would not act out of self-interest. This was mentioned repeatedly in the interviews with direct reports. As one DR said, "Why do I follow him? Because I could put my wallet full of $500 bills on the table and come back a week later and it would still be there. I *trust* him!" (SBJ8, DR2).

The Importance of Culture

> I think that the biggest obligation we have is for the culture.
> (SBJ6)

The importance of the culture and their role in defining it was hugely important to the participants. As one leader said, "The president of the organization is the president of the culture. He achieves the least of the business results" (SBJl). All participants conveyed a very intentional approach to culture and often took swift action to preserve it.

The leaders were aware of how business results and the corporate culture are closely connected and worked carefully not to sacrifice one for the other. Another leader said, "We went out of our way to be fair to people. We went about the merger in a very deliberate way because we were dealing with people's livelihood" (SBJ7). And because these leaders have a highly attuned interpersonal sense, they were aware of subtle inconsistencies between desired cultural attributes and actual behavior on the part of employees.

An Inquiring Communication Style

> If I ran the meeting, it would be all what [I] want. That's what these people will do because [of my position]. And I know I could probably influence them into what conclusion I came to. But that is also not my role. My role is to give them information, coaching, and technical advice for them to make the decision. (SBJ4)

These leaders are very aware of the power of their opinion and use it carefully. They tend to inquire, solicit, and offer ideas rather than issue commands. Several use stories as a way of conveying an idea. They are not oblique, however, and will insert their opinions, if necessary, or state that things must be done a certain way. However, their preference is not to do this. Part of their motivation may be to enhance the problem-solving ability of others through subtle coaching, rather than telling, and thereby grow the organizational thinking capacity. They are also acutely aware that if they tell others what they think too soon, the employees may comply without real buy-in, and it is this long-term commitment they are interested in achieving. This approach requires patience on the part of the leader, and sensitivity on the part of the subordinate. Just because their supervisor isn't telling them what to do doesn't mean he or she doesn't care very deeply about moving in a particular direction. Again, this aspect of leadership style could be misinterpreted by others.

The Judicious Use of Power

> Leadership gives you influence. It does give you power. All kinds of power. I prefer influence to power. (SBJl)

As mentioned above, these leaders are very aware of their positional power, and the researchers were particularly interested in how a modest person deals with the power of the position. The researchers found that power was used carefully, and usually to remove barriers. Speaking to the subtlety of one leader's use of power, a DR said, "He's a bright but soft light bulb. The light is everywhere, but he doesn't blind anyone" (SBJ7, DR2).

The participants were attuned to small but meaningful symbols of power, such as the arrangement of a room. In only one case, for example, did a leader choose to be interviewed behind his desk. One participant spoke of this:

> I am aware that I am a big guy, so I know I can tower over people; so I sit at a table instead of standing. I want the message to be the thing, not my size, not have it be "Here is this big guy staring down at me." . . . [It's more about] "Where is your comfort zone?," not "Come to my office." (SBJ2)

Commitment and Modesty

> One person can't make this happen. It is going to take all of us working very, very hard, and I still don't know if we are going to do it. It's nothing I am going to do. I don't even know how to do it. I'll clear the way. I try to be honest and give my perspective. I'll have opinions of where we ought to go. But on a day-to-day basis, things will shift. (SBJ3)

The two characteristics Collins (2001) ascribes to the level-five leader seem to relate to a number of attributes displayed by the participants. All of them seemed to have strong intellectual horsepower, although this was not directly assessed. In addition, they all possessed a keen intuitive understanding of people, a quiet confidence, and a reflective and principled nature. These leaders understand the situations they encounter at a level of complexity that many others do not. And they are honest with themselves, first and foremost. They understand their strengths and limitations and recognize that they are fallible human beings. They know that others have talents that they don't, and that they need those individuals to be successful. They have a strong sense of duty, and this weighs on them. They recognize that many others depend on them, and they choose their actions carefully. Once committed, they are very clear about the goal and the difficulties facing them. The question of whether commitment and modesty are outward manifestations of a cluster of other attributes would be an interesting topic for another study.

The Five Adjectives Exercise

As mentioned previously, the DRs were asked the question "What are five adjectives you would use to describe this person?" Given that a lexicon of adjectives is frequently used to build personality constructs, this seemed like a useful question. The "Affinity Diagram" is shown here (table 19.2).

As can be seen from the chart, six categories emerged from the analysis: interpersonal, character, problem solving, work habits, inspired leadership, and self-assurance. The largest grouping, by far, was "interpersonal." This was especially interesting, given that the "quiet leader" description did not mention interpersonal capability. The highest number of mentions within the "interpersonal" category was in a cluster labeled "caring," and within that, the words "caring" and "kind" were specifically mentioned 11 times by the DRs. The most widely shared characteristic reported by the participants and most meaningful to the direct reports was the leaders' evident concern for their staff. This more than any other stands out as a defining attribute to the direct reports. The groupings that received the next highest number of mentions were "character" and "problem solving." The portrait that emerges from the adjectives selected by the direct reports is a person who is caring, authentic, dependable, open-minded, employs a thoughtful decision-making style, strives for productivity and results, tends to challenge the status quo, and appears to be self-assured.

Table 19.2. Five Adjectives Affinity Diagram

Interpersonal	Character	Problem Solving	Work Habits	Inspired Leadership	Self-Assurance
CARING	AUTHENTIC	LISTENER	PROMPT	COURAGEOUS	STRONG
Caring (6)	Honest (3)	DOESN'T BLAME	THOROUGH	CHALLENGES THE SYSTEM	EVEN-KEELED
Kind (5)	Leads by example	OPEN-MINDED	DRIVER	INSPIRATIONAL	POLISHED
Understanding (3)	Genuine (2)	Open-minded (2)	Driver (2)	ADVENTUROUS	SELF-ASSURED
Compassionate (3)	Sincere	See others' POV	Results-oriented	ENTHUSIASTIC	
Empathetic (2)	DEPENDABLE	Appreciates diversity	PERFECTIONIST	Enthusiastic	
Loving (2)	Dependable (3)	THOUGHTFUL	Perfectionist	Passionate	
People-oriented	Dedicated	Thoughtful (3)	Demanding		
Big-hearted	Reliable	Analytical (2)	EFFICIENT		
Sympathetic	MODEST	Reflective	Efficient		
Supportive	ADMITS FAILURES	DECISIVE	Good organizational skills		
Encouraging	ETHICAL	KNOWLEDGEABLE			
Nurturing	Ethical/moral	INSTINCTIVE			
Thoughtful gestures	Trustworthy				
ENABLES PEOPLE					
Enables people					
Helps people					

SELF-GIVING

PATIENT

LOYAL

ACCESSIBLE

SOCIAL

EMOTIONAL

LIKEABLE

NICE

FUN(2)
Happy
Jolly

HUMOROUS (2)

FAIR (5)

TRUSTING (4)

SPIRITUAL (3)

VISIONARY
Visionary
Forward-thinking

INTELLIGENT
Intelligent (2)
Smart

CREATIVE

Quantitative Key Findings

It would be inappropriate to draw too many conclusions from the results of the two instruments administered, given the small sample size. However, the instruments were chosen as a way of cross-validating the findings from the interviews and did prove useful in this regard. Several interesting findings will be discussed here for illustrative purposes. As stated earlier, the mean on the OPQ is set at 5.5 stens and the standard deviation is 2 stens. Consequently, any score higher than 7.5 or lower than 3.5 would be more unusual. There were no scales in which the combined mean and standard deviation of our participant group fell outside these boundaries. However, there were four scales that trended high and one that trended low, and these are worth expounding upon (see table 19.3).

Within the "relationships" category, scales that trended high were the "modesty" (a high scorer was defined as someone who dislikes talking about achievements) and the "caring" (a high scorer was defined as being sympathetic to the concerns of others, helpful, and supportive). Within the "thinking style" category, the "behavioral" scale (in which a high score indicates a person who likes to analyze the motives of others and is inclined to take this into consideration in their decisions) was high for the composite group, while the "conventional" scale trended lower (indicating that they are less constrained by tradition than other people and more inclined to follow novel approaches). Finally, within the "feelings and emotions" category, the "trusting" scale was high, indicating that the leaders were inclined to see people as reliable and honest. A "thinking style" scale called "evaluative" was midrange, indicating that their analysis of situations is typical of most people.

These results suggest a servant-leader profile: someone who is compassionate and concerned for people, conveys trust in others, has an interest

Table 19.3. Occupational Personality Questionnaire Notable Scale Results

Scale	Mean	Standard Deviation
Modesty	7.2	.8
Caring	7.1	1.0
Behavioral	7.0	1.2
Conventional	3.8	1.3
Trusting	7.6	1.6

in others' ideas and considers them in a balanced manner, and is likely to deflect attention away from their own contributions. They are likely, as well, to place a high value on a supportive and respectful work environment, in which cooperation is valued over competition with others. The low score in "conventional" may be related to the participants' being from smaller organizations, which are often more nimble. Of note is that the scores related to "sociability" were all average, indicating that while the leaders dislike talking about their accomplishments, they are generally extraverted. Modesty and introversion do not appear to be related.

On the MQ, like the OPQ, there were no scales, which were outside the range of expected scores. However, there were four scales on which the participants scored more highly than would be typical, and three that trended lower (see table 19.4).

In the "energy and dynamism" domain, the composite scores on "power" and "commercial outlook" were high. These scores indicate that the leaders in this study were more motivated by the opportunity to wield influence and authority in a situation with bottom-line impact than was expected, and that these areas are their main sources of energy at work. This is consistent with level-five leaders' drive for business results. This is also likely related to their positions in upper-level management. The "power" score was intriguing, as the topic of power was of key interest in this research. Because the participants are at high levels in their respective organizations, it is not surprising that they are motivated by situations they can drive.

The next set of scales in the MQ is called the "Synergy cluster" and relates to aspects of a work environment, but separate from the task, that may be motivating to people. The participants scored somewhat low on the

Table 19.4. Motivational Questionnaire Notable Scale Results

Scale	Mean	Standard Deviation
Power	7.3	1.9
Commercial Outlook	7.5	2.5
Recognition	3.8	1.4
Ease and Security	3.8	1.6
Personal Principles	8.5	1.2
Flexibility	7.4	2.3
Material Rewards	3.8	1.9

"recognition" and "ease and security" scales, but very high on the "personal principles" scale. In fact, this score was the highest of any scale on either instrument. This would indicate that the participants do not need praise and recognition from others or job security to the degree others do to feel motivated. However, they would find it very difficult to work in an environment with questionable ethics.

In the "intrinsic motivators" category, the participants' composite score was high on "flexibility," indicating they preferred situations without much structure, while in the "extrinsic motivators" category, the leaders in this study were less motivated by material reward than others might be. Their scores on a "status" scale were more typical.

Their scoring pattern suggests that the participants are attracted to leadership roles because they believe they can make a financial impact in a principled organization, rather than because of the external trappings of success. Their relatively lower concern for pragmatic considerations of job security and compensation may be due to their current life situations. The results may be different among level-five leaders who are younger and/or less financially secure.

Examining the OPQ and MQ results together, the pattern that emerges is of an interpersonally oriented leader who elicits trust by conveying a sense of integrity and demonstrates a ready interest in the lives of employees and their ideas. This leader may have a somewhat entrepreneurial orientation and bring innovation to situations. Employees will likely feel that they helped contribute to the organization's success. There is also likely to be encouragement for trying rather than criticism for failing in these organizations. These leaders' ability to both identify and drive for business opportunities while building a loyal group around them that is similarly focused is surely a key factor in their success.

The overall pattern seen in the quantitative results is similar to what the researchers observed in the qualitative research. However, there are some differences that bear mentioning.

Initially, the high "power" score was a bit surprising. The researchers heard repeatedly from DRs that they had not observed the leaders using power. However, it may be that "power" has become a somewhat inflammatory term in business, representing self-aggrandizement rather than using influence and authority for a purpose beyond self-interests.

The midrange score on "status" was also surprising, as the researchers found in the interviews that these leaders seemed quite uncomfortable with status. Business cards and use of titles became a marker for modesty in this study. All the leaders downplayed their titles. One participant did not include a promotion that had occurred a year ago on his business card. Another did not even carry a business card. A typical comment by one of the leaders who happened to be president of his firm was,

> One of the things is that there is no human being better than another. We're all equal. You call me John, you don't call me Mr. [X]. I don't care what your title or role is. The responsibilities might be different, but that doesn't mean you are different. (SBJ5)

The high scores on "modesty" and "personal principles" were encouraging, as these characteristics were in the description and thereby confirmed the sampling approach used in the study. It was also consistent with what was revealed in the interviews. There was a distinct use of "we" rather than "I" in the interviews when discussing achievements. Furthermore, several times subjects mentioned that they had exited an organization because the dominant culture was inconsistent with their values.

A point worth mentioning is that the MQ does not assess developing people/coalescing a team as a motivator. However, this was seen as a very important factor for all the leaders in this study, as discussed earlier.

Conclusions

Most of the characteristics identified by Collins (2001) and Greenleaf (1977/2002) were observed in this research. We found people who, as Collins (2001) stated, worked in a focused and disciplined manner toward the tenacious pursuit of goals. They were quick to deflect praise and credit others. They used a questioning style and engaged others in open debate. They all showed a commitment to high standards. The "ferocious resolve" that Collins found was observed in varying degrees. Some participants were faced with situations that were more dramatic than others. Confidence that they would prevail in the end, coupled with a clear sense of the challenges they faced (termed by Collins the "Stockdale Paradox") was observed. Like Greenleaf (1977/2002), we found that the leaders were reflective and had a strong sense of who they were—their strengths, their limitations, and what was important to them. They were very engaged by the growth of people and facilitating that process. They had a questioning nature and employed it when solving problems and influencing. They cared deeply about people and felt tremendous responsibility for them. We did not uniformly observe prescience or the healing through shared wholeness that Greenleaf discusses. We saw a motivation for both achieving business results (Collins, 2001) and growing people (Greenleaf, 1977/2002). The behaviors observed were consistent with the behaviors outlined in the model proposed by van Dierendonck & Heeren (2006) and many of those by Russell and Stone (Russell & Stone as cited in Rennaker, 2006). In addition, like Russell and Stone, we found organizational culture to be an important aspect of servant-leadership.

To characterize these leaders based on competencies or personality attributes would be inadequate. Character plays a strong role in shaping who they are, consistent with both Collins's (2001) and Greenleaf's (1977/2002) findings. Collins (2001) equivocated on whether this is a leadership style that one can grow into, or whether a level-five leader is born, not made. This study would assert that a principled and discerning nature is essential in this type of leader, and that without it, coaching for development is fruitless. It also suggests incorporating character as an element in the selection process, as the companies in Collins's study did. Although it is obvious how difficult this may be to address, it is a necessary and fundamental element of this type of leader.

In seeking to identify these individuals, it is important to pay attention to the processes people used to achieve goals, not simply the results. This study revealed that these leaders are as concerned with the "how" as much as the "what." Seeking out feedback from direct reports is important as well, since a key element of success for this type of leader is the ability to gain followers through their character and competence and their strong interpersonal capability. Finally, examining the hiring and promotion processes can be revealing. Do the ratings purposely weight people who are skilled at impression management over those who are less self-promoting? It is our hope that this research can be helpful in providing a richer portrait of these individuals so that they can be more readily identified in hiring decisions and talent management discussions.

Although some key findings have been uncovered in this study, there is opportunity for future research. A study that includes more women and minorities is called for. Not only would it allow the key findings to be further validated, but it would also be helpful in developing a statistical comparison between this leadership type and the norms captured by SHL (1995, 2000) on upper-level managers for the OPQ and the MQ. In addition, the concept of modesty in leadership continues to intrigue us and offers many fruitful areas for further study. These leaders appear to be highly self-aware, though this study did not specifically probe this topic. What is the link between modesty and self-knowledge? Is a person who is reflective by nature more modest? How does a belief in a higher being contribute to modesty? Are people who are modest more emotionally intelligent? A new research focus on transcendental leadership that is emerging in the leadership literature (Sanders et al., 2003) may be useful in shedding some light on these questions. Finally, we would encourage more researchers to pay attention to other aspects of the servant-leader besides interpersonal capabilities. While this is an attractive aspect of these leaders, research focused on it alone does a disservice to an effective type of leader by not addressing such important qualities as a drive for business results.

We look forward to future studies on this topic. Like Collins (2001), we found these leaders to be both admirable and enjoyable to meet. We always came away from the interactions feeling uplifted and wishing a bit wistfully that we could work in these organizations. Like the heroic leader, the participants draw people to them. However, while some heroic leaders might become wearisome because of their arrogance, the modesty of the leaders encountered in this study would certainly contribute to steadfast loyalty and trust. And the good news is, if we are willing to put aside mythological beliefs about what good leaders look like, potential level-five leaders abound in business settings: "The problem is not, in my estimation, a dearth of potential level-five leaders. They exist all around us if we know what to look for" (Collins, 2001, p. 37). We hope this study has contributed to advancing that goal.

Note

The authors would like to acknowledge the following organizations and their employees for participating in this study: TDindustries, Dallas, Texas; Twin City Co-ops Federal Credit Union, Saint Paul, Minnesota; American Bank, Saint Paul, Minnesota; North American Membership Group, Inc., Minnetonka, Minnesota; and E. A Sween Company, Eden Prairie, Minnesota. Leaders of this type are distinctly uncomfortable with having attention placed on them. However, they believed in what we were doing, opened up their organizations to us, and gave generously of their time. We are deeply grateful for their assistance.

References

Babbie, E. (2007). The *practice of social research* (11th ed.). Thomson Wadsworth.

Badaracco, J. L., Jr. (2002). *Leading quietly: An unorthodox guide to doing the right thing*. Harvard Business School Press.

Bono, J. E., & Judge, T. A. (2004). Personality and transformational and transactional leadership: A meta-analysis. *Journal of Applied Psychology, 89*(5), 901–910.

Collins, J. (2001). *Good to great: Why some companies make the leap . . . and others don't*. Harper Business.

Covey, S. R. (1990). *Principle-centered leadership*. Fireside.

Covey, S. R. (2004). *The eighth habit: From effectiveness to greatness*. Free Press.

Creswell, J. W. (2003). *Research design: Qualitative, quantitative, and mixed methods approaches*. Sage.

Eisner, E. W. (1991). *The enlightened eye: Qualitative inquiry and the enhancement of educational practice*. Macmillan.

Erlandson, D. A., Harris, E. L., Skipper, B. L., & Allen, S. D. (1993). *Doing naturalistic inquiry: A guide to methods*. Sage.

Fawell, H. W. (2006). Evolving leadership: Servant-leadership in the political world. *The International Journal of Servant-Leadership, 2*(1), 399–426.

Greenleaf, R. K. (1991). *The servant as leader*. The Robert K. Greenleaf Center.

Greenleaf, R. K. (2002). *Servant leadership: A journey into the nature of legitimate power and greatness* (L. C. Spears, Ed.; 25th anniversary ed.). Paulist Press. (Original work published 1977)

Hill, C. E., Thompson, B. J., & Williams, E. N. (1997). A guide to conducting consensual qualitative research. *The Counseling Psychologist, 25*(4), 517–572.

Hogan, R., Curphy, G. J., & Hogan, J. (1994). What we know about leadership: Effectiveness and personality. *American Psychologist, 49*(6), 493–504.

Hogan, R., & Kaiser, R. B. (2005). What we know about leadership. *Review of General Psychology, 9*(2), 169–180.

House, R. J., Spangler, W. D., & Woycke, J. (1991). Personality and charisma in the U.S. presidency: A psychological theory of leadership. *Administrative Sciences Quarterly, 39*(3), 364–396.

Judge, T. A., Bono, J. E., Ilies, R., & Gerhardt, M. W. (2002). Personality and leadership: A qualitative and quantitative review. *Journal of Applied Psychology, 87*(4), 765–780.

Kanungo, R. N. (1998). Leadership in organizations: Looking ahead to the 21st century. *Canadian Psychology, 39*(1–2), 71–82.

Kouzes, J. M., & Posner B. Z. (1987). *The leadership challenge*. Jossey-Bass.

Laub, J. (2005). From paternalism to the servant organization: Expanding the Organizational Leadership Assessment (OLA) model. *The International Journal of Servant-Leadership, 1*(1), 155–178.

Lincoln, Y. S., & Guba, E. G. (1985). *Naturalistic inquiry*. Sage.

Maxwell, J. C. (1993). *Developing the leader in you.* Thomas Nelson.

Miles, M. B., & Huberman, A. M. (1994). *Qualitative data analysis: An expanded sourcebook* (2nd ed.). Sage.

Polkinghome, D. E. (2005). Language and meaning: Data collection in qualitative research. *Journal of Counseling Psychology, 52*(2), 137–145.

Rennaker, M. (2006). Servant-leadership: A model aligned with chaos theory. *The International Journal of Servant-Leadership, 2*(1), 427–453.

Sanders, J. E., Hopkins, W. E., & Geroy, G. D. (2003). From transactional to transcendental: Toward an integrated theory of leadership. *Journal of Leadership and Organizational Studies, 9*(4), 21–31.

SHL. (1995). *Motivation questionnaire manual and users guide.* Author.

SHL. (2000). *OPQ32 Manual and users guide* [CD-ROM]. Author.

Skovholt, T. M., & Jennings, L. (2004). *Master therapists: Exploring expertise in therapy and counseling.* Allyn and Bacon.

Stake, R. E. (2005). Qualitative case studies. In Norman K. Denzin & Yvonna S. Lincoln (Eds.), *The Sage handbook of qualitative research* (3rd ed., pp. 443–466). Sage.

Strauss, A., & Corbin, J. (1998). *Basics of qualitative research: Grounded theory procedures and techniques.* Sage.

Tourigny, L., Dougan, W. L., Washbush, J., & Clements, C. (2003). Explaining executive integrity: Governance, charisma, personality and agency. *Management Decision, 41*(10), 1035–1049.

van Dierendonck, D., & Heeren, I. (2006). Toward a research model of servant-leadership. *The International Journal of Servant-Leadership, 2*(1), 147–164.

Weller, S. C., & Romney, A. K. (1988). *Systematic data collection* (Qualitative Research Methods Series, No. 10). Sage.

Wood, J., & Vilkinas, T. (2004). Characteristics of chief executive officers: Views of their staff. *Journal of Management Development, 23*(5), 469–478.

Yin, R. K. (2003). *Case study research: Design and methods.* Sage.

Chapter 20

Servant-Leadership as a Cornerstone for Restoration of Human Dignity

José Hernández

Human beings are experiencing a loss of dignity that diminishes us as a community of people. Many times the consequences of losing our dignity are not severe, allowing us to recover in a short time; other times, they can be so dramatic that they end up scarring us for a lifetime. Those who lose their dignity ultimately have the choice to find resiliency and recover from their loss. Likewise, those who violate the dignity of others bear the responsibility to choose to live with morality and justice toward others. As Greenleaf (1977/2002) explained, "Because we have a natural authority resulting from our power and freedom to choose, we need to use it in a principled way" (p. 5). An important characteristic of an individual is the innate ability to choose. As humans, we are equipped with the unique capacity to do what no other being can do, endowed with the power to utilize freedom to make our decisions and to choose between alternatives. Viktor Frankl's (1997) idea of a person's freedom to choose gives some perspective to the relationship between human choice and human freedom; he describes it as having an "awareness of freedom and responsibleness" (p. 33).

The purpose of this paper is to consider the idea that humility and seeking forgiveness are key elements of servant-leadership and that these are the elements of servant-leadership that are required for the restoration of human dignity.

An individual's dignity can be stripped as the result of a variety of actions or situations (e.g., berating a child, yelling at a store clerk, beating a homeless person, being unable to afford health care), from a small scale, for example, an isolated instance of verbal abuse of a child, to a large scale, for example, the repeated sexual abuse of a child (Fraser, 1987). Ferch (2003) noted, "People have inherent worth, a dignity not only to be strived for, but beneath this striving, a dignity irrevocably connected to the reality of being human" (p. 2). Viktor Frankl (1963) referred to external powers as barriers to people's enjoyment of freedom. He pointed out that "a creative life and a life of enjoyment are banned [resulting in] . . . an existence restricted by external forces" (p. 106). For most of us, suffering is an ineradicable part of life; generally people have the inner capacity to fight for the preservation of their dignity in difficult times. However, depending on a person's inner strength and circumstances, there are phases when an individual's suffering is perpetrated by external forces that limit him or her to a hopeless life of despair. Frankl also talked about people making decisions in challenging and stressful times:

> Every day, every hour, offered the opportunity to make a decision, a decision which determined whether you would or would not submit to those powers which threatened to rob you of your very self, your inner freedom . . . [and which resulted in your] renouncing freedom and dignity. (p. 104)

Through self-responsibility we are able to grow and have a better understanding of freedom and choice. In choosing to live responsibly, we develop characteristics of servant-leadership within us. Servant-leadership can be a great tool for people of all walks of life to use in meeting the challenge of losing our dignity. Servant-leadership offers an opportunity for each of us, not just those in positions of "power," to respond to the loss of dignity in the world.

An understanding of servant-leadership requires humility and maturity of an individual and a community that truly cares for the good of humanity (Spears, 1998, p. xi). Humility refers to a person's ability to respond with optimism and courage to the challenge of examining his or her inner identity (Palmer, 1998). Palmer asserts, "A leader must take special responsibility for what is going on inside his or her own self, inside his or her consciousness, lest the act of leadership create more harm than good" (p. 200). Having courage in the face of vulnerability is vital in the humbling of one's self, and through the practice of servant-leadership we are opened "toward a more accepting and empathetic understanding of one another" (Ferch, 2003, p. 10). Furthermore, when we live by these principles, we contribute to healing and to a conscious and deeper sense of community. I believe that by humbling ourselves and acting with love and forgiveness toward others, it is possible to move toward desired goals. By doing so, humans may embrace a more dynamic and inviting way of life. Spears and Lawrence (2002) suggested that "servant-leadership is a long-term, transformational approach to life and work . . . a way of being that has the potential to create positive change throughout our society" (p. 4).

Servant-Leadership

A new moral principle is emerging which holds that the only authority deserving one's allegiance is that which is freely and knowingly granted by the led to the leader in response to, and in proportion to, the clearly evident servant stature of the leader. (Greenleaf, 1977/2002, p. 9)

Robert Greenleaf (1977/2002) clearly articulated his vision of the interior qualities of a servant-leader with this assertion. This idea of servant-leadership can be traced back to the days of Jesus of Nazareth (Crossan & Reed, 2001; Greenleaf, 1977/2002; Spears, 1998). Palmer (1998) explains,

A leader is a person who has an unusual degree of power to create the conditions under which other people must live and move and have their being, conditions that can either be as illuminating as heaven or as shadowy as hell. (p. 200).

Within the Christian tradition, the Bible contains many stories that characterized Jesus as a servant-leader. One story involves Jesus washing his disciples' feet. Afterward, He told them,

Now that I, your Lord and Teacher, have washed your feet, you also should wash one another's feet. I have set you an example that you should do as I have done for you . . . no servant is greater than his master. (John 13:13–16)

Jesus taught about the attributes and characteristics of a servant-leader, or simply devoted his time to serving others in numerous ways and for a variety of reasons. Jesus stated, "The Son of Man did not come to be served, but to serve" (Matthew 20:28). Similarly, Buddhism, with its emphasis on a concern for others and an awareness of the suffering of others (Hanh, 1998), has many of the attributes and characteristics of servant-leadership. The essence of the Buddha's teaching proclaims, "If you learn to practice love, compassion, joy, and equanimity, you will know how to heal the illnesses of anger, sorrow, insecurity, sadness, hatred, loneliness, and unhealthy attachments" (p. 170).

Jesus' controversial way of thinking took the entire culture by surprise and challenged the political and religious leadership of the time and region to consider the unexpected and to look at a new and revolutionary idea of leadership (Crossan & Reed, 2001; Sande, 2004). Presently, more than 2,000 years later, this idea of leadership continues to develop and grow significantly. Although it might be difficult to separate the name of Jesus from the divine, many of his deeds as described in the Bible apply to the concept and purpose of servant-leadership. Jesus said, for example, "Whoever wants to become great among you must be your servant, and whoever wants to be first must be slave of all" (Mark 10:43–44).

Robert Greenleaf (1977/2002), founder of the Center for Servant-Leadership and creator of the idea of leader as servant, brought to people's attention a more compelling and holistic approach to leadership—a theory replete with provisions for a brighter future. He noted, "The servant-leader is a servant first" (p. 13). This core notion has opened up opportunities for many people nationwide and around the world (even for those who are not necessarily practitioners in the traditional sense of a leader). It has also stimulated new ways of understanding leadership that may challenge the views of various communities and individuals, especially those exercising traditional models of leadership (Spears, 1998; Wren, 1995). Greenleaf (1977/2002) proclaimed, "It begins with the natural feeling that one wants to serve, to serve first" (p. 13). Greenleaf seems to refer to something more than a natural feeling and deeper than an individual desire to provide a service. The essence of this prophetic-like insight and profound idea is based on the certainty of a promise that can be fulfilled through the ambition of a true leader's actions intended to help and inspire others to "become healthier, wiser, freer, more autonomous, more likely themselves to become true leaders" (p. 13).

I consider the inner attributes of servant-leadership to be similar to the inner beauty that an individual possesses, particularly in terms of the clarity and the quality of insight that exists to empower that individual in moving toward transcendence. Transcendent growth can lead individuals to achieve something beyond themselves, as they seek first to understand and then to be understood (Covey, 1989, pp. 235–260). As a person becomes immersed in the wonders and principles of servant-leadership, new insights and gifted ideas may result in unlimited and creative ways. A servant-leader is "one who seeks to draw out, inspire, and develop the best and highest within people from the inside out" (Spears, 1998, p. xii).

Ideas of human possibility, the loss of dignity, despair, restricted freedom, oppression, and the potential of servant-leadership evoke many images of our humanity. Ultimately, we can hope for the certainty that servant-leadership can be developed and can flourish in people from all walks of life and in all corners of the world. But how do people, communities, cultures, and nations begin to develop and flourish amid the social injustice that is constantly jeopardizing humanity? What are the elements holding humanity back from advancing toward a more fulfilling and prosperous life? What would it take for a circumstance of oppression, chaos, and injustice to be transformed into a condition of restorative justice characterized by servant-leaders and their actions? I envision a process, perhaps a framework, within which to bring about transformation through servant-leadership. This framework consists of four stages:

> Stage 1: Humans experience *restricted freedom and a lack of human dignity.*

> Stage 2: Humans require a response involving *choice and self-responsibility.*

> Stage 3: Humans can choose to act with *love and forgiveness.*

> Stage 4: Humans promote *reconciliation and restorative justice.*

In exploring each of these points in this framework, I consider the idea of affirming servant-leadership as offering hope for reconciliation and the restoration of human dignity.

Servant-Leadership as Cultural Heritage

Before I go on to explore each of the framework's four stages, I would like to describe some of the background and circumstances in my growing-up years that exposed me to servant-leaders and influenced me today to believe in servant-leadership as a personal cultural heritage. It is a heritage that is dear to me, and I embrace it proudly. This heritage is the root of my passion for studying the concept of servant-leadership and pursuing my own development as a servant-leader.

I was very fortunate to be born in a humble home and share it with seven other siblings in my native Venezuela. At the head of the household was my mother, an energetic young widow full of life, a loving person with the overwhelming stress of raising eight children on her own after my father died. Although most of the time she would come across as a strict and unyielding disciplinarian, my mother tried to instill in us from an early age that nothing worth having comes easy and that we needed to work hard and be disciplined to achieve whatever we wanted in life, and to pursue with tenacity any dream we wanted to realize. My mother is a great woman; she was my first and the most important source of inspiration and hope I have known. It was through her hard work, work ethic, humility, and servanthood that we were able to overcome very difficult and challenging times.

As I think back it seems as if it was not as result of fate, chance, luck, or coincidence that I was born into poverty into Venezuela, into my particular family and its circumstances, and with specific talents and gifts to possess and hopefully use during my lifetime. It would be easy for me to wonder about or even resent the difficulties of my childhood and think that it was rather inconsistent on God's part to give me the hopes and the corresponding gifts to play professional sports and a desire to pursue high-level education but to have me be born into a family without the resources to support these aspirations. How could extreme poverty, an illiterate mother, undereducated siblings, or an unsupportive father be part of the intricately designed plan for my life? Despite the difficulty of these obstacles, I always seemed to possess enough motivation and perseverance to overcome them. I always had big dreams for my life. One of the most powerful effects of love is the hope that it plants within us. Hope is as essential to our lives as oxygen. I believe fervently that perhaps through divine intervention and my mother's example a strong hope was planted in me at an early age, which allowed me to hold on, to persevere, and to live my dreams.

It was 1975, I was 10 years old, and the Major League Baseball World Series was taking place. As I listened to the radio broadcasts of every game, it was made clear to me that I ought to pursue learning the English language, to play baseball in the major leagues, and to live in the United States of

America. At first it was just a thought; later it was more like a serious hope; and then it became my biggest and most desired dream. Even though the main reason I wanted to come to the United States was to participate in professional sports, my close second priority was to acquire an education. All of these thoughts and ideas grew so intensely and with so much certainty as I approached my teen years that I had the hope and drive to pursue my dreams with the tenacity and the passion that have helped me to achieve many of my dreams up to this point in my life.

I began dedicating rigorous effort to my English studies in school, as well as finding the inner discipline to become an excellent student overall. I knew that I was preparing myself for the opportunity to study in the United States, and I wanted to be ready whenever that opportunity presented itself. I overcame hunger and found the way to focus and learn despite my physical depletion many times; I rose above economic constraints and somehow always found the way to get the school uniform and supplies I needed for each school year; I prevailed over the doubts that others had about me and found a few good supporters as well as my own personal faith to persevere. In the midst of my demanding studies, I was playing baseball and quickly becoming one of the most talented catchers in the youth league in Venezuela. In my baseball pursuits, I encountered the same barriers and challenges that I faced at school—poor nutrition, financial limitations, and some doubting family members and onlookers. It was difficult to tackle the dream of becoming a world-class athlete without anything to eat some days, without the necessary equipment or money to travel with the team, and difficult to convince coaches and fellow players that such a tall kid could be a catcher. Nevertheless, these challenges were more than just trials for me. They were a daily reality that kept me on my toes and spurred me on to make the decision to either give in to the pessimism of others and my own moments of weakness, or to stick with it and hold tight to my dreams.

When I was recruited by the Boston Red Sox organization to come to the United States at the age of fifteen, I was elated, overjoyed, ecstatic—but not completely *surprised*. I realized that my dreams, and the inner strength to pursue them, were finally taking flight. However, my father would not allow me to accept the Red Sox' offer, and my lifelong dreams seemed snuffed out in an instant. I initially filled the void left by my broken dreams with disappointment and sadness, but all this accomplished was to hold me back from moving forward and keeping myself ready for the next opportunity that might come my way. I quit baseball soon after, and I took up basketball to distract my thoughts from all the disappointment I was experiencing. As the saying goes, "When God closes a door, somewhere He opens a window," and it was quickly apparent that my athletic skills applied to the sport of basketball as well. During the next year, my father died of a sudden heart attack and my family fell into even greater poverty. With my excellent academics and my sports ability, I was able to continue my high school studies and be selected to play competitive basketball on my country's national team, all while working odd jobs to help my mother support our family and raise my younger siblings. I realize in retrospect that God knew that I needed a purpose to drive me and to inspire me to reclaim my dreams—even if some of them were revised. Although I did not know God intimately at that time in my life, He was continually making His presence known in my life, and He was blessing me in ways that allowed me to love and care for others.

After successfully completing high school and teacher's college in Venezuela, in addition to playing for professional basketball teams and my country's national team, I was given the opportunity to come to the United States to play college basketball and pursue the advanced education I had always dreamed about. Fast-forwarding to the most recent years of my life, I speak English fluently, I enjoyed my years as an athlete and can now coach others to achieve their basketball dreams, I am raising a beautiful family in the United States, and I have earned a master's degree and am working toward a PhD.

Freedom and Human Dignity

Experiencing restricted freedom and a lack of human dignity may be a combination of factors leading to a life of despair, chaos, inferiority, and the development of hatred and bitterness among individuals (Ferch, 2005). Individuals may experience these feelings associated with oppression and injustice. Especially when an individual's freedom to choose is restricted, he or she may be at a disadvantage in terms of becoming a complete and productive member of society (C. S. King, 1969). In contrast, when a person can enjoy the true freedoms that a free society offers, that individual may have a better chance to understand the relationship between freedom and choice. With choice comes a sense of responsibility, which Frankl (1997) suggests is a virtue. William Manchester (1983), in his book *The Last Lion: Winston Spencer Churchill*, described how hard and painful World War I was and what happened when Great Britain was finally declared victorious over its enemy. In the story, he tells of the reaction and state of mind of an angry soldier and future leader of the defeated country that illustrates the consequences of failing to recognize self-responsibility and of acting without remorse in doing harm to others:

> "I knew that all was lost. Only fools, liars, and criminals could hope for mercy from the enemy. In these nights, hatred grew in me, hatred for those responsible for this deed. . . . The more I tried to achieve clarity on the monstrous events in this hour, the more the shame of indignation and disgrace burned my brow. What was all the pain in my eyes compared to this misery? In the days that followed, my own fate became known to me . . . I resolved to go into politics." The soldier was Adolf Hitler. (pp. 650–651)

From this story, it is important to point out that when people take self-responsibility for the freedom of choice, it may guide their actions to respect and promote goodness in others. This is what England endeavored to do by sending humanitarian aid to Germany after the war. In contrast, when a person chooses not to be responsible, his or her actions may lead to the denial of the freedom and dignity of other human beings. Because of Hitler's lack of humility, he refused to choose resiliency and recovery as a response to his loss of dignity, which prompted him to use his power in an unprincipled manner. A servant-leader in this type of situation would draw upon his or her humility and both seek and grant forgiveness in the pursuit of restoration.

Choice and Self-Responsibility

Frankl (1997) contended that many people have the tendency to react emotionally in stressful conditions. Occasionally, these emotional tendencies are displayed in an uncontrolled manner, leading an individual to ignore the responsibilities that come with his or her actions. Hence, one's actions can produce both individual and communal harm, including an act of violence or evil toward humanity. Ferch (2003) explained how a person may act without taking responsibility for the self-perpetuated oppression of others:

> When a person is hidden, that person's leadership is also hidden, and he or she tends to use hidden measures such as superiority, dominance, and fear. Such measures can be effective, at times achieving powerful results, but they keep those who are led in darkness, subservient, and oppressed. (p. 2)

In the case of Adolf Hitler, I believe that his experiences in World War I affected him in a significantly negative way, leading him to cynicism and then to nihilism. His choices led him to objectify others to the point of extreme oppression and genocide without remorse. To challenge this way of thinking, and move toward a better understanding of humanity, servant-leadership offers a unique and inviting practice of leadership. Servant-leadership places the good of those led over the self-interest of the leader (Greenleaf, 2003; Laub, 1999). Greenleaf (1977/2002) was confident that natural servant-leaders exist who are willing to lead and to meet the needs of humanity. As he put it, "Leaders will bend their efforts to serve with skills, understanding and spirit, and followers will be responsive only to able servants who would lead them" (p. 18).

Love and Forgiveness

The ability to forgive is one of the characteristics found in a servant-leader. Servant-leaders are willing to seek forgiveness when wronged by others and grant forgiveness to those who have done wrong (Holloway, 2002; Tutu, 1999). Ferch (2003) explained the significance of forgiveness in reconciliation and in fostering human relationships built on love:

> One of the defining characteristics of human nature is the ability to discern one's own faults, to be broken as the result of such faults, and in response, seek meaningful change. Socially, both forgiveness and the disciplined process of reconciliation draw us into a crucible, from which we can emerge more refined, more willing to see the heart of another, and more able to create just and lasting relationships. (p. 1)

There are remarkable leaders whose lives are characterized by love and forgiveness. Among them was Martin Luther King, Jr., who encouraged us to love the oppressor. Desmond Tutu engendered love through forgiveness that could heal violence. Nelson Mandela refused to deny the humanity of those who imprisoned him and those who confessed to the most heinous acts against human dignity. Robert Greenleaf's call to servanthood promoted wisdom and freedom. Finally, President Abraham Lincoln demonstrated redemptive love by hiring his arch-enemy, Edwin M. Stanton. The actions demonstrated by each of these leaders illustrate what Ferch (2003) described as "potent expressions of the interior of the leader oriented toward healing the heart of the world" (p. 3).

The concepts of love and forgiveness are not easy ones for many people to understand and express. Desire and discipline are required to understand them, patience and humility to obtain them, and love and commitment to practice them. According to Ferch (2003), forgiveness "requires a form of personal integrity that is hard-won. A certain lifestyle results, reflected in a humble awareness of one's own faults and the integration of strength, hope, and grace with regard to the faults of others" (p. 3).

Early on in our marriage, my wife and I began to engage in arguments in which we exchanged uncontrolled emotional words that we later regretted. Despite feeling love for one another, at times we did not like each other. I was too concerned with self-righteousness and at times felt that my wife was only critical toward me. My typical response was defensive and fueled by emotional reactivity. My responses prevented me from developing a deep awareness of my wife's emotional needs and kept me from seeing the fundamental flaw in my human nature. Fortunately, I found gifted people, friends and mentors, who helped me to understand what it meant to honor Kim in our relationship with love and freedom, and to cultivate humility by asking for and granting forgiveness. This experience has served as a healer of my interior qualities and has raised my confidence as a servant-leader. Furthermore, it has fortified the key elements of servant-leadership as the forefront of our lives, elements that every true servant-leader should possess. Greenleaf (1977/2002) said that the real motive for healing is for one's own healing, not to change others, meaning that the true motive to serve others is for our own betterment.

In an effort to seek reconciliation with other religious practices, the late Pope John Paul II showed the world a wonderful example of love and humility, which I believe to be special attributes of a servant-leader. He asked the forgiveness of other world religious leaders for any harm they might have suffered in the name of Christianity. He also visited the religion's sacred places and prayed over them. This act demonstrated a sense of love through the act of granting and asking for forgiveness. This story leads us back to the essence of a servant-leader—characterized by humility and committed to seeking forgiveness for the preservation of human dignity. Similarly, Ferch described the notion of love and forgiveness inherent in reconciliation, restorative justice, and servant-leadership: "Movement away from alienation and emotional reactivity into love itself; the depth of love and the integrity . . . is what lifts us to forgive and grow and become deeper, truer people" (personal communication, April 2004).

Nelson Mandela and Martin Luther King, Jr., signified a keen awareness and understanding of Greenleaf's ideas. Although they were both deeply affected by the oppression they personally experienced, they demonstrated love and forgiveness and transformed their liabilities into assets. They recognized the necessity of suffering to promote a righteous cause and guarded against personal bitterness. Mandela and King demonstrated hope and vision and acted upon the opportunity to transfigure themselves and their society in the midst of the ordeals of that time. In 1964, at the opening of his defense before the Pretoria Supreme Court, Mandela (1994) finished his statement to the court with these words:

> During my lifetime I have dedicated myself to the struggle of the African people. I have fought against white domination. I have fought against black domination. I have cherished the ideal of a democratic and free society in which all persons live together in harmony and with equal opportunities. It is an ideal which I hope to live for and to achieve. But if needs be, it is an ideal for which I am prepared to die. (p. 13)

After more than 27 years as a political prisoner, in 1994 Nelson Mandela became the first democratically elected president of South Africa. "From a country of bloodshed and hate, he and those around him effectively built a country of hope" (Ferch, 2005, p. 109). As Mandela was prepared to sacrifice himself for the love he held for the ideals of democracy and freedom, this same love inspired the foundation of the Truth and Reconciliation Commission. Mandela and Archbishop Tutu demonstrated a great love by asking the country to offer forgiveness to those who committed human atrocities during Apartheid.

Similarly, Martin Luther King, Jr., was guided by love and commitment and never stopped advocating for peace, justice, and redemption. Demonstrating an emotionally disciplined approach to conflict, he led nonviolent protests and encouraged us to love the oppressor. Martin Luther King, Jr.

(1963), led one of the most amazing civil rights movements in history. He embodied love and forgiveness as a human being and a great leader. Martin Luther King, Jr., encouraged us to respond to hatred and injustice with love:

> There will be no solution to the race problem until oppressed men develop the capacity to love their enemies. The darkness of racial injustice will be dispelled only by the light of forgiving love. The degree to which we are able to forgive determines the degree to which we are able to love our enemies. (p. 89)

Mandela and King are true servant-leaders who genuinely care for humanity and seek to serve the needs of others. Their leadership is founded in love, not only for those who are oppressed but for all of humanity. Loving the oppressor, as King encouraged, communicates Mandela's ideals of democracy and freedom in the spirit of peace and forgiveness.

Reconciliation and Restorative Justice

On April 27, 1994, for the first time in its history, South Africa celebrated a democratic election in which Nelson Mandela was elected president, marking the end of apartheid. This is the most recent display of servant-leadership, forgiveness, and restoration of hope that humanity has witnessed in modern history. Led by President Mandela and Chairman Archbishop Desmond Tutu, the Truth and Reconciliation Commission (TRC) was created. The TRC set out with a specific and drastic vision, asking people to accept forgiveness and reconciliation as a plan for restorative justice. The commission invited people to come forward and tell the truth regarding political acts of violence. Perpetrators would receive the opportunity to be granted amnesty, and victims' families could find peace in facing and forgiving the perpetrators. There were conditions that perpetrators needed to meet in order for them to be allowed to apply for amnesty (Tutu, 1999):

- The act for which amnesty was required should have happened between 1960, the year of the Sharpeville massacre, and 1994, when President Mandela was inaugurated.

- The act must have been politically motivated. Perpetrators did not qualify for amnesty if they killed because of personal greed, but they did qualify if they committed the act in response to an order by, or on behalf of, a political organization, such as the former apartheid state.

- The applicant had to make full disclosure of all the facts relevant to the offense for which amnesty was being sought.

- The rubric of proportionality had to be observed. In other words, the means were proportionate to the objective. (pp. 49–50)

"If these conditions were met, said the law, then amnesty 'shall' be granted" (Tutu, 1999, p. 50). The commission enacted these conditions into law, giving the process and the nation an opportunity for a positive outcome. The TRC's vision of transforming a country of injustice, retribution, and violence into one of freedom, justice, and hope became a reality. In the present, distanced from the nightmares of the past, South Africa enjoys the liberties and benefits of a democratic nation.

Conclusion

Human beings long for goodness and wholesome leadership in the world. The acts of servant-leaders such as Nelson Mandela and Martin Luther King, Jr., have inspired humanity to seek a new way of living and of dealing with social injustice: to strive for restoration and respect for all human beings. Restricted freedom and a lack of human dignity confine people to a life of despair, hatred, and, ultimately, oppression. Freedom of choice and responsibility release the oppressed, allowing them to act responsibly with care for human dignity. Once committed to a journey toward restorative justice, people can begin to love, to forgive, and to seek forgiveness of others. Laub (1999) connected servant-leadership with the search for common goodness in humanity:

Servant-Leadership promotes the valuing and development of people, the building of community, the practice of authenticity, the providing of leadership for the good of the those led and the sharing of power, status for the common good of each individual, the total organization and those served by the organization. (p. 81)

Servant-leadership is a type of leadership that creates a solid foundation from which people can reach new heights and help others to come and share a deeper understanding of humility and forgiveness on a personal and communal level. I am convinced that freedom and human dignity can lead a person to make good choices and embrace self-responsibility. This commitment can, in turn, lead the person to love, to forgive, and to seek forgiveness. A model of responsible choice, love, and forgiveness may lead to reconciliation on many levels, finally resulting in a state of restorative justice. Once people reach that point in life, servant-leadership can be developed, and it may flourish everywhere. Fundamental strength and courage can be revealed, and only then can goodness be present in every corner of the world.

References

Covey, S. R. (1989). *The seven habits of highly effective people: Restoring the character ethic.* Simon and Schuster.

Crossan, J. D., & Reed, J. L. (2001). *Excavating Jesus: Beneath the stones, behind the texts.* Harper.

Ferch, S. R. (2003). *Servant-leadership, forgiveness, and social justice.* The Greenleaf Center for Servant Leadership.

Ferch, S. R. (2005). Servant-Leadership, forgiveness, and social justice. *The International Journal of Servant-Leadership, 1*(1), 97–113.

Frankl, V. E. (1963). *Man's search for meaning: An introduction to logotherapy.* Beacon.

Frankl, V. E. (1997). *Man's search for ultimate meaning.* Plenum.

Fraser, S. (1987). *My father's house: A memoir of incest and of healing.* Harper & Row.

Greenleaf, R. K. (2002). *Servant leadership: A journey into the nature of legitimate power and greatness* (L. C. Spears, Ed.; 25th anniversary ed.). Paulist Press. (Original work published 1977)

Greenleaf, R. K. (2003). *The servant-leader within: A transformative path* (H. Beazley, J. Beggs, & L. C. Spears, Eds.). Paulist Press.

Hanh, T. N. (1998). *The heart of the Buddha's teaching: An introduction to Buddhism.* Broadway.

Holloway, R. (2002). *On forgiveness: How can we forgive the unforgivable?* Canongate.

King, C. S. (1969). *My life with Martin Luther King, Jr.* Henry Holt & Co.

King, M. L., Jr. (1963). *Strength to love.* Fortress.

King, M. L., Jr. (1964). *Why we can't wait.* HarperCollins.

Laub, J. A. (1999). *Assessing the servant organization: Development of the Organizational Leadership Assessment (OLA) instrument. Dissertation Abstracts International, 60* (02), 308A. (UMI No. 9921922)

Manchester, W. R. (1983). *The last lion: Winston Spencer Churchill.* Little, Brown & Company.

Mandela, N. R. (1994). *Long walk to freedom.* Little, Brown & Company.

Palmer, P. J. (1998). Leading from within. In L. C. Spears (Ed.), *Insights on leadership: Service, stewardship, spirit, and servant-leadership* (pp. 197–208). John Wiley & Sons.

Quest Study Bible: New International Version. (1994). Zondervan Publishing House.

Sande, K. (2004). *The peace maker.* Baker Books.

Spears, L. C. (Ed.) (1998). *Insights on leadership: Service, stewardship, spirit, and servant-leadership.* John Wiley & Sons.

Spears, L. C., & Lawrence, M. (Eds.) (2002). *Focus on leadership: Servant-leadership for the twenty-first century.* John Wiley & Sons.

Tutu, D. (1999). *No future without forgiveness.* Doubleday.

Wren, J. T. (1995). *The leader's companion: Insights on leadership through the ages.* Free Press.

Chapter 21

Greenleaf's Servant-Leadership and Quakerism

A Nexus

CAROLYN CRIPPEN

Two hundred copies of a small thirty-seven page booklet with a bright orange cardstock cover were published in 1970. The author, Robert Kiefner Greenleaf (1904–1990), introduced a paradox in *The Servant as Leader* (Greenleaf, 1970/2008) and presented a new approach to leadership, including followership and service. Today there is an abundance of literature about the concept of leadership in general, and specifically about particular types of leadership, for instance, contingency leadership (Fielder & Chemers, 1974), moral leadership (Sergiovanni, 1992), distributive leadership (Harris & Muijs, 2005), lateral leadership (Fisher & Sharp, 2004), shared leadership (Pearce, 2003), and transformational leadership (Bass & Riggio, 2008). Forty years later, *The Servant as Leader*, and the philosophy of servant-leadership, remains popular and has now been translated into many languages, including Czech, Mandarin Chinese, Turkish, Dutch, French, Spanish, and Japanese. The endurance and popularity testify to the value of the written content. If our belief system guides our values and our behavior, then an examination of Greenleaf's beliefs may reveal the foundation for his servant-leader ideas first penned at the age of sixty-six. In this chapter I initiate a discussion of Greenleaf's concept of servant-leadership and his beliefs and practice of Quakerism. The connection may prove vital.

Defining Servant-Leadership

Greenleaf worked first in Indiana as a telephone lineman and eventually moved into organizational management at AT&T from the mid-1920s to the 1960s. He lectured at the Massachusetts Institute of Technology, Dartmouth, and the Harvard Business School. Greenleaf believed that through strategies of service and stewardship, a leader would be identified by the people as the first among equals, or primus inter pares (Greenleaf, 1976). Greenleaf tells the story of how he discovered the concept of servant-leadership through reading a small book, *Journey to the East*, by Herman Hesse (1956/2000). The book speaks of a band of men who set out on a long journey. Accompanying the men was a fellow named Leo; his job was to care for the band of men by doing all of the menial chores and providing for their comfort. The journey progressed well, until Leo disappeared. At this point, the travelers or band of men aborted the journey, having quickly fallen into disarray without Leo.

Many years later, the narrator of the story encountered Leo. It was at this point that the narrator realized Leo was the titular head of the order that sponsored the journey. He was the leader, but his nature was that of a servant. His leadership was given to him but could be taken away by the band of men. His desire to serve the group of men came from his heart: a desire that was intrinsic, natural, and genuine. Leo wanted to be of service to the band of men. Leo was a servant first by taking care of their basic needs each day while on the journey.

Greenleaf believed the message of the story was that one had to first serve society, and that through one's service a person would be recognized as a leader. Who is the servant-leader? Greenleaf's (1970/2008) response is clear:

> The servant-leader is servant first. . . . It begins with the natural feeling that one wants to serve to serve first. Then conscious choice brings one to aspire to lead. . . . The difference manifests itself in the care taken by the servant—first to make sure that other people's highest priority needs are being served. The best test, and difficult to administer, is: do those served grow as persons;

do they, while being served, become healthier, wiser, freer, more autonomous, more likely themselves to become servants? And what is the effect on the least privileged in society; will they benefit, or, at least, will they not be further deprived? (p. 15)

Greenleaf believed strongly in the equality of all human beings. He worked with educational, business, theological, and industrial organizations, and his goal was for the development of strong, effective, caring communities in all segments of our society (Greenleaf, 1976). There is a common yet narrow conviction that servant-leadership is linked to Christian practice only. Many people see Jesus Christ as the consummate example of a servant-leader. But I would suggest that greater inclusivity is needed in a list of servant-leaders, such as Mahatma Gandhi, Martin Luther King, Jr., John Woolman, Nelson Mandela, Dorothy Day, Stephen Lewis, Parker Palmer, Eleanor Roosevelt, the Dalai Lama, and many other people who are not famous or affiliated with a specific religious group. Frick (2004) clarifies Greenleaf's intent: "Greenleaf, content 'to stand in awe of all creation' when it came to religion, hadn't conceived the servant-leader as part of any particular doctrine" (p. 280).

Greenleaf (1979/2002) recognized an important reality. He noted,

They do not see the servant leadership in action as you saw it. And that may be the fundamental key. Effective servant-leaders can be so subtle about it that all anybody is likely to see is the result. They don't see the cause. (p. 151)

Servant-leaders are, first, human beings with the same frailties as anyone else. They are not perfect. They make mistakes; and, if they are famous, those mistakes are certainly magnified. Greenleaf (1979/2002) wrote about all human beings living out their lives on a continuum: at one end is leadership and at the other end is followership. He contends that we move back and forth along this continuum throughout our lives. As long as one continues to move one way or another there is growth or learning. It is only when one becomes "stuck" in one spot that growth is stifled in status quo.

The term *servant* usually causes a level of discomfort in people. They often ask why another word wasn't used instead, for example, service? Some find it demeaning, and relate it to the concept of one person having power over another. I had a teacher yell out to me in a presentation about the philosophy of servant-leadership, "I am no kid's servant!" In his papers, Greenleaf explained his choice of words:

> I got the idea that the key to the greatness of Leo was the fact the he was first a servant and then a leader, and that's where the term that I have coined from my writing *Servant Leadership* came from. (as cited in Frick, 2004, p. 274)

Frick (2004) carefully explains Greenleaf's concept of servant: "A servant is one who consciously nurtures the mature growth of self, other people, institutions, and communities" (p. 5). Greenleaf believed that a new moral principle was perhaps emerging. People respond freely only to those individuals chosen as authentic moral leaders "because they are proven and trusted as servants" (p. 275).

An Introduction to Quakerism

Greenleaf did not stress specific religions in his writing. He lived the latter part of his life at Crosslands Retirement Center, a Quaker community. Greenleaf's biography reveals that he held Quaker values, beliefs, and ideals (Frick, 2004). What are Quaker ideals? The Quakers, or Friends, were founded in 1652 by George Fox in England. Fox preached that "direct revelation is available to all true seekers, Christian and non-Christian, without benefit of 'steeple houses,' priests or rituals, and is presented to us through the 'Inward Light,'" (Frick, 2004, p. 127). Quakers are pacifists and do not support violence, abuse, coercion, war, or the death penalty (Cox, 1985; Curle, 1981; Lakey, 2004). They are interested in the penal system and the human condition of those incarcerated. Friends support a simple lifestyle and are conscious of the environment. Groups such as Greenpeace, Amnesty International, and Save the Children were initiated and/or supported by Quakers. Wilmer Cooper (1991) writes, "A typical list of Friends' testimonies today includes peace, simplicity, honesty (integrity), equality, community, and care for the environment" (p. 10). Quakers do not believe in converting people to their ways or beliefs. Thus, many people are often unaware of Quakers living in their area. Those who join do so through "convincement" or by being convinced of the truth of the Quaker way through inward reflection and commitment (Hertzberg, 2002; Lamb, 2000).

In Canada, Friends gather in homes or in a meetinghouse on First Day (Sunday) for meeting or worship. There is no official leader. Friends simply enter the meeting room and sit down quietly for about an hour. The arrangement is a circle or a square. All are welcome: children, the elderly, all races and cultures; men and women are treated equally and valued regardless of sexual preference or occupation. There is no hierarchy, no figurehead, just a community of fellow "seekers" of the truth (Curle, 1981). A social time and refreshments follow the meeting, when people connect with each other in their community. Quakers speak plainly and directly and carefully. What do Quakers say?

- There is something sacred in all people.

- All people are equal before God.

- Religion is about the whole of life.

- We meet in stillness to discover a deeper sense of God's presence.

- True religion leads to respect for the earth and all life upon it.

- Each person is unique, precious, a child of God. (*Quaker Faith & Practice*, 1999)

A Nexus

Several scholars have identified servant-leader characteristics in Greenleaf's writing. Spears (1998) lists ten: listening, empathy, healing, awareness, persuasion, foresight, conceptualization, stewardship, commitment to the growth of others, and building community. Barbuto and Wheeler (2006) add "calling" to the list. Recently, Sipe and Frick (2009) have listed seven pillars of servant-leadership: person of character, puts people first, skilled communicator, compassionate collaborator, has foresight, systems thinker, and leads with moral authority. It seems to me that an interconnected web (Wheatley, 2006) provides a frame for servant-leadership: at the center of the web is relationships. Subtle but powerful strands interconnect or support each other to make the web strong. At the juncture of the connecting strands are essential concepts of *caring* (which can be demonstrated through empathetic listening, reflection, stewardship, inclusivity, respect), *tenacious purpose* (including courage, vision, growth, and treating all people as valuable, capable, and responsible), and the *moral imperative* (ethical, thoughtful, selfless, humble, democratic, just, community builder). I agree with Wheatley (2006): "We need to create stronger relationships" (p. 145), a critical step to being a servant-leader. Many of these concepts are embedded in Quaker beliefs.

Quakers stress the importance of *listening*. Notably, hearing one's self is highly valued. Reflective thought and being quiet are stressed:

> This is one of the great things about being a Friend—that we learn how to listen; we learn how to listen to the voice of the spirit inside us; we learn how to be quiet. This is a great art. It's a very uncommon art. (Curle, 1981, p. 4)

"Friends are encouraged to listen to each other in humility and understanding, trusting in the Spirit that goes beyond our human effort and comprehension" (*Quaker Faith & Practice*, 1999, p. 19). Quakers "sit in silence" for an hour during their meetings. Listening and hearing are critical to getting the message right. Taking time to think decisions through carefully, to discern, will lead to better judgment than rushing without input from others or time for pondering outcomes (Smith, 2003). The best communication forces you to listen (De Pree, 1989). Effective leaders are great communicators and must be good listeners, to themselves (through their inner voice), as well as to others. A good servant-leader strives to understand and empathizes with others. Greenleaf wrote that trust could be developed through the use of empathy when he stated,

> Individuals grow taller when those who lead them empathize and when they are accepted for what they are, even though their performance may be judged critically in terms of what they are capable of doing. Leaders who empathize and who fully accept those who go with them on this basis are more likely to be trusted. (Spears, 1998, p. 81)

Noted Quaker scholar Dr. Gray Cox (1985) writes,

> The Quaker ethic is a process meant to be practiced rather than a theory meant to be accepted or a set of dogma meant to be blindly obeyed. It is an activity born of commitment and concern, it is rooted in a coherent set of ideas about the nature of meaning and truth, and is a living discipline. Quaker attitudes towards their concerns—and towards the process by which we

come to act on them—are rooted in fundamental beliefs about truth, meaning, reason, and the self. (p. 4)

Cox (1985) clarifies the four fundamental beliefs as viewed by Quakers (paraphrased):

1. Truth is something that happens; it occurs. Truth is not a dead fact that is known; it is a living occurrence in which we participate.

2. Meaning is communal. Mind is a social activity; meaning is something we do together and share jointly. We may say many different things, and yet somehow speak with one voice.

3. Feeling and reason are viewed as continuous with one another. With feeling we touch, with reason we reach. Feeling is the aspect of immediacy; reason is the aspect or mediation or bridging.

4. The self is inherently social and transitional, becoming. People are aspects of communal processes.

During a Quaker meeting for business everyone listens attentively to the person speaking. They may not agree with what is spoken but they respect the person's right to an opinion and hold them in positive regard. But this understanding should be supportive as opposed to patronizing. "It is a misuse of our power (as leaders) to take responsibility for solving problems that belong to others" (Block, 1993, p. 72). An ethic of care is present (Noddings, 2003) and acceptance.

In Quaker meetings for business there is always a period of silence before the meeting begins, after it ends, and often during the discussion of issues and decisions. Quaker Cox (1985) identifies five aspects in group decision making during a Quaker meeting for business:

1. Quieting impulses

2. Addressing concerns

3. Gathering consensus or seeking clearness (meeting in worship with others often serves to intensify markedly the sense

of being addressed by an issue and by the concerns of our community)

4. Finding clearness (this is the stage of resolve, the stage at which we find ourselves standing in the conviction of some truth) (Clearness usually involves a sense of openness with a wide variety of perspectives. It involves wholeness, an integrity that comes from different positions. There is unanimity and a sense of presence.)

5. Bearing witness—such clearness compels some activity, either demonstrated verbally or by doing, in private or public. (pp. 7–15)

Yes, this takes time, but ultimately all voices are heard, and a sense of collaboration, inclusion, and affirmation prevails in the group. Greenleaf's ideas about persuasion, not coercion, fit well. The servant-leader seeks to convince or persuade others, rather than coerce compliance. One can use persuasive language or persuasive actions. Greenleaf believed that consensus is a method of group persuasion. Frick (2004) acknowledges the source of Greenleaf's consensus/persuasion approach:

In the Quaker practice of consensus, Greenleaf found a proven way of making decisions that honored all voices and used some of his favorite strategies: silence, listening, and a reliance on spirit as expressed through individual insight. He also learned about the critical role of the chair—called the Clerk by Quakers—who makes consensus work. A Clerk is a situational leader, no better or worse than anyone else. He or she is a *primus inter pares*—a first among equals—not a final arbiter. (p. 130)

Autry (2001) states that the transition to a culture of servant-leadership requires time for the development of necessary features or qualities for a servant-leader. Time is an important aspect of healing as directed toward servant-leadership. A servant-leader has the potential to heal oneself and others (Greenleaf, 1970/2008). Quaker Martin (2006) recently wrote, "Instead of entering into the suffering of others, one can imagine those persons in their essential wholeness: visualizing them surrounded by the Light, seeing 'that of God' in them" (p. 70). Sturnick (1998) writes extensively about *healing* leadership and servant-leadership and warns that it is not always possible as a healthy leader to find followers, and she believes that "sick organizations really do contaminate" (p. 191).

Gardiner (1998) suggests that healing can come through just quietly being, and that a "quiet presence is an act of renewal" (p. 122), and Greenleaf (1979/2002), a lifelong meditator, viewed the action of meditation as an act of service because one is taking time to think about things, to reflect, and, often, to solve one's problems. Greenleaf suggests that taking the time to ponder decisions, when possible, is an ethical thing to do. Quaker Murphy (1983) connects the healing concept directly to those in "social services" when she writes,

> The phenomenon of burn-out is characteristic of teachers and social workers who feel they are working against the intractable evil of the world and the incorrigibility of those they try to help. Often they become cynical, or feel they themselves are part of the unjust structure to which they can only apply band-aids. (p. 22)

A young doctor who attended a Quaker meeting sat in silence for an hour. He commented after the time had passed that he "felt refreshed and appreciated the quiet time to just sort things out."

The servant-leader has a general *awareness,* especially self-awareness. Servant-leaders often examine and ponder their values, beliefs, and actions. Quakers develop awareness through self-reflection, through listening to what others tell them about themselves, through being continually open to learning, and by making the connection between what they know and believe and what they say and do. This is called, in the vernacular, "walking your talk" (Bennis & Goldsmith, 1997). "Each Quaker deserves to be a leader, because God is equally available to each as the Light within" (Frick, 2004, p. 129).

Servant-leaders seek to nurture their own abilities to dream great dreams. They are "conceptualizers" and big-picture thinkers and visionaries. Greenleaf (1970/2008) called them "prophets" in his original booklet. I would call them "keepers of the dream." It is interesting that Greenleaf believed at the age of sixty-six that he finally had something worthwhile to put in print. He personally paid for and published those 200 copies of *The Servant as Leader* and distributed them to friends and colleagues and waited for a response to his dream. Greenleaf (1996) describes conceptual talent as

> the ability to see the whole in the perspective of history—past and future—to state and adjust goals, to evaluate, to analyze,

and to foresee contingencies a long way ahead. Leadership, in the sense of going out ahead to show the way, is more conceptual than operating. The conceptualizer, at his or her best, is a persuader and a relation builder. (p. 217)

Experience often helps develop foresight. Frick (2004) paraphrases Greenleaf:

The leader needs to "have a sense for the unknowable and be able to foresee the unforeseeable" through intuition and reflection. Quakers hold their seniors in high regard and often seek their advice, wisdom, and foresight. Foresight, in fact, is the central ethic of leadership. (p. 276)

Greenleaf (1970/2008) states,

Foresight is seen as a wholly rational process, the product of a constantly running internal computer that deals with intersecting series and random inputs and is vastly more complicated than anything technology has yet produced. Foresight means regarding the events of the instant moment and constantly comparing them with a series of projections made in the past and at the same time projecting future events—with diminishing certainty as projected time runs out into the indefinite future. (p. 18)

Greenleaf (1970/2008) believed all members of an institution or organization play significant roles in holding their institutions in trust (caring for the well-being of the institution and serving the needs of others in the institution) for the greater good of society. This is *stewardship*. Fullan (2003) suggests that school principals (and teachers, as well) be mindful that "changing context is the key to deeper change" (p. 21) and seek to ask, What is my role in making a difference in the school as a whole? (p. 21). De Pree (1989) emphasizes the need for us to make a contribution to society: "The art of leadership requires us to think about the leader-as-steward in terms of relationships: of assets and legacy, of momentum and effectiveness, of civility and values" (p. 13). Sergiovanni (1992) explains that stewardship "involves the leader's personal responsibility to manage her or his life and affairs with proper regard for the rights of other people and for the common welfare" (p. 139). The essence of stewardship is moral leadership.

The servant-leader is committed to the individual *growth of human beings* and will answer the call to nurture others. "The signs of outstanding leadership appear primarily among the followers. Are the followers reaching their potential? Are they learning? Serving?" (De Pree, 1989, p. 12). As a Quaker, Greenleaf spoke of being a seeker of truth and constantly growing and learning in the process, and he wished the same for others in any organization. Murphy (1983) wrote, "Education is thought of in its broadest sense [as] the transforming of persons and of society" (p. 34). A Quaker perspective on teaching is as follows:

> We are educators, we do not treat our students as empty vessels to be filled with our superior knowledge. We consider them as equals; we do not try to teach them, but to help what is within them to unfold. (Curle, 1981, p. 12)

Quakers have always been concerned about education and have a history of the development of Friends schools at the elementary, secondary, college, and postgraduate level (Cooper, 1991, p. 22). Sergiovanni (2001) comments on servant-leadership in the context of school:

> The leader serves as head follower by leading the discussion about what is worth following, and by modeling, teaching, and helping others to become better followers. When this happens, the emphasis changes from direct leadership based on rules and personality, to a different kind of leadership based on stewardship and service. (p. 34)

Ultimately, the servant-leader seeks to identify some means for *building community*. There are several approaches to building community outlined in the literature (Starrat, 2003); three approaches mentioned include giving back through responsible service to the community, investing financially into the community, and caring about one's community. Sergiovanni (1992, p. 146) states that caring is an integral part of shared community, a moral act. Cooper (1991) elaborates,

> Integrity creates a sense of togetherness and belonging when applied to persons in community. . . . Individualism, which is preoccupied with doing one's own thing, often with little concern

for how it affects other people, dominates much of our behavior in western society. (p. 21)

When one enters a Quaker meeting, someone greets and welcomes you, and if you are known, then you usually receive a hug. If you are a visitor, then someone will shake your hand and invite you in and make sure you are comfortable and aware of what happens in a meeting. The Quaker meeting is a community, and those who belong are valued as precious members (Garman, 1994; Haight, 1987). Their safety is always paramount. Quakers have a long history of providing safe passage or lodging for those in need—dating back to the fight for the abolition of slavery in the United States, all the way to present-day Quakers who help those fleeing from violent or oppressive situations.

Conclusion

I hope this brief discussion will be a catalyst for a broader investigation into Quakerism and servant-leadership (Greenleaf, 1970/2008). It does seem apparent that Greenleaf's Quaker beliefs have been reflected in his philosophy of servant-leadership. As an educator-administrator for more than forty years and as a student of leadership since 1980, I feel comfortable engaging an analytical process of seeking greater understanding of the concept of servant-leadership. In addition, perhaps my perspective as a Quaker has added to this intentional form of stewardship. Senge (1990) reminds us that organizational change requires a variety of leadership types at different times. It seems to me that the time for servant-leadership is now. What can we learn from this Quaker-Greenleaf servant-leadership nexus? The emphasis on human value and on acceptance and encouragement for the greater good is clear. Moral and ethical leadership (and followership) that builds community and includes all members of society can be the result of an intentional journey into the heart of servant-leadership. Servant-leadership, like Quakerism, is a philosophy grounded in listening, integrity, caring, affirmation, inclusion, and clarity of purpose. Greenleaf's servant-leadership is an intrinsic and humble investment of service to society toward the moral imperative. Servant-leadership is also a philosophical foundation whose ancestry melds comfortably into Quakerism and whose example quietly permeates our world with a legacy of good. May we encourage compassionate leadership-followership today and always.

References

Autry, J. (2001). *The servant leader.* Prima Publishing.

Barbuto, J., & Wheeler, D. (2006). Scale development and construct clarification of servant leadership. *Group & Organization Management, 31*(3), 300–326.

Bass, B., & Riggio, R. (2008). *Transformational leadership* (2nd ed.). Lawrence Erlbaum.

Bennis, W., & Goldsmith, J. (1997). *Learning to lead.* Perseus Books.

Block, P. (1993). *Stewardship: Choosing service over self-interest.* Berrett-Koehler.

Cooper, W. (1991). *The testimony of integrity in the Religious Society of Friends.* Pendle Hill Publications.

Cox, G. (1985). *Bearing witness: Quaker process and a culture of peace.* Pendle Hill Publications.

Curle, A. (1981). *Preparation for peace.* Argenta Friends School Press.

De Pree, M. (1989). *Leadership is an art.* Dell.

Fielder, F., & Chemers, M. (1974). *Leadership and effective management.* Scott, Foresman.

Fisher, R., & Sharp, A. (2004). *Lateral leadership: Getting things done when you're not the boss* (2nd ed.). Profile Books.

Frick, D. (2004). *Robert K. Greenleaf: A life of servant leadership.* Berrett-Koehler.

Fullan, M. (2003). *The moral imperative of school leadership.* Corwin Press.

Gardiner, J. (1998). Quiet presence: The holy ground of leadership. In L. Spears (Ed.). *Insights on leadership: Service, stewardship, spirit, and servant-leadership* (pp. 116–125). John Wiley & Sons.

Garman, Mary. (1994). *Righteousness and self-righteousness.* The Wider Quaker Fellowship.

Greenleaf, R. K. (1976). *The institution as servant.* The Robert K. Greenleaf Center.

Greenleaf, R. K. (1996). *On becoming a servant-leader.* (D. M. Frick & L. C. Spears, Eds.). Jossey-Bass.

Greenleaf, R. K. (2002). *Teacher as servant: A parable.* The Robert K. Greenleaf Center. (Original work published 1979)

Greenleaf, R. K. (2008). *The servant as leader.* The Robert K. Greenleaf Center. (Original work published 1970)

Haight, D. (1987). *Meeting.* Argenta Friends Press.

Harris, A., & Muijs, D. (2005). *Improving schools through teacher leadership.* Open University Press.

Hertzberg, K. (2002). *Doing the work: Finding the meaning.* Argenta Friends Press.

Hesse, H. (2000). *The journey to the east.* Farrar, Straus and Giroux. (Original work published 1956)

Lakey, G. (2004). *New theory, old practice: Nonviolence and Quakers.* Southeastern Yearly Meeting of The Religious Society of Friends.

Lamb, S. (2000). *Friends: A people called to listen.* Wider Quaker Fellowship.

Martin, M. (2006). *Holding one another in the light.* Pendle Hill Publications.

Murphy, C. (1983). *Nurturing contemplation.* Sowers Printing Company.

Noddings, N. (2003). *Happiness and education.* Cambridge University Press.

Pearce, C. (2003). *Shared leadership: Reframing the hows and whys of leadership* (J. Congers, Ed.). Sage.

Purkey, W., & Siegel, B. (2002). *Becoming an invitational leader.* Humanics Trade Group.

Quaker Faith & Practice (1999). Yearly Meeting of the Religious Society of Friends (Quakers) in Britain, London (2nd ed.).

Senge, P. (1990). *The fifth discipline: The art & practice of the learning organization.* Doubleday/Currency.

Sergiovanni, T. (1992). *Moral leadership.* Jossey-Bass.

Sergiovanni, T. (2001). *Leadership: What's in it for schools?* Routledge-Palmer.

Sipe, J., & Frick, D. (2009). *Seven pillars of servant leadership: Practicing the wisdom of leading by serving.* Paulist Press.

Smith, J. (2003). *Friends: A people disciplined to follow.* Argenta Friends Press.

Spears. L. C. (Ed.). (1998). *Insights on leadership: Service, stewardship, spirit, and servant-leadership.* John Wiley & Sons.

Starratt, R. (2003). *Centering educational administration.* Lawrence Erlbaum.

Sturnick, J. (1998). Healing leadership. In L. C. Spears (Ed.), *Insights on leadership: Service, stewardship, spirit, and servant-leadership* (pp. 185–193). John Wiley & Sons.

Wheatley, M. (2006). *Leadership and the new science: Discovering order in a chaotic world* (3rd ed.). Berrett-Koehler.

SECTION IV

THE ART AND SCIENCE OF
SERVANT-LEADERSHIP

Chapter 22

The Significance of Foresight in Vision and Narrative Leadership

Lyna M. Matesi

The purpose of this chapter is to discuss how foresight fuels vision and is deployed through narrative leadership. The underlying premise is Greenleaf's (2003) observation that servant-leaders simultaneously "know the unknowable" and "foresee the unforeseeable" (p. 50). In Greenleaf's writing, intellection, imagination, and insight constitute foresight and fuel vision. Similarly, Sashkin (2004) asserted that leader visions are both mentally and behaviorally constructed. I support both Greenleaf's (2003) and Sashkin's (2004) claims by outlining how mental construction of vision is achieved *through foresight* and how the behavioral construction of vision is achieved through *narrative leadership.*

I pursue this argument by (1) summarizing the role of vision in the transformational leadership literature; (2) linking the transformational leadership description of vision to Robert Greenleaf's (1977/2002) conception of foresight; (3) introducing narrative leadership and discussing its role in foresight; (4) using a Nobel Peace Prize lecture to demonstrate the connected nature of foresight, vision, and narrative; and (5) recommending resources to support leader practice.

Transformational Leadership, Vision, and Foresight

J. M. Burns's definition of transforming leadership has shaped the transformational leadership research (Bass & Bass, 2008). Burns (1978) reported that "leadership acts as an inciting and triggering force in the conversion of conflicting demands, values and goals into significant behavior . . . they act as catalytic agents in arousing followers' consciousness" (p. 38). According to Burns, leadership catalyzes transformation, raises people up, and invites a shared, actional purpose.

Sashkin (2004), in undertaking a review and synthesis of the transformational leadership (TL) literature, examined eight theories from well-known leadership theorists such as James MacGregor Burns, Bernard Bass, Warren Bennis, James Kouzes, and Barry Posner, Elliott Jacques, David McClelland, Robert House, John Kotter, James Heskett, Jay Conger, and Rabindra Kanungo. His analysis considered leader behaviors, leader traits, and situational contexts in an effort to describe common behavioral competencies across the TL school of thought (Sashkin, 2004, p. 191). Through his analysis, Sashkin identified three behavioral elements that span the majority of TL theories. First, the leader behavior of caring, or showing respect for followers, is part of five TL theories. Second, the leader behavior of creating empowering opportunities is evident in seven TL theories. Third, the leader behavior of communicating a vision is embedded in seven TL theories, with the vision being specifically about the *future* (Sashkin, 2004). Most importantly, Sashkin interpreted these three common behavioral competencies of transformational leadership through the primary lens of vision:

> Developing a vision obviously requires that one believes that one's vision can make a difference. Similarly, one would not bother to construct a vision unless one were motivated to achieve that vision through power and influence used to empower members of an organization. Most obviously, developing a vision requires a high level of cognitive power; that is the basis of the ability to construct a vision and is, therefore, the basis for visionary leadership. However, in the absence of behavioral competencies in the leader, the leader's vision will remain nothing more than a dream, for it is with and through people, by empowering them to act in concert toward a common aim, that visions are made real. (p. 192)

In Sashkin's research, vision is "based on the ability to construct the future first mentally and then behaviorally" (p. 186). *Vision*, then, is a broad concept, found across the transformational leadership literature, that employs cognition, communication, and the use of power to make something happen in the future. This combination of power with cognition of and communication toward a future resembles Greenleaf's (1977/2002) definition of *foresight*.

Greenleaf's Foresight

Greenleaf's formative work *Servant Leadership: A Journey into the Nature of Legitimate Power and Greatness* (1977/2002) inspired a now thirty-five-year-old movement to embrace, codify, and enact a theory of servant-leadership. He portrayed the concept of servant-leadership as individually reorienting and socially transforming. He prophesied an urgent need to change social life via the production of enough leaders equipped to serve society into a new way of being (pp. 24–25). Reorienting from a leaders-first to a servants-first perspective is, in Greenleaf's exhortation, paramount to social transformation.

A long string of practitioners and scholars have worked to create and revise a list of the characteristics necessary for an individual leader to be classified as a servant-leader (Buchen, 1998; Farling et al., 1999; Graham, 1991; McGee-Cooper & Looper, 2001; Russell, 2001; Spears, 1998). Nevertheless, none of these research projects have thoroughly explored Greenleaf's understanding of foresight, nor have they explicitly expanded on the dynamic relationship among vision, foresight, and narrative. To help clarify the significance of foresight in the exercise of leadership, Greenleaf's (1977/2002) view of foresight and its relationship to vision will be discussed.

Greenleaf (1977/2002) saw a cultural undercurrent that was questioning anew matters of power and authority. He wondered about the emergence of a new order, one "which holds that the only authority deserving of one's allegiance is that which is freely and knowingly granted by the led to the leader in response, to, and in proportion to, the clearly evident servant stature of the leader" (Greenleaf, 2003, pp. 32–33). He further clarified that "moral principles do not emerge from theory, but from testing and experience. Theories are later built to encase and explain the working principle" (p. 33). Greenleaf thus cast the leader as a moral worker who tests and experiences his or her own orientation to power and authority. Ciulla (2004) observed that the key question at the heart of leadership studies is "What is *good* leadership?" or rather—"What is *morally good* (ethical) leadership?" and "What is *technically good* (effective) leadership?" (p. 13). According to Ciulla, as a normative leadership theory, servant-leadership is concerned with describing and prescribing morally good (ethical) leadership. Moral order in Greenleaf's servant-leadership framework is expressed via individual reorientation and social transformation, which are both to some extent dependent on the order emanating from the leader.

To achieve this moral order, Greenleaf (2003) suggested that the leader requires, among other competencies, the creative cognitive capacity to simultaneously "know the unknowable" and "foresee the unforeseeable" (p. 50). He stated, "In far-out theorizing, every mind, at the unconscious level, has access to every 'bit' of information that is or ever was" (Greenleaf, 1996, p. 314). The leader who serves accesses these patterns of organic unity so that he or she can make ethical decisions, and "the failure of a leader to foresee may be viewed as an *ethical* failure" (Greenleaf, 2003, p. 54; emphasis in original). The failure described by Greenleaf (1998) is grounded in the idea that effective servant-leaders intuitively make sound judgments (p. 124), have a feel for various patterns of human behavior, and generalize based on experience (p. 125) or intuition (p. 124). He suggested that the social failures of war, environmental destruction, and poverty are failures of foresight made one decision at a time (Greenleaf, 1996, pp. 318–319). Without the ability to foresee, a leader is likely to fail to understand the future consequences of present actions. Foresight is portrayed as an ethical, legitimate use of power to "see things whole" (p. 247) or "conjure with the subjective and imponderable as well as with the objective and quantitative" (p. 75).

Greenleaf (1996) clarified that foresight requires cultivation, preparation, and creativity:

> One goes in prepared with strategies, with knowledge, and with as much as can be anticipated . . . [and the] belief that the needed insight will come in the situation is then the supporting faith that relieves one of stress [and] permits the creative process to operate that makes dynamic visionary leadership possible. (p. 324)

Greenleaf's (1998) servant-leadership framework emphasizes the conceptualizing power of leaders, in which foresight is presented as the only genuine "lead" that a leader has (p. 285). His foresight is described as three capacities used in concert to expand awareness so that a leader is ready to "see things whole" (p. 274)—*intellection* is the creative, cognitive capacity of a leader to strategically prepare, analyze, and anticipate; *imagination* is the creative cognitive capacity of a leader to visualize scenarios, pictures, images, or symbols that complement or expand intellection; and *insight* is the creative cognitive capacity of a leader to open her senses to the "imponderable" that lies beyond intellect and image (Greenleaf, 1998). Next, I offer a more detailed description of these three capacities.

Intellection

Intellection is the creative, cognitive capacity of a leader to strategically prepare, analyze, and anticipate. Kim (2002b), in wrestling with Greenleaf's formulation of the ethical imperative of foresight, brought several ideas from the field of system dynamics that clarify the intellection thread in Greenleaf's framework. Kim stated that foresight is "being able to perceive the significance and nature of events before they have occurred" (p. 2). The ethical responsibility of a leader "is to know the underlying structures within her domain and be able to make predictions that can guide her people to a better future" (p. 2). He introduced an important contrast between forecasting and predicting.

In his treatment of Greenleaf's framework, Kim (2002b) explained that forecasting—an attempt to say for certain what will happen in the future—is not feasible, but he emphasized that leaders can offer informed predictions about the consequences of events (p. 2). While informed predictions are certainly part of daily life, what is essential here is Kim's (and originally Greenleaf's) argument that a leader is seen as ethically responsible for developing the foresight necessary to make accurate predictions and to undertake wise action. In Kim's view, a leader who merely meddles by taking poorly envisioned action harms the system and is therefore violating the ethical mandate of leadership foresight. Leaders, in this sense, are called to envision and initiate action that will change underlying system structures in predictable directions (Kim 2002a). The key to accomplishing this task is understanding appropriate action modes and levels of perspective for every action or intervention. To support this claim, Kim described a five-rung ladder consisting of five levels of perspective: (1) events, (2) patterns of behavior, (3) systemic structures, (4) mental models, and (5) vision. These levels of perspective correspond to five distinct levels of action, and each level of perspective is linked to a higher or a lower degree of system or change leverage. Lower leverage is less energizing to change. Higher leverage is more energizing to change (Kim, 2002a). Intervening in vision is a generative mode of action and is cast as having the highest leverage—a vision is used to generate or engender collective action toward a shared ideal.

> As leaders, we must climb higher and see the world from the higher levels and have the skills and capabilities to act in a creative, reflective and generative mode. . . . Exercising foresight is about creating a compelling vision of the future that will tap into the latent aspirations of our people so that they can rise to the greatness within them. (pp. 11–12)

In summary, leader vision is a generative, higher-leverage way to intervene in a system and is fueled by foresight. Exercising foresight is an ethical imperative that employs intellection to see underlying system structures, predict consequences, and inspire others.

Imagination

Imagination is the creative cognitive capacity of a leader to visualize scenarios, pictures, images, or symbols that complement or expand intellection. Stephenson (2009) claimed that public and nongovernmental organization leaders use four interwoven forms of imagination to understand and intervene in social consciousness or identity. His framework coincides with Greenleaf's (1977/2002) understanding of foresight and social transformation, and casts leadership work as requiring leaders to contextually lead adaptation. Stephenson's (2009) four forms of imagination span the full scope of Greenleaf's (1977/2002) foresight. Stephenson's (2009) exploration of these imaginal capacities reveal that intellection, imagination, and insight do not stand each by itself but are in fact intertwined or holographic in such a way that each can be seen from the perspective of the other. His *cognitive imagination* aligns with Greenleaf's (1977/2002) and Kim's (2002a, 2002b) descriptions of intellection and enables leaders to "make sense of their environments at various analytical scales" (Stephenson, 2009, p. 426). The *affective imagination,* seen as the energy behind interpersonal communication, is described as a deep awareness of self and others, and aligns with Sashkin's (1988) findings about the role of empowerment. The *aesthetic imagination* is described as a narrative approach to change that enables leaders "to see possibilities and to discern and develop paths of action that otherwise might go unexplored [and] to undertake these actions in ways that are 'visionary' " (p. 425). Stephenson's (2009) affective and aesthetic imaginations support communication of foresight-informed visions and therefore are essential to narrative leadership. I will address this connection to narrative leadership further in the next section. Stephenson's *moral imagination* is intuitive, creative, and concerned with needs far beyond those of the leader alone. Moral imagination causes a leader to "deepen mutual awareness" and "seek to act in accord with the full weight of history and tradition" (pp. 429–430).

In a similar vein, Lederach's (2005) exploration of moral imagination identified three themes that converge across writings from business, policy, literature, arts, professional practice, and religious tradition (p. 26). He noted that moral imagination sees beyond the physical or rational, beyond the eye into the nature of people, things, and conflict; moral imagination emphasizes the importance of acting creatively to transform and reshape; and moral imagination is more concerned with possibilities than with probabilities. Building on these broad themes, Lederach enumerated four disciplines or capacities that support a turn toward the social transformation of peace.

Lederach's (2005) peace builders lead themselves and others to transcend the violence in their midst by building and mobilizing a moral imagination steeped in relationship, curiosity, creativity, and risk. *Relationship* peace builders visualize self and others, friends and foes, in an interdependent web of relationships. *Curiosity* peace builders pursue a deep, nonpolar understanding of matters with an insatiable curiosity bent toward exploring contradictions and paradox. *Creativity* peace builders invite and hold space for a creative unfolding of the many possibilities that often lie beyond immediate or rational perception. *Risk* peace builders embrace the mystery of the unknown to risk the emergence of peace.

Both Stephenson (2009) and Lederach (2005) added texture to Greenleaf's (1977/2002) foresight. Exercising foresight employs imagination by seeing, embracing, and wrestling with relational or contextual paradoxes, contradictions, and interdependencies to somehow creatively visualize the whole and risk its emergence.

Insight

Insight is the creative cognitive capacity of a leader to open her senses to the "imponderable" that lies beyond intellect and image (Greenleaf, 1996, p. 274). Greenleaf's foresight is a combination of what is known and what needs to be known:

Part of what gives the leader his "lead" is that he knows things that others who accept his leadership don't know. They may have higher IQs and possess more conscious knowledge, but they accept the leader because of his superior insights on matters of vital interest to them. For this reason, he's acknowledged as the one who should go ahead and point the way. (p. 316)

One way to think about insight, then, is to see it as a way of knowing that seems to intensify, magnify, or concentrate intellection and imagination. According to Greenleaf, insight requires the intentional withdrawal, disorientation, and suspension (at least momentarily) of both intellection and imagination to attend to sensory impressions via meditative time (pp. 76–78). There is a rhythm to Greenleaf's foresight—the leader moves between *orienting* through intellection and imagination and *disorienting* through insight. Greenleaf stated that the meditative or reflective stance of insight requires tenuous versus dogmatic knowing (p. 321); invokes an understanding of time that simultaneously spans past, present, and future (p. 319); and is concerned with a multidirectional widening and deepening of perception (p. 322). In his explanation of this leader disorientation, Greenleaf quoted William Blake (1971), who wrote, "If the doors of perception were cleansed everything would appear to man as it is—infinite" (p. 144). For Greenleaf (1996), cultivating insightful awareness expands the decisional or directional resources of a leader, clarifies values, provides armor against the stresses of leadership, and ultimately builds a leader's confidence and composure (p. 323).

Lederach (2005) called this awareness the "discipline of sensuous perception," and he framed it as an act not so much of pulling away, but rather of pulling into the senses. He claimed that peace builders "imagine the whole" (p. 111) and are attentive to or keenly alive in all of their sensual faculties (pp. 108–109). Greenleaf (1977/2002, 1996, 1998), Lederach (2005), and Kim (2002a, 2002b) converged in describing a kind of sense-based insight that is grounded in knowing the order of things and asking koan-like, time-spanning questions to better grasp the whole nature of people, problems, and possibilities: Who am I? Who are we? Where have we been? Where are we? Where are we going? What is the wise way? Exercising foresight, then, employs insight to open awareness and perception through the risk of tenuous inquiry, sensual perception, and purposeful disorientation.

Vision and Foresight

Together, leader intellection, imagination, and insight constitute foresight and fuel vision. Greenleaf (1996) wrote that by using foresight, leaders "fill in the gap" between what is known and what needs to be known (p. 75). If, according to Sashkin's (2004) statement quoted earlier, vision is "based on the ability to construct the future first mentally and then behaviorally" (p. 186), then Greenleaf's (1996) threefold foresight is a useful way to frame the creative cognitive capacities that fuel the generative construction of the future through vision. I will now discuss narrative leadership and its importance in deploying vision (that is fueled by foresight).

Narrative Leadership, Vision, and Foresight

McKenna and Rooney (2008) claimed in their study of leader discourse that

> wise leaders are not only analytical but also imaginative, intuitive and creative. . . . First, leaders need to be agentive, to see the world in different ways, and they need to act on this understanding; second, cognitive complexity is a necessary but insufficient characteristic; third, discourse is crucial in mediating authorized knowledge and its implicit ontology; fourth, as a consequence, knowledge is inherently social. (p. 539)

In this chapter, I have argued that Greenleaf's (1977/2002, 1996, 1998) foresight describes what McKenna and Rooney (2008) framed as agentive seeing and acting on the world. Additionally, I have used Greenleaf's (1996) notions of intellection, imagination, and insight to describe the creative cognitive capacities of leader foresight. Now I turn toward the next aim of this chapter: a description of the narrative leadership that conveys a leader's foresight-informed vision, which is intended to mediate social knowing and acting.

According to Fisher's (1987) narrative paradigm, narrative is the master metaphor of human life. He named our species *Homo narrans* and argued that we use forms of discourse that are essentially all narrative to articulate our reasoning about the nature of self and society (p. 170). He privileged the narration of life and cast our narrative enactments and interpretations of life as the primary form of human knowledge. Knowing, in Fisher's understanding of rhetoric, emerges from narrative rationality, which is a logic that interfuses value and reason to govern what we know through the stories that we hear, tell, and live.

Fisher and Goodman (1995) contrasted objectivist knowledge with praxial knowledge by discussing three broad forms of knowing: (1) knowledge of *that*—knowing the thing; (2) knowledge of *how*—knowing how to use the thing; and (3) knowledge of *whether*—knowing whether to use the thing. Fisher and Goodman clarified that objectivist knowledge focuses on the knowledge of *that* and the knowledge of *how*, assuming that problems are "logic puzzles" that can be sorted by cost-benefit analysis and tend to drive out wisdom by emphasizing information or facts (p. 172). However, they claimed that the knowledge of *whether*, a praxial knowledge, allows for the pursuit of wisdom and includes the knowledge of *that* and the knowledge of *how*. It then transcends and enfolds the merely factual, probable, feasible, or profitable to incorporate an examination of *whether* an idea or action is desirable or of value. Fisher and Goodman stated that regardless of form, objectivist and praxial knowledge is conducted in a storied context, employs narrative rationality, and is grounded in time, history, culture, and character (p. 170). A person's conception of the narrative paradigm is meant to expose the interfused nature of values, facts, and reason and to "restore a consciousness of *whether*" (p. 188), thereby increasing the possibility of the polis being wise.

McKenna and Rooney (2008) and Fisher and Goodman (1995) are attempting to describe a kind of leader wisdom (foresight) that fuels vision and is deployed narratively to create social action. This notion is embedded in the scholarship already presented in the article. To summarize, first, Sashkin (2004) asserted that leadership narrative empowers people and makes vision real; he demonstrated that there is broad agreement across the transformational leadership literature that effective visions must be well communicated. He claimed that vision is mentally constructed (foresight) and then behaviorally constructed (narrative leadership) (Sashkin, 1988; 2004). Second, Kim (2002a, 2002b) described the difference between uninformed meddling and wise, foresight-driven helping and argued that vision via narrative generates collective action and is the highest form of change leverage available. And third, Stephenson (2009) argued that imagination as narrative is a visionary way of seeing, discerning, and undertaking change.

Considered together, these authors support the idea that narrative leadership is the mechanism by which visions of the future, constructed through foresight, are communicated. These concepts are summarized in figure 22.1. This narration of vision can be thought of in two ways: topic and role. First, in acts of narrative leadership, objectivist and praxial knowledge, or the narrated topics or themes, are embedded in a story or a set of stories in the rough forms of Fisher and Goodman's (1995) *that, how*, and *whether*. Second, in acts of narrative leadership, the perspectives or roles that a leader performs are described by Greenleaf (1996) as "historian, contemporary analyst and prophet [or futurist]" (p. 319). These three roles are evident in the narratives that leaders live and speak. Servant-leaders exercise foresight to construct and share a vision of the future that locates the narrated in a situated history, critiques the present, and invites listeners to cocreate a prophetic future. Narrative leadership uses objectivist and praxial knowledge to create a social sense of where we have been, where we are now, and where we are going. Narrative leadership draws out the cognitive, creative, and moral power of the leader through mentally and behaviorally constructing a narrated vision that intends to move, raise, and invigorate the polis. To illustrate these ideas, I provide an example of foresight, vision, and narrative leadership.

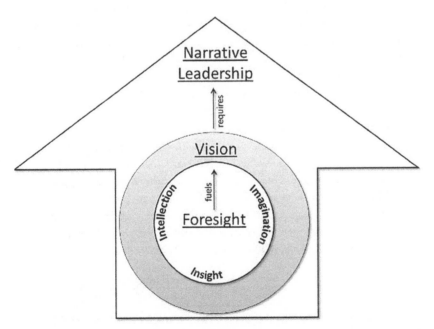

Figure 22.1. An Illustration of the Relationship among Foresight, Vision, and Narrative Leadership.

Wangari Maathai, 2004 Nobel Peace Prize Laureate

Alfred Nobel's (1895) will directed that his fortune be used to fund five annual awards in physics, chemistry, physiology, literature, and peace for those who have "conferred the greatest benefit to mankind." Prizes have been awarded since 1901 in several broad categories: organized peace, humanitarian aid, international law, politics, human rights, and, to a lesser degree, religion and environmental advocacy (Abrams, 2001, pp. 335–337). Upon receiving the Nobel Prize, each laureate has the opportunity to deliver both an acceptance speech and a lecture. These rhetorical opportunities, along with the countless speaking invitations that follow, become a powerful international platform for peace leaders to mentally and behaviorally construct a vision of peace.

Wangari Maathai of Kenya was awarded the Nobel Peace Prize in 2004 "for her contribution to sustainable development, democracy and peace" (Nobelprize.org, 2011). In 2,295 English words, Maathai (2004) delivered a narrative that intertwined the past, present, and future of her childhood, her country, and our world. She simultaneously mourned the environmental conditions that inhibit peace, critiqued the present practices that limit peace, and called on the world to promote peace through a shared vision of democratic environmental sustainability. She exhorted world leaders, governments, industrial institutions, women, and children to realize peace through change. Considering vision, Maathai's narrative invoked Fisher's (1987) *that* (she envisions world peace achieved through environmental sustainability), *how* (each group named above receives a targeted exhortation), and *whether*:

> In the course of history, there comes a time when humanity is called to shift to a new level of consciousness, to reach a higher moral ground. A time when we have to shed our fear and give hope to each other. That time is now. . . . There can be no peace without equitable development; and there can be no development without sustainable management of the environment in democratic and peaceful space. This shift is an idea whose time has come. (Maathai, 2004, para. 28–30)

Considering foresight, as a contemporary analyst, Maathai's vision is rich in *intellection-driven* descriptions of the strategy of her green movement and measurable descriptors of the environmental impact of unchecked deforestation. As a futurist, her vision is *imaginative* in the way she describes the deteriorating richness of her nation and her hope for renewal. She ended her speech by taking the listener to a destroyed stream near her childhood home and envisioning a future where the stream and the surrounding environment are restored, both environmentally and socially. As a historian, Maathai's vision demonstrated *insight* in her allusions to reflection about the devastation she has witnessed and the personal, cultural, and political forces that inspire her. In studying the rhetoric of Maathai's Nobel lecture, Kirkscey (2007) remarked,

> By constructing a narrative of the Green Belt movement in her lecture, Maathai calls on world leaders to examine their own environmental values. . . . Her work illustrates that rhetors can effectively use narrative as an instrument to spread the principles of social movements. (p. 12)

Social movements are often informed by the foresight of individual leaders exercising intellection, imagination, and insight.

Implications for Study

In this chapter, I have drawn on normative, theoretical, and empirical literatures to develop a descriptive model of leader foresight (intellection, imagination, and insight) applied as vision and deployed through narrative leadership. In doing so, I have identified several gaps in the literature. Our understanding of vision is cursory. While there is broad discussion of vision in the transformational leadership school of thought, there is little systematic investigation of what constitutes vision and what deploys vision. My effort to consider the relationship among foresight, vision, and narrative leadership is exploratory at best and leads to a host of interesting research questions. Are intellection, imagination, and insight sufficient and accurate descriptors of leader foresight? Can empirical studies support the notion that leader foresight fuels vision? How can we weigh, measure, or count the significance of foresight-fueled vision in acts of narrative leadership?

Implications for Practice

Narrative leadership draws out the cognitive, creative, and moral power of the leader through mentally and behaviorally constructing a narrated vision that intends to move, raise, and invigorate. To fuel narrative leadership, a leader should consider cultivating foresight and intentionally strengthening intellection, imagination, and insight.

Intellection, the creative, cognitive capacity of a leader to strategically prepare, analyze, and anticipate, can be further developed by learning to collect data for analysis, synthesis, and consequence prediction.

Resources: (1) *Pursue quality certification.* ASQ (2012) offers 17 certifications and has issued nearly 150,000 certifications to professionals worldwide. (2) *Master analytics.* Davenport and Harris (2010) have assembled a collection of text and media resources to help build analytical power.

Imagination, the creative cognitive capacity of a leader to visualize scenarios, pictures, images, or symbols that complement or expand intellection, can be further developed by learning to create and use collaborative workspaces and visual maps.

Resources: (1) *Learn to organigraph.* Mintzberg and Van Der Heyden (1999) offered a straightforward description of how to map the work of any organization. (2) *Learn to prototype.* Schrage (2000) provided an introduction the serious play of collaborative, rapid prototyping. (3) *Learn to visualize data.* Free infographic creation tools are available at visual.ly.com.

Insight, the creative cognitive capacity of a leader to open her senses to the imponderable that lies beyond intellect and image, can be further developed by incorporating cycles of disorientation, renewal, and meditation.

Resources: (1) *Learn to become a corporate athlete.* Loehr and Schwartz (2001) explained how to create energy recovery rituals in their discussion of the corporate athlete. (2) *Learn to be mindful.* Tippett (2009) interviewed Jon Kabat-Zinn in a discussion about the science of mindfulness.

Conclusion

This chapter has argued (1) that foresight fuels vision and is deployed through narrative leadership; (2) that narrative leadership draws out the cognitive, creative, and moral power of the leader through mentally and behaviorally constructing a narrated vision; (3) that there are many interesting, unanswered research questions about foresight; and (4) that leaders can cultivate foresight through intellection, imagination, and insight. Most importantly, the article extends Robert Greenleaf's ideas about the rigor and depth of foresight as a critical element of servant-leadership.

References

Abrams, I. (2001). *The Nobel peace prize and the laureates: An illustrated biographical history 1901–2001*. Science History.

ASQ. (2012). *The value of ASQ certification*. https://asq.org/cert

Bass, B. M., & Bass, R. (2008). *The Bass handbook of leadership: Theory, research, and managerial applications*. Free Press.

Blake, W. (1971). The marriage of heaven and hell. In W. H. Stevenson (Ed.), *The poems of William Blake* (p. 144). W. W. Norton.

Buchen, I. H. (1998). Servant-leadership: A model for future faculty and future institutions. *Journal of Leadership Studies, 5*(1), 125–134.

Burns, J. M. (1978). *Leadership*. Harper and Row.

Ciulla, J. B. (2004). *Ethics, the heart of leadership* (2nd ed). Praeger.

Davenport, T. H., & Harris, J. G. (2010). *Optimize the power of analytics to drive superior performance collection*. Harvard Business School Press.

Farling, M. L., A. G. Stone, & Winston, B. E. (1999). Servant-leadership: Setting the stage for empirical research. *Journal of Leadership Studies, 6*(1/2), 49–72.

Fisher, W. R. (1987). *Human communication as narration: Toward a philosophy of reason, value, and action*. University of South Carolina Press.

Fisher, W. R., & R. F. Goodman. (1995). *Rethinking knowledge: Reflections across the disciplines*. SUNY Press.

Graham, J. (1991). Servant-leadership in organizations: Inspirational and moral. *The Leadership Quarterly, 2*(2), 105–119.

Greenleaf, R. K. (1996). *On becoming a servant-leader* (D. M. Frick & L. C. Spears, Eds.). Jossey-Bass.

Greenleaf, R. K. (1998). *The power of servant-leadership: Essays by Robert K. Greenleaf* (L. C. Spears, Ed.). Berrett-Koehler.

Greenleaf, R. K. (2002). *Servant leadership: A journey into the nature of legitimate power and greatness* (L. C. Spears, Ed.; 25th anniversary ed.). Paulist Press. (Original work published 1977)

Greenleaf, R. K. (2003). *The servant-leader within: A transformative path* (H. Beazley, J. Beggs, & L. C. Spears, Eds.). Paulist Press.

Kim, D. H. (2002a). *Foresight as a central ethic of leadership*. Greenleaf Center for Servant Leadership.

Kim, D. H. (2002b). Leading ethically through foresight. *The Systems Thinker, 13*(7), 1–6.

Kirkscey, K. (2007). Accommodating traditional African values and globalization: Narrative as argument in Wangari Maathai's Nobel prize lecture. *Women and Language, 30*(2), 12–17.

Lederach, J. P. (2005). *The moral imagination: The art and soul of building peace*. Oxford University Press.

Loehr, J., & Schwartz, T. (2001). The making of a corporate athlete. *Harvard Business Review, 79*(1), 120–129.

Maathai, W. (2004). *Nobel lecture.* https://www.nobelprize.org/prizes/peace/2004/maathai/26050-wangari-maathai-nobel-lecture-2004/

McGee-Cooper, A., & Looper, G. (2001). *The essentials of servant-leadership: Principles practice.* Pegasus.

McKenna, B., & Rooney, D. (2008). Wise leadership and the capacity for ontological acuity. *Management Communication Quarterly, 21*(4), 537–546.

Mintzberg, H., & Van der Heyden, L. (1999). Organigraphs: Drawing how companies really work. *Harvard Business Review, 77*(5), 87–94.

Nobel, A. (1895). *Full text of Alfred Nobel's will.* http://www.nobelprize.org/alfred_nobel/will/will-full.html

Nobelprize.org. (2011). *Wangari Maathai biography.* https://www.nobelprize.org/prizes/peace/2004/maathai/biographical

Russell, R. F. (2001). The role of values in servant-leadership. *Leadership & Organization Development Journal, 22*(2), 76–83.

Sashkin, M. (1988). The visionary leader. In J. A. Conger & R. N. Kanugo (Eds.), *Charismatic leadership: The elusive factor in organizational effectiveness* (pp. 122–160). Jossey-Bass.

Sashkin, M. (2004). Transformational leadership approaches: A review and synthesis. In J. Antonakis, A. T. Cianciolo, & R. J. Sternberg (Eds.), *The Nature of Leadership* (pp. 171–196). Sage.

Schrage, M. (2000). *Serious play: How the world's best companies simulate to innovate.* Harvard Business School Press.

Sendjaya, S., Sarros, J. C., & Santora, J. C. (2008). Defining and measuring servant-leadership behaviour in organizations. *Journal of Management Studies, 45*(2), 402–424.

Spears. L. (1998). *Insights on leadership: Service, stewardship, spirit, and servant-leadership.* John Wiley & Sons.

Stephenson, M. Jr. (2009). Exploring the connections among adaptive leadership: Facets of imagination and social imaginaries. *Public Policy and Administration, 24*(4), 417–435.

Tippett, K. (2009, April 16). *Jon Kabat-Zinn: Opening to our lives.* https://onbeing.org/programs/jon-kabat-zinn-opening-to-our-lives/

Chapter 23

Exploring the Intersection of Servant-Leadership and Interpersonal Neurobiology

Hope for Deep-Rooted Mental and Behavioral Transformation

Faith Renae Regh Gilbert

People don't come preassembled, but are glued together by life.

—LeDoux, 2002, p. 3

The principles of interpersonal neurobiology (IPNB)—a rapidly developing field of study that emphasizes relationships, emotions, and the brain (Fishbane, 2007)—can be applied to many leadership styles, be they good or bad. This chapter emphasizes servant-leadership because of the positive characteristics and values it espouses. It introduces some of the fundamental concepts of interpersonal neurobiology and servant-leadership and discusses how IPNB may benefit and encourage servant-leaders as they work toward deep-rooted transformation within themselves, their followers, their organizations, and ultimately society as a whole.

Cozolino (2010) wrote, "Because our brains are social organs interwoven with the brains of those around us, relationships have a direct impact on the biology of the brain" (p. 336). Understanding how relationships literally sculpt the mind and the brain can help servant-leaders comprehend how positive, long-term changes may occur as a result of leader/follower relationships and neuroplasticity. This knowledge is important to the field of leadership studies because it brings a scientifically based tangibility to a discipline that is, for the most part, an intangible one. And that tangibility can bring hope.

Rock and Page (2009) indicated that it is only within the past decade or so that neuroscience has "provided support rather than discouragement for adults who wish to make profound changes" (p. 453). It is now known that even older adults can produce new brain cells as a result of experience. That means there is hope for permanent change that enriches the individual yet benefits society as a whole. This knowledge serves as a foundation for this chapter.

Servant-Leadership and Interpersonal Neurobiology Defined

To scaffold the understanding of how servant-leadership and interpersonal neurobiology tie together, it is important to first explore the meaning behind each term.

Servant-Leadership

Spears (2004) noted that Robert Greenleaf's understanding of who a servant-leader is might be viewed through the lens of 10 characteristics: listening, empathy, healing, awareness, persuasion, conceptualization, foresight, stewardship, commitment to the growth of people, and building community (pp. 13–16). The term *servant-leader* is a paradox. It denotes one who is willing to lead by serving first (Greenleaf, 1977/2002). The servant-leader is empathetic, loving, receptive, responsible, humble, and "concerned with the personal and emotional growth of others" (McClellan, 2008, p. 289). Greenleaf's (1977/2002) test of servant-leadership was encapsulated within his following questions: "Do those served grow as persons? Do they, *while being served*, become healthier, wiser, freer, more autonomous, more likely themselves to become servants? *And*, what is the effect on the least privileged in society? Will they benefit or at least not be further deprived?" (p. 27; emphasis in original).

When servant-leaders are committed to the growth of people and to building community, they will exhibit "a long-term, transformational approach to life and work, in essence, a way of being—that has the potential for creating positive change throughout our society" (Spears, 2004, p. 12). Servant-leadership is a leadership model that correlates well with many of the concepts of interpersonal neurobiology.

Interpersonal Neurobiology

Interpersonal neurobiology is an interdisciplinary and transdisciplinary field that investigates how relationships influence the architecture of the brain (Cozolino, 2014). It involves the study of "wisdom from more than a dozen different disciplines of science to weave a picture of human experience and the process of change across the lifespan" (Siegel, 2006, p. 248). IPNB raises awareness of the need for attunement to the self, others, and the world at large, and it addresses how relationships and experiences shape, strengthen, or modify functional systems within the brain.

New neuroscientific data and the subsequent insights addressed in the burgeoning field of interpersonal neurobiology can be attributed in part to the significant advances in technology that have exponentially increased knowledge about how the human brain processes thoughts and forges new neural pathways. According to Demitri (2007), neuroscientists are now able to view real-time changes in the brain and map brain activity through the use of instruments such as positron emission tomography, electroencephalograms, X-ray-computed tomography, nuclear magnetic resonance imaging, magnetoencephalography, and near-infrared spectroscopy. Camerer et al. (2004) explained, "Feelings and thoughts can be measured directly now, because of recent breakthroughs in neuroscience" (p. 558). Johnson (2009) echoed that thought, "We now have technology in place to picture that inner landscape. . . . These are tools for capturing who we are, on the level of synapses and neurotransmitters and brain waves" (p. 4).

This technology can record changes in brain circuitry as people experience various emotions or engage in specific thoughts or actions. Scientists use this technology to help "pinpoint which brain neighborhoods are active during any given mental activity" (Schwartz & Begley, 2002, p. 22). These technological advances have brought about monumental changes in the field of neuroscience and have helped create numerous subdisciplines, such as neurotheology (Brandt et al., 2010), neuroeconomics (Camerer et al., 2004), neuromarketing (Iacoboni, 2009), and neuroleadership (Ringleb & Rock, 2009).

According to Siegel (2007), interpersonal neurobiology furthers understanding of how the mind and the brain change each other, how personalities and character strengths are formed, how new learning is acquired, and how relationships influence growth. Fishbane (2007) advanced the idea that "interpersonal neurobiology identifies how the brain is wired through relationships and connection" (p. 396), and Siegel (2012a) indicated that IPNB researchers investigate how embodied neural maps generate long-term modifications within relationships, the mind, and the brain.

As the concepts of interpersonal neurobiology are discussed, it will be important to step away from the Cartesian dualism mind-matter debate because, as Shilling (2003) emphasized, "instead of being separate from the body, the mind is located within, and is inextricably linked to, the body" (p. 173). Schwartz and Begley (2002) pointed out that "the neural connections that form brain circuits are necessary for the mind as we know it" (p. 36), and Whitehead held that the "mind and brain are manifestations of a single reality, one that is in constant flux" (p. 45). The nondualistic interface between the mind and the brain is what activates neuroplasticity and results in changed thoughts and behaviors.

Neuroscience can sometimes lean toward reductionism and mechanics, so it is important to keep in mind that humans cannot be reduced to simple biological, physiological, or electrochemical processes. However, Shilling (2012) wrote that certain of neuroscience's "exponents enable us to think creatively about the neurological processes that may inform social actions and interactions" (p. 16). He also emphasized, "Our embodied being is not just a location for society and culture, however, but *forms a basis for* and *shapes* our relationships and creations" (p. 15). The embodiment of a human mind is an important reality, and it should be noted that this embodiment arises within the domain and shelter of relationships.

The Importance of Relationships in Servant-Leadership

Relationships

Leaders place a heavy emphasis on relationships. Burns (1978), one of leadership studies' forefathers, argued that point when he wrote, "The most powerful influences consist of deeply human relationships" (p. 11). Braye (2002) emphasized that "leadership is also based on relationships where people are always considered more important than things. This is a foundation principle" (p. 301).

Servant-leaders understand the value of relationships, and direct their energy toward serving those they are in relationship with. This energy, whether expressed in words, thoughts, or actions, will aid in creating long-term, deep-seated transformation in the minds, brains, and behaviors of both servant-leader and follower.

Relationships encompass internal as well as external experiences, and when those experiences are supportive, they help facilitate positive neuroplastic changes. Relationships have to do with understanding, interconnectedness, and information sharing. They involve "the sharing of the change in energy across time, the patterns of energy flow, that at times contain informational value" (Siegel, 2012b, p. 14). Relationships include the sending and receiving of social signals, and the brain and the mind help regulate those signals.

To understand how servant-leaders can influence or stimulate positive changes in thoughts and behaviors, it can be helpful to understand the perpetual and recursive interactions that take place when systems such as the mind, the brain, and relationships converge. When these three converge, they "form an irreducible triad in producing the flow of information and energy that is human life" (Rock & Page, 2009, p. 26). Understanding the interactions and interdependencies of the mind, brain, and relationships can prove invaluable to a servant-leader who desires to help facilitate new learning and reinforce positive behaviors.

Individuals Are Shaped by Relationships

Relationally oriented servant-leaders can help transform the minds, brains, and behaviors of followers in a manner that enriches lives in personal, organizational, and social ways. That is because significant relationships—expressed through kinships, friendships, affiliations, and mental, emotional, physical, or even virtual connections—can change the mind and the brain due to the fact that the brain has the "capacity to change its patterns of neural connectivity in response to experience" (Gantt & Agazarian, 2010, p. 516).

Relationships are experiences that influence and stimulate changes in the brain. Relationships can include a vast array of experiences in which information and energy are shared, either interpersonally or intrapersonally. This can include experiences such as playing fetch with the family Labrador, sitting in quiet meditation or prayer, cheering with other fans at a football game, or reading a newspaper. A relationship might also involve linking a new idea to a previous idea; it could be experiencing a fiery debate across the boardroom table, or it could be the quiet connection that occurs when one sits silently with someone in their dying hours.

Fosha (2013) stressed the importance of relationships and their healing qualities: "Receptive affective experiences of feeling cared for, loved, seen, and delighted in are transformative" (p. 144). The experience of feeling loved and welcomed can activate a "transformational process in the form of a nonlinear, nonfinite transformational spiral" (p. 145) that allows the mind and brain to change and grow, resulting in transformation of thoughts, emotions, and behaviors.

Humans do not survive or mature without having functional relationships with the environment (both inner and outer) and with other people. While general neural pathways related to basic human functions are connected by the time a baby is born, relationships play a major part in neural growth because, as Cozolino (2014) noted, "The healthy, living brain [is] embedded within a community of other brains: *Relationships are our natural habitat*" (p. 4; emphasis in original). Fishbane (2007) said, "The structure and wiring of our brains require the attunement and attentiveness of others" (p. 396), while Rock and Page (2009) suggested that "the brain cannot become a human brain without social input" (p. 367). Cozolino (2010) stated, "We are born into relationships and come to our individual identity while resting upon social connectivity" (pp. 178–179), and Shilling (2003) noted:

1. The human body at birth is itself the product of evolutionary processes which are affected by social as well as biological processes.

2. As the body develops it is taken up and transformed, within limits, by social factors.

3. The body is not only affected by social relations but forms a basis for and enters into the construction of social relations. (p. 173)

Each of these statements suggests that humans require relationships to survive and indicates that relationships are a necessary part of life.

Relationships involve learning, and what a person learns is a result of where they focus their mind's attention. New learning can ultimately modify the brain because, as Siegel and Soloman (2013) indicated, "where attention goes, neuronal firing occurs" (p. 253). Learning is what forms the tangible neural architecture that enables people to sustain change (LeDoux, 2002).

Fishbane (2007) pointed out that learning (which entails a new experience) can change the brain by causing the formation of new neural circuitry. She said that "experience alters the brain, even as we age. Whenever we learn something new, whether new attitudes, perspectives, or behaviors, we are changing the physical structure of our brain" (p. 397). Her comments on experience and brain alterations explain why each event, movement, glance, or smile can create a trace action in the brain. They reveal how, when behaviors, words, or gestures are repeated, neural connections are strengthened in a way that can forge new pathways, resulting in living neural maps that reflect the life of a relationship.

Social Relationships

DeGraaf et al. (2004) observed that a "community is a sum of its parts," (pp. 159–160). Siegel (2012b) echoed that statement: "The whole of we is greater than the sum of our individual parts. We are embedded in each other and what arises is beyond two separate brains just interacting as isolated entities" (p. 320). Cozolino (2010) wrote that "relationships are our natural habitat, while the isolated brain is an abstract concept" (p. 179). He discussed the emotional circuitry of the human social brain and indicated that "we are born into relationships and come to our individual identity while resting upon social connectivity" (pp. 178–179).

McGilchrist (2013) said, "The brain already understands that the world is a living complex of relations" (p. 85), and Gardiner (1998) described what could happen when individuals come together in community: "In redefining relationship as a *living* reality, instead of a coming together of two selves, a new paradigm is created that serves our emerging collective consciousness" (p. 118). This collective consciousness can create a community.

When individuals form communities, those communities subsequently form a group's social consciousness. This might be termed "the social mind." The "social mind" can emerge when people come together in mind (virtually) or physically. Siegel (2012a) asserted that two or more minds can function as a single system and stated "that a self is part of a much larger interconnected whole: the self can be seen as a 'plural verb'" (p. 387). Buber (1970) expressed the importance of the self living in communicative connection with others: "I require a You to become; becoming I, I say You" (p. 62). Rock and Page (2009) wrote, "Neither human brains nor human minds exist without social relationships" (pp. 25–26), and Siegel (2012a) maintained that "the brain can be considered as a living system that is open and dynamic. It is also a part of a larger system" (p. 27).

The interconnectedness between the mind, the brain, and social relationships becomes apparent in light of Cozolino's (2010) observation that "the brain is a social organ connected to other brains via the social synapse" (p. 195). His definition of *social synapse* is

> the space between us. It is also the medium through which we are linked together into larger organisms such as families, tribes, and societies. When we smile, wave, and say hello, these behaviors are sent through the space between us via sights, sounds, odors, and words. These electrical and mechanical messages received by our senses are converted into electrochemical impulses within our brains. These signals stimulate new behaviors, which, in turn, transmit messages back across the social synapse. (pp. 179–180)

The concept of a social synapse reveals the significance of relationships and social influences. Whether it be in the workplace, family, community, or world, what happens within the social synapse has the power to change minds, brains, and behaviors due to the principles that lay behind the brain's neuroplasticity.

Neuroscientific Foundations

Neuroplasticity

Siegel (2012a) defined *neuroplasticity* as "the ability of the brain to change its structure in response to experience" (p. 53). It is the term used by neuroscientists to describe how "the structure and function of a mature brain remain open to change across the life span" (Moore, 2001, p. 141). Neuroplasticity occurs when neurons are activated through new learning and experience. Neuroplasticity involves new learning and, as Fosha (2013) emphasized, "energy, motivation, curiosity, and pleasure" (p. 145), along with repetition and practice, are vital for strengthening neuroplasticity.

Relationships elicit neuroplasticity by triggering neurochemical events (LeDoux, 2002), and this creates, modifies, or strengthens neural circuitry. When neurons are associated together, learning is facilitated and new thoughts, behaviors, and neural circuitry are formed. Hebb's law states that "neurons that fire together, wire together" (Fishbane, 2007). This law describes why the formation, modification, or strengthening of experience-dependent neuronal connections is possible and why those connections can bring about deep-rooted changes in thoughts and behaviors. It can happen because, as

Panksepp (1998) said, the human brain is "the most complex and most plastic organ in the known universe" (p. 98). This characteristic of the brain is called *neuroplasticity*.

The principles behind neuroplasticity can provide relationally oriented servant-leaders with scientific substantiation that positive mental, emotional, and behavioral changes can become indelible actualities in both servant-leader and follower. LeDoux (2002) pointed out that over the past two decades, researchers have gained significant insights into how experience-dependent neuroplasticity forms tangible neural architecture, enabling people to create and sustain lasting transformation in both thoughts and behaviors. This understanding of the brain's neuroplasticity can bring hope (Leaf, 2013) and added confidence to leaders and followers who would like to experience positive transformation.

Mirror Neurons

Mirror neurons are specialized brain cells activated when a person sees someone engaged in functional behaviors. They give people the capacity to perceive and "share the emotions of others . . . making possible the communication of ideas" (Frith & Frith, 2006, p. 531), and they form neural systems that can mirror or resonate with others. Preeminent neuroscientist Ramachandran (2011) called mirror neurons "the neurons that shaped civilization" (p. 117), and he claimed that they will influence psychology in the same way that DNA influenced biology (Humphrey, 2007).

Mirror neurons play a strong role in relationships and emotional awareness, and they "demonstrate the profoundly social nature of our brain" (Siegel, 2007, p. 166). They can activate in response to communicative gestures, and they are thought to be intricately involved in how humans perceive the actions of others. They are stimulated not only by actions but also by emotions (Frith & Frith, 2006). The mirror neuron system offers insights into social behavior, imitation, and empathy (Siegel, 2006), and they "undoubtedly provide, for the first time in history, a plausible neurophysiological explanation for complex forms of social cognition and interaction" (Iacoboni, 2009, p. 6).

Cozolino (2014) indicated that "mirror systems are suspected of being involved in many social functions" (p. 52), such as learning, gestures, and speaking. He also stated that mirror neurons help people "link up across the social synapse" (p. 187). Keysers (2011) observed that mirror neurons open doors between a teacher and a student. He noted,

> The discovery of mirror neurons made it clear to me that our brains are indeed almost magically connected to each other. We are not born with a brain that deals exclusively with ourselves, but with one capable of feeling with other people. Our brain is set up to resonate with the people around us. (pp. 61–62)

Mirror neurons "might be thought of as 'sponge neurons' because they help us sponge up the feelings of others . . . (allowing) us to feel part of what he or she feels, not to become them" (Siegel, 2012b, p. 137). These neurons can be found in many areas of the brain, and they play an important role in interpersonal attunement and empathy, a highly valued servant-leadership characteristic.

According to Siegel (2007), the mirror neuron system and resonance circuitry are intertwined. When these two systems are activated, people can mirror actions and moods, and they can "simulate another's internal state and imitate that person's behavior. Mirror neurons link what we see from others with what we feel and what we do" (Siegel, 2012a, p. 79). Consistent mirroring will cause neuroplasticity to occur. This can create neural maps that embed the values and attributes of the leader into the minds and brains of followers.

The Mind

The mind can be defined in many ways. Siegel (2011) defined it as "a relational and embodied process that regulates the flow of energy and information" (p. 52), while Bateson (2002) described it as "an aggregate of interacting parts or components" (p. 85). Solomon and Siegel (2003) emphasized that the mind is not stagnant; it develops throughout a person's lifespan in response to experience. Additionally, Siegel (2011) noted that the mind helps people feel, think, talk, and create meaning, and that the "mind arises in both our bodies and relationships" (Siegel, 2012b, p. 7).

While the mind is not synonymous with consciousness, it still requires consciousness, which, according to Bandura (2001), "is the very substance of mental life that not only makes life personally manageable but worth living" (p. 3). Damasio (2003) described consciousness as "the process whereby a mind is imbued with a reference we call self, and is said to know of its own existence and of the existence of objects around it" (p. 184). Schwartz and Begley (2002) defined it as "more than perceiving and knowing; it is knowing that you know" (p. 26; emphasis in original), and Donald (2001) portrayed it as "a multilayered, multifocal capacity and a deep, enduring cognitive system with roots far back in evolution" (p. 10). He claimed consciousness "is the governor of mental life" (p. 47).

The Brain

The brain's work does not lie solely in the provenance of the skull; it unceasingly sends and receives signals via axons, dendrites, hormones, and neurotransmitters that work deep within the many complex systems of the body. It is an organizational, relational, social, and associational organ composed of over a hundred billion neurons that sit amid trillions of support cells that wire and fire together in a weblike network (Hanson, 2013). Each neuron has around 10,000 synaptic connections with other neurons, creating a potentially astronomical number of on-off firing patterns in the brain. Even with all the activity of billions of neurons and quadrillions of synaptic connections, the brain weighs only two to three pounds and is small enough to fit into the palm of the hand.

The brain is considered a dynamic system because its neural network is not static; it changes based on experiences encountered. It is a vital part of a larger complex system that consists of the mind (regulation), brain (mechanism), and relationships (sharing) (Siegel, 2012a). This system allows a person to self-regulate, engage in relationships, and create meaning out of experience.

There is an intimate, reciprocal connection between the brain and the mind. Siegel (2012a) noted that "the mind emerges at the interface of interpersonal experience and the structure and function of the brain" (p. xiii). Johnson (2009) described the brain as the "fingerprints of the mind" (p. 217), while Leaf (2013) wrote, "When you think, you build thoughts, and these become physical substances in your brain" (p. 25). The energy that flows through the mind is held in the brain. Together, the mind and brain form a complex communication system that sends energy and signals throughout the entire body as well as between the self and others (Siegel, 2007).

Myers (2011) emphasized that "everything psychological—every idea, every mood, every urge—is simultaneously biological" (p. 35) (see figure 23.1), and, according to Solomon and Siegel (2003), the mind and brain depend on one another because "the mind can alter the brain and the brain can alter the mind" (p. 9). Rock and Page (2009) indicated that the mind and brain develop at the same time, and Leaf (2013) stated that "thoughts have

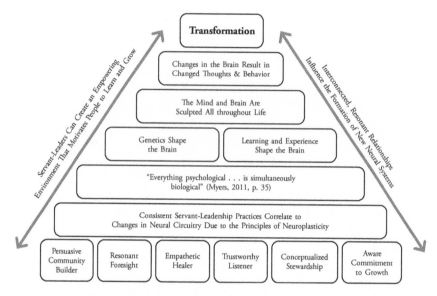

Figure 23.1. Servant-Leadership and Transformation.

Note. Transformation results when the mind and brain are sculpted through genetics and experience. Myers (2011) explained, "everything psychological—every idea, every mood, every urge—is simultaneously biological" (p. 35). Consistently exhibited servant-leadership characteristics can serve as a foundation for neural change due to neuroplasticity and resonant relationships (Gilbert et al., 2012).

the power to change the brain. The brain is changing moment by moment as we are thinking. By our thinking and choosing, we are redesigning the landscape of our brain" (pp. 32–33).

The interconnections of the mind, the brain, and relationships result in a one-of-a-kind individual. This is due to the formation and modification of neural pathways that occur continuously when relationships, minds, and brains merge, emerge, and reciprocally influence one another.

Seeing Servant-Leadership Characteristics through the Lens of Interpersonal Neurobiology

Applications

The purpose of this section is to suggest ways in which servant-leaders can help modify brain circuitry and promote positive, deep-rooted change in both the self and others. Based on the information mentioned earlier, the material below includes some examples that may aid a servant-leader who would like to understand ways to work *with* the brain rather than *against* it in the areas of empathy, resonance, change, insight and inspiration, foresight, and awareness.

Empathy

Empathy is one of the characteristics of a servant-leader. Greenleaf (1977/2002) stated that empathy "is the imaginative projection of one's own consciousness into another being" (p. 33). He observed that a servant-leader who empathizes with and accepts others for who they are will most likely be trusted. When servant-leaders exhibit empathy, mirror neurons are activated. They can feel some of what their followers feel and that can help create a sense of resonance between the leader and the follower. This resonance can make room for trust and growth in the relationship, a key concern for leaders.

Empathy is not just an emotion; it is an embodied experience. It is both emotional and physical, and it carries with it copious definitions. It "means experientially recognizing and understanding the states of mind, including beliefs, desires, and particularly emotions of others without injecting our own" (Rock & Page, 2009, p. 431). Burns (1978) described empathy as "the vital leadership quality of entering into another person's feelings and perspectives" (p. 100). Siegel (2007) said empathy "requires that we reflect on our own internal states" (p. 169), and Gunnarsson and Blohm (2011) suggested that empathy tells people, "I want to see things from your perspective to understand how you can develop as a person" (p. 70). These definitions are certainly not all-encompassing, but they provide solid insights into the value of being an empathetic leader.

Servant-leaders who exhibit empathy can help families, communities, organizations, and societies actively meet more of their goals because, as Boyatzis and McKee (2005) said, empathy "helps us get things done" (p. 178). Empathy can be "a radical force for social transformation" (Krznaric, 2012, p. 1) whenever it activates prosocial behavior and motivates people to try to alleviate pain or distress. It can encourage people to take action and create positive change; it can actually ensure physical survival. As Hall (2010) noted, the notion that "our neurons bristle harmonically with an external reality—is not simply an interesting concept that offers a possible route to explaining the biology of empathy: it likely represents an aspect of biology that has a very long evolutionary history" (p. 129).

Empathy is a "key business survival skill because it underpins successful teamwork and leadership" (Krznaric, 2012, p. 5) and it significantly aids in relationship building. Empathetic leaders are compassionate and emotionally intelligent, and they resonate with others. "They know that emotions are contagious, and that their own emotions are powerful drivers of their people's moods, and ultimately performance" (Boyatzis & McKee, 2005, p. 4). They are mindful of how their subtle emotional attitudes and nonverbal mannerisms might affect their followers, and they are willing to take on the work required to "read their world" (p. 123).

Bridges of communication and understanding can be created when people interact with an empathetic mindset. The result can be closer relationships, deeper understanding of the self and others, and positive modifications of negative thoughts and behavior. These changes can be accomplished at least in part due to the mirror neuron system and the brain's resonance circuitry.

> *Example:* According to Krznaric (2012), a leader can learn how to empathize with others by practicing six habits: (1) cultivating curiosity about strangers, (2) challenging prejudices and discovering commonalities, (3) trying another person's life, (4) listening hard—and opening up, (5) inspiring mass action and social change, and (6) developing an ambitious imagination.

Resonance

Physicists describe resonance as "a sympathetic vibration between two elements that allows these elements to suddenly synchronize signals and act in a new harmony" (Johnson, 2009, p. 273). The mirror neuron system and the resonance system become activated through relational interactions, and they can give rise to significant changes in thoughts and behaviors. Resonance between people indicates a certain harmony between them—a harmony that goes strong and deep—and harmony between people is a boon to any family, organization, or society.

Boyatzis and McKee (2005) discussed how "resonant leaders are in tune with those around them" (p. 4). This attunement helps build a sense of trust into the relationship between a servant-leader and a follower. That trust can help people remain open to relationships and to new learning.

Siegel (2012b) wrote, "We resonate with each other, mutually influencing each other's neural and mental realities as we connect with each other along our walk" (p. 320). A person doesn't lose his or her individuality when empathizing or resonating with others. As Siegel (2011) observed, "resonance requires that we remain differentiated—that we know who we are—while also becoming linked" (p. 63). He noted that resonant leaders can influence others best by maintaining their own internal states rather than being identical to others.

> *Example:* When people resonate with each other, the mirror neuron and resonance systems are active, allowing people to soak up what others are feeling or doing (Siegel 2012a). For example, a child who is afraid of the dark can sense and absorb her mother's calmness. Over a period of time, the child can learn to calm herself like her mother does. In much the same way, servant-leaders can resonantly "lend" their healthy emotional resources to others and help them shift into a more positive state (Rock & Page, 2009). When this type of harmonic connection happens, positive changes can take place, benefitting any relational structure—personal, organizational, or social.

Change

Change occurs as a result of the neuroplastic wiring and rewiring of the brain that takes place when the brain reconfigures itself based on what it learns (Ratey, 2002). Leaders can have hope and confidence, knowing that their lives are making a difference when they consistently interact with others in ways that facilitate positive, healing changes.

Servant-leaders do not exert control over others to resolve problems or create change. Rather, they purposefully remain committed to being humble, open, tolerant, honest, and empathetic—willing to acknowledge that they do not always have the "right" answers. Senge (1977) emphasized that a leader should humbly embrace uncertainty and doubt as they decide what course of action to commit to:

> Without uncertainty or doubt, there is no foundation for tolerance. If there is one "right view," which we will generally see as our own, we have no space for the possibility that a different point of view may be valid. Because of that, we have no empathy for those with different views. (p. 354)

Change involves a certain sense of uncertainty, and Zohar (1997) observed that it is important for leaders in the workplace to realize that some people are more at ease with uncertainty than others. She shared statistics that indicate that in a large company, 85% of the people, when "properly led, *will* change" (p. 93). Approximately 5% of the large company will never change, and about 5 to 10% will be the company's top innovators, creators, and leaders. These statistics indicate the importance of knowing how to lead in ways that help people accept change.

Change can create stress, but fortunately, stress is not always a negative. Cozolino (2010) indicated that "the power of mild to moderate levels of stress to trigger neural plasticity is a key element in the success of . . . any learning situation" (p. 21). Leaders can learn how to integrate change activities into their relationships and organizations that incorporate just enough stress to activate "neural growth hormones supportive of new learning" (p. 20). In this way, leaders may facilitate the growth of new neural circuitry that can alter thoughts and behaviors.

Servant-leaders who introduce change into a relationship, community, or organization need to realize that the brain loves novelty in small doses, but if the brain's "error-detection circuitry fires too often, it brings on a state of anxiety or fear. This partly explains humanity's universal resistance to wide-scale change: big changes have too much novelty" (Rock, 2009, p. 51). When a leader appreciates that too much new information can overwhelm the brain and cause people to become resistant, he or she can approach change processes more effectively.

> *Example:* Servant-leaders can help those who are resisting change by engaging in a process called "chunking" (Rock, 2009). This process enables a person to consider and experience change in smaller doses, and it helps reduce the sense of threat that can accompany the thought of wide-scale change. When leaders chunk information, they shift people's attention to things the leader wants them to focus on. Purposefully focusing on smaller bits of information reduces the sense of threat and decreases resistance to change because the brain is engaged in an appropriately novel way. This will help people function more effectively and more willingly during times of change.

Insight and Inspiration

Greenleaf (1977/2002) equated insight with inspiration. Rock (2009) defined *insight* as a moment that brings about change because that moment carries with it a burst of dopamine and adrenaline that provides a person with energy and a sense of courage. Although the rush of neurochemicals is rather short-lived, it can powerfully motivate a person to take action.

Greenleaf (1977/2002) emphasized the importance of attaining insights, personal enlightenment, and inspiration:

> The forces for good and evil in the world are propelled by the thoughts, attitudes, and actions of individual beings. What happens to our values, and therefore to the quality of our civilization in the future, will be shaped by the conceptions of individuals that are born of inspiration. Perhaps only a few will receive this inspiration (insight) and the rest will learn from them. The very essence of leadership, going out ahead to show the way, derives from more than usual openness to inspiration. (p. 28)

Greenleaf (1977/2002) indicated that people need more than leaders with inspiration. They need leaders who are willing to take up the challenge of the insight, saying, " 'I will go; follow me!' While knowing that the path is uncertain, even dangerous" (p. 29).

> *Example:* Leaders can create space for insights to occur in ways that will access brain circuitry and facilitate change. Rock (2009) said that when considering how to solve a problem or create a different scenario, a person can be encouraged to set aside thoughts or problems for a moment and become only lightly aware of them. This will result in a state of reflection that allows a person to look at the thought process and perceive concerns from a less-detailed perspective. He further stated that engaging in this activity activates areas in the right hemisphere and moves the brain into a dreamier state that helps form different connections that can lead to moments of insight. During these moments of insight, the brain experiences a burst of gamma band brain waves, indicating that different brain regions are in communication. An awareness of this neural process can help leaders serve others more effectively.

Foresight

To make changes to the self, relationships, an organization, or a society, decisions informed by foresight must occur. Greenleaf (1977/2002) described foresight as the ability to "go forward or backward from the instant moment . . . [it] is the essential structural dynamic of leadership" (p. 39). Additionally, Greenleaf (2003) indicated that "prescience, or foresight, is a better than average guess about *what* is going to happen *when* in the future. It begins with a state of mind about *now*" (p. 53; emphasis in original).

Rock and Page (2009) described how neural connections and neurotransmitters allow a person to "gather information from 'out there,' beyond our brain/body; to coordinate our different brain/body functions; to participate in sharing information; and to link past, present, and future" (p. 188). Experiences and relationships create mental maps (memories) that can be accessed when one is seeking to answer questions concerning the present or the future. These "mental maps enable us to add past experience to present perception so as to guide future behavior" (p. 256).

> *Example:* Siegel (2012b) discussed how the prefrontal area of the brain "can make maps of time, connecting the past, present, and future. This is called mental time travel" (pp. 72–73), and it enables humans to "carve out maps of the future based on what happened in the past." Servant-leaders realize the importance of living with their attention focused strongly on the here and now, even as they remain aware of the past and the future. They will draw on the mental maps created by experiences in the past, both good and bad, and will apply the lessons learned as they make current decisions that can positively influence the future.

Awareness

Greenleaf (1977/2002) said awareness is "value building and value clarifying . . . it is a disturber and an awakener" (p. 41). Awareness brings the "here and now" into consciousness. It is a process of knowing and knowing that you know. When this knowing is shared, it "can be at the heart of creating large-scale shifts in human culture" (Siegel, 2012b, pp. 33–34). Shared awareness can create a sense of closeness to others. It can help people become conscious of their own or others' needs and desires. It can also help a person "learn new skills and even change the structure of the brain itself, and to reflect on what has meaning. Awareness makes choice and change possible" (Siegel, 2012b, pp. 2–3).

Greenleaf (1977/2002) surmised that "awareness has its risks, but it makes life more interesting; certainly it strengthens one's effectiveness as a leader" (pp. 40–41). He discussed the things that block one's ability to be fully aware, such as the disappointments encountered in life's journey, but he admonished people to lose those disappointing "blinders" so that they might have the opportunity to "be given the secret of the kingdom: awe and wonder before the majesty and the mystery of all creation" (p. 340). His reference to these mysteries could certainly be thought to include those mysteries of the mind and the brain and the healing relationships that are forged by aware servant-leaders.

> *Example:* When a person has encountered an impasse, such as how to perform a task at work or interact with another person, they should first quiet their mind. Then they can lightly think on their impasse from a more peaceful, generalized bird's-eye view. "This activates right hemisphere regions that are important for insight, and allows loose connections to form" (Rock, 2009, p. 82). Quieting racing thoughts can help bring unconscious answers and insights into conscious awareness.

Conclusion

In this chapter I introduced a potential intersection between several characteristics of servant-leadership and the concepts of interpersonal neurobiology. I discussed the significance of neuroplasticity and the important connection between the mind, the brain, and relationships. I also introduced some basic techniques that can help modify brain circuitry and promote transformation.

Humans are intricately intertwined with others and with their environment. As Siegel (2007) said, "We have human minds dancing with our human brains within our social experiences of the shared construction of human culture" (p. 95). Understanding the concept of neuroplasticity and the fact that relationships literally sculpt the mind and the brain can bring a sense of optimism to relationally oriented servant-leaders. That is because these concepts provide scientific substantiation that transformation occurs as a tangible reality in the brain. This knowledge is important to the study of servant-leadership because it brings a sense of tangibility to a field that is, for the most part, an intangible one. And that tangibility can increase hope in servant-leaders who desire to see deep-rooted, long-lasting transformation occur in the families, organizations, and societies they serve around the world.

References

Bandura, A. (2001). Social cognitive theory: An agentic perspective. *Annual Review of Psychology, 52*(1), 1–26.

Bateson, G. (2002). *Mind and nature: A necessary unity.* Hampton Press.

Boyatzis, R., & McKee, A. (2005). *Resonant leadership: Renewing yourself and connecting with others through mindfulness, hope, and compassion.* Harvard Business School Press.

Brandt, P. Y., Clément, F., & Re Manning, R. (2010). Neurotheology: Challenges and opportunities. *Schweizer Archiv Fuer Neurologie und Psychiatrie, 161*(8), 305–309.

Braye, R. H. (2002). Servant-leadership: Leading in today's military. In L. C. Spears & M. Lawrence (Eds.), *Focus on leadership: Servant-leadership for the 21st Century* (pp. 295–303). John Wiley and Sons.

Buber, M. (1970). *I and thou.* Touchstone.

Burns, J. M. (1978). *Leadership.* Harper and Row.

Camerer, C. F., Loewenstein, G., & Prelec, D. (2004). Neuroeconomics: Why economics needs brains. *The Scandinavian Journal of Economics, 106*(3), 555–579.

Cozolino, L. (2010). *The neuroscience of psychotherapy: Healing the social brain* (2nd ed.). W. W. Norton.

Cozolino, L. (2014). *The neuroscience of human relationships: Attachment and the developing social brain.* W. W. Norton.

Damasio, A. (2003). *Looking for Spinoza: Joy, sorrow, and the feeling brain.* Harcourt.

DeGraaf, D., Tilley, C., & Neal, L. (2004). Servant-leadership characteristics in organizational life. In L. C. Spears & M. Lawrence (Eds.), *Practicing servant-leadership: Succeeding through trust, bravery, and forgiveness* (pp. 47–69). Jossey-Bass.

Demitri, M. (2007). Types of brain-imaging techniques. *Psych Central.* Retrieved on July 14, 2014, from http://psychcentral.com/lib/types-of-brain-imagingtechniques/0001057

Donald, M. (2001). *A mind so rare: The evolution of human consciousness.* W. W. Norton.

Fishbane, M. D. (2007). Wired to connect: Neuroscience, relationships, and therapy. *Family Process, 46*(3), 395–412.

Fosha, D. (2013). "Turbocharging" the affects of innate healing and redressing the evolutionary tilt. In D. J. Siegel and M. Solomon (Eds.), *Healing moments in psychotherapy* (pp. 129–168). W. W. Norton.

Frith, C. D., & Frith, U. (2006). The neural basis of mentalizing. *Neuron, 50*(4), 531–534.

Gantt, S. P., & Agazarian, Y. M. (2010). Developing the group mind through functional subgrouping: Linking systems-centered training (SCT) and interpersonal neurobiology. *International Journal of Group Psychotherapy, 60*(4), 515–544.

Gardiner, J. J. (1998). Quiet Presence: The holy ground of leadership. In L. C. Spears (Ed.), *Insights on leadership: Service, stewardship, spirit, and servant-leadership* (pp. 116–125). Wiley and Sons.

Gilbert, P., McEwan, K., Gibbons, L., Chotai, S., Duarte, J., & Matos, M. (2012). Fears of compassion and happiness in relation to alexithymia, mindfulness, and self-criticism. *Psychology and Psychotherapy: Theory, Research and Practice, 85*(4), 374–390.

Greenleaf, R. K. (2002). *Servant leadership: A journey into the nature of legitimate power and greatness* (L. C. Spears, Ed.; 25th anniversary ed.). Paulist Press. (Original work published 1977)

Greenleaf, R. K. (2003). *The servant-leader within: A transformative path* (H. Beazley, J. Beggs, & L. C. Spears, Eds.). Paulist Press.

Gunnarsson, J., & Blohm, O. (2011). The welcoming servant-leader. In S. R. Ferch & L. M. Spears (Eds.), *The spirit of servant-leadership* (pp. 68–85). Paulist Press.

Hall, S. J. (2010). *Wisdom: From philosophy to neuroscience.* Alfred A. Knopf.

Hanson, R. (2013). *Hardwiring happiness: The new brain science of contentment, calm, and confidence.* Harmony Books.

Hatfield, E., Rapson, R. L., & Le, Y. L. (2011). Emotional contagion and empathy. In J. Decety & W. Ickes (Eds.), *The social neuroscience of empathy* (pp. 19–30). MIT Press.

Humphrey, N. (2007). The society of selves. *Philosophical Transactions of the Royal Society, 362*(1480), 745–754. https://doi.org/10.1098/rstb.2006.2007

Iacoboni, M. (2009). *Mirroring people: The science of empathy and how we connect with others.* Picador.

Johnson, S. (2009). Extravagant emotion: Understanding and transforming love relationships in emotionally focused therapy. In D. Fosha, D. J. Siegel, & M. F. Solomon (Eds.), *The healing power of emotion: Affective neuroscience, development and clinical practice* (pp. 257–279). W. W. Norton.

Keysers, C. (2011). *The empathic brain: How the discovery of mirror neurons changes our understanding of human nature.* Los Gatos.

Krznaric R. (2012). *Six habits of highly empathic people.* http://greatergood.berkeley.edu/article/item/six_habits_of_highly_empathic_ people1

Leaf, C. (2013). *Switch on your brain: The key to peak happiness, thinking, and health.* Baker Books.

LeDoux, J. (2002). *Synaptic self: How our brains become who we are.* Penguin Books.

McClellan, J. (2008). The emergence, expansion, and critique of servant-leadership as a leadership philosophy. *International Journal of Servant-Leadership, 4*(1), 281–302.

McGilchrist. I. (2013). Hemisphere differences and their relevance to psychotherapy. In D. J. Siegel & M. Solomon (Eds.), *Healing moments in psychotherapy* (pp. 67–88). W. W. Norton.

Myers, D. G. (2011). *Exploring psychology* (8th ed.). Worth Publishers.

Moore, D. S. (2001). *The dependent gene: The fallacy of "nature vs. nurture."* Henry Holt and Company.

Panksepp, J. (1998). *Affective neuroscience: The foundations of human and animal emotions.* Oxford University Press.

Ramachandran, V. S. (2011). *The tell-tale brain: A neuroscientist's quest for what makes us human.* W. W. Norton.

Ratey, J. J. (2002). *A user's guide to the brain: Perception, attention, and the four theaters of the brain.* Vintage Books.

Ringleb, A., & Rock, D. (2009). NeuroLeadership in 2009. *NeuroLeadership Journal, 2*(1), 1–7.

Rock, D. (2006). *Quiet leadership: Six steps to transforming performance at work.* HarperCollins Publishers.

Rock, D. (2009). *Your brain at work: Strategies for overcoming distraction, regaining focus, and working smarter all day long.* HarperCollins Publishers.

Rock, D., & Page, L. J. (2009). *Coaching with the brain in mind: Foundations for practice.* John Wiley & Sons.

Schwartz, J. M., & Begley, S. (2002). *The mind and the brain: Neuroplasticity and the power of mental force.* Harper Collins Publishers.

Senge, P. M. (1977). Afterword. In L. C. Spears (Ed.), *Servant leadership: A journey into the nature of legitimate power and greatness* (pp. 343–359). Paulist Press.

Shilling, C. (2003). *The body and social theory* (2nd ed.). Sage.

Shilling, C. (2012). *The body and social theory* (3rd ed.). Sage.

Siegel, D. J. (2006). An interpersonal neurobiology approach to psychotherapy: Awareness, mirror neurons, and neural plasticity in the development of wellbeing. *Psychiatric Annals, 36*(4), 248–256.

Siegel, D. J. (2007). *The mindful brain: Reflection and attunement in the cultivation of well-being.* W. W. Norton.

Siegel, D. J. (2011). *Mindsight: The new science of personal transformation.* Bantam Books.

Siegel, D. J. (2012a). *The developing mind: How relationships and the brain interact to shape who we are* (2nd ed.). The Guilford Press.

Siegel, D. J. (2012b). *Pocket guide to interpersonal neurobiology: An integrative handbook of the mind.* W. W. Norton.

Siegel, D. J., & Solomon, M. (2013). Therapeutic presence: Mindful awareness and the person of the therapist. In D. J. Siegel & M. Solomon (Eds.), *Healing moments in psychotherapy* (pp. 129–168). W. W. Norton.

Solomon, M. F., & Siegel, D. J. (2003). *Healing trauma.* W. W. Norton.

Spears, L. (2004). The understanding and practice of servant-leadership. In L. C. Spears & M. Lawrence (Eds.), *Practicing servant-leadership: Succeeding through trust, bravery, and forgiveness* (pp. 47–69). Jossey-Bass.

Zohar, D. (1997). *Rewiring the corporate brain: Using the new science to rethink how we structure and lead organizations.* Berrett-Koehler.

Chapter 24

Vision and Poetry

Nadine Chapman

The poet uses imagery arising from the concrete, from observation, and from responses to specific people. Through the power of metaphor and symbol, poetry can capture the unique ethical relationship between human beings and their relationship with the physical world. A dream, a dirt road, or the face of a stranger may gain unforeseen depth. Robert Frost's poetry affected Greenleaf's understanding of journey. Other poets, such as Yeats, T. S. Eliot, and Whitman, inspired him as well. He freely acknowledged his debt to these writers for their creative language and vision.

Greenleaf (1977/2002) emphasized the need for prophetic voices and prophetic vision in servant-leadership. He called for liberating visions in leaders (Greenleaf, 1998). This is the task of poetic imagination. Ethical response to another person or persons in distress gains the capacity to project a new path through the poet's voice and language. Poetic practice draws on the words people speak to disclose often hidden meaning, to bring the mystery of human desires to light. It struggles against one-dimensional uses of language that limit the freedom of that voice.

Poetic imagination can illuminate suppressed powers of the human spirit and provide the language for ethical and spiritual growth. Rather than controlling expression, it seeks a changed vision of personal and political reality or historical understanding based on the fullness of language. New words, or words given new meaning, combined with creative courage, can weave from memory and experience alternative ways for humans to interact. This is an effort of hope.

References

Greenleaf, R. K. (1998). *The power of servant-leadership*. L. C. Spears (Ed.). Berrett-Koehler.

Greenleaf, R. K. (2002). *Servant leadership: A journey into the nature of legitimate power and greatness* (L. C. Spears, Ed.; 25th anniversary ed.). Paulist Press. (Original work published 1977)

Chapter 25

The Poetry of Servant-Leadership
What Is This Passion for Journey

NADINE CHAPMAN

What is this passion for journey
we share   as if distance
miles can cajole new words
from hoarse throats

In the town of seven volcanoes
and Mission San Luis Obispo
we leave morning sun for twilight
settled behind timbered doors
—one cool space that teeters
between the earthly and ethereal
A garland—bold rose and blue flowers—
travels white plastered walls
There's nothing shy about St. Francis
                              or his disciples
Here big prayers require large candles
You light one   ask help
for my blood-starved heart

Perhaps we won't go home at all
but take the way of a pilgrim
                          the cherubinic wanderer
disperse our sheltered past
                          among relatives
and join composers of heartsongs
for this war-scarred world

Chapter 26

The Poetry of Servant-Leadership

They

PATRICIA VALDÉS

Miners of Chile who live in the depths of hell.
Children snatched from mother's arms.
Continuous links of chain
started hundreds of years ago . . .

Children whose future is accountable to none.
Orphans who roam the streets of Brazil,
abandoned, ignored, the "problem,"
left to fend for themselves . . .

Families of the "disappeared ones" who refuse to forget.
Mothers who daily, for years, plaza walk
in memory of the dead . . . calling
for justice so that we may not forget . . .

Women who provide, cook, care, and sometimes love.
Hired help, sirvienta. Campesinas and campesinos
covered in sweat, bent in pain.
Sunup to sundown. Working for crumbs,
harvesting food that will evade them.

447

Invisible people who work diligently, daily.
Prisoners of war who are whispered about,
"They must have done something . . ."
Yet they hold on a little longer
with insurmountable strength
that equality, justice, and freedom prevail.

About the Editors

Jiying Song, PhD, PMP

Jiying (Jenny) Song is an assistant professor at Northwestern College. After earning her master of engineering in China and working in the field of IT for 14 years, Jenny came to the United States to pursue a master of divinity from George Fox University. After completing her second master's degree, she earned a PhD in leadership studies from Gonzaga University. Through this process, she has discovered that she has a passion for both effective leadership and academic work.

During her career in China, she served as the operation director of an IT company and managed the operation service enter and marketing department for seven years. She obtained a project management professional (PMP) certification and an IT service management certification and worked as a project manager for more than 10 years. During her graduate study at George Fox University, she worked as teaching assistant for Dr. MaryKate Morse, teaching and tutoring graduate students in New Testament Greek. She has been active in ministry to international students and visiting scholars at George Fox University since 2013. She graduated from George Fox University and received the Dean's Award for "superior academic achievement, exemplary Christian character and extraordinary potential for service as a Christian scholar." At Gonzaga University, she worked with Dr. Chris Francovich as a data analyst for the National Science Foundation's ADVANCE project. She taught project management and spiritual formation at George Fox University. Currently she is an assistant professor of business and economics at Northwestern College and serving as associate editor with Dr. Shann Ray Ferch and Larry C. Spears for the *International Journal of Servant-Leadership*. She enjoys reading servant-leadership studies and essays from all over the world.

Joe Walsh

Joe Walsh is doctoral student with Gonzaga University's School of Leadership Studies. Prior to becoming a full-time doctoral student, he earned his master of arts degree in organizational leadership from Gonzaga University, and a bachelor of arts in philosophy from the University of Minnesota, Twin Cities. Joe is passionate about leadership education and adult development, and volunteers his time with the University of Minnesota's marching band and leadership minor. He firmly believes that leadership is the means by which the human condition can be improved, and hopes that with thorough investigation into our own lives, everyone can realize their full potential.

Kae Reynolds, PhD

Kae Reynolds is a university lecturer based in the United Kingdom, an expert in ethical leadership development, women's leadership, gender, and feminist theory, as well as a dedicated mentor for early career researchers.

Before becoming an academic Kae was based out of Berlin, Germany, where she led large-scale Internet-based projects for business consultancy, online marketing, and internal communication for international corporations in the automotive, telecommunications, publishing, and public sector. She became interested in the fields of servant-leadership and gender while pursuing her master of organizational leadership at St. Ambrose University. On this journey she discovered her passion for research and writing, which led her to obtain her PhD in leadership studies from Gonzaga University.

Kae is a recipient of the Greenleaf Scholars Award in 2010, which provided grant funding for her PhD thesis exploring the theoretical compatibility of servant-leadership and the feminist ethic of care. Kae has also attracted research funding for a doctoral student bursary to develop a measure of moral reasoning orientation for leaders and a small research project to explore gendered communication in popular radio feature interviews of prominent professionals. Her coauthored paper on women's motivation to lead in small social enterprises was awarded the "Best Paper on the Gender in Management Track" at the international conference of the British Academy of Management 2019.

Kae's international academic career has spanned roles at universities in Germany, the United States, Saudi Arabia, and the United Kingdom. She has gained esteem in the field of servant-leadership through invitations as a keynote speaker for conferences and guest lectures in the United States, United Kingdom, and Germany. Kae also serves on the editorial board for the *Journal of Leadership Education* and the trilingual (Spanish, Catalan, and English) journal *Asparkía* for gender and feminist theory and as a peer-reviewer for a number of international journals in the fields of leadership and human resource development.

Jennifer Tilghman-Havens

Jennifer Tilghman-Havens is a teacher, writer, speaker, facilitator, and spiritual director who serves as the director of the Center for Jesuit Education at Seattle University. Her doctoral work in interdisciplinary leadership studies at Gonzaga University has inspired her to publish research on servant-leadership, diversity and equity, transformative pedagogy, women's leadership, and environmental sustainability. As the founding director of the Women's Center at Boston College in 2003, Jennifer developed programming and partnerships to support women's holistic development. Since that time, she has spent her career at the intersections of gender, race, meaning making and leadership. She teaches undergraduate and graduate courses on spirituality and leadership and Ignatian leadership and race, and facilitates several faculty development workshops to foster active, inclusive, and reflective pedagogy. She also serves on the steering committee for the National Science Foundation ADVANCE Institutional Transformation grant at Seattle University, and cochairs the President's Committee for Environmental Sustainability. She presents regularly to audiences large and small on topics of spirituality, transformative education, and liberatory leadership. She has a loving partner and two children who challenge and delight her daily.

Shann Ray Ferch, PhD

Shann Ray Ferch is a husband, father, author, and leadership consultant. In his work as professor of leadership with the internationally recognized PhD program in leadership studies at Gonzaga University (www.gonzaga. edu/doctoral), his emphasis is on how servant-leadership honors personal and collective responsibility, and self-transcendence across the disciplines. As a poet and prose writer, his work has appeared in some of the nation's leading literary venues, including *Poetry, McSweeney's, Narrative Magazine,*

Story Quarterly, Best New Poets, and *Poetry International* (www.shannray.com). He has received Pushcart, Best American, and O'Henry nominations for his short fiction from *McSweeney's* and *Montana Quarterly,* and is a National Endowment for the Arts Fellow. Shann is the author of the American Book Award–winning collection of short stories *American Masculine;* a leading book of creative nonfiction and political theory, *Forgiveness and Power in the Age of Atrocity: Servant Leadership as a Way of Life;* and three books coedited with Larry Spears, Jenny Song, and others titled *The Spirit of Servant Leadership, Conversations on Servant-Leadership,* and *Servant-Leadership and Forgiveness.* He is also the author of an additional collection of short stories, *Blood Fire Vapor Smoke;* the novel *American Copper;* the High Plains Book Award–winning volume of poetry *Balefire;* and two additional poetry collections, *Sweetclover* and *Atomic Theory 7.* After earning a PhD in psychology from the University of Alberta in Canada, he earned a dual MFA in poetry and fiction from the Inland Northwest Center for Writers at Eastern Washington University. Dr. Ferch has also served as a research psychologist with the Centers for Disease Control for the US government, as a panelist for the National Endowment for the Humanities, and is a systems psychologist in private practice. His work regarding executive leadership, organizational culture, and the human will to forgive and reconcile has appeared in scientific journals internationally. As a lead consultant for Leadership Spirit International, in partnership with principal consultant Paul Nakai, he designs and implements comprehensive executive coaching programs for CEOs and their leadership and management teams. His work with executives and organizational culture involves performance-enhancement coaching, team building, leadership development, personal effectiveness and resilience, and relational discernment. Dr. Ferch has conducted leadership initiatives in nonprofit and for-profit sectors that include business, health, government, and public service organizations in the United States, South America, Europe, Asia, and Africa. The editor of the *International Journal of Servant-Leadership,* Dr. Ferch, in collaboration with senior advisory editor Larry Spears, CEO of the Spears Center for Servant-Leadership, publishes essays, science, and scholarly work dedicated to the wisdom, health, autonomy, and freedom of others. The advisory board for the journal includes the following leaders and scholars of international influence: Margaret Wheatley, Peter Senge, Stephen Covey, Warren Bennis, Danah Zohar, Ron Heifitz, Peter Block, and David Cooperrider. Considered the foremost journal in the field, the *International Journal of Servant-Leadership* has published the work of Robert Greenleaf, Larry Spears, Peter Block, Peter Senge, Danah

Zohar, Myrlie Evers-Williams, and Margaret Wheatley, as well as scholars from around the world.

Larry C. Spears

Larry C. Spears is president and CEO of the Larry C. Spears Center for Servant-Leadership, Inc. (www.spearscenter.org), established in 2008. From 1990 to 2007 he served as president and CEO, and as senior fellow and president emeritus of the Robert K. Greenleaf Center for Servant Leadership. Spears has previously served as director or staff member with the Greater Philadelphia Philosophy Consortium, the Great Lakes Colleges Association's Philadelphia Center, and with the Quaker magazine *Friends Journal*. Spears is also a writer and editor who has published hundreds of articles, essays, newsletters, books, and other publications on servant-leadership. Dozens of newspapers and journals have interviewed him, including *Fortune*, the *Indianapolis Business Journal*, the *Philadelphia Inquirer*, the *Washington Post*, and *Advancing Philanthropy*. A 2004 television broadcast interview of Spears by Stone Phillips on NBC's *Dateline* was seen by 10,000,000 viewers. Larry is the creator and editor of a dozen books on servant-leadership, including the best-selling *Insights on Leadership*. In addition, he has contributed chapters and forewords to seventeen books edited by others. Larry serves as the senior advisory editor for the *International Journal of Servant Leadership* (2005–present). In 2010, he was named the Gonzaga University Servant Leadership Scholar, a title granted in recognition of his role as one of the leading scholars in leadership worldwide, and he currently teaches graduate courses in servant-leadership for Gonzaga University. Among several honors, in 2002, Larry received the Outstanding Leadership Award from Chapman University in California. In 2004, he received the Dare to Lead Award from the International Leadership Network. In 2008, Larry was honored by his alma mater, DePauw University (Greencastle, Indiana), with its Community Leadership Award. In 2015, he was honored by the Greenleaf Centre for Servant Leadership–UK. In 2018, Larry was the inaugural inductee into Gonzaga University's School of Leadership Studies' Hall of Honor. Larry has forty years of experience in organizational leadership, entrepreneurial development, nonprofit management, and grant writing, having envisioned and authored thirty successful grant projects.

Contributors

Judy I. Caldwell is a psychology professor at Camosun College, Victoria, British Columbia, Canada. She obtained her PhD at the University of Victoria, British Columbia, in cognitive psychology, with a particular focus on human memory processes. She also completed an MEd in leadership studies in the Faculty of Education at the University of Victoria in 2015 under the supervision of the late Dr. Carolyn Crippin. Judy is the former chair of the Psychology Department at Camosun College and has also served as acting dean of the School of Arts and Science at the College.

Nadine Chapman (in memoriam) was a poet whose work appeared in literary journals and other venues throughout the United States. Described as a "gift of voice, story, and memory," her chapbook of poems *On Solitude* is noted for both its subtlety and its evocative understanding of the human condition. Her work is printed here with love and respect. She taught at Whitworth College, in Spokane, Washington. She lived the life of a poet beloved by many. Her spirit continues to shape the servant-leadership community with grace and dignity.

Carolyn Crippen (in memoriam), PhD, was a professor in leadership studies at the University of Victoria, British Columbia, Canada. She also previously served as the assistant dean of education at the University of Manitoba. Carolyn had a lengthy background in K–12 administration and teaching. She designed and taught several courses on servant-leadership and servant-followership. Her research areas included servant-leadership, senior administration, and Icelandic culture. She published and presented globally. Carolyn worked collaboratively with public, private, and nonprofit organizations and was particularly focused on the creation of caring, effective, inclusive, learning communities. Her life was a gift of love and care to others. With dignity and authentic power her spirit continues to bless the servant-leadership community worldwide.

Erin Davis is a PhD candidate in the Doctoral Program in Leadership Studies at Gonzaga University. She lives and writes near the Little Spokane River and is a professor of English at North Idaho College, where she serves as the writing center coordinator. Her work has been featured in *Assay: A Journal of Nonfiction Studies*, *Trestle Creek Review*, and in anthologies published by Thoughtcrime Press and the Spokane County Library District.

Carmen dela Cruz is a Southern African American writer. Currently, she lives in Spokane, Washington, with her husband and works in Gonzaga University's Graduate Enrollment Management Department. She is also a student in Gonzaga's PhD in Leadership Studies program. Before working in higher education, she worked for some years in the media world with Turner Broadcasting in Atlanta, Georgia. She has a bachelor's in film production from Georgia State University and an MFA in creative writing fiction from Chatham University.

Faith Renae Regh Gilbert, PhD, is a writer and educator whose passion revolves around the study of neuroleadership, specifically as it relates to the intersubjective connections that lie between servant-leadership and the complex principles of interpersonal neurobiology and "languaging." She is a graduate of Gonzaga University's internationally renowned Doctoral Program in Leadership Studies in Spokane, Washington, where she also earned her MA in organizational leadership. Additionally, she studied at the Neuroleadership Institute and Fuller Theological Seminary. Dr. Gilbert is an adjunct professor who teaches leadership courses as well as courses in physiological psychology. She has two children and lives in beautiful northwest Montana with her husband.

Lucia M. Hamilton is a leader in healthcare ministry and a board-certified chaplain, serving as the director of spiritual care for the Ascension Indiana ministry market. Prior to ministry, Lucia was a psychological consultant specializing in the selection and development of leaders for business organizations. Through her work, she was privileged to hear the stories of over 1,100 people. She also served as adjunct faculty at Loyola University of Chicago. In addition to her professional experience in organizational psychology, Lucia has a deep knowledge of the business world gained through twenty years in corporate management positions. She has a long-standing interest in effective leadership practices. Her current research interests include the dimensions and development of character in leaders.

José Hernández was born and raised in Caracas, Venezuela, and has lived in the United States since 1987. He received an MS and a PhD in leadership studies from Gonzaga University. An avid reader of leadership, theology, and social issues, José is a quiet activist in conversations over racial injustice and immigration policies related to the developing world. He is the fitness director at Gonzaga University and an independent sports psychology consultant.

Charlotte M. Knoche's education includes masters' degrees in German and library science and a PhD from the University of Minnesota's Educational Policy and Administration Department. After careers as a German instructor at University of Wisconsin-Milwaukee and a librarian for Portage County, Wisconsin, she joined the Concordia Library and the local CLIC consortium in 1986, beginning as cataloger and reference librarian and moving to library director in 2007. She was an adjunct professor in the Concordia School of Graduate & Continued Studies, School of Accelerated Learning, School of Human Services at Concordia University She's been a member of the ALA(American Library Association), MLA (Minnesota Library Association), ARLD (Academic and Research Division of MLA), ACRL (Association of College and Research Libraries), CALD (Council of Academic Library Directors), MACAE (Minnesota Association for Continuing Adult Education), MVAEA (Missouri Valley Adult Education Association), Minnesota Coalition for Intellectual Freedom, and the Minnesota Literary Council. During this tenure she was honored with several awards and wrote 10 successful grants. In 2007 she was granted the honor of writing the article "Modesty in Leadership: A Study of the Level-Five Leader" with an esteemed colleague, Lucia Hamilton.

Lyna M. Matesi prepares leaders to thrive in disruptive environments. She directs an MBA program at the University of Wisconsin–Stevens Point, teaches professional and academic courses and serves as an on-call facilitator for the Center for Creative Leadership, and is invited to speak with leadership teams in for-profit, nonprofit, and government organizations. Lyna developed her leadership skills in the cellular telecommunications industry, where she was challenged to lead others in navigating significant, ongoing industry disruption. Over the last 25 years, Lyna served in change management, leadership development, and curriculum development roles at US Cellular, and business planning, project management, and communication technology roles at Motorola. Lyna earned a PhD in leadership studies from Gonzaga University, an MA in whole systems design focused on change leadership and organizational development from Antioch University, and a BA in leadership and management from Judson University. In addition to being certified to administer many leadership and organization development assessment instruments, she holds a certificate in organizational systems renewal and is qualified to design and facilitate system-wide change within organizations and communities.

Marcia Newman is president of Marcia Newman and Associates, LLC, located in Indianapolis, Indiana, where she actively engages the hearts and lives of individuals and organizations through coaching and consulting. Working in the field of leadership for the last 25 years, Marcia was previously the director of the Speakers Bureau for the Greenleaf Center for Servant Leadership and a speaker and trainer herself. Marcia's focus is congruence of spirit, voice, confidence, and presence as a catalyst for fulfillment in serving others. Her transformational work has influenced universities, executives, medical professionals, nonprofits, and those in career transition. Marcia's great enthusiasm for people focuses on truth, beauty, goodness, and unity to move them to revelation and Yes! You may find her at www.marcianewmanassociates.com or on LinkedIn.

Kathleen Patterson, PhD, serves as professor and the director of the Doctor of Strategic Leadership program at Regent University, where she has been since 1999. Dr. Patterson is noted as an expert on servant-leadership and has cocoordinated three Global Roundtables, in the Netherlands, Australia, and Iceland, with Dr. Dirk van Dierendonck. Additionally she is involved in numerous consulting projects nationally and abroad, and sits on the boards of the Larry C. Spears Center, CareNet, Millennials for Marriage, and the MENA Leadership Center.

Carla Penha-Vasconcelos is a multilingual scholar and practitioner who promotes knowledge and awareness around collaborative process, intersectional justice, DEI, and women, feminisms, and leadership. Her work cultivates and creates collaborative projects and meaningful connections among diverse communities of practice and knowledge. Dr. Penha-Vasconcelos's background includes serving as a graduate course and leadership training designer for

Gonzaga University, as an adjunct professor for the University of San Diego, and as an independent consultant designing and facilitating training and awareness projects for La Casa, Colective Feminista Antirracista de Barcelona and the North County of San Diego Womxn's March.

Patricia Valdés spent her childhood in Mexico, made a home in Spokane, where she raised her children, and now delights in her grandchildren, family, friends, and community. She served as a therapist in the community, worked as an administrator and taught at Eastern Washington University, and currently serves as the supervisor and bereavement counselor at Hospice of Spokane.

Margaret Wheatley, EdD, began caring about the world's peoples in 1966, as a Peace Corps volunteer in postwar Korea. In many different roles—speaker, teacher, consultant, advisor, formal leader—she acts from the unshakable conviction that leaders must learn how to invoke people's inherent generosity, creativity, and need for community. As this world tears us apart, sane leadership on behalf of the human spirit is the only way forward. Since 1973, Meg has taught, consulted, and advised an unusually broad variety of organizations on all continents (except Antarctica). Her clients and audiences range from the head of the US Army to twelve-year-old Girl Scouts, from CEOs and government ministers to small-town ministers, from large universities to rural aboriginal villages. She has served as full-time graduate management faculty at two universities, and been a formal advisor for leadership programs in England, Croatia, Denmark, Australia, and the United States. Through Berkana, she has advised leadership initiatives in India, Senegal, Brazil, Zimbabwe, South Africa, Mexico, Canada, and Europe. Meg received her doctorate in organizational behavior from Harvard University, and her masters in media ecology with Neil Postman from New York University. She studied at University College London and the University of Rochester for her bachelor's degree. She has authored 10 books, from the classic *Leadership and the New Science* (1992, in 19 languages) to *Who Do We Choose to Be: Facing Reality, Claiming Leadership, Restoring Sanity* (2017). Her new work is a CD plus a book, *The Warrior's Songline*, a journey into warriorship guided by voice and sound. Since 2015, she's been training leaders and activists from 35 countries as Warriors for the Human Spirit. This is the work of the rest of her life. Her websites are designed as rich libraries of materials for those seeking to lead and organize in life-affirming ways: www.margaretwheatley.com and www.berkana.org.

Matthew Williams is a multidisciplinary scholar, researcher, and educator who recently completed a year of service with LINK Community Charter School in Newark, New Jersey, and the Jesuit Volunteer Corps. He holds a BS in mathematics with concentrations in film studies and physics from Gonzaga University. He is grateful for the support, encouragement, and discomfort (leading to growth) provided by his friends, family, and mentors.

Danah Zohar was born and educated in the United States. She is a UK citizen and resides in Oxford. She studied physics and philosophy at MIT, and then did her postgraduate work in philosophy, religion, and psychology at Harvard University. She is the author of the best-selling *The Quantum Self* and *The Quantum Society*, books that extend the language and principles of quantum physics to a new understanding of human consciousness, psychology, and social organization. In 2016 she published *The Quantum Leader: A Revolution in Business Thinking and Practice*. Her most recent book, *Zero Distance: Management in the Quantum Age*, was published in 2021. Danah Zohar is the originator of quantum psychology, quantum social theory, SQ (spiritual intelligence), and quantum management theory. Zohar is currently honorary professor of quantum philosophy at the Centre for Confucian Entrepreneurship and East Asia Civilization, Zhejiang University, Hangzhou, China; a visiting professor in the School of Economics and Management at Tsinghua University (Tsinghua SEM), Beijing; and a visiting professor at the China Art Academy, Hangzhou. She has been a visiting fellow in Australia and the United Kingdom, and lectures widely throughout the world. Described by Financial Times Prentice Hall as "one of the world's top 50 business minds," and named by the *Tsinghua Business Review* as China's "top innovation management thinker of 2018," Zohar is active in management education and consultancy. In September 2018 she received the Haier RenDanHeyi Medal "for her scholarly contribution to the Haier Business Model."

Index

CPSIA information can be obtained
at www.ICGtesting.com
Printed in the USA
BVHW081858090223
658229BV00003B/34

9 781438 490168